HARVARD ECONOMIC STUDIES

Volume XXXIX

The studies in this series are published by the
Department of Economics of Harvard University.
The department does not assume responsibility
for the views expressed.

Interregional and International Trade

By

BERTIL *Gotthard* OHLIN

REVISED EDITION

HARVARD UNIVERSITY PRESS
CAMBRIDGE, MASSACHUSETTS
1967

Library of Congress Catalog Card Number 67–17317

Printed in the United States of America

To My Parents

Preface to the Revised Edition

I was happy to accept the offer to have this treatise republished in a somewhat abbreviated and updated form to bring it into line with recent developments. The changes in this revision are various. In Parts One and Two they are confined mostly to modernizing the terminology and removing minor ambiguities. In the rest of the book such changes are coupled with the omission of outdated empirical material and repetitive arguments. Chapters XI, XXII, and XXIV and Appendices II, III, and IV of the original edition have been discarded altogether. Chapters XV, XX, and XXII of this new edition are considerably abridged from their earlier versions. Finally, in order to give the reader a general indication of my present views, I have added as Appendix II a new essay, entitled "Reflections on Contemporary International Trade Theories."

I wish to express my thanks to all those involved in making this new publication possible. In particular, I am very grateful to Cynthia Travis (Mrs. William P.) for her competent and skillful editing of this new edition and for the great interest she has taken in it.

Bertil Ohlin

Stockholm College of Business
November, 1966

Preface to the First Edition

In this volume I have endeavored to make a contribution toward solving the following problems:

(1) To build a theory of international trade in harmony with the mutual-interdependence theory of pricing—and thus independent of the classical labor theory of value. Since it has been worthwhile to substitute the interdependence theory, as developed by such authorities as Walràs, Menger, Jevons, Marshall, Clark, Fisher, Pareto, and Cassel, for the classical labor value theory, there is every reason for also giving up the labor value analysis of international trade problems. I have started from Cassel's form of the general price theory, but I think my theoretical system will also harmonize with the other interpretations.

(2) To demonstrate that the theory of international trade is only one part of a general location theory, wherein the space aspects of pricing are taken into full account; and to develop certain fundamentals of such a theory as a background for a theory of international trade, wherein the influences of local differences in the supply of factors or production and transportation costs *within* each country are duly considered. In this field collaboration between economists and economic geographers is urgently needed. The fact that the latter have received so little help and stimulus from the former seems chiefly due to the scanty attention economic theory has given to location problems.

(3) To analyze the domestic and international movements of the factors of production, particularly in their relation to commodity movements.

(4) To describe the mechanism of international trade variations and international capital movements under conditions of fixed foreign exchanges, e.g., a gold standard or gold exchange standard regime. This analysis will demonstrate that, among other things, (*a*) changes in the total *buying power* of each country are an essential part of such a mechanism, and (*b*) the fundamental problems of foreign exchange (which after World War I were chiefly discussed with the purchasing power parity theory as a starting point) are integral parts of a theory of international trade.

This book will, I hope, prove that I have learned from the economists of all schools who have dealt with international problems—although

ix

references in footnotes are not numerous. My indebtedness to two schools of economic thought should be expressly stated. Anyone conversant with the writings on international trade by members of the Harvard School of Economics will find here many traces of their influence. Above all, the works of Professors Taussig, Viner, and Williams, as well as discussions with them and with Mr. W. Gardner inside and outside the classroom, have deeply influenced my views. My general theoretical background is colored entirely by the ideas of the Stockholm group of economists, Professors Bagge, Brisman, Cassel, Heckscher, and Myrdal, as well as of Professor Knut Wicksell. Like Dr. Rohtlieb of Stockholm and Professor Birck of Copenhagen, they also helped me with fruitful criticism of earlier versions of this book. Mr. Carl Iversen of Copenhagen read the manuscript, and Mr. Tord Palander read the second proof; both made numerous highly valuable observations and criticisms. Messrs. Karl L. Anderson and J. T. Day corrected the English, and Miss Mona Williamsson compiled the index. My thanks are due also to the Swedish Academy of Science, the American Scandinavian Foundation, and the Rask-Orsted Foundation for financial aid in the preparation of this volume.

Bertil Ohlin

Stockholm College of Business
January 20, 1931

Contents

CHAPTER XIV

CHAPTER XV

CHAPTER XVI

PART FIVE

MECHANISM OF INTERNATIONAL TRADE
VARIATIONS AND CAPITAL MOVEMENTS

CHAPTER XVII

Interregional and International Trade

Introduction

The theories of value, price, and distribution presented in modern treatises on economics may appear to differ greatly, but as regards the nature of pricing, the differences are largely superficial. The theory of supply and demand is universally accepted as a system of general equilibrium, in which the principle of mutual interdependence is fundamental. Special consideration, however, is given to the phenomenon of time, which renders analysis in terms of equilibria inadequate and necessitates a more dynamic approach. The time element is probably the chief cause of the obstacles in the way of a clear-cut presentation of fundamental economic principles. "The difficulties of the problem depend chiefly upon variations in the area of space, and the period of time over which the market in question extends; the influence of time being more fundamental than that of space." [1]

No doubt every author of a treatise on general economics would agree especially with the last part of this quotation, for the time element has in most cases been more or less fully considered throughout their analyses, whereas the space element was at first almost completely neglected—only touched upon in the theory of rent—and was later dealt with only from a special point of view in the theory of international trade. In fact, the general theory of pricing is almost exclusively a *one-market* theory,[2] wherein the idea of space, i.e., different local markets, hardly figures at all. It assumes the existence of only one local market for all the factors of production except natural resources. Their total supply, not their distribution over a given area, is regarded as one of the basic data of the problem. Therefore, in most treatises the problem of location of industry never arises.[3]

[1] Marshall, *Principles of Economics* (London, 1920), V, xv, §1.
[2] In the theory of price discrimination and noncompeting groups, different markets are considered but not different *local* markets, i.e., geographical conditions and distances are not the basis of the discrimination.
[3] The characteristic of a market is that the contacts between buyers and sellers are so intimate that only one price exists for each thing traded. Beside this narrow "single price market" may be set a wider concept: the "multiple price market." Communication between its parts is hampered by costs of transport and other obstacles, and the prices of a certain commodity or factor of production may differ between parts of the market exactly by the costs of overcoming these obstacles. The former is the sense in which the term "market" should be used when one speaks of a "world market" for certain goods; if prices differ because of the costs of overcoming the obstacles, one has to deal with different markets, although they may be indirectly communicating.

1

As a matter of fact, the geographical distribution of productive factors is important. Industrial activity must be adapted to the varying supply of such factors in different places, for only to a limited extent can the supply itself be adapted to the demands of various industries. It is true that some of the factors are, under certain conditions, freely mobile, but some are not, and all those placed in the group called "nature" are completely immobile. Prices of commodities, as well as of productive factors, in such an analysis will be different from what they are under the one-market assumption. Commodities move with more or less difficulty, chiefly because of the cost of transport, which is another element of fundamental importance but is little considered in the general treatises, except in discussions of international trade.

The one-market doctrine evidently needs a superstructure to deal with geographical price variations, i.e., the location of industry, and of trade between places and districts of various types. A theory of *international* trade alone is inadequate, for location is relevant to pricing within countries also. Thus, the theory of pricing must be extended to include *a number of more or less closely related local markets.* To effect such an extension is the object of the theory of interregional and international trade, which is therefore an integral part of the theory of pricing and is built upon the foundation laid by the one-market analysis.

This book assumes the existence of several markets and treats the difficulty of moving productive factors and commodities locally, i.e., from one place to another, not with price discrimination in one place. Such a development of the one-market theory includes both the theory of rent[4] and the theory of international trade as integral parts.

In the presentation of this theory it is convenient to start with a somewhat simplified form of the one-market theory, based on the assumption of full mobility. In Chapters I and II the simple theory is extended to cover *several* local markets through the introduction of a simple form of immobility of the productive factors between geographical districts or regions. Thereby some of the fundamental influences of space are laid bare, and light is thrown upon certain aspects of the location of industry and certain characteristics of interregional trade. Special characteristics of trade between regions (international trade) are studied in Part Two. In Parts Three and Four the influence of obstacles to movements of commodities and productive factors is studied under realistic assumptions, and the theory is applied to domestic and international trade; in other words, the general space aspects of trade are considered. Last, Part Five deals with the mechanism of international trade variations and capital movements.

[4] I have discussed this problem in "Some Aspects of the Theory of Rent: V. Thünen vs. Ricardo," *Carver Festschrift: Economics, Sociology and the Modern World,* ed. N. Hines (Cambridge, Mass., 1935).

Part One

Interregional Trade Simplified

I

A Condition of Interregional Trade

§ 1. *Simplifications.* Space is important in economic life for two chief reasons: the factors of production are to some extent confined to certain localities and move only with difficulty; and costs of transport and other impediments prevent free movement of commodities. Let us first consider the factors of production. It would be difficult, however, to analyze the influence of their geographical distribution and of their lack of full mobility without the aid of some initial simplification.

For many reasons it is convenient to think of the productive factors as located not in certain *places* but in certain *regions*. To be significant, such a region must be in some respects a unit, which requires that it should be different from other regions from a certain point of view, and the differences within the region should be smaller than those between them. In other words, there should be some kind of natural distinction between regions. In this book the principal criterion used is its endowment with factors of production. Hence, regions have different factor endowments, while the factors within a region are essentially similar. In Part One I shall for the sake of simplicity think of a factor as belonging to a region but disregard its location within the region. The most typical case of this kind is one where the factors are confined entirely to a certain region, i.e., are unable to flow over to another, whereas they are fully mobile within the region (their situation in the region being therefore of no consequence). Such a case begins the analysis. In other words, it is assumed that the factors of production are interregionally immobile but *intraregionally* freely mobile. The object of Part One is to explain the nature of trade between such regions, i.e., to describe how their existence makes necessary a modification of the one-market theory of production and prices. Later the interregional mobility of the factors, as well as the lack of such mobility and its bearing upon trade, will be taken into account.

The impediments to commodity movements are disregarded altogether throughout Part One, which deals with the general aspects of interregional trade. In the section on special types of regions, the obstacles to commodity movements across the borders as well as the costs of transport in general will be given attention.

5

§ 2. *Interregional differences in productive factor endowment.* What are the causes of division of labor in general? Why do individuals trade with each other, instead of each one producing his own requirements? Why does division of labor increase the total efficiency of production? The reasons may be grouped under two headings: "varying ability" and "advantages of specialization."

First of all, some individuals have greater ability for certain tasks than others. Varying natural aptitudes make one more fit to be an engineer, another better suited for the work of a physician or a lawyer. Some people take greater interest in gardening than in other occupations, and hence probably make better gardeners than others. Examples could be multiplied.

Second, even if all individuals had exactly the same natural abilities, it would still be advantageous to have specialization in one or a small number of occupations. In this way much greater skill can be acquired than if everyone produced everything for himself. Furthermore, the workman who constantly attends to one task wastes no time changing over from one occupation to another. In short, there results an increase in skill and a saving of time when each individual is occupied in the production of a large number of one particular article instead of cooperating in the production of a small quantity of many different articles. This is one aspect of what are generally called the "economies of large-scale production." About these economies and their influence on inter-regional trade more will be said in Chapter III. The discussion here is confined to the other side of the question, the differences in natural aptitudes.

Turning from individuals to regions, one finds that the latter, like the former, are very differently endowed with facilities for the production of various articles. One reason is that they are differently supplied with productive factors. One region may have plenty of iron and coal but little land for wheat-growing, while another has plenty of wheat-land but a scanty supply of mineral resources; clearly the former is better adapted to iron production and less well adapted to wheat-growing than the latter. It is the proportion of the factors in a region that determines its fitness for specific industries.

This may need further elucidation: a region cannot, of course, produce goods requiring factors of production which do not exist in that region. Copper ore cannot be produced without copper mines, nor can machines be constructed without technically trained and educated labor. Tropical plants, like pepper, can only with extreme difficulty be grown in countries with a temperate climate.

Many other important differences in endowment of productive agents are not of this type. Often a supply of the factors needed for a particular article is to be found in each region, at least if it is of a fairly large size, but some regions have relatively more of one set of factors and less of another. Australia has more agricultural land but less labor, capital, and mines than Great Britain; consequently, Australia is better adapted to the production of goods that require great quantities of agricultural land, whereas Great Britain has an advantage in the production of goods requiring considerable quantities of other factors. If both countries produced their own total consumption, agricultural products would be very cheap in Australia, but manufactured articles would be relatively dear, and the reverse would be the case in Great Britain. Because of its scanty supply of land, each acre would have to be intensely cultivated with much labor and capital to provide the necessary amount of food. The utmost economy would have to be exercised with land and, because of the tendency to diminishing returns, the yields of wheat, etc., from the last units of capital and labor would be very small. In Australia, however, the abundance of land would lead to an extensive method of cultivation, with very little labor and capital being expended on each acre; hence, the yield from each unit of capital and labor would be great.

No further illustration is needed to show how interregional variations in the proportions of factors of production result in different regional adaptations for the same type of production. In brief, each region is best equipped to produce the goods that require large proportions of the factors relatively abundant there; it is least fit to produce goods requiring large proportions of factors existing within its borders in small quantities or not at all. Clearly, this is a cause of interregional trade, just as varying individual ability is a cause of individual exchange.

By such general observations the cause of interregional trade is by no means fully analyzed. The immediate cause of trade is always that goods can be bought cheaper from outside in terms of money than they can be produced at home, and vice versa. It remains to be shown why some goods can be more cheaply produced in one region than in another. In other words, the real problem is to demonstrate what lies behind such inequality in prices or, more precisely, to show in what way differences in equipment come to be expressed in differences in money costs and prices.

§ 3. *Differences in relative commodity and factor prices as conditions of trade.* First, it should be noted that one region cannot possibly be superior to others in the production of *all* commodities, in the sense that it is able to produce all of them at lower *money costs*. For the sake of simplicity, consider two regions only, each having a free paper currency. It is assumed that they have no economic relations with each other beyond the import and export of goods; capital movements, tourist expenses, etc., are thus excluded. Under these conditions, imports are paid for by exports, and it is clearly impossible, except in the very short run, that one region (A) should be able to produce all articles cheaper than the other region (B). There would in that case be a flow of goods from A to B, but not in the other direction. How could this import be paid for? B's demand for "foreign" bills could not be supplied, since nobody in B would be able to export anything and acquire a claim on A. The price of A's currency in terms of B's (the rate of exchange) would be forced up; hence, all A's prices would rise in terms of B's currency until some of them were higher than B's prices. A point of equilibrium would be reached when B was able to export sufficiently to pay for the import from A.

If the relative commodity prices in A and B are equal in the isolated state, no trade is possible and no exchange rate between their currencies is conceivable.[1] In other words, inequality as to the relative commodity prices in the isolated state is a necessary condition for the establishment of trade.[2]

Under what circumstances will relative commodity prices actually be different in two isolated regions? To begin, all prices—of goods as well as of factors—are ultimately, in each region, at any given moment, determined by the demand for goods and the possibilities of producing them. Behind the former lie (1) the wants and desires of consumers, and (2) the conditions of ownership of the factors of production, which affect individual incomes and thus demand. The supply of goods, however, depends ultimately upon: (3) the supply of productive factors, and (4) the physical conditions of production. These latter conditions—the natural and unchanging properties of the physical world that are everywhere the same—determine the combinations of factors, i.e., the technical process, with due consideration of their prices, and

---

[1] Economies of scale are ignored for the present.

[2] This simple statement, which is nothing but a starting point for the analysis, is evidently quite different from the classical doctrine of comparative cost. The statement in the text concerns prices and expenses of production, whereas the distinction between expenses and costs is fundamental in the classical theory. Yet reasoning in terms of prices comes to very much the same thing as reasoning in terms of "opportunity costs." Cf. Cournot, *Recherches sur les Principes Mathematiques de la Theorie des Richesses* (Paris, 1838), and Pareto, *Cours d'Economie Politique* (Lausanne, 1896-97). See also a recent paper by Haberler, "Die Theorie der Komparativen Kosten und ihre Auswertung fur die Begrundung des Freihandels," *Weltwirtschaftliches Archiv* (1930), No. 2. The opportunity cost of one unit of a commodity B is the extra quantity of another commodity A that one would obtain if one unit less of B, and a greater quantity of A, were produced, assuming the output of other goods is unchanged. In the same way the cost of C can be expressed in terms of A. This, of course, comes to the same thing as reckoning in prices if A is used as the monetary unit. A price scale like the one mentioned in the text counts exactly the same as a scale of opportunity costs. If C costs $10 and B costs $2, then *on the margin* a reduction of the output by one unit of C permits an increase of the production of B by five units. Such reasoning explains very little unless connected with a mutual interdependence price system and is as different from the doctrine of comparative cost as anything can be.

thus influence the translation of demand for goods into demand for such factors.

In each region, then, there is a price mechanism, resting on these four basic elements, which determines simultaneously the prices of commodities and of factors of production. When the relation between these elements is different, relative commodity prices are also different, and interregional trade comes into existence.

The situation in the two isolated regions A and B can be compared with regard to these four elements. The first two elements, which govern demand for goods, will be dealt with under one heading: demand conditions. The physical conditions of production are everywhere the same; consequently, differences as to relative commodity prices depend upon the supply of industrial agents and upon demand conditions. Such differences are bound to exist, unless supply and demand conditions are exactly the same in A and B, or unless a difference between the regions as to productive agents is just balanced by a corresponding difference in the demand for commodities. Otherwise, differences in relative commodity prices in the isolated state will exist and will lead to interregional trade, each region specializing in goods it can make cheaper than the other.

It is not possible to say much in general of the relation between the demand and supply elements under which trade will exist. One thing, however, may be pointed out: if the relative prices of the factors of production in the two isolated regions are the same, these factors will be combined in the same way in various industries in one region as they are in the other. Costs of production of all commodities will be the same in both regions, i.e., relative commodity prices will coincide.[3]

Thus, instead of saying that inequality as to relative commodity prices in the isolated state is a condition of trade, one may say that inequality with regard to the relative prices of the factors of production is a necessary—but not sufficient—condition for the establishment of trade (under the simplified assumptions made above). But neither statement explains much. Both commodity and factor prices form part of a system of mutual interdependence. Behind the prices of commodities

---

[3] Differences in technique are clearly unthinkable if the relative prices of *all* factors are the same, for the proportions in which the productive factors are combined—the technical coefficients—are functions of relative factor prices. The quality of the factors being the same, which is so far assumed, *the forms of these production functions* must also be identical in the two countries. If relative factor prices coincide, the technical processes must be alike in A and B. However, the technical and organizing labor may be different and therefore organize production differently, even if the relative prices of all *other* factors agree. In that case the difference in technique is due to the fact that relative prices of *all* factors are *not* the same. The technical and organizing factor in region A is missing in region B, whereas the quality to be found in B is missing in A. These qualitative differences are important and will be analyzed in detail in Chap. V.

and factors alike lie the basic elements of pricing, and a searching analysis must therefore consider the nature of the whole price mechanism.

Coincidence in the relative prices of the factors of production in A and B of course assumes the same relation between supply and demand conditions in each region. It is not necessary that the equipment of industrial agents should be exactly the same in A as in B. Nor is it sufficient; for if demand is different, the relative price of the agents will also be different. One can only say that if differences in supply between the regions are balanced by differences in demand, the relative price of all factors and relative commodity prices will be the same.

In regions with very dissimilar factor supplies this condition can never be fulfilled. There is no reason why demand in a scantily populated region should turn especially to goods requiring much land and little labor—wheat, for instance—and thus raise rent, relative to wages, above its price in a densely populated region, where, as people cannot after all do without food, land is necessarily scarce.

As a matter of fact, little attention need be given to the theoretical possibility of two isolated regions having the same relative commodity prices,[4] in which case no interregional trade could arise. Unless there is in a given case some special reason for the opposite supposition, one is justified in assuming that conditions of supply of factors and demand are such that the relative scarcity will be different in the two regions in an isolated state—differences in supply being probably as a rule more important than differences in demand. In a loose sense, therefore, differences in equipment of factors of production will be the cause of trade. But one must be careful to remember the qualification implicit in the possible influence of differences in demand conditions, for the ultimate determinant of interregional trade, as of all price phenomena, is the relation between the factor supply and the demand conditions.

Interregional trade means that foreign demand is brought to bear upon the domestic factors and commodities, and vice versa; consequently, everything that affects this demand is to be included among the elements that govern interregional trade. The conclusion is obvious: since prices of both goods and factors in all regions affect this reciprocal demand, and since interregional trade is governed by the same basic elements that govern pricing in the isolated region, their position in all regions affects the price system and trade in each, and any statement concerning the nature of interregional trade which refers only to one, or not to all, of these elements is necessarily incomplete.

§ 4. *The price system in isolated and trading regions.* It may be worth while to illustrate this interdependence (of goods and factor prices in

---

[4] Neither is it necessary to discuss the conceivable combinations of different relative factor prices that would yield equal relative commodity prices. See Appendix I.

each of the trading regions) a little further by means of a simplified picture[5] of the price mechanism based on the atomistic assumption of full divisibility. According to this assumption, the price mechanism is always in equilibrium, for there is an instantaneous readjustment after all disturbances. Consequently, the following six relations hold true.

(1) Demand for commodities is equal to supply, i.e., to production.

(2) To produce a certain quantity of each commodity, a definite quantity ("technical coefficient") of each factor of production is needed, if the technique is given. The total requirements of each factor in all industries equal the supply of this factor.

(3) However, the technique is not given a priori. The technical coefficients depend upon the physical conditions of production and the prices of the factors of production.

(4) Commodity prices are equal to the costs of production, which are obtained by multiplying the quantity of each factor required by its price.

(5) Demand for commodities depends upon their prices and upon individual incomes and tastes.

(6) Incomes are governed by the prices of the productive factors and the conditions of ownership.

These conditions suffice to determine factor prices, and prices and produced quantities of commodities, if the supply of factors is known. The technical coefficients—the quantities of each factor used in each industry—are functions of the factor prices (3), the form of the function being determined by the physical conditions of production, which form part of the known data. Similarly, the forms of the functions in (5) and (6), where demand and incomes are functions of the prices of goods and factors, are determined by the wants and desires of consumers (the psychology of demand) and the conditions of ownership of the factors of production. These also are known data. The basic elements are thus the three function forms and the supply of productive factors.

Instead of assuming the supply of factors to be given, one may regard it as a function of factor prices, the form of the function being determined by the inclination of man to work and save (the psychology of effort and sacrifice), which then becomes one of the four known data that govern the price system in one isolated region under these simplified conditions.

Now assume two regions trading with one another. What will the price system be like? Evidently it is not much changed in character. The total demand for each factor of production, in (2), springs not only from production for domestic consumption but also from production for export. At the same time, a part of the domestic consumption is supplied by imported goods; consequently, demand is not equal to pro-

[5] It resembles closely the one presented by Cassel for the one-market theory. For the relation to other descriptions—e.g., that of the Pareto school—see Appendix I.

duction, in (1). Instead, one must posit: demand minus imports is equal to production minus exports. The demand for productive factors is consequently changed.

If imports and exports are known, the equations in (1) and (2) can easily be adjusted. But when they are not known, they depend upon the relation between commodity prices in the two regions *and the foreign exchange rate,* by means of which these prices can be compared. Each region exports the goods it can produce cheaper than the other region, and imports the rest. Thus, given certain prices, the foreign exchange rate determines which goods are imported and which exported. A new variable is thus introduced into the problem: the foreign exchange rate. There is also a new condition: the value of imports and exports must balance, capital movements being left out of account. In this way the price system is determined.[6]

§ 5. *Character of interregional trade.* With this picture of the price mechanism in mind, it is possible to develop the ideas concerning equipment of productive factors a little further. Region A has a relatively large supply of some factors, which are therefore comparatively cheap—unless this inequality of supply is balanced, or more than balanced, by an inequality of demand—and it has a relatively small supply of other factors, which are thus comparatively dear. A will be able to produce cheaply those commodities that require for their production a large quantity of cheap factors, but the other commodities will be relatively dear if produced in that region. In B, where the factors scarce in A are relatively abundant, the cost of production of commodities requiring large quantities of B's abundant factors will be comparatively low. Other goods will be relatively dear.

When an exchange rate has been established, prices and costs of production can be compared directly. Goods requiring a large quantity of factors cheaper in A than in B, and only a small quantity of other factors, can be produced at a lower cost in A and will therefore be exported to B. On the other hand, commodities requiring a large quantity of the latter factors and a small quantity of the former can be more cheaply produced in B and will be imported from that region to A. *Each region has an advantage in the production of commodities into which enter considerable amounts of factors abundant and cheap in that region.*

Australia has an abundant supply of agricultural land but a scanty population. Land is cheap and wages are high in comparison with most other countries; therefore, production of goods that require vast areas of land but little labor is cheap. This is the case with wool, for example. Sheep-raising requires great areas of land but little labor, and the shearing is a relatively simple process; hence, wool can be produced

[6] If some goods can be produced in both regions, the relations become somewhat more complicated, but not fundamentally different. See Appendix I.

at a lower cost than in countries where land is expensive, even if wages in the other countries are somewhat lower than in Australia. Similarly, regions with an abundant supply of labor, technically trained as well as unskilled, and of capital will find it profitable to specialize in manufactures, for labor is cheaper in such regions than in Australia.

In this line of reasoning, however, there is a risk of misinterpretation. To assert that one factor is in the isolated state relatively abundant and cheap in A—compared, of course, with the conditions in B—is not conclusive. Even if a factor is cheap relative to most other factors—using its price in the other region as a basis of comparison—it is not certain that, after the establishment of an equilibrium exchange rate between the currencies, it will be cheaper in the one region than in the other, measured in the currency of either. That necessarily depends upon the exchange rate, which is determined not exclusively by the series of relative factor scarcities in the isolated state but also by A's demand for B's goods (and vice versa) when trade has been opened up. Indeed, this reciprocal demand alone exercises a direct influence upon the rate, although the nature of the demand will of course depend partly upon price conditions in each region. This uncertainty is an inevitable consequence of the mutual interdependence of all the elements touched upon here, which forbids unqualified reasoning in one direction from cause to effect. It may be clearer if put in another way.

§ 6. *The exchange rate and interregional price differences.* A may very well export to B a much greater *number* of commodities than it imports, in spite of the fact that the *value* of imports and exports must balance. In other words, the cost of production of the majority of goods may be lower in A than in B. It is naturally also possible for a majority of factors to be cheaper in A than in B. The list of relative factor prices in the isolated state does not reveal how high the exchange rate will be, and therefore it cannot be said which or how many factors will be cheaper in the one region than in the other.

For example, call A's currency *sterling* and B's currency *dollars*. One dollar can buy certain quantities of B's factors during isolation. How much do *these quantities* of factors cost in A in terms of sterling? This question can be answered even in the isolated state, and we can draw this figure:

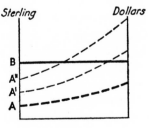

Fig. 1

The curve *B*, a straight line, indicates the prices of these quantities of factors in region *B;* they all cost one dollar. The curve *A* indicates the prices in sterling of the same quantities of the same factors in region *A*—in the isolated state, of course. The cheapest factor in *A*, relatively, is placed at the left, then the next cheapest, and so on. If the exchange rate that trade will establish is £1 = $2, the *A*-factor price curve in terms of dollars will be *A'*, but if the exchange rate is £1 = $3, then the corresponding curve will be *A''*. In the former case almost all factors are cheaper in *A*; in the latter the situation is reversed. Whether one or the other will emerge cannot be foretold a priori, since it depends upon the conditions of equilibrium between imports and exports and thus upon the intensity of reciprocal demand.

The factor combinations on the extreme left of the figure, i.e., very cheap in *A* relative to B in the isolated state, will necessarily be cheaper in *A* than in *B* when trade has started and an exchange rate has been established. Similarly, the factors on the extreme right, which are very dear in *A*, will certainly be dearer than in *B*. Therefore, *B* will export goods requiring large quantities of these factors for their production, and *A* will export goods containing much of the former factors. Of the intermediate factors one can say nothing a priori.

To sum up, the nature of interregional trade is determined not only by the supply of productive factors, or by the relative scarcities which that supply in relation to demand has created in each isolated region, but also by the play of demand in each region for goods from the other—the reciprocal demand. In fact, a fundamental aspect of trade is that it places the demand of one region in touch with the supply of productive factors in the other. (Cf. § 4 and Appendix I.)

No essential part of the above need be changed to apply to the case of several trading regions. To know which factors are relatively abundant and cheap, one must compare their prices in many regions instead of in one only. This will no doubt make it more difficult to say a priori of any one of the productive factors or commodities that it will be cheaper in a certain region than in the others when trade has been opened. In other words, it will be more difficult to say anything a priori as to which goods each region is to export. Nevertheless, the supply of productive factors is sometimes sufficient to determine the ensuing trade in concrete cases.

It remains, however, that even in such cases both the supply of factors and the demand conditions in each region produce price discrepancies that make interregional exchange profitable. The real nature of interregional trade—the conditions of its existence as well as its consequences—cannot be adequately explained by referring to the factor supply only, or to any other single element in the great interdependent system of pricing. That system, as developed in the one-market theory, must be modified and completed through the introduction of demand from abroad. In this way it becomes valid as an explanation of pricing in a number of trading regions.[7]

It may be helpful to give here a few concrete examples of the influence of differences in the supply of productive factors. It will then be seen that, in spite of the effect of different demand conditions, the differences in equipment between regions are sometimes so considerable that they determine the fundamental nature of trade. The simplified reasoning used in the discussion of the Australian case is therefore justified if to it is added a tacit qualification as to the influence of demand.

§ 7. *Illustrations.* One example is wheat-growing in Europe. If one excludes those countries that, like Finland and Norway, almost entirely lack the kind of climate necessary for wheat, the rest may be divided into two classes: those that export wheat or at least produce enough for their own consumption, and those that to a large extent are dependent upon foreign supplies. It is then seen that nations belonging to the former category have a relatively scanty population and much arable land per head, but the output per hectar sown with wheat is low. In 1925 Russia had an output per hectar of 8.3 decitons, and Rumania's was 8.6 decitons. Hungary showed a considerably higher figure: 13.7. The wheat-*importing* nations, however, had a much denser population, i.e., a scanty supply of wheatland per head, but produced much more per hectar—on an average fully twice as much. The figures for Holland and Denmark were 28.4 and 33.1, respectively. This is just what one would expect. Regions with a relatively large supply of land that can be used for wheat-growing produce wheat cheaply and export it to other regions, where prices are higher and much capital and labor is expended on each acre of land. A comparison between the three exporting countries and the two importing countries is significant because in neither case does the existence of special facilities for manufacture confuse the issue. The wheat-exporting regions outside of Europe—Argentina, Canada, and the western states of the United States—like those in Europe, have a large supply of arable land per head and a small output per acre.

[7] The doctrine of comparative costs as presented by Ricardo and Mill is unsatisfactory, not only because the scale of labor costs is built upon extreme simplifications, which cannot be abandoned without bringing down the whole edifice, but also because it neglects the influence of demand conditions on these scales themselves. The mutual interdependence is lost sight of. A simple description of certain conditions of production in terms of comparative cost schedules is put forward as determining the nature of international trade, but the play of reciprocal demand is given a secondary place as influencing only the extent of trade and the barter terms. As a matter of fact, the scale of comparative costs is not given a priori but is affected by the play of reciprocal demand, as demonstrated already by Mangoldt, *Grundriss der Volkswirtschaftslehre* (Stuttgart, 1863).

In Uruguay, animals and products thereof supply more than 95 percent of the total exports. This country has plenty of land and a climate that makes it excellent for cattle-breeding, but it has a small supply of labor and capital, and no coal.

Another good example of how the supply of natural resources dominates production and trade may be found in Finland. This country has a relatively ample supply of land, which is suited for another kind of vegetation—soft wood. It has a scanty supply not only of agricultural land but also of other gifts of nature, such as iron ores and coal fields. The result is that in the early 1930's more than 90 percent of its exports consisted of wood, pulp, and paper. In 1922, 43 percent of Canada's exports were vegetable products, 18 percent were animal products, and 24 percent were wood and paper. The influence of the large supply of wheatland, forests, and power is apparent.

The production of manufactured goods requiring much labor but little of other factors is found in fairly densely populated countries that are poor in most natural resources and where labor is consequently the most abundant factor. Many hand-made rugs, for example, come from southwestern Asia. Although a great many countries have a large supply of land suitable for raw-silk production, many of them have little or none of this industry because it consumes too much labor. This is true especially of the United States, a country with a scanty labor supply.

The growing of flax is also a laborious process. In the nineteenth century it was located chiefly in western and central Europe, but almost the whole European supply now comes from Russia and the Baltic countries. Hemp, another labor-consuming plant, is chiefly cultivated in Italy and Russia.

The sugar beet can be grown in most European countries and almost everywhere in the United States so far as soil and climate are concerned, but it must be given excellent care by human hands, which machines have not so far been able to supplant. It therefore tends to be produced in countries with a large supply of unskilled labor, such as Russia, Poland, Czechoslovakia, and eastern Germany; little is grown in the United States or Canada.

Like sugar beets, potatoes require much labor—a great deal more than wheat. They may also be grown on poorer soil and in a colder climate. Large quantities of potatoes are therefore naturally grown in the very countries in Europe that produce much sugar. This is not exclusively owing to the abundance of labor and the relative scarcity of first-class agricultural land in these countries; the character of demand exercises an important influence. The relatively low standard of living and the absence of cheap grain—both consequences of the supply of productive factors—naturally turn demand largely toward the cheap, plentiful potatoes. Indirectly, this large consumption of potatoes means a great demand for labor and relatively poor land and tends to increase the scarcity of these abundant factors; hence, the relative scarcity of the various factors becomes more similar to that in other regions than a mere study of the differences in equipment would lead one to suppose. A complete investigation into the location of potato-growing would entail a discussion of other circumstances, such as the feeding of hogs and the costs of transport, which is not necessary at this stage of the analysis.

The reaction of demand may also be seen in other examples. In Argentina, land is abundant and much of it can be used to produce beef cattle with little expenditure of its scarce labor and capital. As a result, meat there is relatively cheap, and its consumption is unusually great. In some densely populated countries, however, with little land per capita and few other natural gifts, cattle-breeding is also an important industry, which seems to contradict the first statement. The contrast is only apparent; such regions, e.g., Denmark, go in for milk cattle, which must be well taken care of and require much labor, but which can to a large extent be fed with oil cakes from other regions and thus require little land.

These examples of the influence of varying supplies of labor and arable land suffice to illustrate the fundamental idea. A significant passage from Russel-Smith's *Industry and Commerce*[8] presents a vivid picture of the situation in this respect, although some expressions are open to criticism:

The sparse population seizes upon the raw products of nature, or produces raw materials requiring the least labor. A dense population, having few raw materials per capita, must fabricate them to a high degree to make value. In the new forest lands, one person to two or three square miles, will make a satisfactory living by trapping fur-bearing animals and gathering gums, herbs, and roots. A population slightly more dense will cut down the forest and sell logs as lumber. A sparse population upon the open plain will employ itself in tending herds of sheep and cattle, and will export wool, hides, and animals. If the population increases and the climate is suitable, the level plain will be carelessly plowed up and sown to grain, which will be exported to the densely peopled regions in exchange for manufactures. This, in brief, is the explanation of the great commerce of the second half of the nineteenth century and the present. The European peoples settling the comparatively empty lands of America have been producing wheat and sending it back to the better yielding wheat lands of Europe; they have been sending beef and pork to the European countries, where the pastures are better and cattle more numerous per square mile; they have been exporting lumber to the countries where forests are better kept, because the European population is dense and the American population has been, and still is, relatively scanty. This is the chief explanation of the commerce of the newly settled lands in Dakota, Nebraska, or Saskatchewan with the older settlements to the eastward, whether in England or New England.

[8] Russel-Smith, *Industry and Commerce* (London, 1925), p. 661.

It must be kept in mind, however, that it is the supply of *all* factors in a region that counts, and that capital and various mineral resources and other factors are sometimes as important for the division of labor and trade as the supply of land per capita. Furthermore, the density of the population is itself to a large extent a result of the supplying of other factors like coal and iron mines in favored regions. It is necessary to consider each region's equipment as a whole in every analysis pretending to be more than an exemplification of certain special tendencies. Professor Smith overlooks this fact when stating: "It is a surprising fact that the United States with all its land and agricultural wealth has not become an important exporter of dairy products." [9] As a matter of fact, the rich supply of all sorts of natural resources and capital per capita in the United States—or its relative scantiness of labor, which is the other side of the same thing—suffices to explain why labor-requiring dairy products are expensive and neither have been nor probably will be exported from that country in the future.

The examples so far have been chosen only from cases where the supply of labor and arable land has a decisive effect on the division of labor and thus on trade. In that way it has been possible to keep the reasoning very simple. It might be useful here to add an example of the influence of the relative scantiness of the supply of capital. The period between the two World Wars offers a great number of such examples because of the extreme scantiness of capital caused in some countries by the destruction of war and the unsettled conditions of peace. Poland and the Baltic countries had a rate of interest for business credits varying between 15 and 30 percent after conditions became sufficiently stabilized for a comparison with money rates in other countries to have real meaning. In Czechoslovakia rates were somewhat lower, but still out of proportion to quotations in Western Europe. The influence of this scantiness of capital on the direction of industrial development was conspicuous. To take one instance only, new sawmills were started everywhere in the numerous forest districts in those countries, in spite of the fact that the quality of wood was poor in many places. Pulp factories, which can use second-grade wood, developed much less simply because they required large amounts of capital, whereas the cost of sawmills of modern construction was far lower.

Finally, in studying the factor supplies in a region, one must consider not only the scarce factors that have a price but also to some extent the various kinds of land or "nature" that command no price. This may seem paradoxical from the standpoint of the ordinary one-market price theory, in which it is usually considered self-evident that factors which are not scarce fall outside the economic analysis and there is no need for economizing with them. Yet after some reflection

[9] *Ibid.*, p. 88.

it becomes clear that in a study of pricing in many communicating markets attention must be given to factors that are scarce in some regions, even if they are free in others. This is only an extreme case of relative scarcity; factors may in some places be so cheap that they command no price at all. Land of a certain quality is practically free in some parts of Australia and Argentina, whereas it is scarce and expensive in other parts of the earth, and this fact influences the inter-regional distribution of production.

§ 8. *Summary*. The first condition of trade is that some goods can be produced more cheaply in one region than in another. In each region the exported goods contain relatively great quantities of the factors cheaper there than in the other regions, whereas the goods that can be more cheaply produced in other regions are imported. In brief, commodities containing a large proportion of dear factors are imported, and those containing a large proportion of cheap factors are exported.

In this analysis it must be borne in mind that whether a factor is cheaper or dearer in region *A* than in region *B* can be ascertained only when an exchange rate between the two currencies has been established; and that rate depends upon *the conditions of reciprocal demand*, i.e., upon all the basic elements of pricing in all regions. Nothing less than a consideration of all the elements that constitute the price mechanism—the system of mutual interdependence—can adequately explain the nature of interregional trade. If this condition is kept in mind, the simplification can be carried even further. There is no doubt that varying factor supplies are the main cause of the inequalities in costs of production and commodity prices that lead to trade. One region compared with another has a very large supply of certain factors but little of others. When demand conditions do not counteract this inequality of supply, the outcome is an inequality in relative prices of factors and goods in the isolated state; and after the establishment of an exchange rate a situation arises where *A*'s abundant factors are found to be cheaper there than in *B*, and the scantily supplied factors dearer there than in *B*. Keeping these qualifications in mind, one may in such cases use the words "abundant" and "scanty" where the words "cheap" and "dear" would be more exact.

Australia trades wool and wheat against manufactures because the former products require much land of grades found in large quantities in that region, whereas manufactures require large quantities of labor and certain gifts of nature, such as coal and iron mines, which are scantily supplied in Australia. Thus, certain grades of land are exchanged for labor and for other grades of land. In a strict sense, Australia exports goods containing much land not because land is abundant but because land is found to be cheaper there than in other regions after trade has started; but this evidently comes to very much the same thing. Only if demand conditions were so peculiar that land—in spite of the abundant supply—was not cheaper than in regions with a scanty supply, could circumstances be different. Failing such extraordinary demand conditions, one can say that trade implies an exchange of abundant factors for scantily supplied factors.

§ 9. *Notes on similar viewpoints in works by earlier writers.* It is noteworthy and peculiar that the viewpoint in this chapter was generally neglected in earlier treatises on international trade. The fact that the productive factors enter into the production of different commodities in very different proportions, and that *therefore* (relative prices of the factors being different in different countries) an international specialization of production is profitable, is so obvious that it can hardly have escaped notice. Yet this fact was long ignored in international trade theory. There can hardly be any other explanation than the dominance of the Ricardian labor cost theory—in the form of the doctrine of comparative cost—which is built on the explicit assumption of proportionality among the quantities of all factors except land in all in-dustries. This assumption precludes the study of varying proportions. In a consistent mutual interdependence theory of the international aspects of pricing, however, the idea is necessary and self-evident.

It is not surprising, then, to find it first touched upon not by the English classical school but in French works. Viner[10] has drawn attention to an interesting passage in Sismondi's *De la Richesse Commerciale.*

Il y a certaines manufactures qu'un très petit capital suffit pour mettre en mouvement, parce que la matière première est de peu de valeur, et qu'elle en acquiert une très considerable par le travail d'un seul artisan. Le point de la France et d'Alençon, la dentelle de la Flandre et celle de Mirecourt sont des exemples de cette espèce de manufactures. Les femmes qui les travaillent ne gagnoient que 25 à 40 centimes par jour suivant leur habileté . . . Le bas prix de la main d'oeuvre permet donc toujours aux pays pauvres de vendre certaines productions à meilleur marché que les pays riches; aussi l'Angleterre, la nation la plus riche de l'Europe, a-t-elle toujours besoin de celles qui ont moins de capitaux qu'elle, non-seulement pour les productions qui ne sont pas propres à son climat, mais encore pour celles dont le prix est surtout composé de main d'oeuvre; tandis qu'elle peut vendre meilleur marché que toute autre nation celles dont le prix est surtout composé de profit; elle tire des dentelles et des toiles de la France et de l'Allemagne, de la bonnèterie de l'Ecosse, et elle distribue des étoffes, de la quincaillerie, et des marchandises qu'elle a importées des Indes, et non ouvré elle-même, à tout l'occident.[11]

Sismondi did not develop the idea further; that was done three decades later by Longfield, an Irish economist of considerable originality. From his *Lectures on Political Economy* I make the following quotations:

[10] Angell, "Theory of International Prices," *Journal of Political Economy* (1927), p. 622.

[11] Sismondi, *De la Richesse Commerciale* (Geneva, 1803), I, 256.

Suppose two countries between which existed a perfect freedom of inter-
course, let them be similarly circumstanced as to soil and climate, but in one
the inhabitants are all free, while in the other the laboring part of the population is in a state of slavery. The commerce between those countries will
necessarily consist of exchange of the products of harsh disagreeable labor
from the country of slaves, for the result of skilled and educated labor from
the land of freemen. The master will not employ his slaves in a more agreeable kind of labor, when he can gain a little more by a different sort, whatever be the hardship and disagreeableness. But the freeman will not sell so
cheap this additional sacrifice of ease and comfort; but as his own interests,
not those of his master, are concerned, he will learn every kind of skilled
labor with greater facility and less expense than the slave.[12]

Further on Longfield asserts:

I have also shown that in a highly civilized society, skill, intelligence, and
integrity will be more general, and therefore will have a less effect in increasing wages; while on the other hand, the laborer already in possession of all
the necessaries and comforts of life will not easily be induced to engage in a
disagreeable and unhealthy occupation. To induce him to do so he must be
highly paid for the hardships he encounters, and in consideration of the higher
qualities which are employed . . . Hence, independent of every difference of
soil or climate, *the exchange between two countries, such as I have described,
will consist principally of articles produced by that species of labor which in
each country is relatively cheapest.*[13] The one will export articles where skill
and integrity are required on the part of the workman and where intelligence
and capital are required on the part of his manager.

Longfield then proceeds to demonstrate that this country will have a low
rate of interest and will export goods that require much capital. He
continues:

But the case will be different in the less civilized country, where life and
property are insecure, and capital therefore scarce, and profits high and the
laborer needy, ignorant, and dishonest. The exports of this country will consist
of articles produced by the most unwholesome and disagreeable labor, but in
making which skill and honesty are not required from the laborer; such exports, in short, as in a lecture of last term I said were naturally produced in
a country where slavery was allowed.[14]

Curiously enough, John Stuart Mill, although he must have been
familiar with Longfield's writings, seems never to have touched upon
this line of reasoning. Not even Cairnes, who stressed the influence of
noncompeting groups on prices in general, analyzed the effects on international trade of different scales of remuneration in different countries. Although later writers touched upon the question, they did not,
so far as I know, make it the subject of any analysis.[15] It is significant

[12] Longfield, *Lectures on Political Economy* (Dublin, 1834), p. 70.
[13] Note that Longfield does not think of cheapness relative to effectiveness, as
did the classical economists. The italics are mine.
[14] Longfield, p. 240.
[15] See Nicholson, *Principles of Political Economy,* II (London, 1897), p. 313;
Bastable, *The Theory of International Trade* (London, 1903), p. 32.

that Bastable did not mention this viewpoint in the chapter entitled "The Influence of Foreign Trade on the Distribution of Income," which considers only variations in the scarcity of land relative to that of other factors, and not the changes in relative scarcity of productive factors in general. The influence of the classical approach, with its fixed scale of remuneration, etc., is evident.

Del Vecchio's *Teoria del Commercio Internazionale* contains some similar ideas. Europe has low wages and America low rents. Each district exports the products that require much of the cheap factors. Thereby, the demand for labor is increased in Europe and the demand for land is increased in America:

Complessivamente sono favorite quelle forme di rimunerazione che in un paese sono piu scarse, e sono diminuite quelle che sono piu alte; la concorrenza internazionale essendo rivolta ad esportare quei prodotti che sono ottenuti con fattori di produzione piu a buonmercata. Si tende ad una relative livellamento per il fatto che sono favoriti nelle importazioni poco rimunerati.[16]

It is somewhat surprising to find that this idea is not followed up at all in the chapter on the effects of international trade on the distribution of wealth. In that chapter, he discusses the relation between rents and other incomes just as in the orthodox classical analysis.

Later, some well-known writers gave close consideration to this set of problems. Taussig[17] decided that the "modifications" of the classical theory that they make necessary are not very important. Eight years earlier, Heckscher published in Swedish a more comprehensive and very important analysis under the title *The Effects of Foreign Trade on the Distribution of Income.*[18]

Both Heckscher and Taussig regard their discussion as a modification and addendum to the classical theory. Heckscher, for instance, looks upon his paper as an analysis of "the antecedents of the law of comparative costs." I cannot share this view. As a matter of fact, I do not think that it can be fitted into the classical labor cost theory at all. The assumption that the productive factors, except land, enter in the *same* proportion into *all* goods is vital to the classical theory. It cannot be ignored in any attempt at modification.

For the mutual interdependence theory of pricing, the situation is quite different. No such assumption is made, so that a comparison of the price systems in two isolated countries that open up trade leads *immediately and necessarily* to conclusions concerning the influence upon the causes and effects of international trade of the different proportions in which productive factors enter into different commodities. This at

[16] Del Vecchio, *Teoria del Commercio Internazionale* (Padova, 1923), p. 12.
[17] Taussig, *International Trade* (New York, 1927), pp. 50-75.
[18] Heckscher, *Ekonomisk Tidskrift* (Stockholm, 1919). Trans. in *Readings in the Theory of International Trade,* ed. Ellis and Metzler (Philadelphia, 1949).

least was my experience when working out a sort of interdependence theory of international trade.[19] As to the method of dealing with this question I was naturally much influenced by Heckscher's paper.[20] It goes without saying, however, that the point of view first emphatically introduced by Heckscher in international trade theory cannot well be dealt with in the same way when it is an attempt to modify and explain the real contents of the law of comparative costs as when it is a part of a mutual interdependence theory of international trade, where this "law" in the classical sense does not figure at all.

[19] Ohlin, *Handelns Teori* (Stockholm, 1924). Cassel's treatment of this problem in Part V of *Theoretische Sozialökonomie*, 4th ed., which was added in 1929, is largely the same as that in my book, which he indicated in a generous footnote.

[20] My starting point, when in 1921 I began to try to revise the theory of international trade, was to build on a mutual interdependence theory of the Walràs-Cassel one-market price theory type. Only a little later did I realize that a "factor proportion theory" fitted in very well. Heckscher in a preface to the English translation of his paper commits a slight error of memory on this point.

II

On Some Effects of Interregional Trade

§ 1. *Tendency toward equalization of factor prices.* The most immediate effect of trade under the conditions that have been assumed to exist is that commodity prices everywhere are made to tally. So long as there are no costs of transport or other impediments to trade, all commodities must command the same prices in all regions. Trade has, however, a more far-reaching influence on prices and on the use of productive factors—in brief, on the whole price system. To explain this influence is the object of the present chapter.

A very abstract and simple case is one where only two regions and two factors, which may be called labor and land, are considered. One region with an abundant supply of land but a scanty supply of labor finds it advantageous to import goods requiring much labor, since they can be more cheaply produced "abroad," and to export goods requiring much land. Industries that use great quantities of labor are reduced or disappear; hence, the demand for labor is diminished. Industries that use great quantities of land expand; therefore, the demand for land is increased. The scarcity of labor is thus reduced and that of land is increased. In the other region, which has an abundant supply of labor but little land, the concentration on industries that use much labor means greater relative scarcity of labor and lesser relative scarcity of land. In both regions the factor that is relatively abundant becomes more in demand and fetches a higher price, whereas the factor that is scantily supplied becomes less in demand and gets a relatively lower reward than before. *The relative scarcity of the productive factors is reduced in each of the two regions.*

This reasoning also holds good for a greater number of factors. Some of the factors are relatively abundant in *A*—in the sense that they are, after the opening up of trade, cheaper there than in *B*. Their prices are raised in *A* and lowered in *B*. With the other factors the change is, of course, the reverse. If one compares prices in the two regions directly, one finds that factors cheaper in *A* than in *B* have become more in demand and have risen in price in *A* but have become less in demand and have fallen in price in *B*, whereas the factors that are dearer in

A than in *B* have risen in *B* and fallen in *A*.[1] The effect of inter-regional trade is a tendency toward equalization of the prices of productive factors.[2]

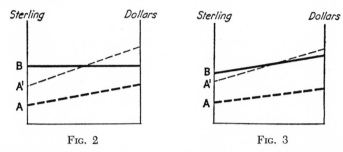

FIG. 2   FIG. 3

A graphic illustration may help to make this point clear. Fig. 2 reproduces Fig. 1 in Chapter I to illustrate the position before trade has had any influence on prices. Fig. 3 shows the change in factor prices brought about by trade, if the rate of exchange is assumed to be £1 = $2. It is seen that prices of the factors in *A* have relatively and absolutely approached their prices in *B*. The curves *A'* and *B* are closer. The factors that were cheaper in *A* than in *B* (the left portion of the curve *A'*, below *B* in Fig. 2) now command a higher price in *A* and a lower price in *B*, whereas the other factors (to the right of the point of intersection) are now cheaper in *A* and dearer in *B*.

It is here assumed that the number of factors is considerable but that there are only two regions. Evidently there is nothing in this reasoning that will not apply also in the case of several regions.

It is easy to give examples of this price equalizing tendency of trade. Forests are cheap in northern Scandinavia, and therefore wood products are exported. But if there were no export of such goods, the Scandinavian forests would certainly be much cheaper still. They would not, as they do now, feel the influence of the demand from other parts of the world. In the United States, on the contrary, forests are fairly dear, but they would be still more so if wood products could not be imported from Canada and Scandinavia.

In the case of Australia, agricultural land would evidently be cheaper than it is now if no agricultural products could be exported. The same would be true of Argentinian beef. In Europe the situation would be the reverse, agricultural land reaching very high price levels if no food could be imported. Thus, trade has raised the price of Australian and

[1] Compare, however, § 4 below, where it is shown that the fall is only *relative* to the price change of the same factor in the other region. In terms of goods, its price may rise.
[2] Cf. Heckscher, "The Effects of Foreign Trade . . ."

Argentinian land but lowered the price of European land. *Relative to the price of land,* wages have been lowered in Australia and raised in Europe.

§ 2. *No complete equalization.* This tendency toward an equalization of both factor and commodity prices is the natural consequence of the fact that *trade allows industrial activity to adapt itself locally to the available factors of production.* Industries requiring a large proportion of certain factors gravitate toward regions where those factors are to be found in large quantities and therefore at low prices. Producers, no less than consumers, look for the cheapest market. In brief, an uneven distribution of productive factors will, unless it is balanced by a corresponding geographical unevenness of demand, cause factor prices to be different in the various regions, and bring about a certain division of labor and trade between them. Some commodities are produced exclusively in one region and exported to the others. If in actuality there were no costs of transport (the assumption underlying the present analysis), many commodities would belong to this group. But because of the many impediments to trade several regions produce the same commodity, some of them importing a little of it, others exporting. It is even conceivable that a region will produce exactly what it needs of a certain article. A discussion of these cases can be undertaken more profitably after the impediments to commodity movements have been considered.

It has been shown that trade tends to counteract the original price inequality and bring about a more uniform price formation among regions. One might ask whether trade can in this way make prices in the various regions coincide exactly. In such a situation trade would not disappear, as one might be inclined to think at first, since the old price inequalities would immediately reappear. On the contrary, price equality assumes a certain adaptation of demand to the supply of factors, i.e., the maintenance of a certain interregional division of labor and trade.

Complete equality of factor prices is, however, almost unthinkable and certainly highly improbable. The location of industry and thereby the demand for factors cannot completely adapt themselves to factor supplies in each region, chiefly because industrial demand is always the "joint demand" for several factors and because factors are not completely mobile. The combination cannot be varied at will; on the contrary, the most economical combination is determined by prices of the factors and physical conditions. Consequently, the best adaptation of production to the geographical distribution of industrial agents, which would be the result of trade under the simple assumption here, cannot lead to a complete interregional factor price equalization; some factors will still command higher prices in one region and lower prices in others, and vice versa.

It is not worthwhile to analyze in detail why full equalization does not occur;[3] in any case, when the costs of transport and other impediments to trade have been introduced into the problem, such an equalization is obviously impossible. Consequently, the following analysis recognizes that prices of productive factors vary from one region to another even after the establishment of interregional trade.

In this connection one thing should be noted. When a concrete case of trade is analyzed, it is easy to point to the existing factor price discrepancies as the cause of trade. Australia and Argentina export wheat, partly at least because wheatland is cheaper in those countries than in Great Britain. Scandinavia exports wood products because forests are cheaper there than in most other countries. China, Japan, Turkey, and some other countries export raw silk not only to the United States but also to France because silk requires much labor and wages are low in the former countries. In brief, each region produces and exports commodities requiring relatively large quantities of factors that are at present cheaper there than in other regions.

This argument is, however, not quite satisfactory. The present price situation is in itself a result of trade, i.e., of the conditions of demand that are called forth by trade. A valid explanation must go further back to the question of why wages or the price of forests are lower in certain regions than in others. On the whole it can be said that wages of ordinary labor are low because the supply of other factors is very scanty, i.e., because labor is the relatively abundant factor. Similarly, forests in Scandinavia and wheatlands in Australia are cheap because they are abundant.

§ 3. *Gain from interregional trade.* A complete local adaptation of production through interregional factor movements and the resulting complete price equalization would make prices just the same as if there were only one region and no geographical distribution of the industrial agents. The joint supply of factors would be used and combined just as in the one-market theory. Space would be of no consequence. In such a state prices would be different from what they are when there are a number of isolated regions. Clearly, the price changes caused by interregional trade under the assumptions here lie somewhere between the two extremes of isolation and complete equality. The tendency is to push prices from the complete independence state to the complete equalization state, but it is not completed. Factor price differences are reduced but they do not disappear.[4]

The great inequality with regard to factor equipment in the case of

---

[3] Cf. Appendix II.

[4] The conditions under which a complete equalization of factor prices occurs have been analyzed by Paul Samuelson in "Prices of Goods and Factors in General Equilibrium," *Review of Economic Studies,* 21:1-20 (1953-1954).

no trade means an enormous loss,[5] for it is not balanced by a corresponding inequality in demand. In one region wheat must be produced by an intensive application of labor and capital on each little bit of land; in another region vast areas of land are barely used at all or cultivated with a very small amount of labor and capital. The condition in the second region involves a comparatively wasteful use of land, whereas capital and labor are used wastefully and inefficiently in the first region. Had there been only one region with the same total supply of productive factors as in all the existing regions together, the use of the factors would be more efficient. The total production of all goods taken together would be much greater. One would not in one place spend a great deal of capital and labor to increase production a little when the same result could easily be obtained through a slight increase in the cultivated area, while in another place land is wasted for lack of demand. Instead, labor and capital would be transferred from places where their marginal productivity is low to places where it is higher. The prices of these factors would everywhere be the same, which would mean a much better utilization of them than would obtain in the case of a number of isolated regions.

When trade allows industry to adapt to local conditions of production, somewhat the same result is reached as if only one region existed. If the prices of factors are completely equalized interregionally, the combination of factors in the various industries is exactly the same as in the case of one region only. As has been stated already, space would be of no consequence if production could be adapted perfectly to the available facilities. Even though as a matter of fact there is only a *tendency* in this direction, prices in each region being moved somewhat in the direction they would take in the case of one region only, yet a similar gain from better utilization of the industrial agents through trade will of course ensue. Land will still be cultivated more intensively in one region than in another, but some capital and labor in the region poor in land will be withdrawn from wheat-growing. Wheat will be imported from regions which have an abundant supply of land and are therefore able to increase their production of wheat by adding comparatively little capital and labor. Much wheat for the British Isles is grown in Argentina with the use of less capital and labor than it would require in Great Britain. At the same time many manufactured articles for Argentine consumption are produced with a similar saving in Great Britain with its wealth of coal, iron, and labor.

Were the mobility of the production factors among the regions free, a leveling of their prices and a more efficient combination of them

---

[5] "Loss" is a reduction and "gain" is an increase in the real national income in terms of commodities.

could be brought about through a movement from a region where some of them were cheap to others where they were dearer. This movement would diminish their supply and thus raise their prices in the former region and increase their supply and lower their prices in the other regions. For example, a transfer of British coal and iron mines and labor to Argentina would tend to equalize their factor supplies and their prices.

There are, however, many different obstacles to such movements (which will be discussed later). There is nothing to do but to use the factors where they are and to locate production so that it suits the geographical distribution of the factors as well as possible. At the same time, factor inputs are adjusted so that in this indirect way a certain equalization of prices takes place through the interregional exchange of commodities. The total volume of production is increased. Thus, *the mobility of goods to some extent compensates for the lack of interregional mobility of the factors;*[6] or (which is really the same thing), trade mitigates the disadvantages of the unsuitable geographical distribution of the productive facilities. This is the cause of gain from interregional trade under the simplified assumptions made so far.

§ 4. *Effects upon factor prices in terms of commodities.* There remains one most troublesome question concerning the effect of interregional trade on price relations. The discussion so far has considered only its influence on the relation between commodity prices in various regions —a complete equalization as a result of trade—and on the relation between prices of productive factors in various regions, finding here a tendency toward equalization. One must study the no less important question of the effects of trade upon the relation between commodity prices and factor prices in *each* region.

The amount paid for the use of all the productive factors is always equal to the total value of the goods produced. Since trade and interregional division of labor mean a more efficient production and a larger volume of commodities, the prices of the factors must obviously rise in terms of commodities. If the commodity price level in each region has been kept constant, factor prices expressed in terms of money must rise. Suppose, for instance, that as a result of trade an index number of factor prices for all regions taken together has risen by 50 percent, i.e., that the total output of goods has increased to this extent. Is it certain that an index number for factor prices in any one region has risen?

[6] In a discussion of trade between two countries of which the one has skilled, the other unskilled, labor, Longfield observes, "Commerce which exchanges the production of human labor has the same effect as if the laborers themselves could remove from one country to another, without greater expense or inconvenience than attends the removal of the goods which they manufacture." *Lectures on Political Economy*, p. 239.

What determines the extent of that rise? Evidently this amounts to asking whether all regions reap a gain from trade and what determines the amount of gain that goes to each of them.

First, is it conceivable that a certain region A might gain nothing at all, its factors being as an average neither dearer nor cheaper than before? The answer is in the negative. The change in production caused by trade implies a change in the relative scarcity of A's factors, with those contained mostly in A's exports rising relative to the others. Consequently, if A exports agricultural products and imports manufactures, the terms of trade between these two classes of goods must now be more favorable to agricultural goods than they were when A was isolated. If the price level has been constant, such goods are dearer, whereas manufactures are cheaper than before. This is an advantageous situation, for a region that concentrates upon agriculture will receive more manufactured goods through imports in exchange for agricultural exports than it could produce for itself. In the same way, the region that exports manufactures will also benefit.

Only if trade did not change the relative scarcity of factors in A at all would it be conceivable for the terms of trade to be unaffected and for A to reap no gain at all. But such a case is impossible, for trade cannot fail to cause some change in the relative scarcity of the factors.[7] In fact, no change in the use of A's factors can take place except under the stimulus of a change in commodity prices in favor of its export goods. Nonetheless, interregional trade is inconceivable without such a change in production.

Whereas it is inevitable that each region should reap some gain, with its price level for factors rising as a result of trade, nothing has indicated how the gain will be divided among the regions. Indeed, the whole idea of dividing the gain caused by trade is of doubtful value. Neither does it seem very fruitful to ask under what conditions one region gains *more* than another, considering the unfeasibility of quantitatively measuring the gain. The question assumes a much more realistic aspect in a discussion of how far certain *trade variations* are advantageous to one region and disadvantageous to another, which will be considered later. At present it is enough to know that the total value of all productive factors in terms of goods will rise in all regions as a result of trade. In other words, it can be taken for granted that the level of factor prices will rise in all regions. Consequently a relative decline in the

---

[7] Bastable and others think it quite likely that the large region derives no gain whatsoever. This erroneous conclusion is the outcome of their disregard of changes in the relative prices of the factors of production other than those that have to do with rent, and their consequent assumption of constant cost as a normal case. Cf. Bastable, *Theory of International Trade*, ii. Note, however, a realistic analysis must consider economies of large sale. See Chap. III. In the classical analysis—even in Taussig's writings—there is a certain confusion with regard to these economies and "increasing return."

price of one of them, say labor, compared to another, say land, does not necessarily mean that the wage level is lowered in terms of goods. Should Australian labor be worse off because of international trade? Of course not.

Rent is usually a fairly small part of the total national income. Assume that it is 5 percent and rises to 10 percent, while the total income of the region increases by 50 percent. In terms of goods, rent is then three times as high as before. If wages are reduced from 65 to 60 percent of the total income, then labor's absolute share will still be much larger than before (60 percent of 150 being 90 as compared with 65). In terms of commodities, rent has risen 200 percent and wages 38 percent. Wages are such a substantial part of the total income that it is almost unthinkable that a considerable rise of the latter could fail to raise total wages also, even if the percentage going to the laborers became somewhat reduced.

Other factors are in this respect probably in a very different position from labor. Import of foodstuffs into Great Britain has probably lowered the rent of agricultural land not only in a relative sense—its percentage of the national income being much smaller than it would be in isolation—but also absolutely, in terms of commodities.

Unfortunately, this kind of reasoning about the total gain from interregional trade and its division among the various regions and productive factors is subject to such serious qualifications that it can claim only a limited interest. First, use of the concept "constant price level" in an investigation into any fundamental change of the economic conditions is open to strong criticism. For that reason a comparison between the isolated state and a state of interregional trade will always be somewhat lacking in concreteness. On the whole, a comparison of two cases of differing amounts of trade—after, for example, a reduction of tariffs or costs of transport—is likely to be more profitable. An analysis of the results of the opening of trade between regions that have before been isolated does nevertheless seem necessary as an introduction because it throws some light upon certain fundamental relations.

Second, the total supply of productive factors would certainly not be the same in an isolated state as it is, for example, in Great Britain. Many people would have starved to death before the population reached anything like its present figure. Clearly the effects of interregional trade cannot be studied independently of that trade's influence on the supply of productive factors. The analysis in the present chapter merely paves the way for a fuller discussion later on.

§ 5. *Generalization of one idea underlying classical law of comparative costs.* There is one aspect of the interregional division of production that has always attracted much attention and been the subject of much intricate analysis, although it is in fact only one of a large class of phenomena, and easily explainable as such. According to the classical theory of value the possibility that a country may import certain goods, although they could have been produced with less labor at home than in the exporting country, has naturally been considered as an extremely important, even as *the* fundamental, problem of international trade. Viewed from a consistent equilibrium theory of prices it is not so.

It has been found that each region will export the goods it can produce cheaper in *money* costs than can other regions. The cheapest possible combination of productive factors is of course used under all conditions, insofar as their location allows. This minimum cost combination naturally depends upon the prices of the factors. If one factor is too expensive, another one will be used. Although the cheaper factor renders less service than the more expensive one, the difference in price may more than make up for this, and the costs of production will therefore be lower.

In Central Europe the land that would yield the largest crop of rye per acre—if a certain amount of capital and labor were spent on it—is practically never used for rye but for wheat-growing. The reason is simple: wheat can afford to pay a higher rent. The cost of rye is found to be lower when grown on land that is not good for wheat. It yields less per acre, but this lower yield is more than compensated by the lower rent to be paid. Similarly, when wheat and wine compete for the same land, the latter is often the stronger. Demand for wine is so insistent that wine can afford to pay a higher rent than wheat. Such is the case in many places in Southern Europe, where wheat is grown on land that yields less than vineyards would if they were used for wheat.

The same applies to labor. A man with a $10,000 salary will not be used at a job that a $3000 man can handle almost as well. A banker does not do his typing himself even if he is better at it than his typist. One will always prefer to use a greater quantity of a cheaper factor than a smaller quantity of a dearer one if the total costs are lower that way. The combination of raw materials and half-finished goods follows the same principle.

The only case dealt with so far has assumed that the factors or elements to be used are all found in one region. The truth of the statement that the minimum (money) cost combination is chosen is therefore evident; there is nothing peculiar or calling for special "laws" in explanation. The ordinary price theory is clearly sufficient. It is difficult to see why it should be otherwise when the factors or materials are situated in different regions. The land that is best for rye, in the sense that a given amount of capital and labor will yield more rye there than on other sorts of land, may be used for wheat, while rye is imported from regions that only have land of second-rate quality. This is exactly what happens in Northern Europe: to produce lace, fine cutlery, or surgical instruments, costly American labor will not be employed, even though it might produce a greater quantity of goods per day with the aid of a certain amount of other resources than Belgian or German labor. The low wages of the latter more than make up for their lower efficiency.

In the same way, using the classical terminology, one may say that a unit of productive power—whatever that might mean—in one country can produce a greater quantity of a certain commodity than a unit of productive power of a different sort in another country, but that the commodity may nevertheless be exported from the latter to the former. The price of the unit of productive power in the former country is too high—which is a way of saying that its superiority is greater still in other industries.

In this analysis there is nothing peculiar. A mutual interdependence theory of interregional trade—based on money costs (prices) and not on real costs—has no use for a special law of comparative cost, which gives a flavor of paradox to a fairly simple relationship while being from other points of view a result of unnecessarily extreme simplifications. Indeed, this so-called law is only a special instance of the tendency to find the cheapest possible combination of productive factors.

Regional borders influence the "minimum (money) cost combination," and thus the location of production, because it is impossible to combine factors located in different regions. This circumstance makes it necessary to extend the one-market theory to cover pricing in several interrelated markets.[8]

Consider the growing of wheat and potatoes, wherein the latter requires much more labor than the former. The best wheatland would yield more potatoes per acre than does the poor land that is actually used for potato-growing; but its rent is higher, which makes the present distribution of land between the two crops economical. Assume that such a district is divided into two regions, of which *A* has all the wheatland and *B* has all the potato land. Clearly it is still advantageous to use the land as before, unless the supply of the other factors causes a change. Assume that rich iron ores and coal mines are discovered in *B*. Labor becomes relatively scarce in that region, and wages rise above their level in *A*. This tends to give *A* an advantage in both potato- and wheat-growing, especially in the former, which requires plenty of labor. The outcome may well be that all the potatoes and part of the wheat are grown in *A*, whereas *B* concentrates upon manufactures and some wheat-growing, applying very little labor to each acre of cultivated land.

In this case the inability to move labor from *A* to *B* prevents the

---

[8] The tendency to use the minimum cost combination is at work as before. Thus, no dualism in the treatment of the price problem need arise. When the classical labor value theory is applied to the phenomenon of international trade, the law of comparative cost—of which one has, curiously enough, heard nothing in the analysis of domestic trade—is introduced as a *deus ex machina*.

most economical use of the land. The various qualities of land cannot be utilized as they would be if they were located in the same region, for the cooperating factors are not to be found in the desired quantities. The minimum cost combination will still be chosen, but since the relative prices of the productive factors are different from what they would be if there were only one region, it will be a different combination from that in the one-region case. Only a study of the price mechanism in a world of trading regions can throw light upon the nature of the "distortion" of relative prices and the use of the factors which results from the location of factors in different regions.

§ 6. *Summary.* A condition of interregional trade is that the fundamental elements of pricing in each region, the supply of factors and the demand for commodities—behind each of them *two* basic data—have such a relation to each other that after trade certain factors are cheaper in one region than in the others and the cost of production of certain commodities is lower. That this condition is fulfilled is chiefly owing to the great differences in factor supplies. Keeping in mind the influence of demand, one may say that a "sufficient" condition of trade is an inequality in the endowment of factors of production, for this inequality is never exactly balanced by the same inequality in demand.

The effect of interregional trade is to equalize commodity prices. There is also a tendency toward equalization of prices of the factors of production, which means a better use of them and thus a reduction of the disadvantages arising from any unsuitable geographical distribution of productive factors. From each region goods containing a large proportion of relatively abundant and cheap factors are exported, and these factors therefore become scarcer than before, whereas goods containing a large proportion of scarce factors are imported, and the latter factors therefore become less scarce. The same result could be obtained by a transfer of the factors. As it is, interregional trade serves as a substitute for such interregional factor movements.

In addition, the price of the factors that become relatively less scarce may well rise in terms of commodities, for the total volume of goods increases, owing to the more efficient use of the productive facilities made possible through trade, and the *average* prices of all productive factors consequently rise in all regions. The nature of the price mechanism is essentially the same as in the one-market theory, but its "construction," i.e., the relations that determine the actual prices, is different. Only a study of the whole price system can explain the interregional division of labor or any other phenomenon of pricing.[9]

[9] For a mathematical presentation of the analysis in Chaps. I and II the reader is referred to Appendix I, which readers who are not afraid of mathematics should study before Chap. III.

III

Another Condition of Interregional Trade

§ 1. *Modifications of the atomistic price theory.* The doctrine in the two preceding chapters has been built on the basis of a one-market theory of pricing, assuming *full* general mobility and divisibility. It must now be modified to reflect conditions that are more characteristic of the modern economic world. Most books on economic principles recognize such a modification in several respects but ignore or pass over it in interregional trade. The object here is to indicate the special significance of the lack of general mobility and divisibility for interregional prices and thus to give a more realistic picture of trade. However, without an exact description of the kind of regions under analysis, the picture must necessarily be lacking in concreteness. The generality of interregional trade theory is abstract, and this can only be remedied when it is applied to special cases.

First, one cannot assume, as has been done above, that commodity prices are everywhere equal to costs of production—both expressed in money. A considerable amount of friction will make prices deviate for shorter or longer periods from the cost of production. Nor can one assume the prices of the factors of production to be uniform throughout a region. Unskilled labor in one industry will sometimes receive a much higher wage than labor of the same quality in another industry. This also is owing to circumstances which may be grouped together as "economic friction."

A tendency toward equality exists, however; when inequalities occur, the price mechanism tends to restore them. Such reactions require more or less time. For this reason, every explanation of pricing that attempts more than a statement of certain equilibria must consider time, and this is the chief cause of the difficulties encountered by a concrete theory of pricing. Even if no new disturbances occur, prices will not return to the equilibrium that existed before this special disturbance happened, for during the "disturbed" situation the basic elements determining the equilibrium are changed.

Another modification, but of a somewhat different character, is necessary. The equilibria toward which prices tend in a society characterized by friction do not correspond to the equilibria in an "atomistic" society;

35

the variations or disturbances do not oscillate around the full-mobility equilibrium, i.e., they do not balance each other but show a net movement in certain directions. A most important example is the use of productive capacity. An industry's output may oscillate, for instance, from 60 to 100 percent of capacity, giving an average of about 80 percent. The prices of the products therefore tend in the long run to equal the costs of production when only 80 percent of the capacity is used, whereas in an atomistic society full capacity would always be used. The existence of overhead charges is hence of great importance for pricing under dynamic and frictional conditions.

The equilibrium toward which prices tend in a friction-dynamic society thus differs in important respects from that which is advanced under the atomistic theory. To enter upon a detailed analysis of the question would be inappropriate here. I must suppose that the general theory of pricing is known and investigate how far the modifications that friction introduced in this theory have special bearing on the interregional aspects of pricing.

Three cases are of special importance. First, the temporary existence of unused capacity affects price policy. For instance, producers may sell at different prices in different markets. This price discrimination is significant for interregional pricing because space permits a number of more or less sharply distinguished markets. The question will be dealt with in detail after the obstacles to commodity movements have been considered.

Second, a considerable amount of risk is inevitable when the productive factors are directed toward certain uses, for they cannot easily be turned into other channels. This is particularly the case when capital is invested in capital goods or in training human labor. Such risks, and the consequent losses when things go wrong, must for society as a whole be compensated for in higher returns when conditions are normal; at least a tendency of this sort exists. Some of these risks are considerably greater in certain regions than in others, a fact that exercises some influence upon the interregional division of labor. Since the only regions of importance in this respect are nations, the problem can best be dealt with later in connection with international trade.

Third, lack of divisibility makes production on a large scale more efficient up to a certain point than production in small quantities. Here is an element of fundamental importance for interregional trade; in fact, a revision of the doctrine explaining same becomes necessary.

§ 2. *Lack of divisibility.* Although no parallel is entirely satisfactory, it may be said that regions, like individuals, reap certain advantages from specialization, quite independently of any difference in their productive equipment. Specialization in certain commodities makes production on a large scale possible; and only when production is so organized can there be an economical division of labor using machines and tools of the most efficient size.

Most regions would be forced to produce a great many articles on a small scale if they imported nothing from "abroad." If manufactured for small "home markets" only, cash registers, dyestuffs, complicated machines, tools, and many other things could be had only at considerably higher cost than at present, when they are produced for the world market. Clearly the economies of large-scale production make interregional division of labor profitable, irrespective of differences in the prices of the factors of production. In other words, the advantages of specialization resulting from large-scale production encourage interregional trade. Commodities that can be produced very cheaply in huge factories or in large groups of factories, and which when located together reap benefits from external economies, are spread over large markets, each factory or group of factories being sufficient to satisfy the demand of a large number of consumers. On the other hand, commodities that can be produced with the same or greater efficiency in small establishments, e.g., made-to-order clothing, generally do not travel very far; they are produced where they are in demand, even if the demand in each region is comparatively small. The former kind of articles figures prominently in interregional trade, but not the latter.

It is not my purpose to enter upon a general discussion of the nature of these economies of large-scale production; for this I refer the reader to books and articles by Bullock, Carver, Landry, Taylor, Frank Knight, and John M. Clark. Only a few observations need be made here. If all original productive factors—raw materials, tools, and implements—were completely divisible, any combination of them could be established, irrespective of their absolute quantities. The most economical combination—that which gives the lowest cost of production per unit of commodity—would be equally possible on a small or a large scale. An optimum proportion would exist—dependent, of course, upon the prices of the factors—but no optimum size.

As a matter of fact, the size of the factory or establishment is very important. Only when fairly large quantities of certain factors and implements are used can the minimum cost combination be reached. This may be because the least unit of certain instruments is large, or because a larger unit is relatively more "efficient" than a smaller one. In short, so-called internal economies are the result of a lack of divisibility.

External economies of production are similarly attended by incomplete divisibility. For example, the advantages an industry derives from concentration in a certain locality are to some extent dependent upon the existence of a well-organized labor market. If textile factories, for instance, were scattered over a large area, manufacturers could not be certain of finding instantly a sufficient supply of the special type of skilled labor they required. In other words, the labor market must be of a certain size to be efficiently organized; clearly this can be termed a sort of incomplete divisibility.

There are, of course, many other advantages to a geographical concentration of industry, but a well-organized labor market is often the most important one, particularly in industries where the skill of the workman is great. The little town of Pforzheim in Germany, for example, had 1000 jewelry factories and about 30,000 jewelry workers in the late 1920's. It is not necessary to give further examples. Enough have been given to indicate that the various economies of large-scale production are the result of a lack of divisibility.

§ 3. *Large-scale economies as a cause of trade.* It was earlier pointed out that the advantages of producing a large quantity of a single commodity instead of a little of all commodities must lead to interregional trade. Each region has a limited supply of productive factors and is unable to produce efficiently everything it wants. By specializing in certain articles, it can produce more cheaply and export a part of its output in exchange for other goods. To demonstrate the importance of this, assume that a number of regions are isolated from each other, and that their factor endowments and their demand are so balanced that the relative prices of factors and commodities are everywhere the same. Under the assumptions of Chapter I, no trade is then possible. As a matter of fact, insofar as the market for some articles within each region is not large enough to permit the most efficient scale of production, division of labor and trade will be profitable. Each region will specialize on some of these articles and exchange them for the rest. The character of this trade will be entirely a matter of chance if factor equipment is everywhere the same, for it doesn't matter whether a certain region specializes in one commodity or another, just as uniformly endowed individuals can with equal advantage specialize in any kind of work.

Trade of a different sort will also ensue. The demand for productive factors must vary in the industries where large-scale production is economical. Some industries require relatively more labor, others require more capital. Consequently the different growth of these industries in different regions causes a shift in the demand for factors of production and makes their relative scarcity unequal; certain factors become cheaper in one region than in the others. This makes further division of labor profitable. Each region will also export other goods that contain relatively large quantities of the factors that are now cheaper there than "abroad." If a region has some large-scale industries requiring much capital and certain gifts of nature, like iron and coal resources, labor and agricultural land will be less in demand and cheaper than otherwise. Consequently industries using much of the latter factors will grow up as in a sense "supplementary" to those using much of the former ones.

This case would, of course, never occur in reality. Factor endowments and conditions of demand are always such that relative prices of both factors and goods are unequal; therefore trade arises from both sources. The tendency toward specialization because of differences in factor endowments is strengthened by the advantages of large-scale production. The location of an industry in one region and not in another might simply be due to chance, the industry having gained strength in that particular region and having reached an efficient scale. Since it cannot profitably be carried on in every region because the total demand is too small, it tends to remain where it was first located. However, although such cases should not be ignored, they are probably not very important. On the whole, it is certainly the differences in factor supplies that determine the course of interregional trade—unless regions are small—whereas the advantages of large-scale production are more in the nature of a subsidiary cause, carrying the division of labor and trade a little further than it would otherwise go, but not changing their main characteristics.

If the actual location of production is not that which the available factors would seem to indicate, the usual explanation is that this location was natural in earlier times, and when certain industries have once been established in a place, there is a tendency for them to remain there. Friction of various kinds here is responsible; examples will be discussed later, e.g., the tendency of the glass industry to remain in regions with ample supplies of wod after coal, a much cheaper fuel, became available in other regions. As time goes on, however, the tendency toward a more economical location and trade will break through. Indeed, it is more surprising that industries move about as easily as they do in spite of all deterrent elements than that they tend to remain for some time where they have developed.

Industries are not equally sensitive to the advantages of large-scale production. Some derive practically no advantage from it once they have reached a certain small size. Others can produce at competitive prices only with large factories, so that smaller establishments either become large or are quickly eliminated. The boot and shoe industry is often mentioned as a rather surprising example of the former case, and the automobile industry is of the latter type. The most important industry in which the small unit is supposed to be as good as or better than a bigger one is agriculture. Great caution, however, is needed in every discussion of this question. Even in typical large-scale industries, small firms often seem to do quite well for considerable periods of time. Nowhere is the importance of large-scale organization more conspicuous than in agriculture; indeed, the entire Danish farming industry is in important respects one unit. Scientific experiments, control of the quality of the products, the manufacturing and marketing of eggs, butter, and bacon, and many other functions of essential importance are performed by the farmers' cooperative associations, which form large economic units in close cooperation with one another. If it is true in a sense that the smallest productive unit for making eggs is a hen, and that it is also the most efficient one, one may say with equal justice that the entire Danish poultry industry is the economic unit, and that it would be relatively less efficient if it were only 10 percent or 1 percent as large. Thus, Danish agriculture in a way reaps many advantages from large-scale organization; and the fact that it was first organized on that basis still gives it a superiority over farming industries in some other countries—an advantage lost slowly, if at all, as the latter industries attain a similar organization.

§ 4. *Effects of trade due to economies of large-scale production.* What effect has interregional trade—or rather the extension of trade—caused because of indivisibilities leading to economies of large-scale production? Such trade means that industry is organized so as to use the industrial agents more efficiently. In other words, the disadvantages arising from the lack of divisibility are substantially reduced. For various reasons, however, this tendency toward the most efficient use of factors cannot be fully realized. An extension of the scale leads not only to better use of the industrial agents but also to waste in several respects. Beyond a certain point the disadvantages more than outweigh the advantages; consequently the optimum size does not give the perfect balance that would characterize the case of full divisibility.

This conclusion that interregional trade reduces the disadvantages of indivisibility corresponds to the previous conclusion that trade mitigates the disadvantages of an unequal geographical distribution of productive agents. If they were completely mobile, demand would govern their distribution; as it is, trade, or the mobility of goods, compensates to some extent for the lack of interregional mobility of factors. Combining these two results leads to the conclusion that interregional trade has a tendency to reduce the disadvantages of both the lack of mobility and the lack of divisibility of the factors of production. However, the earlier formulation can perhaps be regarded as including the latter; if the productive factors were completely mobile, they could be brought together in such a way that the lack of divisibility would mean the least possible advantage. Interregional trade caused by the lack of divisibility has a similar tendency. Thus, all interregional trade, whether due to the one cause or the other, might be regarded as a substitute for geographical mobility of the productive factors. However, it is more clarifying to say that trade is caused by the uneven distribution of the factors (relative to demand) and their lack of divisibility, and that it tends to reduce the disadvantage caused thereby.[1]

[1] To avoid misunderstanding, it should perhaps be pointed out that the tendency of commodity prices to coincide with average costs may be weak if many firms are below the optimum scale of output; marginal costs—i.e., the cost of an increase in output—then fall below average costs. Such a situation is not compatible with long-run equilibrium, but it has to be analyzed in connection with international trade variations, especially in their relation to the business cycle, and in connection with the influence of unused capacity, both of which questions will be dealt with briefly later.

IV

A Variation of Interregional Trade

§ 1. *Relative factor prices and terms of trade after a change in demand.*
In order to demonstrate the nature of interregional trade as clearly
as possible, it was necessary to compare a state of complete isolation
with one of trade. However, more light can be thrown upon the nature
of existing trade and the price mechanism in trading regions by studying
some familiar variations of the above theme. Therefore, the reactions
of the simplified price mechanism to a change in demand will be briefly
discussed as a preparation for a more concrete analysis on the basis of
less abstract assumptions.

Imagine two regions in which all commodities are either import or
export goods. Under free trade, this is the most probable situation,
although it is conceivable that the costs of production of some commodities may be the same in both regions and that these goods are
not traded. It is also possible that some goods are used in only one
country.

Now suppose that B's demand for some of A's goods increases; the
relative scarcity of the factors required for the production of those
articles is also increased. To such an expansion of the demand for some
goods there is a corresponding slackening in the demand for other
goods[1] and a reduction of the relative scarcity of the latter's productive
factors. The owners of the first factors get higher incomes than before,
compared with the incomes of others. Since most of these factors belong
to A, its total income rises in relation to the total income of B. A buys
more of the joint product of both regions than before, and B buys less.
Assume, for instance, an increase in B's demand for paper, pulp, and
wood from A. The forests in A must necessarily rise in value and afford
their owners an increased income. If the total money value of the
product of both regions is kept constant, A will get a higher money
income and B will get a lower one than before.

This analysis holds good for two groups of productive factors in a
single region. When demand changes in favor of the productive factors

[1] I assume that this reduction in demand is evenly distributed over all other
goods, whether produced in A or in B.

42

(e.g., manufacturing labor) belonging to a group of individuals, called A, their income rises and that of other people (e.g., farmers), called B, falls. A is able to buy a greater quantity of goods produced with B's factors than before, whereas B has to be satisfied with a smaller quantity of its own goods, perhaps a smaller quantity of A's goods, and certainly a smaller volume of all goods taken together. Neither of the two groups can buy for more or less than its total income—unless one of them lends to the other—so there is nothing peculiar in the maintenance of equilibrium between the "imports" and "exports" of each.

The change in the distribution of the joint product of A and B has a special character when A and B are two separate regions, e.g., a wood country and a wheat country. B's increased demand for wood products from A raises the relative scarcity not only of A's forests but also of other factors, e.g., labor, which combine with forests in the making of such products. Even if B has as great a supply of labor as A—and no other reason for buying products of A's labor than its favored position in a forest district—the general wage level in A will rise compared with that in B. Demand for commodities is indirectly a *joint demand* for certain productive factors. In this case B's greater demand affects not only the forests' rent but also A's labor, which receives higher wages, whereas in the case of one region the mobility of labor between A and B prevents an unequal development of wages.

Thus, on the one hand, the scarcity of all A factors regarded as one group is increased in relation to the scarcity of all B factors. On the other hand, the factors used in relatively large quantities in A's wood industry grow more scarce compared with other factors in A. If the price level for factors in general in A and B taken together is kept constant, the share of A factors rises and the share of B factors drops. But certain A factors—not used in the wood industry—may be cheaper than they were before.

Not only wood but other goods of A become more expensive than formerly if they use factors of the same sort as the wood industry. Goods not using these factors become cheaper, but the price level for commodities produced in A and exported therefrom rises. The level of prices for B's goods, on the other hand, drops. The terms of trade move in favor of A.

The balance of trade is automatically kept in equilibrium, in spite of the increased value of B's wood imports from A, because A has a greater buying power[2] and B has a smaller one than before. Neither

[2] The term "buying power" is used in preference to "purchasing power" to escape the risk of misunderstanding because the latter is most usual in the expression "the purchasing power of money." Buying power is the total gross income, increased by borrowings and reduced by loans, and expressed in terms of money with reference to a *period* of time.

of them can buy for more or less than its gross income. *B*'s income is reduced, yet a greater amount than before is spent on wood products, so that a smaller amount remains for purchases of other goods from *A* and of *B*'s own goods. *A* gets a larger and *B* gets a smaller share of the joint product of both regions than formerly.

This analysis of the readjustment of the trade balance differs from the orthodox one, according to which the increased demand for wood products tends to give *B* an unfavorable balance of trade, its imports being in excess of its exports. To induce *A* to buy more of *B*'s goods and thus maintain the balance, *B* must offer its goods at a cheaper price: in Mill's language, it must "force an increased demand for their exports, by offering them at a lower value." [3]

Mill and his followers tacitly assumed that the buying power or the total demand of each region is the same as before. In other words, they assumed that the demand curves in terms of money, like those of Edgeworth and Marshall, are unaltered, apart from the original variation that forms the object of the analysis. Only on that condition would *B* offer to *A* more tempting terms of trade in order to increase its exports. This assumption is clearly contrary to the facts. The original change in the direction of demand will change the relative scarcity of *A*'s and *B*'s productive factors—each considered as one group—in favor of the former; thus, the total buying power of *A* is increased and that of *B* is reduced. It is an essential part of the interregional price mechanism that the total buying power in each region, and thus its demand curves, is altered; to overlook this is to ignore a most vital connection. This will be demonstrated in detail later during a closer study of capital movements and the monetary mechanism of other variations. [4]

One aspect of this classical analysis of variations in demand has been frequently discussed. *B*'s reducing the price of its goods, in order to balance its increased imports, may induce *A* to buy a greater quantity of them; but if the elasticity of demand is less than one, the total value of *B*'s export does not rise but falls. In that way, it is argued, no equilibrium of trade can be established. Defenders of the classical theory assert that if all goods are taken together, the demand for them cannot be less than one. This may or may not be so; but even if the elasticity were much less than one, equilibrium would be restored through the influence exerted on the quantity of commodities demanded

---

[3] *Principles of Political Economy*, ed. Ashley (London, 1920), III, xviii, § 4. This same view lies behind Keynes' pessimistic attitude toward the feasibility of war indemnity payments. *The Economic Journal* (1929).

[4] The fact that people with increased incomes in *A* may buy considerably more or less of *A* goods than would the people with reduced incomes in *B* is not considered.

because of the increase in *A*'s buying power and the reduction in *B*'s.

§ 2. *Reactions of factor supply.* No attention has here been given to the existence of economic friction, except insofar as the economies of large-scale production are concerned. Friction blurs the line of the analysis and makes it necessary to consider the time needed for the transfer of productive factors from one industry to another, and similar problems. Furthermore, the reaction of the factors in each region has been ignored, and a tacit assumption has been made that they are unaffected by the price alterations involved. On that condition the enhanced demand will raise the price of the goods and of the productive factors concerned. The general tendency is that greater quantities can be obtained only at increasing cost—cost meaning the same as expenses of production in terms of money—although this tendency may be more or less modified through the influence of the economies of large-scale production. A short time after the original change, however, this influence is probably not very great. The rule is certainly that in the short run increased demand leads to higher prices.

As time goes on, economies of scale in industries producing the articles that have come into greater demand tend to reduce expenses more or less. Of still more importance, *the supply of many productive factors reacts to the stimulus of increased reward.* Labor that has received increased pay may appear in larger quantities, and its price may tend to fall; although it is not impossible also that the supply may be reduced, and a higher standard of living may make people less inclined to undertake hard and disagreeable work. In this "price sensitiveness" of the factor supply lies the chief difficulty of the problem. To handle it adequately in general terms is clearly impossible. It is necessary to take concrete cases and inquire, for example, how far economies of large-scale production and the increased supply of factors cause a tendency toward price reductions for the goods in great demand—a tendency in the reverse direction from that characteristic of the first stage.

To study the reactions of the supply of productive factors thus becomes of paramount importance. I have entirely neglected it previously on the assumption that the basic conditions of pricing—factors, supplies, desires and wants in general, physical conditions of production, and ownership of the productive factors—do not react to the opening of trade or to variations thereof. As a matter of fact, not only *the supply of factors* but also the *desires and wants* are subject to change under the influence of trade and its fluctuations. The increase in *population* in various regions, to take only one example, has perhaps been more affected by trade than by any other single circumstance; and trade has been potent in creating a new demand for new goods. The effects of present trade and of variations in trade are felt in all economic life, and the forces that govern the supply of productive factors and the demand for various articles, i.e., *the so-called basic elements, do not remain untouched by it.* Their reaction is, of course, largely a question of time. Every analysis of trade effects must in this respect be a description of a *time-using process.* This will be demonstrated clearly during the presentation of concrete cases of special types of regions, above all, of different countries.

Part Two

International Trade Simplified

V

International Comparisons of
Productive Factors

§ 1. *Introduction.* Part Two contains an application and modification of the doctrine presented in Part One. Just as nations are certainly the most significant of all regions, so the theory of international trade represents the chief application of the general theory of interregional trade. The most important border lines for the movement of industrial agents are the national frontiers; and mobility *within* the various countries is no doubt considerably greater than international mobility. The analysis in Part One will therefore be helpful in a study of trade between nations, which fulfill so well the conditions established for regions. It cannot, of course, be applied without important modifications, for it was built upon drastically simplified assumptions. Above all, the supply of productive factors is not given once and for all, and it is affected by price variations as well as by circumstances that have nothing to do with trade and pricing. Various labor qualities, for instance, are trained only insofar as they are needed and *because* they are needed. In short, the supply of industrial agents may sometimes be described more adequately as the *result* of trade rather than as its cause.

Another simple assumption in Part One—that regional borders offer no obstacles to commodity movements but exclude interregional transfers of factors—will not be relinquished in favor of a more realistic conception until Part Three. There the influence of frontiers on commodity movements will be considered, as well as the international mobility of productive factors and its significance for international trade. Part Two proves that many essential features of international trade may be explained before including the former considerations, the cost of transport, or the international immobility of factors of production.

On the whole, Part Two applies the theory of interregional trade to a special case, one in which the regions are different countries. It emphasizes traits that are characteristic of conditions in such regions. The previous assumptions concerning factor supply are generalized. For the moment, complications arising from the international monetary mechanism are bypassed.

49

§ 2. *Different groups of labor.* Labor has so far been regarded as one factor, just like capital, while several types of land have been mentioned. There are cases, as shown in the examples, where no finer classification of the factors of production is necessary, at least so long as one is content with broad outlines. Yet it cannot be overlooked that the various groups of labor perform different tasks and receive unequal wages, and that the flow of individuals from one group to another is not free and easy. Should not such groups of labor be regarded as different factors of production? Since some of them receive relatively much higher pay in one country than in another, this must have something to do with the international division of labor. Countries with a large supply of labor having high technical skill are able to produce many manufactured goods more cheaply than other countries. A rich supply of individuals with a good general education who receive salaries not much higher than the wages of unskilled labor—while in other countries they receive twice or three times as much—makes for a superiority in industries requiring plenty of educated labor. In brief, if differences in wages among groups of workers in a country last for a sufficient period of time, these groups may well be regarded as separate productive factors, just as are different qualities of land.

A fine distinction between a great number of labor groups, however, meets with the difficulty that transition is comparatively easy. Laborers belonging to one trade may leave it and go to another without any preparatory training, or with only a short one, if the requirements for skill are moderate. Such movements are likely to follow when wages in one trade rise considerably above wages in others of the same general standard. Considerable wage differences among laborers of the same grade cannot last very long unless some kind of monopolistic policy interferes; in other words, the groups are not entirely noncompeting. This is true to some extent even for groups of different abilities. Unskilled labor may become skilled, and skilled labor of one kind may— sometimes easily—acquire the skill needed for a different sort of work and thus change over to another group. The supply of the various grades is consequently, within certain limits, able to adjust itself to the demand; and the state of supply on a certain date is not of great significance since it can be changed. It will not determine the location of industries but will itself vary to suit the kind of production that other and more permanent elements call forth.

The question of where to divide labor into separate factors depends upon the nature of the special problem under discussion. When a relatively short period of time is considered, the discrimination may be fine. The change in supply that can take place in the short run is relatively small and need not impair the conclusions. However, a study of thoroughgoing changes in international trade and the conditions of production, i.e., of the fundamental determining elements, can be based only on a broad division of labor into large groups. Although such groups do not form watertight compartments, the transitions from one to another either are small or can be considered separately.

In other words, the reason for making a distinction between various labor groups is that changes in their relative incomes may occur and last for a considerable time, which will influence production and trade. The basis for drawing a border line between them must be the difficulty of transfer. If it is very easy to go from one trade to another, the factors should be regarded as part of the same group because no important variation in relative wages is likely to arise, or at least to last any length of time.

In most cases a broad division into three factors only will suffice: (1) unskilled labor, (2) skilled labor, and (3) technical labor. The second group comprises mechanics, foremen, office clerks, etc., and the third represents the technical and administrative leadership required in production. For some industries female and child labor is of special importance; in a study of the location of such industries these two kinds of labor must be treated as separate factors. Countries with a rich and cheap supply of them will attract such industries if the conditions of production are in other respects comparable. "Being able to use in greater degree the labor of women and children, the silk industry has tended to move to the regions where such labor is easily got and the laws regulating it are loose or loosely enforced." [1]

In some cases unskilled labor consists of two or more distinct groups having different qualities and recognizable as separate factors of production. A typical example is found in countries with a population composed of several races. South Africa, for instance, has a considerable number of both black and white unskilled workers, drawing extremely unequal wages. There the qualitative difference is notorious, and since a transition between the two groups is excluded, they should be regarded as separate factors of production, although they no doubt complete for certain types of work. It is doubtful, however, how far white labor in South Africa should be called "unskilled." In such a case the difference in usefulness between white and black labor is in most occupations not exactly offset by the difference in wages, so that there is a tendency for the native labor to take over almost exclusively the unskilled work, whereas the white population concentrates on semi-skilled and skilled work. In South Africa, the "field of unskilled work has passed entirely out of white hands, and the field of semi-skilled toil is passing . . . The white man demands, indeed needs, a very much larger wage than the native African . . . In periods of industrial depression the employers find it necessary to close down or to dilute their

[1] Taussig, *Some Aspects of the Tariff Question* (Cambridge, 1915), p. 232.

white labor with black. And wherever the economic pressure is acute, it is only a matter of time before the white man will be ousted." [2]

When such a process has been completed, the difference between wages in the unskilled trades, which are practically reserved for native labor, and the skilled trades, in which native labor plays an insignificant part, is much greater than in countries with a racially uniform population. This affects the location of production and international trade. South Africa has become a place for manufacturing industries that can use great quantities of low-grade unskilled labor. For instance, a part of the gold-mining industry is largely dependent upon the supply of cheap native labor.

It is clearly necessary to regard black and white labor as separate factors of production. Relative scarcity of black labor will—in the same way as relative scarcity of natural resources—react unfavorably on the wages of the white man. The two labor factors are more "cooperative" than "competitive."

Special importance must be attached to the closed-shop policy of trade unions. Not long ago it was considered impossible for trade unions to establish sufficient obstacles to movements among unskilled trades to create and maintain for any length of time considerable wage differences. Experiences have since shown that this policy can succeed. The closed-shop policy has proved to be still more successful in the case of skilled trades. First, transition from one to another is naturally difficult since it often requires a long time and special training. Second, the trade unions are able to exercise a considerable influence on the ability of young labor to enter such trades and thus increase the supply. The latter fact is of great significance, for variations in supply brought about by wage discrepancies do not always take the form of a real flow from one trade to another, but simply of a tendency on the part of the rising generation to turn especially to favored trades, with the influx into the others declining. In fact, by restricting the free choice of occupation, trade unions are often able to influence the supply of labor both in skilled and unskilled trades and thus to affect the relative wage levels. These wage discrepancies may last long and affect noticeably the international division of labor.

Examples are not difficult to find. Strong trade unions often raise wages in prosperous industries much above the level for similar work in other industries; they do, in fact, sometimes succeed in expropriating a part of the business profit, though as a rule only after severe and costly industrial warfare. The result is that the development of the industry is much hampered, whereas it may expand or fail to decline in countries that have less favorable conditions but pay a reasonable wage for labor on this general level. The special increase of wages for

[2] *The Nation* (January 14, 1928).

labor in the former country has exactly the same effect on the location of industry as a scanty supply of labor in general in the latter country. In the last resort the closed-shop policy attempts to create an artificial scarcity of labor for certain jobs. There seems to be little doubt that some Australian trade unions—e.g., the wool shearers—have forced their wages to such a height that the expansion of certain "natural" industries has been seriously retarded.

In some countries the trade unions have raised the wage level in manufacturing industries considerably above the level of agricultural wages. This cannot but check the development of manufactures and maintain a greater volume of production in agriculture; the supply of industrial workers is evidently restricted, and that of farm laborers is increased. These two groups should in such a case be dealt with as separate factors of production. In one country the wage discrepancy is probably greater than in another, which affects seriously the lines of economic development and the course of trade.

When important differences continuing over fairly long periods exist between various groups of unskilled labor, it is evidently convenient and fruitful to regard them as separate "subfactors," although all are parts of the same factor—unskilled labor. Skilled labor should, whenever necessary, be treated in a similar manner. There are many sorts of skill, and a lasting scarcity of one sort relative to others may make it advantageous to regard them as separate subfactors. Often a distinction between skilled labor in a narrow sense and so-called semiskilled labor is of great importance.

In the case of technical labor it may also prove necessary—especially in investigations of developments during fairly short periods of time—to use many different subfactors. Electrical engineers and shipbuilders cannot do the same work, nor can mechanical engineers and chemists. A scarcity of electrical engineers, for example, may hamper the development of a new electrical industry even in a country where the conditions for that industry are in other respects excellent, and in spite of a great supply of chemists.

In discussing the broad characteristics of international trade and its long-run tendencies, however, the influence of wage differences within labor groups on the same general level—e.g., mature unskilled men or engineers with a university training—may as a rule be ignored. The three labor factors mentioned above (unskilled, skilled, and technical) may suffice perhaps as well as any other broad division. Nevertheless female and child labor must be taken into account in special cases, just as must the existence of various labor groups caused by trade union policy or other kinds of monopolistic regulation.

It is evident that no clear-cut lines can be drawn and that, whatever border lines are drawn, no factor is ever perfectly uniform throughout.

Unskilled labor covers a great many different types receiving varying wages, although the differences are not always so substantial as to necessitate a subdivision into minor groups. At one time a certain trade may get a slightly higher pay than the others, and at another time the situation may be reversed. Variations occur all the time, and economic friction prevents a smooth and instantaneous adjustment. Industries in one part of a country may be more prosperous at one time than those in other parts and therefore able to pay higher wages, and such wage discrepancies are reduced slowly. It must be kept in mind that labor is not perfectly uniform and that, in spite of all qualifications, the distinction between various groups of labor is important. It seems best to recognize this clearly from the beginning.

§ 3. *Different natural resources.* The productive factors usually called by the general name "nature" should be separated. No description is necessary to show that natural resources differ immensely in quality—in fact, they have hardly anything in common except that they are all gifts of nature. Although many of their differences are from an economic standpoint unimportant, a sufficient number of economically essential inequalities remains to necessitate a division of natural resources into a great number of factors. Such a procedure does not present the same kind of difficulties as does the subdivision of labor into several separate factors. Whereas transition from one labor group to another is in many cases comparatively easy and materially affects the supply within each group, such a transition between different factors of nature is possible only by means of capital investment. Even when long periods of time are considered, a fine division into an arbitrarily great number of factors is possible.

It is usually convenient to handle a more limited number of groups, each containing factors essentially similar, and to disregard their inequalities. Such a grouping of natural resources may be effected in more ways than one—e.g., on the basis of usefulness for various economic purposes. It is not necessary to consider qualities so common that they are found almost anywhere, such as the fact that the surface of land is in most places level and firm enough for the building of houses. Such qualities need be considered only in special cases. A simple way of finding out which properties of nature are generally relevant is to examine them from the point of view of various industrial activities. Five classes readily present themselves: (1) agriculture and forests, (2) fishing and hunting, (3) the production of minerals, (4), the production of water power, and (5) transport activities. The establishment of a small number of qualities from each of these categories gives a bird's eye view of the equipment of natural resources in different countries and some idea of the division of production and trade among them. The grouping is not invalidated by the fact that coal and water power, for instance, can replace each other. So can labor and nature to a large extent.

In almost all cases, however, it is of paramount importance to reckon with a much greater number of factors to understand the conditions governing international trade. The possibilities of qualitative differences in soil, climate, wind, humidity, or surface are immense. It is therefore practical further to divide each factor into a number of subfactors. They differ in many ways; their differences are in some cases of little economic importance and may be disregarded, but in others they are essential.

§ 4. *Different capital factors.* For purposes of comparison, the capital available in a country is expressed as a sum of money that represents the cost of reproducing the capital goods in existence after deduction for depreciation and obsolescence. The price of this capital during a period of time is the rate of interest.[3]

The rate of interest varies with the conditions of the transaction. A sum of capital may be available during longer or shorter periods, and this influences its employment, for the combination of a series of short-time loans cannot fully make up for the capital's being lent for only a brief space of time. The "waiting" done by the capitalist may be said to be of a different quality if he has the right to stop it on short notice than if he promises to wait a certain definite period of time. His reward—the rate of interest for "short" capital—is as a rule lower than the long-time rate of interest. In some respects this difference resembles the inequality between a home laborer and a factory laborer. The former is not unwilling to work in a factory, but he wants the right to use his own labor at home any time he pleases. This difference between "long" and "short" capital must be recognized in some cases by treating them as separate factors of production.

In the same way, capital available for risky undertakings is rendering a different service than is capital for safe investments only and may with advantage be treated as a separate factor. The distinction is similar to that between "long" and "short" capital. It seems not at all unlikely that the comparatively slow economic development in France before World War I had something to do with the French capitalists' preference for safe investments, such as Russian state bonds, ironical as it may seem in the light of subsequent experience.

To avoid misunderstanding, it should be added that the expression "mobility of capital" refers to abstract capital, not capital goods. The incomplete international mobility of capital is due to the preference of capitalists for home investments and not to the difficulty of moving capital goods, which is discussed in the analysis of the incomplete

---

[3] The fact that many existing capital goods have a technical form that differs considerably from what is most economical at present will be considered later.

mobility of commodities. However, an upper limit to the *net* movement of capital from one country is set by the domestic supply of liquid capital, which comes from new savings and from the gradual release of savings that were invested in capital goods during earlier periods.

It is unfortunate for an analysis of interregional and international trade that the one-market theory of the Walràs-Cassel type has given so little attention to the question of defining and limiting the various productive factors and has thus left no familiar conclusions upon which the present many-market theory may build. This lack is the reason for the foregoing remarks on the meaning of the term "factor of production" with regard to labor, land, and capital.

§ 5. *International comparisons of unskilled labor.* To make international comparisons of factors is extremely difficult because of their thousand and one qualitative differences. One of the principal advantages of the classical three-factor approach is that these difficulties come to the fore and must be faced at the outset. This may seem to make the theory of international trade more complicated, but it is certainly conducive to greater clarity in the long run, for an apparent simplicity gained at the expense of fundamental aspects of the problem must ultimately prove a disadvantage.

To begin with labor, is unskilled labor in one country the same as unskilled labor in others? Or, are there qualitative differences of importance? The answer to the latter question is of course in the affirmative. A Javanese cannot render the same service as a Dutch worker, and an Indian is not so useful as an American. Even unskilled labor calls for a combination of qualities rarer among some people than among others. Some degree of reliability, honesty, discipline, general education, and other attributes is required in modern production both in and outside of factories. Deficiencies in one or several of these respects are reflected in lower productiveness.

There are international differences in the "efficiency" of unskilled labor, but it is difficult to say whether they should be attributed to differences in its quality or to a greater supply of cooperating factors. An American worker in a cotton mill produces more than an English worker, at least in the lower grades of goods; the superiority of the English over the Italian is perhaps still greater. But an Italian immigrant in the United States will, after adapting himself to the new conditions, produce more than the English worker in an English mill and probably as much as his English and American fellow workers in the American mill. To account for this by a change in his education does not seem practical. A much better way is to classify all individuals as belonging to the same labor group if under similar conditions as regards machinery and organization they are fairly equal in efficiency, disregarding minor individual differences. This can probably be said of Italian, English, and American workmen, provided they live at a certain standard and have received a similar education.

The United States Tariff Commission states that the higher efficiency of American labor in cotton-weaving is a matter not of individual superiority on the part of the American weaver but of difference in industrial organization. It is natural, therefore, to regard unskilled labor in Italy, Great Britain, and the United States as one and the same productive factor, notwithstanding inequalities in productivity arising from differences in the technical milieu created by other factors and larger markets. The output per head is greater in a country like the United States where comparatively large quantities of skilled labor, technical labor, and capital cooperate with each unskilled worker and where production can be organized on a large-scale basis. Clearly, the qualitative differences are not so numerous and important as they look at first sight, but enough of them exist to make it necessary to deal with unskilled laborers of widely different capacity as separate factors of production.

In an analysis of present trade it is not worthwhile to ponder to what extent observed inequalities in ability are due to environment and to what extent they can be mitigated through training or a higher standard of living.[4] It suffices to know that these differences may exist for a period of time amply sufficient to influence radically the location of industries and the course of international trade.

Unless the number of subfactors is made very great, which would not be practical, some inequality in usefulness exists even between laborers belonging to the same subfactor. However, the fact that Danish and Swedish labor, for example, are not of exactly identical quality can be taken into account through the use of different technical coefficients. Even if the relative prices of all factors in the two countries were the same, their combination in production would differ; consequently, the technical coefficients cannot in all countries be expressed as the *same* functions of the relative factor prices. On the contrary, differences in quality as well as differences in productive organization affect the forms of functions and the costs of production in each country.

Yet certain differences in the equipment of productive factors may be so dominating—and therefore certain to express themselves in a definite way in prices—that significant conclusions concerning international trade can be drawn from a brief comparison of the factor supply in various countries, even if the comparison is made without considering all qualitative inequalities. For example, Italy has a relatively greater

[4] Cf. Taussig, *Some Aspects of the Tariff Question*, pp. 194-196.

source of labor and a smaller supply of natural resources than does Australia. This fact is not invalidated by the fact that labor in Italy and Australia is not quite the same.

§ 6. *International comparisons of other labor qualities.* The difficulties in making international comparisons of other groups of productive factors are similar to those of unskilled labor, and the method of presenting them is consequently more or less the same. Skilled workers in the United States and Germany, Italy and Russia, do not perform the same tasks. One reason is that they have different abilities, but a still greater reason is that they work with different equipment of other factors, as a result of differences in the size of the home market. Although the qualitative differences among skilled labor in various countries are important, they can usually be regarded as the same factor.

All backward countries have some kind of unskilled labor, often different from unskilled labor in the leading manufacturing nations. However, they are often devoid of workers corresponding fairly well to skilled workers in the latter nations. Hence, whereas various sorts of unskilled workers must be regarded as separate factors, skilled labor can be dealt with as one.

Skilled labor must of course be divided into a number of subfactors, and this circumstance must sometimes be given much attention, but it should be emphasized that the differences between its subfactors—e.g., Italian and American skilled workers—are less than they seem at first because they are in a different technical milieu. When such workers are moved to places with similar industrial conditions, their usefulness varies surprisingly little.

Higher grades of labor, called "technical labor," may be dealt with similarly. Although it is obvious that their qualitative differences are more numerous and important than those of skilled labor, it is also true of technical labor that their differences are less than they seem. The efficient organization of production in the United States is probably due only to a small extent to its technical labor being different from that of Europe. Engineers emigrating from Europe are able to do exactly what American engineers do; at home they get less opportunity to organize production on a large-scale basis.

The fact that before World War I the supply of technical labor in Germany was more abundant and relatively cheaper than in the United States was one of the most powerful reasons the German chemical industry had a marked superiority. Similar observations are possible without considering qualitative differences of factors. As a rule, however, greater accuracy is required. One must take into account that technical labor takes many different forms. Electrical engineers cannot easily do the work of mechanical engineers, and vice versa. They are therefore best dealt with as separate subfactors except in a very general analysis. In international comparisons of the productive facilities for various industries it is often important to note that one country has a greater supply of certain types of engineers, whereas another country has more of other sorts. Such differences may be only temporary, but they exercise an influence similar to that of the noncompeting groups of unskilled labor and cannot be wholly neglected.

Great attention must also be given to those qualitative differences that cannot well be described even by a great number of various subfactors. Electrical engineers with fairly equal education and training in Germany and the United States are best dealt with as the same subfactor; yet their qualities may differ in important respects. Technical as are the costs of production of commodities and international trade. processes and the whole organization of production are thus affected,

This circumstance affects the mutual interdependence system of pricing in the same way as do the qualitative differences of other factors. The technical coefficients in each country are not determined exclusively by the relative prices of the factors and subfactors but also by differences in quality; consequently these coefficients may be expressed as functions of the relative factor prices only if the forms of these functions in the various countries differ so as to include the inequalities among workers (whether they are more or less skilled) who are treated as the same subfactor.

Ability to take the initiative, to do new things, is in some ways allied to inventive talent. Like the latter, it is more marked in some countries than in others, not only in the case of technical labor but in the lower grades as well. It is a most valuable quality, which may powerfully affect the location of new industries and trade between nations.

§ 7. *Comparisons of capital factors and natural resources.* International comparisons of capital equipment present difficulties like those of comparing labor factors. It has already been pointed out that for some purposes capital may be regarded as a homogeneous factor of production, whereas for others it must be divided into several subfactors, e.g., "long" and "short" capital. Each of these species can be further divided into capital for "safe" or for "risky" investments. Although no sharp limits exist between such subfactors, the relation between their prices affects the location of industry.

The terms "capital," "long," "short," and "risk" have a universal meaning. Thus, international comparisons of capital are simple enough. Comparing France, Great Britain, and the United States before World War I, for instance, one may say that France had relatively more "safe" capital than did Great Britain, and that the latter country had relatively more of it than did the United States. France had little capital for risky enterprises, whereas in Great Britain a more substantial part of the total capital was so invested—but far less than the corresponding share of American capital. This state of things considerably affected the economic development of these nations and almost dominated the character of prewar international capital movements.

Greater difficulties arise when for a certain period of time capital takes the form of special capital goods. In the long run it can acquire new forms, but the period that elapses before this is possible may be considerable and may influence the international division of production and international trade.

In comparing the productive equipment in various countries, one must give much attention not only to the quantity of capital but also to the technical form of the capital goods. To describe this situation in a country or to summarize the differences among countries in simple terms is clearly impossible; the inequalities are too numerous and of widely different character.

One possible method would be to treat capital goods in the same way as natural resources, although the division into a number of separate factors and subfactors would refer only to a definite period of time. Such a procedure resembles that used in treating allied labor groups between which transition is possible but slow. This method would, however, prove unnecessarily complicated; a country can always establish factories containing capital goods according to the most economical technique. Its ability to "compete" with other countries is determined by the costs of these goods and the current rate of interest, not by the costs of capital goods of an unsuitable kind, e.g., old machinery. These have value only to the extent that they can compete with new machinery. Consequently, contrary to the businessman's impression, factories with old equipment, if they have any value at all, can produce as cheaply as can those with new equipment. Thus, the fact that at a certain time some capital goods have an unsuitable technical form can hardly make a country *less* suited for production of the commodities in question than the height of the current rate of interest would imply.

It is possible, however, that new factories using capital goods of the most economical type are not remunerative in such a country, whereas old factories are so long as their old buildings and machines are not worn out. For a time a country may therefore have a *greater* competitive power in some industries than the height of the rate of interest and the prices of other factors would seem to indicate. This fact should be considered a modification of the theory that has been built upon an assumption of only one or two capital factors.

Striking illustrations of this kind are not difficult to find. The spinning of coarse cotton yarns in Great Britain no doubt benefited after World War I because of the large plants constructed before or during the war in anticipation of a growing market.

In international comparisons of natural resources there are difficulties similar to those encountered in the case of unskilled labor. The best method of comparison is to adopt a similar procedure, grouping the natural resources into a number of factors, each comprising some subfactors.

§ 8. *International differences in the stability of productive conditions and risks.* International production may vary not only in respect of the supply of capital and labor available for more or less risky enterprises but also in respect of the risk involved in a certain enterprise. The same type of production may mean a much greater risk in one country than in another; unforeseen losses and the *need* of risk-bearing may vary, even though the character of production in other respects is uniform.

The more stable the conditions, the more easily all significant risks may be anticipated, and the lower will be the losses, *ceteris paribus*. In some countries the dangers of destructive frosts, plant diseases, or floods increase the losses involved in agriculture, whereas manufacturing industries are less affected. The effect is naturally to discourage agriculture in comparison with other industries.

Frequent revolutionary upheavals exercise a similar effect in the opposite direction. They often cause the loss of such capital as buildings and machines, or established markets, and are therefore a greater burden on manufacturing industries than on agriculture. This fact has some connection with the slow expansion of manufacturing industries in South American countries.

Fraudulent and inefficient government, partial or powerless courts, low business morals, and many other factors also increase the losses involved in carrying on business in a country. The danger of war and of consequent interruptions of normal economic activity and loss of property is perhaps the best example of such influences. First-class foreign firms in the Baltic countries in 1926 were paying 15 to 18 percent interest on English loans, but the same firms could borrow English capital at 6 percent or less for investment in Scandinavia. The difference—a "premium" of 9 to 12 percent—was required chiefly to cover the risk of war with Russia.

It is true that many risks have something to do with the qualities of the natural resources and the population. Land under rapidly shifting climatic conditions is more uncertain in yield than is land of equal fertility in all other respects but in a more equable climate. A detailed description of the various qualities of productive factors therefore takes account of the fact that the use of some of them leads to sudden losses and that they can be combined only with capital of the risk-bearing type. Similarly, bad government and a danger of revolution and war are "social" conditions of production that affect costs and create a need of risk-bearing.

Nevertheless, it seems best to regard *this variability of the productive conditions,* i.e., the absence of stability, as a special aspect of the equipment of productive factors and the social conditions of production at a given moment.[5] Whether dealt with in one way or another, losses owing to instability and difficulties of making correct forecasts vary internationally and must be considered in a study of international trade.

[5] Differences in the social conditions of production can be regarded either as causes of differences in the forms of the functions that govern the technical co-efficients or as additional cost elements of a special sort. See Appendix I.

VI

Some Fundamentals of International Trade

§ 1. *Summary of certain conclusions in Part One.* This chapter will be mainly concerned with a restatement and modification of the conclusions in Part One concerning the nature and effect of interregional trade. Simple reasoning must be abandoned in favor of a more complicated analysis on the basis of the results arrived at in the previous chapter concerning the meaning of the term "factor of production" and the possibilities of comparing the productive equipment in various countries.

The most exact description of trade—whether between countries or regions—is obtained by analyzing a mutual-interdependence system of pricing, which takes account of the existence of several markets for the productive factors. Interregional trade assumes that relative costs of production and prices would vary in different regions without trade; i.e., it assumes a different relation between the supply of factors and the demand for goods in each country. Differences in relative costs of production in an isolated state express themselves after the opening of trade in price differences of such a nature that some goods become cheaper in each region than abroad (prices being expressed in terms of one currency by means of the foreign exchanges).

Part One showed that inequality in the prices of factors in the isolated state is sufficient to cause different commodity prices and thus to cause trade. This condition is fulfilled when the factor supplies are distinctly different in various regions, for it is practically inconceivable that a corresponding difference in the consumers' demand, being indirectly a demand for factors of production, should exactly offset the difference in factor supply.

Generally, abundant factors are relatively cheap, scanty factors are relatively dear, in each region. Commodities requiring for their production much of the former and little of the latter are exported in exchange for goods that call for factors in the opposite proportions, Thus, indirectly, factors in abundant supply are exported and factors in scanty supply are imported.

This is, however, only one aspect of interregional trade. The economies of large-scale production also cause an interregional division of production; they must be considered along with trade due to different factor supplies. The proportions in which the factors are used in the production of a commodity depends not only upon their prices but also upon the quantity to be produced. Consequently, different technical combinations may be used at the same time in different countries to produce the same commodity.

§ 2. *Influence of qualitative differences within the same subfactor.* Although the factors actually mentioned in Part One were comparatively few, the analysis is in no way weakened if finer breakdowns are used, as was seen in Chapter V. Certain qualifications, nonetheless, must be examined whenever it appears that abundantly available and cheap factors will be exported. Knowledge of the equipment of factors is not always sufficient to permit an opinion as to whether one of them is relatively abundant or not, i.e., whether it would be relatively cheaper than most other factors in a country in an isolated state. Conditions of demand also exercise their influence. This is, of course, only one way of saying that the supply of one productive factor must be seen in its relation to the supply of the others and to the demand for the commodities to be produced.

More serious qualifications are called for because of qualitative differences between productive elements treated as identical subfactors.[1] In general, these qualifications mean that the analysis and conclusions can make no such claim to precision as Part One seemed to imply.

In most cases the qualitative differences are a minor element. One can say that Australia has a greater supply of land and less capital and labor than England without bothering much about the considerable differences in the quality of the land. This is an extreme case, it is true; but when a fine distinction in a number of factors and subfactors has been made, the qualitative differences may for most purposes be wholly ignored or considered afterwards as a slight modification.

One may object that in other cases the qualitative difference is the deciding element. A few engineers in one country may have a special knowledge of a particular technical process—or may have patent rights to its exclusive use—and may for that reason be able to produce more cheaply than other countries. In such cases it is no doubt best to regard the different kinds of technical service rendered as an expression of such an important qualitative difference between the engineers that they must be treated as separate subfactors. Indeed, the principle underlying the grouping of various industrial elements into factors and subfactors is that a "factor" shall comprise elements that are fairly similar and a subfactor shall comprise elements that are similar in practically all economically relevant respects. It follows *ex definitione*

---

[1] Similar difficulties arise for the one-market theory.

that qualitative differences between elements belonging to the same subfactor are of only minor importance.

§ 3. *Qualitative differences of commodities and services.* In the previous section account was taken of the international differences in the qualities of productive factors and the consequent impossibility of making a clear-cut, simple analysis sufficiently realistic. It may be practical in this connection to mention that varying qualities of the same commodities are traded.

The case of commodities is indeed parallel to that of factors of production. Just as unskilled labor in different countries is seldom of identical quality, so articles produced in different places show more or less significant inequalities. In fact, competing firms—whether in the same or different countries—rarely produce absolutely identical articles. In many cases the differences are so slight as to exercise little or no influence on trade; in others they are of considerable importance.

English and Czechoslovakian boots for ordinary wear cannot be called identical; nor can one say that the former are "worth," for example, 10 percent more than the latter. If their price is 10 percent higher, a certain number of people will prefer the one kind and the rest will prefer the other. If the price difference increases to 20 percent, some people will continue to buy English boots; if it disappears, others will still buy Czechoslovakian ones. Sales are no doubt affected by price changes, but only to a certain extent and after a certain time.

It has hitherto been assumed that a country exports things it can make cheaper than other countries and imports the rest. This statement clearly assumes that the goods are identical in quality; as soon as this condition changes, the relationship between prices and international trade becomes more complicated.

Similar examples are numerous. Motor cars, cotton cloth, tea, even goods of standardized quality like wheat and iron, exhibit many differences important enough to affect international trade. English pig iron is not quite the same as German; wheat from the United States and from Argentina differs widely; American and Egyptian cotton differs even more.

One should treat all these as different commodities, or as "subcommodities" to indicate that they belong to the same class. Two types of wheat are more similar than wheat and rye and compete more closely for the consumers' demand. Although their relative prices on a certain market may vary, there are as a rule narrow limits for such variations —limits that do not exist for the relative prices of completely different goods.

According to customs statistics, in many countries the same sort of commodity is both imported and exported. This is partly due to the costs of transport, partly to the fact that the imported and exported commodities are of different quality. For instance, before World War I Denmark imported butter from Siberia and exported Danish butter to Great Britain, because of the marked difference in taste. A study of international trade statistics reveals many similar cases.

To understand the conditions of competition in international trade, then, one must often regard articles produced in different countries as different commodities, which are closely related because they are able to satisfy similar wants. In other cases the qualitative differences are so slight that they are best disregarded at the beginning of an analysis; later a modification to include them can easily be made.

§ 4. *Qualifications of the observation that trade tends to equalize factor prices.* It is now advisable to turn from an analysis of the nature of international trade to a description of its *effects*. The most general and exact description may be obtained by comparing the price systems in isolated countries with prices in a number of trading countries. Such a comparison shows the price changes brought about by trade; they consist of an equalization of commodity prices and a tendency toward equalization of the prices of factors. All of this of course is expressed in terms of their relative prices, for no rate of exchange between the currencies can exist without trade, and the absolute prices in one country cannot be compared with the prices in another. The tendency toward equalization of factor prices is explained as follows: goods containing a large proportion of relatively abundant and cheap factors are exported and these factors become more scarce, whereas goods containing a large proportion of scantily supplied and expensive factors are imported and the latter becomes less scarce. Trade consequently acts as a substitute for the movements of productive factors and reduces the disadvantages arising from their immobility. The possibilities of producing on a larger scale reduce the disadvantages of their imperfect divisibility.

These conclusions hold good, with some important modifications, even when factors exhibit such great differences in quality that they seem not to be comparable. Does the fact that the productive factors are *numerous* complicate the question? The tendency toward an equalization of their relative prices is most obvious when only two factors exist; when their number is great, the effect upon some of them may be the reverse. It is conceivable that a scantily supplied factor, relatively dear in the isolated state, should be more in demand to produce export goods that also require large amounts of factors that are abundant and cheap. The abundant factor's cheapness may more than offset the high price of the scanty factor. Trade consequently means increased scarcity of the expensive factor whenever it must cooperate with cheap factors in production for export. Such cases are certainly the exception. There can be little doubt that the general tendency under the given circumstances is to effect a price equalization.

Since the qualities of the productive factors and of the various commodities differ, this beclouds the observation that trade has a tendency toward international price equalization.[2] If an article can be more cheaply produced in one country than in others with the use of a similar technical process, i.e., similar productive factors, clearly some factors must be cheaper there than abroad. But what does it mean to say that some of them are cheaper when their quality in different countries is not identical? There is, of course, no other way than to compare their prices with due regard to their quality and usefulness. Since differences in this respect depend upon the conditions under which the factors are used, and these conditions are not the same everywhere, the comparison lacks a firm basis. In many cases, however, fairly narrow limits for the difference in usefulness may be drawn. A factor in one country may be from 10 to 20 percent more useful than the same factor of a slightly different quality in another country. If the better factor costs 40 percent more, one may say with due regard to quality that the country with the least efficient kind has the cheapest supply of this factor.

Before World War II unskilled laborers in Estonia received about one-third the wages of Swedish workers. Their lower standard of living and deficient education made them less useful, but under the conditions of production prevailing in most industries the difference in usefulness was not so great as to invalidate the relative cheapness of unskilled labor in Estonia. For instance, the most up-to-date Swedish newspaper machine was attended by nine Estonian operatives in 1926. Since the Estonian workers received one-third as much as the Swedes, the labor bill was the same as if three Swedes had been employed. The normal number of operatives in Sweden for a similar machine was five. Thus, in this operation the least efficient labor was the most economical, although the superior technical management in Sweden may have offset this in part.

Similarly, after World War I the Danish superiority over Germany in the machine industry was too insignificant to offset the great difference in wages. German skilled labor received much lower wages than their counterparts in Denmark, which resulted in a large German exportation of machinery to Denmark. The demand for machine workers was thus increased in Germany and reduced in Denmark so that there was a tendency to price equalization of the productive factors.

§ 5. *Further qualifications.* The case is much the same if the qualitative differences of the factors in a certain industry in various countries are

---

[2] A similar lack of precision is found in almost all parts of economic theory, e.g., the law of variable proportions, the principles of overhead costs, and the analysis of price level variations.

so great and durable as to make them subfactors. In order not to make the analysis unnecessarily complicated, a case involving two countries only is considered.

Assume first that certain subfactors are used in country A and others in country B to produce the same or closely similar commodities. Two qualities of land may be so different that they are best dealt with as different subfactors, although both are used for the growing of wheat. Country A has much land of quality q, which is superior, and a little land of quality k, which is inferior. B has little of q and much of k—which under the circumstances in the two countries represents a less valuable endowment. If only k is considered, B has much the greater supply of it. But if both qualities are considered together—wheatland as a whole—A is clearly better endowed. For this reason the land k—and naturally q—is relatively cheaper in the isolated state in A than in B, in spite of the larger supply of the former factor in the latter country. Furthermore, A is able to produce wheat more cheaply than B, *ceteris paribus,* and export it to the latter country. As a result of trade, the price of both qualities of land is increased in A and reduced in B. This may be called a tendency toward equalization. Clearly the supply of good and poor land must be considered together to form an opinion of the "natural" course of trade.

The condition is essentially the same from an economic point of view if the competitive character of the various subfactors arises from the fact that they produce, not goods of a similar quality, but goods that serve as substitutes for each other in consumption. Assume that country A in the isolated state grows not wheat but rye on its poor land. The consumption and cultivation of rye is given up when wheat can be imported from B, and other uses are made of the land. The effect upon factor prices is the same as in the case above. A price equalizing tendency occurs, however, only in cases where the same subfactors exist in the various countries. If A has only good land and B has only poor land, the term "price equalization" has a somewhat different meaning. However, as long as subfactors belonging to the same factor group are concerned, this term conveys an impression of some of the effects of trade. High-grade Swedish iron ores are exchanged for good German coal, because Sweden has nothing but very poor coal mines, and Germany lacks ores of the highest quality. One has to consider the two sorts of coal mine subfactors together, and the two sorts of iron mine subfactors in the same way. Through trade German coal mines and Swedish iron mines get higher prices, whereas Swedish coal and German iron ore are cheapened. This is a sort of price equalization. In other words, when subfactors are highly competitive, they may be considered together, in which case a certain price equalizing tendency of trade is not to be denied.

§ 6. *Exceptions to the rule.* Trade does not tend to equalize factor prices when quite different factors are closely competitive, being used in one industry to produce the same or a similar commodity while otherwise rendering quite different services. This case is by no means rare; on the contrary, a great many goods are produced by means of widely different technical processes.

Consider a few examples. Wheat is grown on large American farms with complicated and expensive machinery, much land, but little unskilled labor. How different from the Arab's old-fashioned methods of cultivation in North Africa, which require fifty or one hundred times as much unskilled labor per bushel! Rice is produced in China and Japan in very much the same way as it was hundreds of years ago. In the early part of the century its cultivation began in the United States by means of newly invented machinery. In spite of the enormous wage difference, the United States exports a significant amount of this grain to Eastern Asia. A similar case is flax-growing, which requires much unskilled labor. It long had its stronghold in countries with very low wages, like the Baltic countries and the parts of Russia bordering on them. In Scotland cultivation declined because wages were too high. Since World War I, however, the invention of labor-saving machinery for pulling and threshing the flax has led to a considerable cultivation of it in the United States and Canada.

The glass industry also offers good examples. For centuries window glass has been blown with the same simple tools, the only substantial improvement in methods of production being in the melting of ingredients. In the twentieth century American methods of machine blowing and Belgian methods of drawing the glass in sheets have been so much improved that they have driven out the old methods, at least in high-wage countries. For glass bottles Owen's blowing machine effected a similar revolution. Yet both window glass and bottles are still produced in considerable quantities by the old methods.

This is not the place to dwell upon the problem of why some commodities can be produced by radically different methods while others cannot, at least profitably. It suffices to know that many important articles are produced in various countries by means of widely different technical processes. In such cases the increased demand, when production is increased for the sake of exports, affects quite different factors from those that feel a lessened demand in the importing country when home production is rendered superfluous. An analysis of these cases when only two countries—e.g., civilized and noncivilized countries—are involved will introduce similar cases when the number of trading nations is considerable.

First, assume that two factors, *q* and *k*, both of which can be used to produce a certain commodity at the same cost under present conditions, *exist in both countries.* Trade in that commodity has for some reason or other been prohibited but is suddenly liberated. In country A the factor *q* is much cheaper than in country *B,* whereas the factor *k* is a little more expensive. Consequently, *A* uses the first factor and *B* uses the second one to produce this article. Under these conditions *A* has lower costs of production than *B* does and exports the commodity to the latter country. Demand for *q* is increased in *A* while demand for *k* is reduced in *B.* So far as *q* is concerned, the price difference between the two countries is reduced; but for *k* it is *increased.* The latter factor becomes still cheaper in *B,* although it was already cheaper there than in *A.*

This is, of course, not the entire effect of the trade. Goods must be exported from *B* to *A* to pay for the new imports, which increases the demand for some *B* factors. It is conceivable that the factor *k* will be used so much in industries producing these exports that its price in *B* relative to its price in *A* will be maintained, but it is not at all certain that this will be the case. The possibility remains that trade will increase the discrepancy between *k*'s price in *A* and in *B,* although it reduces this discrepancy for *q.* This is an important exception to the general rule.

In the theory of the optimum combination of the productive factors, i.e., the analysis of the laws of increasing and decreasing returns, the basic thesis is that a relative increase in the quantity of one factor in production (which means, of course, at the same time a relative decrease in the quantity of other factors) leads to lower relative scarcity and thus lower wages for the former and greater relative scarcity and wages for the latter. The important exception to this thesis is that some factors are so closely competitive that an increased quantity of one of them may lower the marginal productivity, and thus the wages, of the rest. The conclusion regarding the effects of international trade is entirely parallel to the above. The factors may be so highly competitive that relative prices may move in a direction opposite to what the general rule would lead one to expect.

How important are such exceptions? Are they so numerous and significant as to invalidate the usefulness of the general statement of the price equalizing tendency of trade? This is the same as asking whether the various productive factors are mainly cooperative or competitive. In order to answer these questions, one should bear in mind that the productive factors may be competitive, not only if they produce the same or a similar commodity, but in general if one of them is used in industries rendered superfluous because of imports of goods produced by another factor.

It makes no difference, in the hypothetical cases offered above, whether the commodity produced partly by the aid of *q* in one country is quite different from the commodity no longer produced by k in the other country. Production of certain goods is given up or reduced because of imports, and production of other goods is increased for the sake of exports; relative factor prices are thereby affected. But the commodities that B now imports are not all the same or of exactly the same quality as those that B has ceased to produce; hence, the increased demand for factors in A does not affect the same factors as the reduced demand in B. There is no reason for assuming a tendency toward equalization of factor prices insofar as the changes in industry are of this sort.

If trade did not influence the type of goods consumed in each country, i.e., if imports served only as substitutes for identical goods formerly produced at home, the scope for substituting different factors for each other would be relatively limited. However, since many commodities are imported which would not be produced at home, and since the production of other goods is reduced or given up altogether, *the chances of an increase in the international price differences through international trade become much greater.* The strengthening of demand in the exporting country may chiefly concern factors other than those affected by the reduction of demand in the importing one.

For example, in Finland imported German coal takes the place of domestic wood for fuel. The price of forests is reduced, although they are already much cheaper there than in Germany. This discrepancy implies that forests have other uses; otherwise they could not be dear in Germany. Trade in wood products is likely to have an equalizing effect. This is certainly the case with the Finnish export of lumber, pulp, and paper. There can be little doubt that international trade as a whole increases the scarcity of forests in Finland and reduces it in Germany, which brings about a certain equalization.

Thus, the fact that most factors can be used in many different ways and that international trade comprises many commodities increases the possibility that the price equalizing tendency will dominate. It seems certain that a substantial restriction of trade would increase the international differences of the prices of productive factors. In a study of special cases of trade one must, however, include the opposite result as a possibility.

All these circumstances call for another qualification of previous statements as to the effects of trade on commodity prices. The conclusion that a complete price equalization is brought about as soon as obstacles to commodity movements cease to exist is an expression of complete equalization of the supply of commodities. If the fact is now considered that some goods are not produced at all in one country and some are not produced in the other in the isolated state, the equalization of supply conditions becomes something more than a price equalization;

it involves also the supply of new goods that could not profitably have been produced at home. The costs of production of tea in Scandinavia, e.g., would be exceedingly high, many times as high as import prices. But since tea would not be used without importation, it is perhaps somewhat artificial to place all the effects of trade into the formula of price equalization. If this expression is used in the following pages, for the sake of brevity, it must be taken to include all the effects of trade so far as equalization of commodity supply is concerned.

§ 7. *Trade as an equalizer of costs of production.* The statement that trade tends to equalize factor prices internationally refers only to countries where the factors in question are to be found. Many factors exist in certain countries only. Take the case of copper mines. The countries without such mines are in almost the same situation as countries having very few of them, where the price of this factor is naturally lowered by trade; their economic life is affected in virtually the same way.

Consider the case where one country has a world monopoly of a certain factor. Trade raises its value because world demand turns to it, but trade cannot, in a strict sense, lower the value of this factor abroad because there is no supply of it outside the borders of the one country. Thus, one cannot speak of a tendency toward international price equalization in respect of this factor, although the economic effects in countries lacking the factor altogether are similar to those in countries with a small supply of it.

One inclusive statement for the cases in which one of the trading partners has a monopoly of the good or the factor must run in terms of an equalization of the costs of production, actual and potential. Countries without a supply of this factor may be able to use entirely different factors to produce the same commodity, although at higher costs. If the commodity is imported, the prices of these factors and the potential costs of production are reduced. Evidently, in the cases touched upon in the previous section, where the same commodity is produced in different countries by means of a radically different technique and no factor price equalization ensues, one may speak of a tendency to cost equalization. The cost at which a commodity is produced tends to rise in the exporting country as a result of the increased demand for the productive factors, whereas the potential costs in the importing countries drop, owing to the smaller demand for the factors that would otherwise have been used to produce the import commodity at home. It is only to the extent that importation of one commodity replaces the production of entirely different goods at home that the tendency toward cost equalization fails to operate. This qualification should be kept in mind but is probably of little practical importance in a study of concrete trade variations, e.g., those due to tariff changes.

§ 8. *Trade and economies of large-scale production.* More or less independently of the different equipment of productive factors, international trade is called forth by the economies of large-scale production. A certain geographical division of production becomes natural. Trade reduces the disadvantages arising from the incomplete divisibility of the factors, for it renders possible production on a larger scale. This is especially important for small countries; without trade they would have to produce all of their needs, which could be done only in small technical units with comparative inefficiency.

The trade brought about by the economies of large-scale production influences the international relations of factor prices. Because trade and division of production are carried further than they would be otherwise, the demand for the factors used in the industries existing in each country is increased. It is quite possible that factors which are relatively cheap in one country (causing certain industries to locate there) come into such demand, as a result of large-scale establishments, that their prices rise above prices abroad—but not so much as they would have risen in other countries, if these industries had been situated there.

Economies of large-scale production strengthen the tendency toward international division of production due to the varying equipment of productive factors. They consequently increase the trend toward price equalization. They may even go further and cause *new* international price differences for the productive factors as indicated in § 6.

In any consideration of the conditions of production in various countries, special attention must be given to the qualities of the productive factors with respect to their greater or smaller divisibility. Relatively indivisible factors—i.e., those that can advantageously be used only in combination with large quantities of other factors—command relatively low prices when production is carried on by small firms. By making large-scale production possible, international trade increases the demand for them relative to other factors. In other words, trade favors the factors that count chiefly in large factories, e.g., certain types of technical and organizational labor. This is confirmed in that these factors get a relatively much higher reward in countries with a large home market than in small countries. In brief, international trade turns world demand in the direction of factors that count for much in large-scale enterprise.

There may be some international differences not easy to characterize in terms of incomplete divisibility. Does American technical labor, working in a different technical and economic milieu from the European, possess qualities that can be made full use of only in large undertakings? Is this one reason that large-scale production plays a much larger role in the United States than in other countries? Or is that role due solely to the larger market, the different relative factor prices, and the youth of the United States as a manufacturing nation? To these questions no definite answer can be given. But it is difficult to deny that the answer to the first one *may* be in the affirmative. If so, international trade must tend to raise the prices of American factors relative to factors in other countries.

It must be emphasized that the economies of large-scale production and the different equipment of factors are not independent "causes" of trade; on the contrary, their effects are intermingled in several ways. The most suitable equipment of factors for the production of a certain commodity depends upon *how much* of it is to be produced, for a larger scale means a different technique. However, the economic advantages of large-scale production are influenced by the relative prices of the factors. In countries with high wages for skilled labor this factor must be utilized to the utmost in large factories; small firms are unable to compete. In low-wage countries the superiority of the big firm is as a rule not so considerable.

It may be worthwhile to reemphasize in this connection that an increase in the volume of production in certain industries through expansion of trade, and reduction of corresponding industries in importing countries, need not affect costs of production in the same way as do factor prices. Although prices of the factors used in large quantities in these industries fall in the importing countries and rise in the exporting ones, costs of production of the commodities concerned need not rise in the exporting countries; the increased economies of large-scale production may more than offset the higher factor prices. Thus, while trade tends to equalize actual and potential costs of production in different countries, this observation must be qualified with regard to changes in the scale of production.

§ 9. *Differences in the stability of economic conditions.* It remains to consider the influence of risk upon international trade. Two aspects of risk were dealt with previously. First, the various sorts of capital and labor have a different capacity or inclination for risk-bearing. For instance, a distinction is made between capital available for risky enterprises and capital whose owners want to invest it safely.

In countries with an abundance of capitalists willing to take risks, the difference in interest between risky and safe investments is relatively small; for that reason risky enterprises are undertaken there rather than elsewhere. As the risk is especially great when large sums of capital may be lost, industries that require much capital and are also risky are located in such countries. The demand for risky capital is increased in such countries while it is reduced abroad. Trade thus has an obvious tendency to equalize the prices of capital internationally. However, capital is more mobile internationally than is perhaps any other factor of production. It can easily move to places where the conditions of production are best in other respects. The supply of such capital does not for that reason exert so great an influence upon the international location of industry as it otherwise would.

The second aspect of risk already mentioned is that conditions vary internationally with regard to economic stability. In some countries the risk of making wrong forecasts and incurring losses is much greater than in others. Wars, revolutions, bad government, and the like may have this effect. Two results follow: (1) the need of risk-bearing is greater in countries of the former type, and (2) commodity prices in such countries must be sufficient to cover not only a normal profit but also a *risk premium*. Whenever things go well, there must be a surplus over and above the ordinary costs of production, including the reward for risk-bearing, to offset the losses that occasionally occur because of unforeseen changes. These risk premiums, which are similar to premiums for insurance against fire or accident, in the long run constitute no income for the producers; they are exactly balanced by the losses. But they are important elements of the costs of production.

Unstable countries naturally need risk-bearing more than countries where conditions are unlikely to be much disturbed. The price for risk-bearing will be very high in such countries, and they will specialize in relatively safe industries. The greater need of risk-bearing by itself will tend to discourage industries for which instability means the greatest amount of "uncertainty."

Risk premiums are predictably high in unstable countries, like the Central American states, where they add to the costs of production more than in other countries. This tends to keep down the prices of the productive factors in unstable countries. Industries for which the risks and the necessary risk premiums are relatively small tend to develop in such countries, whereas industries that feel the instability more, and consequently must charge a higher premium, work under a handicap and tend to be located elsewhere.

On the whole, manufacturing industries producing on a large scale and using much fixed capital are likely to be most adversely affected by forms of instability like revolutions, wars, and unreliable governments. Agriculture and similar industries will feel their effects less. This international division of production evidently diminishes the losses arising from the various disturbances; in other words, trade reduces the total amount of the risk premiums.

§ 10. *Effects on trade of differences in taxation and other social conditions of production.* It is obvious that the effectiveness of industry and the height of the costs of production are considerably affected by such factors as social institutions. A spirit of cooperation between employers and employees, for instance, may in the long run contribute much to a greater output from the enterprise. Especially important in this area is the system of taxation. Since taxation weighs more heavily on certain industries than on others, it affects the course of production and trade.

Taxation is not only an extra cost item; it affects as well the height of the various factor and commodity prices that function as normal elements of cost. The whole price system in an isolated country is changed by taxation. Few generalizations can be made since everything depends upon how the taxes are imposed, the psychological reaction of the business world, and the like,[3] so that no attempt to analyze such problems will here be made

In brief, taxation also affects the character of international trade. Import and export duties constitute only one special sort of tax. The tendency of increased trade to equalize the prices of the productive factors internationally is supplemented by a trend in each country toward increased demand for the factors that "cooperate with low taxation," i.e., that are used in industries relatively little taxed. Differences in tax cost may make a commodity move from country *A* to country *B*, or vice versa; the tendency toward factor price equalization is thus to some extent checked. To what extent this occurs depends upon how greatly differences in taxation affect costs of production in various industries and countries.

Other social institutions that influence production and trade are prohibitions and monopolies. Even if they do not directly affect international trade, they affect prices in general and thereby international trade.[4] Monopolistic regulation of international trade is common in many branches of industry. The principal exporting firms in industries producing such articles as matches, telephones, and artificial silk make agreements concerning the division of foreign markets; and when they compete, financial strength has as much to do with success in obtaining important orders as the quality of the products and their prices. The nature of the laws regulating patent rights in certain countries is another element influencing location; production of the commodity in question within the national borders is a condition of the maintenance of patent rights. Such influences play an important part in international trade today, and their importance seems to be growing.

§ 11. *Summary.* The circumstances governing the character and effects of international trade are more numerous, many-sided, and difficult to describe in precise terms than those governing interregional trade.

---

[3] A satisfactory analysis of the incidence of taxation must include the dynamic character of economic life—perhaps even more than must the analysis of most other price problems. See Appendix I. Bertil Ohlin, "Taxation and International Trade," *Social Aspects of European Economic Cooperation,* I.L.O. (Geneva, 1956).

[4] Trade unions sometimes exercise a monopolizing influence and affect relative costs and international trade. So do producers' monopolies which, however, often use price discrimination.

The observation that the tendency of trade is to equalize factor prices internationally must be qualified in several respects. The difference in quality between productive factors in different countries, the possibility of using entirely different technical processes, the economies of large-scale production, and differences in economic stability and taxation not only blur the outlines of the previous analysis but make it uncertain to what extent international trade as a whole actually tends to equalize factor prices. This uncertainty arises also because the kind of goods consumed within trading countries may be radically affected by the opening of such trade. These circumstances affect much less the conclusion that trade tends to equalize the actual and potential costs of production in different countries. Yet even this conclusion has to be modified, chiefly with regard to the possible influence of economies of large-scale production in each special case.

VII

Reactions of Demand for Goods and Supply of Productive Factors

§ 1. *Reaction of taste.* It has been emphasized that the earlier analysis of the nature and effects of international trade is in part artificial, being based on a comparison between a state of isolation and one of active trade. If the primary elements of pricing (the demand for commodities, behind which lie individual tastes and possessions; and the commodity supply, behind which lie the supply of productive factors and the physical qualities of nature) were unaffected by the existence of trade, such a comparison would tell the story.[1] As a matter of fact, they are not; both supply and demand are radically influenced by the international division of production and trade. Evidently, then, only one aspect of trade has so far been studied. Dealing with one subject at a time, I have studied first the effects of international trade as they would be if the character of demand and supply of industrial agents was unaffected. I now turn to a brief discussion of the changes brought about in these conditions, starting with those of demand.

Trade affects the individual's demand by changing his *taste* but exercises no direct influence on his possessions. It is self-evident that in a particular country many goods would not be produced at home if they were not imported; there would thus be no supply of them at all, and no demand for them. The supply of imported spices, for example, creates a new demand. In general, international trade has been an extremely powerful factor in extending civilization, and civilization consists partly in the creation of "artificial" needs. This kind of influence is obvious even at closer view. Traders make it their task not only to supply goods people want but to make people desire the goods they want to sell. A study of the foreign trade of China in the last half-century brings out this fact very clearly.[2]

On the whole, the demand for commodities adapts itself more or less

[1] This takes into account the fact that individual incomes are changed through a change in factor prices, and that for this reason consumers' demand varies.
[2] See, e.g., Remer, *The Foreign Trade of China* (Shanghai, 1926).

to supply. Countries with poor facilities for wheat-growing but with a climate more favorable for the cultivation of rye acquire the habit of eating rye bread—a rare thing in countries not producing rye. This is indicated by the fact that only 2½ percent of the total world production of rye passes national frontiers, whereas the corresponding figure for wheat is 16 percent. The larger part of the exported rye goes to countries that grow some rye themselves, like Czechoslovakia and Scandinavia. The enormous consumption of rice in eastern Asia is another example.

These circumstances imply a more far-reaching influence of international trade than was indicated in previous chapters. Nevertheless, they tend to make the effects of a disappearance or serious reduction of trade less disastrous than they would otherwise be. Man adapts himself to circumstances. His change in tastes as supply conditions vary is only one aspect of this adaptability, which naturally renders him less susceptible to disturbances and changes.

§ 2. *Reactions of factor supply.* In the relationship between international trade and the supply of productive resources,[3] the influence of the former rests partly on the fact that changes in the prices of the factors of production alter their supply. As international trade affects factor prices, it must also affect factor supply. To understand the nature of this influence, the elasticity of factor supply in general must first be noted. For the sake of clearness, two sorts of reactions of factor supply are distinguished, namely, toward changes in their *relative* prices and toward changes in the price of a certain factor in *terms of commodities.*

Consider the supply of the various labor factors (unskilled, skilled, and technical, or a more detailed breakdown). A change of wages in favor of one factor tends to increase its supply. The greater the difference, for instance, between wages of skilled and unskilled labor, the more profitable it is to acquire the necessary training to become a skilled worker. It is probably the general rule that in this way supply reacts positively toward changes in relative wages, although it may take a long time for any substantial effect to be produced. When considering the quantity of the supply reaction, one must above all keep in mind that it is small in the beginning and grows as time goes on. A quickly passing improvement in the economic position of a certain labor group may fail entirely to attract new members.

It is evident that supply of one type of labor may be affected as much—or more—by a variation in the wages of other groups as by a change in its own economic position. Higher wages for female factory workers will probably increase the number of women willing to go into the workshops. Yet a substantial improvement in wages for male

[3] See Heckscher, *The Effects of Foreign Trade.*

workers will almost certainly tend to reduce the number of wives and daughters who undertake factory work. Thus, a general increase of wages may reduce the number of workers.

To return to the influence of changed *relative* wages, the smaller the labor groups treated as separate factors, the more important—relatively —are the supply variations. The transfer of individuals from one small group to another of a similar type is easier than the increase by the same percentage of people in a large group, e.g., skilled labor. Consequently, the greater number of labor subfactors considered, the more attention must be given to supply reactions, even during relatively short periods.

The most important exception to this rule is probably due to the closed-shop policy of trade unions. A small but powerful union may succeed in forcing up its wages and regulating the number of its members. Higher wages for masons will not necessarily increase their number. In some countries the existence of strong unions pursuing successfully a policy of this kind is too important to be ignored in a description of their equipment of productive resources. It may powerfully affect the earnings and development of various industries and the character of international trade. For instance, industries using extensive buildings may be much handicapped (especially in countries with a harsh climate, where the buildings have to be strong) if the building workers force their wages considerably above the normal wage level in the country.

This leads to the question of a change in the price of labor in terms of commodities—a change in the standard of living not in relative wages—brought about, e.g., through an increase in the real national income engendered by international trade or its expansion. It is by no means certain that a higher wage standard all round will increase the total quantity of labor through an increase either of population or of the working part of it; nor is it certain that there will be an increase in the number of hours worked per worker or of their "efficiency," whatever that may mean. A higher standard of living may take the form partly of more leisure time. It may lead to a restriction of the number of children and thus, in the long run, of the population, and to a reduction of the percentage of the population prepared to work. The only important conclusion that can be reached concerning such difficult problems without detailed analysis and painstaking collection of facts seems to be that practically nothing is known of supply reactions toward higher wages in terms of commodities.

To turn to another group of productive factors—natural resources— it is tempting to state simply that the supply of nature does not react at all to price changes. This may be correct in a sense. One has to remember, however, that investments of capital often bring about practically the same result as increased quantities of nature. Drainage or irrigation, for instance, increases the surface of the world available for agriculture. Holland has won considerable areas of land from the sea by means of a system of costly walls. The higher the price of land, the more profitable such enterprises will be and the more likely they will be carried through. An increasing value of gold, copper, and the like will cause more energy to be used to find new mines, and poorer and poorer mines will be put into use and worked with a great outlay of capital. In this sense the supply of nature is increased.

It is very doubtful how far and in what direction the supply of capital is affected by changes in the rate of interest. A very low rate probably reduces savings in the long run, whereas a very high rate increases them. But variations in the neighborhood of the usual level may fail to have any influence at all or may lead to a change in the opposite direction, a negative reaction; lower wages, greater savings. Here again, nothing is known for certain. I should, however, think it extremely probable that whatever the long-run reaction may be, the short-run effect of a lower interest rate will be reduced savings, and vice versa, for the simple reason that a considerable part of saving is generated by interest incomes, when the source itself is diminished or increased, the flow into capital channels is likely to be correspondingly affected.

Capital available for risky enterprises will almost certainly appear in greater quantities when a change in its favor, compared to rates on safe capital, takes place. The greater the extra reward for uncertainty, the more willing are people to carry it. The same applies to the supply of labor in occupations where the return is very uncertain. Extra pay for the uncertainty increases the flow of individuals into these occupations.

§ 3. *Increases in international differences in factor supplies caused by trade.* International trade, through its influence on the prices of the factors of production, inevitably affects their supply, which in turn influences the character and extent of trade in a way which will now be subjected to a brief analysis. Inequalities in the equipment of productive factors call forth trade, which tends to a large extent to raise the prices of the relatively abundant and cheap factors and to depress the prices of the rest.[4] How does this affect the supply of factors? In most cases it is probable that the reaction will be positive. The increased prices of the relatively cheap factors will call forth a still greater quantity of them, although they were already plentifully supplied. The reduced relative prices of the scantily existing factors will probably reduce their quantity. Evidently the outcome is *greater un-*

[4] This statement refers to *relative* factor prices. In terms of commodities, all or the large majority of them may receive a higher reward as a result of trade.

evenness internationally as to factor supplies, and a strengthening of the tendency to trade.[5] Insofar as the existing differences in factor supply are increased, the character of trade will remain about the same, but its volume will be greater. The division of production among the various countries will be carried further.

In the beginning of the nineteenth century Great Britain had more capital and highly educated labor than any other nation. That was one reason (its good transportation facilities and coal and iron mines being probably the most important of the others) that manufacturing industries began to develop in England and Scotland. Demand for capital and technical labor was increased. The high price paid for these factors called for their increasing supply, and the differences against other countries was increased.

This division of production brought so many advantages to Great Britain that most factor prices were raised in terms of commodities, even if some of them held a relatively less favorable position than before. As the tendency toward higher wages became apparent it was met by an extremely powerful reaction of supply; population increased by leaps and bounds. Because even small children were used in factories, the increase in the number of industrial workers was rapid, and land rents rose in the long run. The expansion of international trade in the first half of the twentieth century in a great many countries helped to sustain the trend toward the concentration of manufacturing industries in Great Britain and the increase of its population. There can be little doubt that if for some reason this far-reaching international division of production and trade had not been possible, the population in that country would have grown much less rapidly than it actually did.

There are also somewhat less revolutionary variations. Wages of technical labor are lower in Germany than in Great Britain or the United States. Since many modern technical processes depend upon the use of great quantities of such labor, Germany secures an advantage in the production of goods manufactured by these methods. For example, it exports chemical products that contain a relatively large quantity of technical labor. International trade increases the demand in Germany for this factor and tends to raise its price. But at the same time, the supply of such labor tends to grow under the influence of rising wages. The same circumstances that once made supply large (educational facilities, frugal living in the middle classes) call forth an increasing number of skilled technicians. Growing demand and supply go hand in hand. Consequently, in periods of increasing demand no rise in wages of this sort of labor need take place. Relative to other wages they may even fall if it is assumed that the standard of living in the middle classes is kept fairly constant through

[5] This effect was stressed by Heckscher, *The Effects of Foreign Trade.*

the increase in their numbers. Yet the wage level for less educated labor qualities may rise in terms of goods as a result of the development of chemical and other industries, as in Germany. Apparently international trade, through its tendency to equalize factor prices internationally, calls forth supply reactions that lead to greater international inequality in the equipment of labor factors. The supply mechanism thus tends to counteract the price-equalizing tendencies of trade.

With respect to capital, countries with cheap capital attract industries that require much of this factor, the demand for it is increased, and interest rates in these countries tend to rise, while falling in other countries. If savings react positively, the result will be increased international differences in the supply of capital.

Although the supply of nature does not, perhaps, react in the strict sense of the word, the investment of capital can increase the supply of most types of natural resources. Thus one can draw a close parallel with the positive reaction of various labor factors. Equalization, more or less, of the value of natural resources will tend to restrain investments in countries poor in such resources and increase them in countries where they are plentiful. The equipment of productive facilities is consequently made more uneven.

Clearly, as in the case of labor, the supply of other factors establishes a sort of resistance to the price equalizing tendency of trade. This resistance is of varying strength, according to the *elasticity* of the factor supply. The elasticity may be called complete if the same relative factor prices are maintained over time in spite of the opening of trade. The German case presents an illustration. It is quite possible that wages of technical, skilled, and unskilled labor are not in the long run changed in favor of the technical factor, even though the demand for it relative to the other two may be greatly increased through trade. A growing supply may entirely make up for the increased demand. "In the colder North nature demands more of man. He will take factory work as readily as other work, for it is all strenuous. In the South people ask higher wages for factory work, for it is disagreeable relatively." [6] *Ceteris paribus*, factories are concentrated in the northern countries, where a large part of the population becomes factory workers.

Such cases of complete elasticity of supply are probably rare. The rule seems to be that trade exercises a certain equalizing influence on factor prices, and that *supply reactions can only make it less considerable than it would otherwise have been.*[7]

[6] Russel-Smith, *Industry and Commerce*, p. 175.
[7] Taussig (*International Trade*, p. 56) is of a different opinion. He thinks it unlikely that foreign demand will change the scale of remuneration, partly because this demand is small compared to domestic demand, partly because of the reactions of supply in various labor qualities. "The social stratification that results

Assume that an extension of international trade leads to an expansion of one industry and a reduction of another in a country, and that these two industries employ laborers of different qualities. Skilled and technical labor in one industry has not the same training and experience as the labor in the other. A rise of wages in the expanding industry relative to wages in the declining one will occur unless there is a continued flow from the labor groups in the declining industry to those in the expanding one. If the actual flow is smaller than this needed quantity, the reward to the labor groups in the expanding industry will rise in relation to wages of other groups, especially those in the declining industry.

This analysis of elasticity of supply can be extended to cover not only factors of production in the strict sense but also the various forms of capital goods. The price of productive instruments naturally tends to equal their cost of production. In times of great demand they usually rise above this level, and this increased cost of capital goods has the same effect upon output and costs of production as does a temporary scarcity of essential labor. However, the price of productive implements often falls below their cost of production, sometimes for considerable periods. If they cannot be used in industries other than those for which they were originally intended, the existing supply will be available even though prices fall very low. The elasticity of supply of implements is greater upward than downward.

Another important conclusion from this analysis is that *the fundamental conditions of international division of production and trade cannot be described in terms of the actual supply of factors at a given moment.* The elasticity of the supply reaction is related to the *length of the time* that has passed since the original change in factor prices. In some cases little or no change of supply can be brought about in a year; in other cases a year suffices to reestablish the old relative prices, from which only temporary deviations of a few months' duration are possible. When individuals can pass freely and quickly from one group of labor to another, price discrepancies are naturally of short duration. This is also the case when new labor can be directed easily into the channels where reward has increased. Clearly, when dealing with elasticity of supply and supply reactions toward changes in international trade, one must refer to a certain period of time. In general, the longer the time the reacting tendency has to work, the more it offsets the effects on prices of an original change. Investigations into variations of international trade thus tend to be descriptions of *time-using processes,* in which both demand for commodities and supply of productive factors vary more or less as time goes on.

---

from the domestic conditions is well established and seems to be deeply rooted." It is clear, however, that foreign demand is important in small countries, although not perhaps in the United States.

In summary, international trade, through its influence on the prices—both relative and in terms of commodities—of productive factors and implements, evokes supply reactions that as a rule tend to offset the price equalizing tendencies of trade by increasing the inequality of the productive factor endowment. The nature of trade influences on productive factors is therefore complicated and permits of no sweeping generalizations.

§ 4. *Changes in quality of labor and capital caused by trade.*[8] The above analysis concerning the elasticity of factor supply covers only the most direct of the effects of international trade on productive equipment. International trade changes the fundamental facts of economic life in trading nations and cannot fail to affect in a thousand and one ways the factors governing the output of labor and capital. The far-reaching nature of the indirect influence is best realized if it is asked what the world's population and the capital equipment would be like if there had been no international trade, and how different it would be from the present situation. One can only say that the difference would be enormous and that it cannot be adequately dealt with in quantitative terms. Trade changes the *quality* of the people, teaches them to consume new things and to use old things in new ways. Technical knowledge is largely the result of specialization, which trade has made possible. The character, not only of so-called technical labor, but also of skilled and unskilled labor is affected.

From a closer viewpoint more precise conclusions may be drawn. Trade means specialization and large-scale production, and this influences the character of the various labor factors. Engineers specialize in automobiles in the United States, in dyestuffs and other chemicals in Germany, and in textiles in Great Britain. The direction in which labor is educated and trained is to some extent governed by trade. In this way a division of production, for whatever reason it has come about, tends to create differences in productive resources, which in turn tend to maintain the existing organization of production. This is one of the advantages that "old" manufacturing nations have as a result of their early industrial development. It becomes necessary, in a study of present-day trade, to take into account the conditions of production and trade some decades ago.

The adaptation of labor to the requirements of industries where it is employed becomes a cause of *extended* trade. Acquired, no less than inherited, qualities that involve differences between the productive resources of various nations lead to specialization along different lines, i.e., to international trade. Trade thus engenders more trade for two

[8] The outstanding treatment of this question is Taussig's *Some Aspects of the Tariff Question*, which is in my opinion the most important contribution to the analysis of international trade since Mill, *Principles of Political Economy*. I have made no attempt to summarize Taussig's conclusions here, which would be difficult if not impossible, and refer the reader to the book itself.

reasons: it causes variations in the qualities of labor, and it tends to increase the unevenness of the international distribution of factors of production. The former influence, like the latter, means that international differences in factor equipment are increased.

The effects of trade on the technical form in which the capital goods appear are in some way analogous to the effects of trade on labor quality. In each country this form is determined by the requirements of the industries that have existed and do exist there. The difficulty of changing the technical form of capital goods tends to make present trade follow the same current as earlier trade, even though the price of liquid capital would make changes profitable.

§ 5. *Trend of future international trade.* The preceding analysis leads to an interesting question, which has long been the subject of discussion among economists: Will international trade continue to attain larger and larger volume, or is the trend toward less and less trade?

The influence of international trade on the productive resources in various countries will, so far as it has been touched upon above, tend to increase the volume of trade in the future. But there are other elements that decidedly tend to bring about a greater international self-sufficiency. Up to now, only a few nations have had manufacturing industries of any importance long enough to acquire the knowledge and training necessary for efficiency. Other nations still remain at a more juvenile stage or have not started to walk. As time goes on, however, and the young industrial countries grow older, their working populations learn the traditions of factory work, acquire skill, and become technically educated in increasing numbers. The superiority of the older nations is reduced or disappears. In the middle of the last century Great Britain held a position in industrial development far in advance of any other nation. At present, several countries have already caught up or surpassed her.

This is not the place to analyze the dynamic forces responsible for this development. International trade probably helps to bring it about. The importation of machinery into a young manufacturing country is a necessary condition for a quick growth of factory production. Both directly and indirectly the stage in which machines can be produced at home is brought nearer.

Some well-known economists believe that in the future an increasing number of nations will catch up with the pioneers in manufacturing. If that happens, the character of international trade will be greatly altered, for trade between countries in the same phase is different from trade between countries on a different level of industrial development. Backward countries export raw materials and agricultural products and receive in exchange manufactured products. When they have advanced to the next stage and taken up production of the simpler qualities of manufactures, their imports consist of high-grade finished and half-finished products and of machinery, for which they pay with the same products as do backward countries. Countries at the advanced manufacturing stage export highly specialized prod-ducts like motor cars, electrical machinery, and chemicals.

For an illustration, consider some figures concerning trade between certain leading manufacturing countries. In 1927 no less than 17.3 percent of the exports from the United States went to Great Britain, and 9.9 percent went to Germany; about one-fourth of the German foreign trade was with the United States, Great Britain, and France; one-fourth of the British trade was with the other three countries; and more than one-third of French foreign trade consisted of imports and exports to the United States, Great Britain, and Germany.

Such figures lend no support to Marshall's opinion that "the per-centage of the world's trade which is governed by differences of in-dustrial phase, and of aptitude for particular sorts and grades of manufacture, is less than formerly." [9] Marshall probably underesti-mated the importance of the fact that economies of large-scale pro-duction and specialization increase rapidly and that they make one country better adapted to manufacture certain goods, while other countries specialize in others. An examination of the trade in ma-chinery between the leading manufacturing nations brings out this fact clearly.

In addition, natural differences of the human factor, whether in-herited or acquired, are hardly less important than differences in natural resources—a fact that has been emphasized by Marshall himself. Con-cerning America, he wrote:

The history of the Eurasian continent reproduced itself in America with great speed. Those districts which yield wealth least easily are now the richest; the northern states are richer than the southern; and the southern are much richer than those still nearer the Equator, which are peopled by races from Southern Europe. This stratification of human energy from north to south in the two continents largely influences the present courses of trade; but it is itself effect, rather than ultimate cause. For, in the long run, national wealth is governed by the character of the population more than by the bounty of nature.[10]

If that is so, human differences will continue to affect not only wealth but the direction of production and international trade, inde-pendently of differences in natural resources. A people with little disposition for thrift and foresight and no genius for organization or invention will always, however much they can learn from other peo-ples, be inferior in capital equipment and technical labor. It will pay

[9] Marshall, *Money, Credit and Commerce* (London, 1923), p. 105.
[10] *Ibid.*, p. 99.

them to specialize in goods that require little of these factors and to import the rest. Industries adapt themselves locally to the qualities of man as they do to the qualities of nature.

One might, however, put forward as an argument in favor of Marshall's view about the dominating influence on trade of differences in natural resources the fact that human inequalities are to some extent due to different natural surroundings. Climate and soil influence character; a benevolent nature has so far tended to make man less energetic, indeed, made it less tempting or more difficult even for those who are energetic to work hard. "Climatic conditions have controlled the nature of man almost as much as that of vegetables." [11]

On the other hand, natural differences are also due to some extent to man. The qualities of nature that are unknown or useless are as if they did not exist; an extension of the knowledge of how to use nature means—in a certain sense—that nature has changed its qualities.

§ 6. *Summary.* In spite of the variability of the supply of productive factors, which is constantly undergoing variation in reaction to price changes, the nature of trade is determined, *inter alia,* by the *actual* supply which is an element in the mutual-interdependence system of pricing, which represents a snapshot of the existing situation. If one goes deeper it becomes apparent that factor supply is greatly affected by trade and its variations. Past trade has much to do with the nature of present trade. The basis of the international division of production is not so much the actual supply of productive factors as the conditions that govern its supply—such as psychological elements, social habits and institutions, educational facilities, and the like.

The nature of trade depends also upon the demand for commodities. Here, too, it is the actual demand that counts at a given moment, but the development of the demand is deeply influenced by international trade.

The essence of the matter is that international trade, supply of productive factors, and demand for commodities react upon one another. Pricing and trade are nevertheless the outcome of actual demand and supply conditions, as was explained earlier in the analysis of the mechanism of pricing.

In each concrete case one must examine how far supply and demand reactions necessitate a modification of conclusions reached without them. In general, investigations into minor variations of trade need give little attention to these reactions unless the period of time considered is very long; such variations do not make much difference in the supply of productive factors considered as broad general groups. The development of the German chemical export industry is the result of a great supply of cheap intellectual labor of a certain quality; the

[11] *Ibid.,* p. 100.

reaction of the supply of such labor is a matter of comparatively small importance so long as the question involves the explanation of the growth of this special industry. It is true, no doubt, that the growth of the chemical industry has made people study chemistry, but it can have exercised little influence on the supply of intellectual labor in general. The existence of a middle class with a capacity for methodical, painstaking work is probably intimately connected with the general economic development in Germany and thus with international trade, but it is not fundamentally dependent upon the existing German chemical export industry. There is much more reason for saying that the supply of intellectual labor is one of the causes of the chemical industry than that this industry is the cause of the rich supply of intellectual labor.

The nature of supply reactions to variations in international trade is a complicated question. The facts of the case are also very little known. Consequently, no sweeping generalizations can be made. There undoubtedly is a tendency toward a positive reaction in the case of many grades of labor (higher relative reward = greater supply). Thus, insofar as trade tends to equalize factor prices internationally, it also tends to increase the international inequality of equipment of productive factors, so that the first tendency is more or less counteracted. Although the strength of the factor price equalizing tendency is somewhat uncertain, the tendency to equalize actual and potential costs of production is clear. To the extent that the factor supply reacts positively, this tendency is also diminished. The trade called forth by economies of large scale affects factor supply as explained in Chapter VI.

International trade affects not only the quantity of the productive factors but also *their quality*. This influence is largely such as to lead to an extension of trade, but coupled with other general dynamic forces, it may lead to a reduction of the international differences of labor with respect to skill and training.

One fact is certain and of paramount importance in any study of concrete problems: the reaction of factor supply, like that of demand for goods, varies with the length of time it has to work itself out. If one is interested in the short-run effects of certain variations, these reactions may be ignored. A study of the simple price mechanism—the economies of large-scale duly considered—then tells the essential story; the relations determining prices exercise a dominating influence. The further ahead one wishes to look, the more attention must be given to factor supply reactions. In the long run they play an increasingly important, perhaps a dominating, role.

§ 7. *Gain from international trade.* In general, these effects of international trade involve a "gain": the volume of goods is increased.

But this word lacks meaning when the *character of demand* undergoes a change. When individuals want new goods or goods in different proportions, the weaknesses of the index methods come to the fore. Take the case of China in the 1930's, which Remer[12] summed up as follows: "China is undergoing an economic revolution which may well be looked upon as the cumulative effect of the penetration of foreign trade. In its consequences China's trade is by no means a fact of little importance. It is rather the first and most easily measured of the whole interrelated set of phenomena which will make the China of tomorrow as different from the China of the past as is modern Europe from the Europe of the Middle Ages." How impossible to describe the effects of trade in terms of gain!

Most serious of all is the fact that the *number* of subjects change. An increased volume of production may mean less goods and services per head. Is it to be called gain if the output grows apace with the population, in spite of a fixed supply of natural resources? Evidently, since trade affects the character and number of the economic subjects, it is arbitrary and valueless to talk about the total gain, much less to *measure* it. It follows that the old question of how the gain from international trade is divided between the trading nations is artificial and of little if any theoretical or practical importance.

The concept of gain has real meaning—like consumers' surplus—only when it refers to a minor variation of trade. It may then be possible to assume the character and number of subjects unaffected by the variation without too much violence to the facts. Strictly speaking, one must assume also that the distribution of income is not much changed. Under these conditions the increase of an index of production or an index of available goods (national income in terms of commodities) conveys real meaning—an improvement in the economic position—and the measure of the increase may be taken to represent the size of the gain. Clearly one has to ask, not for the total gain from international trade, but for the gain from an extension of trade or for the loss from a reduction.

§ 8. *Cases of location.* A few examples concerning the location of industry may give a more realistic impression of the relationships described earlier. The following cases are designed to demonstrate not only how production and trade are determined by the equipment of productive factors but also how trade influences that equipment. Brief descriptions of a few simple cases must suffice by way of illustration. In these cases the existence of a certain industry is explained, *not* the character of the economic life of the country. Consequently, the location of all other industries is considered as a known datum.

If a certain industry is located in one or a few countries and not in

---

[12] Remer, *The Foreign Trade of China*, p. 241.

others, it must be because costs of production are lower there than in other countries, since certain factors are cheaper there than abroad. How far the supply and the price of the various factors are the outcome of the particular industry's location in the given country must also be considered. In some cases it may be necessary to go further and examine the circumstances behind the factor supply in general.

Such an analysis of international location is similar to the investigation a businessman would make before deciding where to place a factory. He considers first the various cost elements in each place (wages, prices of natural resources, etc.), then the influence that the location of his factory there might have upon them, taking into account not only the effects his demand would have upon prices, if the actual supply of factors remained constant, but the possible effects of his activity upon that supply.

Consider the textile industry, for example. Practically all countries that have any manufacturing industry at all produce a considerable quantity of textile goods. The first phase of modern industrial development is textile production by means of up-to-date machinery. Why has it proved so much easier to establish this production in industrially young countries than to establish other industries? The answer is partly the tariff policy and the cheap transport of raw materials, but chiefly the fact that the necessary supply of labor is to be found almost everywhere. The carrying on of hand spinning and weaving for centuries has made a large part of the population, especially in textile production centers, familiar with the handling of wool and flax and their manufacture into cloth. Relatively little skill and training are needed for a textile worker, however difficult it may be to acquire first-rate skill, as compared to the machine industry, where workers are of little or no use unless they meet a definite standard of performance.

In view of the ease with which textile industries can be established, it is at first sight somewhat surprising that Britain acquired the dominant position. It is partly due to the advantages of an early start: by means of newly invented machinery, production had been firmly established on a modern basis in Great Britain long before it commenced under similar conditions in other countries. A skilled labor supply appeared, and organization on an unprecedented scale brought many advantages.

Some of these causes of superiority have disappeared, especially as far as coarse cottons and low-grade woollens and worsteds are concerned. Several other countries, among them Japan, Germany, Italy, France, and the United States, now have the same advantages of production; they possess a good supply of trained labor and use the same machinery as British firms. Evidently an equalization of production conditions in the textile industry of various nations has taken place, except that wages vary widely from one country to another.

In goods of high quality the position of the British industry still appears strong. The supply of specialized skill among workers and engineers cannot be matched in many other countries. The influence of an early start, i.e., its effect on productive conditions, is still a source of superiority which compensates for the disadvantages of high wages.

The linen industry presents a particularly interesting example. The north of Ireland and the south of Scotland grew much flax a century ago and manufactured it on hand looms, but for a long time they have grown very little flax, its culture having passed to low-wage countries like Belgium and the Baltic group. Nevertheless these two areas of Ireland and Scotland are centers of the world's finest linen factories. For generations their technical skill has been turned into this channel, and the consequent supply of labor has been such a source of strength that the manufacturing industry has remained even though the production of the raw material has emigrated.

The standard of living, social conditions, habits, and other elements affecting the supply of labor are important factors in determining the international location of production. For example, the sugar beet is cultivated in Germany, Poland, and Czechoslovakia by means of much cheap female and child labor. Similarly, the great supply of home workers at low rates in poor countries or countries with distinct social habits is an important location factor. Toys in Germany and Austria, glass in Bohemia, and lace in Belgium are produced so cheaply that they can be exported even to the United States over the high tariff wall. In such cases the "inherited" skill is also of importance. The supply of cheap home labor may be especially dependent upon the existence of other industries that use labor chiefly at certain seasons of the year or at certain times of the day. The Belgian peasants make lace in the intervals between their farm work.

In general, the existence of one industry can sometimes be explained only by the conditions of a *supplementary* industry. The supply of productive factors must be considered from the point of view of both industries, or rather, the fact that conditions are suitable for one is due partly to the existence of the other, and vice versa. Agriculture in northern Sweden stands and falls with the forest industry: the farmers work in the woods in the winter, cutting and transporting the lumber as long as the snow lasts, and concentrate on agricultural work during the brief summer.

It is evident that within limits a country may specialize in any one industry as well as in any other. Chance plays a significant part in determining the location of industry. An invention in a particular country may give rise to the manufacture of certain machines, whereas other machines are produced in other countries, partly as a result of inventions there. A different distribution of inventions would have caused a different location of production.

There are, however, strict limits to such influences of chance. No invention will make a country an important producer of the article in question if the productive facilities are not fairly good. Moreover, the direction in which inventive and administrative labor turns depends much upon the existing industries and the natural facilities of the country in question. For this reason *inventive and administrative genius will not so much affect location in an unpredictable way as it will complement existing tendencies toward division of production.*

In the 1930's Great Britain, Germany, Japan, and Switzerland had the largest net per capita export of manufactures. The first two have plenty of labor of all sorts, capital, iron and coal mines, but a small supply of agricultural land and other natural resources. The other two lack mines and have slight natural resources but possess an abundant supply of labor and capital. This supply of labor and capital is largely the result of earlier trade, which brought an increase in population. Without imported food, manufacture for export would have been impossible. Indeed, a very large proportion of the productive factors would have been required to work in relatively inefficient food production. As a result, little wealth could have been amassed.

It is clear that *the location of manufacturing industries in the twentieth century is to a large extent governed by earlier establishment of the labor and capital supply.* The supply of nature is less subject to change, for which reason industries requiring the use of rare natural resources have a more stable location. This is the case in the production of many raw materials, as opposed to their manufacture into finished products. Once ready, raw materials may be transported long distances to manufacturing plants. Manufacturing is relatively independent of climatic conditions, although an unhealthy or a hot climate is a great drawback. For these reasons manufacturing industries may in the future spread over much wider areas than will raw material production.

Part Three

Commodity and Factor Movements

VIII

Interregional Costs of Transfer of Commodities

§ 1. *Introduction.* Ever since the classical economists erected that marvelous structure, the theory of international trade, the relative immobility of the factors of production has justified a separate theory, independent of price theory in general. This opinion has been accepted by almost all later writers with the exception of Sidgwick, who suggested that what necessitates a special theory for international values is not the imperfect mobility of labor but "the fact of distance, which renders international exchange costly." [1]

This observation cannot of course be accepted without qualifications; domestic trade is sometimes not less costly than international trade but more so. Nevertheless, Sidgwick's impression that too little attention had been given to the various costs of transport was well founded. Modification of the general price theory is necessary because of such costs no less than because of the immobility of productive factors. Both these elements make themselves felt in international as well as in domestic trade. The important distinction is therefore not between domestic and international trade theories but between a *one*-market and a *many*-market theory of pricing.

There are different markets for goods and for productive factors, and all the obstacles to movements among these markets are of importance for a general theory of location. It is true that in a study of location in international trade the lack of factor mobility is perhaps the most important element (although there are also special obstacles to international commodity movement that must be reckoned with); but *international trade theory cannot be understood except in relation to and as a part of the general location theory, to which the lack of mobility of goods and factors has equal relevance.*

§ 2. *Preliminary analysis of the influence of obstacles to interregional commodity movements.* One can build directly upon the simplified theory of interregional trade that was developed in Part One, while keeping the qualifications from Part Two in mind, and introduce the

[1] Sidgwick, *Principles of Political Economy* (London, 1883), p. 229.

complicating elements step by step. First to be considered are the obstacles to interregional commodity movements.

Between various regions commodity prices tend to differ by the costs of transfer. But this is true only of goods subject to interregional trade; if the costs of transfer are greater than the differences in the costs of production in the various regions, naturally each region will produce such goods itself and will not enter into interregional trade. Such goods are here called "home market goods" as opposed to import and export commodities, which together are called "interregional goods." This is a useful distinction, although no fixed border lines exist between the two groups of commodities. Later in the analysis it will sometimes be convenient to divide home market goods into two classes: those that compete closely with import or export commodities, and those that meet little competition.

Goods and services that must be produced in the immediate neighborhood of the place of consumption are naturally home market goods, the word "goods" being taken in a wide sense and including personal services. As a matter of fact, personal services form a large and important part of home market goods, e.g., domestic services and the distribution of commodities to consumers. Other examples of home market goods are heavy and bulky commodities, such as bricks and milk, whose transfer costs are high in relation to their price.

The most important transfer cost is costs of transport, where the term "costs of transfer" indicates transportation costs as well as the costs of overcoming other obstacles, such as tariff walls. Costs of transport vary greatly for different commodities: some are bulky, heavy, or easily spoiled; others may be sent round the world for an amount that is insignificant compared to their value.

What are the effects of costs of transport on interregional trade? In other words, what changes in the price system as presented in simplified form in Part One are required when the costs of interregional transport are taken into account? These costs vary with other elements of the price system. The transfer of commodities from one region to another can be done only by means of certain productive factors; transportation requires the use of such factors as much as does production in a narrow sense. From this point of view, transportation services hold the same place in the price system as do other services and commodities.

There are, however, more important differences. In Chapter I the relations governing the price system under simple conditions were set forth;[2] additional elements must be considered when transportation services are introduced. The total demand for each factor of production

[2] See also Appendix I.

comes not only from production for domestic consumption and export but also from transport activities. Costs of transport, like other services and goods, are governed by the prices and quantities of the factors required. Demand for "foreign" goods is based on their price abroad plus the costs of transport and is, therefore, at the same time a demand for interregional transport services.

Furthermore, the relation between costs of production at home and the supply price of "foreign" goods, i.e., costs abroad plus transportation costs, determines whether a given commodity is to be imported, exported, or produced for the home market. It fixes the volume of imports and exports. Similarly, the prices of productive factors determine, through their effect on trade, the amount of transportation services that each region will supply. Such services affect the balance between imports and exports. By means of these relations, a simplified picture of the price system for productive factors, goods, and transport services is obtained.

Transportation between regions *A* and *B* may require the use of productive factors in other regions as well. This is often the case when land transport is used: railroads carry goods through region *C* at costs that depend upon the quality and price of *C*'s transportation factors. Although it is true that the costs of transport are governed by the prices and quantities of the factors required, the factors in all regions must be included. There are, of course, many alternative routes and methods of transport between *A* and *B*; as with production, selection is made on the basis of cost.

Being part of the price system, transport services naturally vary with it under the influence of changes in demand, supply, and other elements. A study of railroad tariffs or shipping rates reveals clearly that the charges for different goods depend upon the general demand for and supply of transport facilities. Freights may be cheaper or dearer in one direction than in the other, according to the demand for transportation. Inward and outward freights are an example of joint supply; a relatively great demand for transportation in one direction raises its price compared to the price in the opposite direction.

Great Britain has as a rule high export shipping rates and low import rates, since the export of coal requires more tonnage than do other important goods. In the British trade with Scandinavia, however, inward freights are higher than outward freights, for Scandinavian articles like timber and pulp are so bulky as to require even more tonnage than British coal.

In the nineteenth century the volume of goods exported from Europe to South America was much greater than the volume of goods imported. Hence, freight rates to South America were generally higher than rates in the opposite direction. This situation has now changed because South America exports large quantities of grains, a comparatively bulky commodity.

Costs of interregional transfer other than transportation charges may be similarly dealt with, e.g., the cost of overcoming special difficulties in trade with regions where "economic customs," laws, and language are different. Duties on imports or exports belong to a special category. Payment in money is necessary to overcome these obstacles, but the sum is not given as a reward for the use of certain productive factors, as in the case of transportation costs; consequently there arises on this account no demand for factors, except a few customs officials and clerks and laborers for the extra work required by compliance with customs formalities. This special contingency should be kept in mind in considering interregional transfer costs as part of the price system. All of them can be dealt with as analogous to costs of transportation.

It is now easy to explain the influence of costs of transfer upon interregional trade. Naturally, if there were no such costs, trade would take place in all or practically all commodities. Costs of transfer thus reduce trade and weaken its tendency to equalize commodity and factor prices.

The reduction of interregional trade caused by high costs of transfer affects many industries by reducing their scale of production. In certain of these cases the affected industries are as a result unable to achieve economies of large scale. The costs of transfer limit the size of markets and of units of production much more in some cases than in others. Since certain regions are much larger than others, this considerably affects the character of trade between them.

The technique, i.e., the proportions in which the factors are used, varies with the scale of production. In the small technical unit most commodities are made by hand with little machinery; large-scale enterprise has been able to substitute automatic and semiautomatic machinery for manual labor to a surprising extent. It follows that one region may be able to produce a commodity on a small scale cheaper than another, since it has cheap manual labor, whereas the other is able to produce the same commodity cheaper on a large scale, owing to its command of a great supply of capital and technical labor. Evidently the size of the market, around which interregional costs of transfer raise a wall, is a condition of some importance to trade.

The transfer of goods requires productive factors in other proportions than do other sorts of economic activity. Long-distance transport probably requires relatively great quantities of capital, iron ore mines, and coal mines, so that the growth of long-distance trade has doubtless tended to raise the relative scarcity of these factors. Much transport makes use largely of natural resources employed little or not at all in industry, e.g., seas and rivers. These are very often "free"; the traffic is unable to make them scarce, i.e., to give them a price.

§ 3. *Distance and the character of trade.* Another aspect of the influence of costs of transfer is what may be called the "transfer relations" of trading regions. First to be considered is the distance to the market. It is assumed for the sake of simplicity that costs of transfer are in proportion to the distance covered and that trade takes place only in finished goods, i.e., that the whole process of production is carried out in one region.

Two regions, *A* and *B*, are situated close together; a third, *C*, lies further away. *A* concentrates upon manufactures, whereas *B* and *C* are predominantly agricultural. The former naturally exports manufactured goods to the other two, which send agricultural products in exchange. They do not, however, export precisely the same sort of farm products to *A*. The long distance from *C* to *A* puts the former at a disadvantage in the export of heavy, bulky, and easily spoiled commodities; consequently, *B* exports chiefly such products, and *C* sends agricultural goods that are more easily transportable. Thus, the difference in trade between *A* and *B* and *A* and *C* may be considerable, even though *B* and *C* have practically identical productive factors. Trade between *A* and *C* is much less lively than between *A* and *B*. *C* will produce for herself the same manufactured goods that *B* imports from *A*. Evidently not only exports from, but also imports to, the two agricultural regions are different.

Examples of the influence of distance are easy to find, although affected by many varying circumstances at the same time. If Denmark exports butter and eggs to Great Britain, and Australia sends wool, the explanation is partly to be found in the different distances to market.

Transfer costs are of course affected by conditions other than distance—for instance, the character of the earth's surface over which the transportation takes place. *C* may not lie further away from *A* than does *B* but must use expensive land communications for its exports to *A*, whereas *B* is able to use the cheaper sea transport. The economic result, however, is the same.

§ 4. *Relation between transfer costs for raw materials and finished goods.* The problem is more complicated when the transfer of raw materials, auxiliary materials, or machinery, to the places of production is concerned. In many cases the process of production is divided between several regions; iron ore, for instance, may be produced in one place and smelted in another. Evidently costs of production at the higher stages of the process include the costs of transferring raw materials from the various sources of supply.

Whether a certain commodity f is to be produced in the region A for the home market or is to be imported depends not only upon how cheaply f can be manufactured from the raw material r but also upon the relation between the costs of transferring f and r from the region B, where r is produced. If it costs more to transfer r than f, manufacturing of the latter in B, which has the local supply of r, means a saving compared to the manufacturing of f in A. If, nevertheless, this commodity is manufactured in A, the reason must be that production in A is so much cheaper than in B that it can offset the higher transfer costs. On the contrary, if the finished good f is more difficult to transfer than r, production for A's consumption tends to be located in A, unless there is some more than compensating disadvantage that raises the costs of production in this region.

There is a tendency for the commodity most difficult to transfer to govern location. When it is f, production takes place close to the market; when it is r, it is better carried out in the neighborhood of the raw-material resources. If the costs of transfer are equally high for both f and r, both regions and all others on a straight line between them are equally suitable. However, this is true only of production of f for consumption in A. The situation is different when the most favorable location—in A or B—for export of f to region C is to be determined. In this case the manufacture of f in A and its transport to C entails extra costs of transfer, unless A is situated on the line of cheapest transportation from B to C. If the same factory is to export to many places, A cannot be as good a location as B. In general, transfer relations tend to make the region with raw material supply the most favorable for the location of industries manufacturing for export to other regions.

In cases where production on a large scale is more efficient and cheaper than output in small quantities, and the market in each region is not very great, the superiority of raw material regions for production for export may give them advantages of scale that other regions are unable to obtain. For this reason they may be able to do the manufacturing so cheaply that they can export even to regions where the supply of productive factors is equally suitable for these industries but where production has not reached the optimum scale. This situation, together with the fact that raw materials are often more difficult to transfer than goods made from them, explains why manufacturing processes are in so many cases concentrated in the regions with raw material supply.

Usually, however, the transfer relations between various regions are much more complicated. The raw material r is perhaps produced not only in B but also in D, and at different costs. Whether C is to import f from A, B, or D depends not only upon the costs of manufacturing and the costs of transfer in these regions, but also upon differences in the supply of r. To be at some distance from a cheap supply of raw materials may be as advantageous as to be close to a more expensive source.

Furthermore, in many cases several raw and auxiliary materials and several sorts of machinery are required for the manufacture of *f*. It may be cheapest to import them from different regions. *A* may have a cheaper supply of some of them than *B*, whereas the latter may have a corresponding advantage with regard to others. The iron industry is dependent upon easy access to ore, coal, and markets. Given their location, one can easily compute where the iron industry must be located in order to realize minimum costs of transfer.

To each location of production of *f* corresponds a certain location of production of raw materials and certain total costs of transfer. One must compare the costs of the *total* process of production, even though it may be divided between several regions, plus all the costs of transfer, in all possible different cases, before one can know anything about the minimum cost location. If there are other cost considerations they must also be considered.

When location of industry and interregional trade are in equilibrium, they are characterized by the fact that no enterprise can reduce costs of production, with due regard to transportation costs, by choosing another location. The demand of one region for producers' goods from other regions is a function of the location of industry, and this demand determines what sorts and quantities of raw materials or machinery are needed. This demand has to be added to consumers' demand in the "equation of reciprocal demand" and is still another modification of the system of equations presented in Appendix I to illustrate the price mechanism.

A change in the relation between costs of transfer of goods at lower stages of production and goods at higher stages may radically affect location. An obvious example is the effect of import duties on finished goods; they make it cheaper to import raw materials and manufacture the finished goods within the protected region. Thus, to some extent the later stages of production are moved from the raw material region to the market region. Trade in raw materials takes the place of trade in finished goods. Pulp instead of paper may go from Scandinavia to Great Britain.

The height of the costs of transfer is also greatly affected by the volume of trade. Trade connections become more intimate and transportation becomes cheaper between regions that exchange great quantities of commodities. In this way regions that are densely populated and rich in capital and therefore carry on a large volume of trade are, so to speak, brought economically "nearer" to their markets than are poor regions with a scanty population but otherwise in a similar position.

No simple formulation of the influence of transfer relations upon location and trade is possible. Similarly no exact description can be given of the nature of the trade among a number of regions with different facilities for production. In the latter case, however, if certain qualifications are kept in mind, it may be said that each region tends to specialize in commodities requiring relatively large quantities of the productive factors that are relatively abundant there. As to transfer conditions, no corresponding statement seems possible. One must be content to know that they take their place in the mutual interdependence system of pricing by which trade, costs of transfer, and the interregional distribution of production and markets are all determined.

§ 5. *Interregional prices.* Turning now to the price relations of trading regions, for the sake of simplicity I shall assume two regions only and study commodity prices on that basis. Differences in costs of transfer between regions will cause the price of a good that is traded to vary from one region to another. Such differences in the costs of transfer may be due to the fact that A imports goods that are easier to transport than those B imports, or vice versa. Or they may be due to lower freight rates to A as a result of a lesser demand for transportation in that direction. Import duties may also raise interregional prices in B widely over A's level. There is thus no foundation for the widespread impression, prevalent in the post-World War I monetary discussion, that international differences in price levels must be due to differences in home market prices.

Whereas interregional prices tend to differ between regions by the full amount of the costs of transfer, prices of home market goods usually differ *less* than these costs. This is, of course, the reason that they are produced in both regions, i.e., are home market goods. Otherwise, they would be produced exclusively in one region and traded to others. Within the limits set by the costs of transfer—which are often relatively higher for home market goods than for interregional goods—prices of the former may move differently in different regions. There is nothing to prevent houses from becoming cheaper in Sweden at the same time that they are becoming more costly in Great Britain. However, home market prices in one region are in several ways indirectly tied up with home market prices in other regions. This is a complicated question, which should be considered in some detail. The question may be put in this way: To what extent are interregional discrepancies in home market prices kept within narrow limits not only through the potential trade in these goods that would come into existence if interregional price differences exceeded the costs of transfer, but also through the actual trade in *other* goods.

It should be noted that goods in different stages of production—

raw materials, half-finished goods, auxiliary materials like tools and machines, finished consumers' goods—are subject to interregional exchange. In some cases only the finished products are traded; in other cases, only the raw materials. Nevertheless, prices of all categories tend to be equalized. The cost of a house in *A* and *B* will differ less when the import of timber from *A* to *B* reduces the price difference for this commodity to the costs of transfer than when timber is produced in *B* at high cost. The price of bread in various regions differs less now than it would if there were no interregional trade in wheat. Interregional trade in butter tends to prevent large differences in milk prices, in spite of the fact that milk hardly enters into such trade at all. In regions that produce some butter themselves although they import large quantities of it (i.e., Great Britain), the price of milk holds a fairly definite relation to the price of imported butter. The price of milk in the exporting region (i.e., Denmark) is also governed by the same butter price, after deducting the costs of transfer. In this way the butter trade keeps the interregional difference in milk prices within narrow limits.

Evidently trade in goods in the earlier stages, including machinery, tends to make costs of production and prices of home market goods in later stages of production more nearly similar in various regions than they would otherwise be. Similarly, trade in goods in later stages affects the price of home market goods in earlier stages. In cases of joint supply, when different products are made from the same raw material, the price equalizing tendency will affect all these goods. Cheap furniture and building timber, which are both made from fir wood, afford an example.

The case is similar when two or more commodities are manufactured in one process of production out of a common raw material; their prices are naturally intimately related. If in certain countries only one of them enters international trade, the prices of the others belonging to the home market group are affected by this trade. Increased demand for the traded commodity and its higher price in these countries will tend to increase the prices of the home market goods. In other words, home market prices tend to vary in the same way in all countries.

There is another influence of a similar although still more indirect character. The factors of production are not subject to international trade and resultant price equalization; factor prices thus hold a position analogous to that of home market prices. But trade in commodities of whatever sort tends to bring factor prices in various countries closer to each other; and costs of production of goods that do not enter international trade—home market goods—are thereby brought more into harmony. The price at which an apartment can be rented depends greatly upon the rate of interest. If the interregional differences in interest levels are reduced through trade, other things being equal, a tendency toward equalization of the price of apartments is clearly brought about. In brief, insofar as prices of interregional goods and productive factors in one region are made to differ less from such prices in other regions, costs of production and prices of home market goods are also made more nearly equal.

Assume that demand for home market goods falls off in A and increases in B. Home market prices will fall in A and rise in B, and the prices of the various factors of production will be affected in the corresponding direction. As a result, the production of and trade in international goods is necessarily influenced. Thus, the variation in factor prices is counteracted, and the change in home market prices is kept within more narrow limits. Assume further that the impediments to interregional trade are considerably reduced and the prices of interregional goods are consequently more nearly equalized in various regions. Insofar as these goods enter as costs in the production of home market goods, the prices of the latter also approach equality.

This analysis concerns the supply aspect of home market goods; it is necessary to consider also the demand conditions that tend to maintain a connection, albeit an elastic one, between home market prices in different regions. Prices of home market goods naturally cannot differ much from prices of import or export goods if the latter offer intense competition. If the price of domestic electrical machinery is raised above the import prices for the same articles, the machinery will be imported. Thus, demand for "competing home market goods" easily counteracts any tendency toward price variations in one region exclusively. Although a certain commodity is an export commodity in A (exported to C) and a home market commodity in B, the prices will not vary arbitrarily; a special case of this sort is "rival demand," which exists when one commodity can be substituted for another. International trade in margarine tends to prevent great differences in butter prices between countries where the latter is a home market commodity.

Furthermore, prices of competing home market goods in B and C, which can both import similar products from A, will move more or less in harmony. If competition between imported and domestic goods is very close, home market prices in B and C tend to be equal and to exceed A's export prices by the costs of transfer.

Special attention should be given to one category of home market prices, the prices of personal services. Most of them are only slightly affected by trade in commodities that enter into the costs of production of the services because practically the whole cost consists of wages. Thus, prices of services in various countries are affected by trade only through its effect on the prices of productive factors—in this case, labor's wages. It is clear that wages are by no means equalized interregionally and that for this reason the prices of personal services, as every traveler knows, vary from one region to another more than almost any commodity price.

Evidently the relation between home market prices in different regions is governed (1) by the prices of the productive factors affected by trade and (2) by the possibilities of trade in goods that compete with, can be substituted for, or are joint products with the home market goods. On the whole, therefore, the interrelation of home market prices in different regions is more fixed than appears at first sight.[3]

This analysis of home market prices applies to the case of many trading regions as well. It remains to describe briefly the relations between prices of traded goods between two regions.

§ 6. *Interregional prices, continued.* Consider four regions. *A* imports goods from *B*, and *C* obtains the same goods from *D*. Costs of production in *B* and *D* may differ considerably, perhaps by as much as the costs of transfer between these regions. The costs of transfer from *B* to *A* and from *D* to *C* may also differ, although not more than the costs of transfer between *B* and *D*. Interregional price relations are affected by the costs of transfer between the regions that trade with one another in the goods concerned.

Evidently, even if the group of commodities called "interregional goods" contains the same articles in *A* and *C*, the level of interregional prices in these two regions may differ, not only because of differences in the costs of transfer, but also because of the existence of more than one exporting region. Costs of production and export prices may be much higher in the region supplying *A* than in the region supplying *C*. Most European countries buy pulp from Scandinavia, but certain of them buy from their neighbors, e.g., Hungary from Czechoslovakia. Prices in both these countries are lower than Scandinavian prices plus costs of transport.

These remarks lead to a conclusion that has been often ignored.[4] To say that prices of interregional goods tend to differ by the costs of transfer is saying nothing. Such a statement refers only to a certain exporting region and the regions importing from it. It is not true of a comparison between prices of this commodity in the various importing regions; the price differences are often less than the costs of transfer between them. Neither is it true of a comparison with re-

---

[3] For certain variations in their relations, see Chap. XXII.

[4] E.g., see Keynes, *A Treatise on Money* (London, 1930), v, sec. 2, where the viewpoints on international price relations are otherwise similar to those in this book.

gions belonging to a different group, i.e., not trading in this commodity with the first group. One can only say that the price differences will be less than or equal to the costs of transfer to the farthest point.

Often, however, different exporting regions have common markets that connect their prices. This is the case with pulp: price variations in Scandinavia not only affect import prices in regions that import pulp from Scandinavia but also indirectly offset pulp prices in other exporting regions and thus throughout the world.

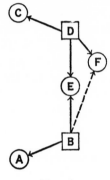

Fig. 4

The relation between prices in various producing regions is nevertheless far from fixed, even if variations in costs of transfer are disregarded; the position of the common market may vary. In the above figure, *B* and *D* have a common market in *E*. If *A*'s demand falls off, prices decline in *B* and *E*. *D* may be forced out of this market by *B*, and *B* may invade *F*, which used to buy only from *D*. If it is assumed that the exporting regions quote the same prices at the factory for all their customers, prices will fall more in *A*, *B*, and *E* than in *C*, *D*, and *F* because of costs of transport. Evidently it is not justifiable, except in the case of goods produced in one region only, to refer to a world market price, to which the costs of transfer are simply added in order to know the price in a certain region.

Knowledge of interregional price conditions implies knowledge of the costs of production in the various producing centers, and of the currents of trade from these centers to the various importing regions. A bird's-eye view of interregional price relations is secured through a system of equations that take the interregional costs of transfer into account.[5] The analysis given above shows that in such a price mechanism general price levels and interregional prices are far from equal.[6] Prices in all trading regions are interrelated, but not in such

[5] For the character of such a system, see Appendix I.
[6] The discussion of foreign exchange problems after World War I suffered a great deal from impractical assumptions about equality of price levels. Even

a simple fashion. The interdependence is closer for home market goods and less close for interregional goods than appears at first sight.

§ 7. *Difficulties with price indices.* In connection with this analysis certain difficulties in comparing price indices among regions should be mentioned. One special reason for care in using the concept of the "level of interregional prices" is that the commodities entering interregional trade are not identical in all regions. Not only are there many differences in quality that impair the accuracy of price comparisons, but much more serious is the difficulty arising from the fact that a commodity belonging to the home market group in one region may belong to the interregional group in another. A price index for all interregional goods in *A* is therefore not comparable to a price index for all interregional goods in *B*. As a rule, the distinction between home market and interregional prices and the price level concept in general is of greater use in comparisons of conditions on two different dates in the same region than in comparisons between different regions.

Difficulties inherent in the index method also make themselves felt. The result depends upon how the weighting is done. In a strict sense, all comparisons rest upon the tacit assumption that the commodities or groups of commodities, or productive factors or factor groups are fairly equal in the various regions. The costs of living, for instance, can be compared if the budgets used are identical or similar. The greater the difference between the things to which the sum of prices refers in various regions, the less significant the comparison can be.

If some goods play a much more important role in the budgets of *A* than of *B*, and other goods are consumed only in one of the regions, a comparison of the costs of living becomes artificial. However, if there are fundamental similarities, two indices of the costs of living for each region may be computed by means of the budgets used; in case the relation of the index in *A* and that in *B* is similar for the different computations, the result attains a certain validity.

Comparisons of the absolute heights of the general wholesale price levels in various regions are often much less significant. The aggregates of goods that must be used as a basis for the computation differ considerably if the weighting is to be based upon the economic importance of the goods in each region. Since a comparison of price indices is nothing but a comparison of the total value of a certain "bale" of commodities in the various regions, the result is

---

writers like Hawtrey and Cassel were responsible for such analyses. See their writings of 1926: Hawtrey, *The Economic Problem* (London, 1926), p. 113, and Cassel, "The Foreign Exchanges," *Encyclopedia Britannica*, New Volume I, p. 1080. For a view related to that in the text, see Wicksell, *Geldzins und Güterpreise* (Stockholm), x; and Keynes, *A Treatise on Money*, vii.

devoid of interest when the aggregate of goods is not approximately
equal. If identical aggregates are chosen, they are not necessarily
satisfactory representatives of economic life in the different regions.

Evidently, general price indices for regions with considerable inequalities in their economic structure do not throw much light on
price conditions. A statement that the general price level of commodities or productive factors in *A* is 10 percent higher than that in
B can be meaningless. If comparisons are to be made, they must be
based on special indices, constructed for some special purpose. If, for
instance, the food habits of the populations are similar, one may
say that an index of food prices is 10 percent higher in *A* than in
B. Again, if a certain industry uses the same raw materials in both
regions and practically in the same proportions, the height of the
raw material prices may be expressed by means of indices. Similarly,
with regard to factor prices, they may be compared interregionally
only if they refer to factors or groups of factors that are approximately
equal in the various regions.

It is important to distinguish the problem of comparing the absolute
height of prices with that of comparing price *variations* in different
regions. In the latter case the comparison is not between prices in
A and prices in *B*. Instead, one wishes to know whether prices in
A have changed more or less than prices in *B*. The computation of
the change in the price index involves only a comparison between
conditions at two different times in the *same* region. From 1900 to
1914, for example, the general wholesale price level may have risen
by 20 percent in *A* and by 10 percent in *B*. Such a comparison is
permissible even if *A* and *B* produce and use many different goods,
or if the goods used are more important in one region than in the
other.

Different indices can be employed also for different purposes. It
is particularly interesting to compute the change in the net money
value of all goods produced. This computation gives the same result
as a comparison of the value of all productive factors used in the
region during two periods of time, including profits, i.e., the change
in the national income expressed in money. The fact that this income fluctuates more in one region than in another, when certain
changes in the economic situation occur, has great significance.

The price *changes* of productive factors, individually or by
groups, can of course be compared, like commodity prices. The
wages of manual workers may be said to have risen by 20 percent
in *A* and by 30 percent in *B* even if the proportion of skilled and
unskilled workers is different in the two regions, for the comparison
does not assume that the figures refer to identical objects.

§ 8. *Prices of productive factors in different regions.* This relation can best be illustrated by an analysis of hypothetical cases. Suppose that of the three regions A, B, and C given in § 3, B and C have similar productive factors (farmland, etc.). C is either situated further away from A than is B, or its means of communication with that region are for other reasons not as good as those of B. Costs of transport for import and export goods are assumed to be about equal.

It follows that B's productive factors will be in relatively greater demand by A than C's—in other words, that their prices will be higher. The general level of commodity prices, as measured by a wholesale price index of the ordinary type, is therefore also higher in B than in C. It is true that import prices are higher in C, but export goods common to these two regions command higher prices in the ports of B than in C, since they are closer to the market in A. The consequent relative cheapness of C factors tends to make home market goods in C also cheaper than in B.

Observe, however, that some home market goods in C are *import* goods in B and may well cost more in C therefore than in B. Yet certain goods that B is able to export are home market goods in C and will probably cost less there than in B. These two qualifications do not impair the conclusion that the general price level, as commonly computed, is lower in a region far from its markets than in another region with similar productive factors but situated closer to the main centers of trade. The fact that import goods from A cost more to C than to B means that C obtains less for its exports and pays more for its imports than does its rival. Evidently, the long distance to A is a disadvantage to C.

In general, productive factors situated close to the market for their products—or so situated that these products can be easily moved there—obtain higher value than more distant factors. Out-of-the-way regions have cheap factors, for which reason they produce for themselves many commodities that more favorably situated regions with higher income levels would import. This is one way in which interregional trade is restricted by the costs of transfer.

The trade with A obviously affects the prices of factors and commodities differently in B and C. Relative prices in these two regions may differ more when actual trade is going on than otherwise. The assertion that trade tends to equalize the prices of the factors of production therefore refers to the situation as a whole[7] but need not be true of relative factor prices in any two regions. Yet if trade occurs between two arbitrary regions (in this case B and C) it cannot but exercise an equalizing influence on prices in *these* two regions.

[7] The price equalizing effect may be measured by an index of interregional factor prices. For reasons analogous to those discussed above with reference to commodity prices, it is not worthwhile to give much attention to such measurements.

§ 9. *Differences in factor supplies and prices.* It is evident that the prices of traded goods in different regions are so profoundly influenced by the transfer relations that any explanation which disregards this aspect of the problem is inadequate.[8] It is equally clear that the differences in factor supplies, described in terms of the quantities of factors in each region and irrespective of their local distribution within it, affect interregional prices. Other things being equal, home market prices will be low in regions where the factors of production important to home market industries are cheap.[9]

The influence of productive equipment is particularly clear in regions with an uneven supply of natural resources; they have a high general price level, as measured by a wholesale price index of the ordinary type, for they lack many of the factors that play a leading role in home market industry. In the southern part of Argentina almost nothing but oil is produced; consequently it is cheap, whereas almost everything else is expensive. This illustrates the influence of both the costs of transport and the supply of factors of production.

Another case is found in gold-producing districts. Alaska, for instance, is a rather barren country apart from its gold mines. Almost everything has to be imported and is, therefore, more expensive than in the places where it is produced. Gold, on the other hand, is a little cheaper than elsewhere, though very little indeed, but this does not lower the general price index because gold is not among the commodities included in the general price index.

§ 10. *Friction and interregional prices.* There are a number of reasons, in addition to those already mentioned, why the differences in prices among interregional goods cannot be explained simply in terms of the costs of transfer. First, commodities do not, so to speak, sell themselves automatically. It is not easy to sell a product in a new market without incurring heavy initial marketing expenses; hence, the differences between the prices of such goods in different countries may much exceed the combined costs of transport, duties, and similar expenses.

As for the relation between home market prices, much of what has been written here concerning the connection between prices in different regions is valid only when interpreted as referring to long-run tendencies. Prices of home market goods in different regions are connected only loosely by reactions which, when changes occur, may come about slowly and with little precision.

Consider first elements on the supply side that tend to cause a parallel development of home market prices in several regions. Raw materials and other factors, or intermediate products used in industries

[8] Cf. Taussig, *International Trade*, v.
[9] See Chap. XIV, where this reasoning is further pursued and illustrated.

manufacturing certain goods, may be subject to interregional trade and their prices may therefore tend to move more or less in harmony. This influence is doubly indirect and, from a short-term point of view, uncertain. The cheapening of a certain factor in region A may lead to a reduction of wages given to this factor employed in region B's export industries. But for some time, at least, the same factor in B's home market industries may retain their old pay because of trade union policy or other friction. For the time being, home market prices in B may fail to move downward as they have in A.

From a short-term point of view factors used in home market industries are different from the factors employed in export industries. It is clearly only insofar as the same factors are used in these two groups of industries that trade in interregional goods can affect directly factor prices and costs of production in home market industries.

With regard to demand, as certain home market goods compete closely with interregional goods, price variations in the latter tend to be reflected in the prices of the former. This does not happen instantly. A drop in import prices may bring a corresponding change in the prices of competing home market goods only after some time, when an attempt to maintain prices has led to reduced sales and increased imports. However, trade in goods in a late stage of production (e.g., paper) is probably often effective in bringing about quick reactions in the prices of raw materials (e.g., wood), even if they are not subject to interregional trade. Even in this case some time may pass before the expected variations occur.

Differences in the supply of a product generally explain temporary discrepancies in the prices of the product in different regions. Factor and raw material prices affect the supply of a product only indirectly, through their influence on costs of production. Although in the long run this influence is no doubt decisive, and the simple assumption of coincidence between costs and prices is justified, it is equally clear that temporarily production costs and prices often differ considerably. Profits are high in certain industries, but others are working at a heavy loss. If profits tended to develop in a similar manner in all regions, commodity prices would also tend to move in harmony. As a matter of fact, it often occurs that while a certain industry is prospering in one region and declining in another, costs are falling in both. Similarly, a variation in costs between regions in an industry need not at once make selling prices move in a parallel direction.

Last, it should be mentioned that costs of production relating to individual commodities are not exact quantities. The division of overhead costs between different products of the same process or between different "bales" of goods even when of identical quality is more or less arbitrary. This opens up possibilities for a price policy that may be developed along different lines. The most conspicuous example is the use of "dumping," or price discrimination in general. Electrical energy, for instance, is sold to private households and factories at different prices, according to the use made of it. The traditions of such discrimination in Sweden and Norway are different; it is therefore quite possible that a reduction in costs would not affect the prices of electricity in the same way in these two countries. Private householders might reap the chief benefit in one, and factories in the other.

§ 11. *Summary.* This chapter has analyzed the influence of interregional costs of transfer on trade. It has been demonstrated that transfer costs not only hamper interregional trade but change its course and, to some extent, its effects. The relation between commodity and factor prices in different regions has been illustrated and described in view of transfer costs. The connection between prices of interregional goods has been shown to be less direct and that of home market goods to be more so than might be assumed at first sight. From a long-term point of view the price system of mutual interdependence ties them firmly together, but considerable discrepancies in their development in different regions are temporarily possible.

IX

Interregional Factor Movements and Their Relation to Commodity Movements[1]

§ 1. *Factor Movements as an alternative to trade.* Having dealt with the influence of obstacles to interregional commodity movements, I now come to the question of interregional movements of productive factors. So far these factors have been assumed to be completely mobile within the regions but unable to move at all between them; in neither regard does the assumption correspond to reality. One must consider not only the possibility of transferring factors from one region to another but also the obstacles to their movement within the regions. These obstacles, and the corresponding difficulties in the way of intraregional commodity movements, are discussed in the next chapter. At present I shall examine the interregional factor movements and their influence on interregional trade, as well as the effects of trade on such factor movements, ignoring the price discrepancies that exist *within* the regions.

The obstacles to interregional factor movements vary to some extent with the sort of regions under consideration. They are generally more important when the regions are individual countries than when they are parts of the same country. A realistic description of these obstacles is consequently possible only in a study of a special sort of region. I shall return to this question in the chapters on international trade. In general it may be said, however, (1) that natural resources are immobile, (2) that obstacles to labor movements consist not so much in actual expenses of transporting the laborer, his family, and his personal property as in a psychological aversion to change, particularly change to something more or less unknown, and (3) that obstacles to capital movement are similarly psychological.[2] Such ob-

---

[1] The fact that international movements of labor and capital had been much neglected in orthodox treatises and that a theory of such movements need not be subordinated to a theory of commodity movements was drawn to my attention by Professor John H. Williams during my studies at Harvard University in 1922-23. Cf. his very important paper, "The Theory of International Trade Reconsidered," *Economic Journal* (1929).

[2] The difficulties of adjusting the trade mechanism to include capital movements are another matter; see § 5.

stacles therefore cannot, as in the case of commodities, be reckoned in definite costs of transfer.

However, the stimulus that makes laborers and capitalists overcome the obstacles is chiefly a desire to receive a higher price, i.e., higher wages or interest rates. The difference in price sufficient to induce a transfer of labor or capital is insufficient to call forth a greater transfer. Thus, if the height of the obstacle is measured by the stimulus necessary to overcome it, it is clear that different laborers and different units of capital meet obstacles of differing heights. In this respect they are not comparable to the obstacles to commodity movements such as difficulties of transportation and duties that from an economic point of view appear as costs of transfer. In other respects, however, the obstacles to factor movements may be dealt with in an analogous manner.

As factors move from regions where their prices are relatively low to regions where they are dear, their scarcity and therefore their rewards in the former are increased, whereas their prices in the latter fall, unless there is at the same time some counteracting tendency. Interregional mobility tends to make prices more uniform in the regions concerned, just as the interregional movements of commodities were found to do.

These tendencies, being in the same direction, cannot but affect one another. Through the exchange of commodities not only *their* prices but also those of the productive factors are to some extent equalized; i.e., interregional discrepancies in factor prices are reduced, and interregional factor movements are thereby less compelling. The movement of goods to some extent takes the place of factor movements. In other words, if no trade took place, the price discrepancies and consequently the movements of the productive factors would be more considerable. Trade renders unnecessary in part—in some cases wholly—the international movement of capital and labor.

Nevertheless, the exchange of goods cannot bring about a complete equalization of factor prices. Interregional differences remain and call forth factor movements whenever the difference is great enough to overcome the obstacles. Factor prices are in this way brought closer together in the different regions; the need for interregional trade and consequently its volume are reduced. Factor movements act as a substitute for the movements of commodities. Interregional price equalization seems to be furthered either by both movements or by the one that meets with less resistance.

If the mobility of the factors increases, a new transfer of them will take place, and the consequent greater harmony between their prices in different regions will obviate part of the exchange of commodities. However, a reduction in the costs of transport through improvements in the technique of transportation will increase trade, and the often resultant decrease of the factor price discrepancy may diminish interregional factor movements. Everything depends upon the intensity of the reaction of factor prices and therefore factor movements when trade varies, and upon the intensity of the reaction of commodity prices and therefore trade when factor movements vary.

In some cases the exchange of goods may operate alone. It may cause such a high degree of price harmony between regions that no interregional movements of capital and labor are called forth. The margins between wages and interest rates in different regions may be too small. Under such circumstances the mobility of the productive factors has only potential importance: it does not affect production and prices but would do so if either the factor price discrepancies or the mobility increased.

It is theoretically conceivable that in other cases factor movement, but no trade, takes place between two regions. Both may find it profitable to trade exclusively with other regions, but this may be compatible with such different factor prices that factors move between the two regions. For all practical purposes, however, one may assume that either commodities alone or both commodities and factors move between the various regions.

A study of variations in interregional trade—whether the cause be changes in demand, technique, or anything else—must consider the reactions of both these tendencies toward price equalization. Variations that would increase price discrepancies are counteracted both by a change in trade, which directly affects commodity prices and indirectly affects factor prices, and by a change in factor movements, which affects factor prices directly and commodity prices indirectly. The tendency toward price equalization thus operates in two ways.

§ 2. *Influence of factor movements on volume and character of trade.* The reactions of trade when the primary cause of the economic variation lies in a changed factor mobility may now be considered, and also the reaction of factor movements when the primary cause is a change in the obstacles to trade. Assume that the interregional mobility of productive factors is for some reason considerably increased and that under the circumstances the existing discrepancy in factor prices is large enough to cause factor movements that contribute to the equalizing of interregional factor prices. When price differences have in this way been reduced, the factors will again become stationary. What will be the situation with regard to trade?

One would suppose from the previous analysis that the volume of trade would be reduced, since it has been partly obviated through the direct equalization of factor prices, implying in many cases greater similarity in the equipment of productive agents. Such is the case, for example, if *A* exports capital to *B* while *B* sends labor to *A*. If the total income in *A*, i.e., the sum of the prices of all productive factors, maintains about the same relation to that of *B* as before, trade is reduced.[3] However, the redistribution of productive factors increases the real income in both regions taken together—in terms of commodities[4]—and this condition, *ceteris paribus*, tends to increase trade. It is conceivable that this tendency would be stronger than the one just mentioned.

The outcome is still more uncertain when the total income in one region increases compared to the total income in the other. If *B* is a new country with plenty of natural resources, the movements of factors may go one way only, with both labor and capital flowing to *B* from *A* or from several other regions. The total income is increased in *B* but reduced in *A*. If income in *B* has been considerably smaller than in *A*, a more even distribution of income between them must tend to increase trade. There can be little doubt that trade between Europe and South America has been greatly increased through the flow of labor and capital from the former to the latter, in spite of the fact that these movements have made South America's equipment of productive agents more like Europe's than formerly. Economic life in South America has experienced an enormous growth, which would have been impossible without the influx of labor and capital.

The volume of trade is dependent upon the absolute quantity of productive agents in the various regions, not alone upon the inequality of their endowment. Better, the strength of the demand, which is governed by the quantity, prices, and conditions of ownership of productive factors in the various regions as well as by the taste of its inhabitants, affects the volume of trade no less than do the conditions of supply. Trade between England and Iceland, despite the great inequality in their factor supplies, is smaller than between England and Holland, where factor endowments are more nearly identical.

Of course, if the total income in *B* is greater than in *A*, an increase in factor movements from *A* to *B* tends to reduce interregional trade. The more productive factors, and thereby consumers, are concentrated in one region, the less is the need for interregional trade, at least if this concentration means at the same time a step toward factor price equalization.

As a matter of fact, labor and capital have usually gone to regions with scanty supplies of these factors and relatively low aggregate in-

---

[3] Under dynamic conditions national income may differ from the sum total of factor prices. For the present purpose this fact need not be considered.

[4] The concepts "volume of trade" and "volume of production" must be used with caution. Cf. Chap XV.

comes. The migration has considerably increased total income and has thus tended to increase interregional trade. It seems probable that in many cases this trend has been stronger than that toward reduction in trade because of greater similarity in factor prices. Nevertheless, factor movements have in most cases almost certainly reduced the volume of interregional trade.

There is no fixed relation between the size of incomes and trade. Factor movements imply not only changes in productive techniques but also, at least in some cases, a change in the direction of demand. The immigrant laborer need not demand the same goods as did the expatriated capitalist.

In brief, apart from costs of transfer of commodities, the volume of trade depends upon (1) the inequality of factor supplies, (2) the size of the respective aggregate incomes, i.e., the volume of demand in different regions, and (3) the direction of demand. Factor movements affect all three[5] of these elements, and they affect the second in two ways; they may change the *relations* between total incomes in various regions; and the redistribution of factors means increased effectiveness in their utilization, i.e., tends to raise the volume of production and income everywhere.

§ 3. *Influence of factor movements on trade, continued.* A few similar subjects remain to be considered. The first has to do with the so-called "economies of large-scale production" in the widest sense of the expression. Under certain conditions the prices of the factors that increase in quantity through influx from other regions need not fall relative to the prices of factors that are not augmented at all. A region with a great supply of natural resources may receive an influx of capital and labor without any reduction of interest rates and wages. It is well known that when the quantity of one factor is increased and the quantity of other cooperating factors is constant, the return per unit of the former may in the beginning increase. Four thousand men will probably produce more than twice as much in a new country as two thousand men. The tendency to diminishing returns as regards the factor that is increased only makes itself felt after a certain point has been reached. A new region with a scanty supply of labor and capital may, owing to external economies, get a higher output per head and unit of capital when the supply of labor and capital is increased, which has been abundantly illustrated by economic history.

The point where a further influx of labor reduces wages may not be reached, even though the tendency to diminishing returns is active

---

[5] The volume of trade is, of course, governed by all the basic circumstances in the price system, but some of them, like conditions of ownership, are not affected by factor movements and therefore are not touched upon here.

in the individual enterprises. Density of population is necessary for the opening and maintenance of communications, educational facilities, etc. Although each farm would get less output per head by employing one more man, indirect advantages would come to all of them from an increase in density. It is quite possible, therefore, that the flow of labor and capital into South America toward the end of the last century had no tendency to reduce wages or even interest rates—at least, in the beginning—but on the contrary raised them relative to rents. The change in factor prices during this period may thus have been in the same direction there and in Europe, where the outflow of labor and capital must have raised wages and interest rates. If that is so, factor prices have not moved closer together, and trade has had no tendency to decrease.[6] Nor have factor movements had any tendency to change the character of trade; goods containing relatively great quantities of natural resources have always been the natural export articles of South America.

After a certain point has been reached, however, wages and interest fail to rise as fast as rents. Relative factor prices at this point tend to be equalized interregionally. This must be the case still more when wages and interest rates tend to fall under the influence of increased quantities of labor and capital.

The last qualification is that the large-scale economies effected when the market is enlarged through the influx of labor and capital affect the various industries quite differently. If these economies are felt chiefly in export industries, trade tends to increase. However, increased effectiveness, particularly in industries that produce goods competing with import commodities, must have the opposite effect on the volume of trade. It is impossible to say which of these alternatives is most probable in new countries receiving both labor and capital from abroad. It is true that internal economies are greatest in manufacturing industries and tend to reduce imports of manufactures in new regions. But external economies are perhaps even more important in agriculture and tend to increase exports. The higher factor prices, in terms of goods, which must follow counteract these tendencies, and a balance between imports and exports is maintained; the volume of trade can just as well be increased as reduced. The same thing may be expressed by saying that the proportions in which productive factors are needed change as a result of large-scale economies. This may affect the character and volume of trade in a way impossible to describe in general terms. Evidently, the number of acting and counteracting tendencies set at work by international factor movements is great, and the net result on the volume and character of trade is correspondingly varied.

[6] On the contrary, trade must have grown as a result of the increase in the national incomes.

It is often but not always true that factor movements tend to equalize factor supplies in the various regions. The stimulus to factor movements lies in the interregional price differences, which would exist even if the factor supplies were the same. Differences in demand, transfer conditions, social conditions, and the like, cause differences in factor prices which might be sufficient to call forth factor movements.

Consider three regions *A*, *B*, and *C*, of which the last two are similarly equipped, whereas *C* lies much further away from *A* than *B*. *A* being an important market for the goods of the other two regions, the prices of most factors tend to be higher in *B* than in *C*; consequently, some of them may move from the latter to the former, and the equipment of *B* and *C* will then differ more than before.

When factors migrate, they induce changes throughout the economies affected, of which change in the conditions of production is only one facet. Variations in factor supply and factor prices also change the costs of transfer in two ways which affect the distribution of industry and interregional trade. In the first place, costs of transfer naturally depend upon the prices of the productive factors needed for transportation. By influencing factor prices, interregional factor movements also affect costs of transfer. Transport services hold a place in the price system analogous to that of other services and commodities. Second, large-scale economies affect transport services in much the same way as commodity production. Since factor movements to new countries, for instance, increase production there, they also cause an expansion in the transportation services and a cheaper supply of them is made possible. Harbors and railroads, for example, may be built and cheaply operated, which must markedly affect the volume and character of trade.

So much for the different effects of interregional factor movements upon interregional trade. Although no general statement can be made, the foregoing analysis throws light on the relations between factor and commodity movements.

§ 4. *Influence of changes in transfer conditions on factor movements.*[7] Because factor movements depend upon interregional price differences, any variation in the basic elements of the price system may affect factor movements. The costs of transfer, i.e., the prices of transfer services, whose place in the price system is similar to that of other services, have been analyzed. Productive factors at certain

---

[7] The expression "transfer conditions," which is convenient in many cases, refers to the physical conditions of production and transportation in all regions, regarded from the point of view of transfer of commodities. The quality of the surface of the earth in various parts of the world is, perhaps, particularly important, together with the distance between the regions. The term "conditions of production" refers to the supply of factors in the various regions and to the physical conditions of production and transportation, both regarded from the point of view of production.

prices must be used, their quantity depending upon the qualities of the factors and commodities, i.e., the natural properties of the materials. In other words, the same physical conditions govern production in a narrow sense as those that control transportation.

Interregional factor movements require small amounts of transfer services. A little shipping room for emigrants is perhaps all.[8] Whether capital movements require extra means of transportation is doubtful. They need not increase the total volume of trade since they may reduce commodity movements in one direction as much as they increase them in the opposite one. At any rate, the consequent demand for transportation services is analogous to the demand for them for purposes of travel and the like.

The previous section investigated the effects upon the price system, and particularly upon the volume and character of trade, of primary changes in factor mobility that induce interregional factor movements. Analysis of the effects of primary variations in the price system, with special attention to the reactions of interregional factor movements, is postponed to Part V, with the following exception: those basic changes in transfer conditions are particularly interesting. They affect interregional trade directly and thence other parts of the price mechanism, e.g., factor prices and interregional factor movements, indirectly. This is evidently the reverse of the case considered in the previous section; a change in factor mobility can influence nothing but factor movements directly and trade, etc., indirectly. The latter case has been discussed; discussion of the former begins with the influence upon factor movements of changes in trade due to technical improvements in transportation.

The effect of such changes may be for factor prices to be so nearly equalized that factor movements which would otherwise have taken place are rendered superfluous. Yet it is quite possible that out-of-the-way regions may become natural locations for certain industries and will, therefore, attract labor and capital, whereby interregional factor movements are increased. Interregional discrepancies in factor prices may well be widened in some cases and reduced in others, with diverse effects upon factor movements. This holds good for both reductions and increases in the costs of transfer—for instance, the effect upon factor movements of a policy of high protection.

It has been demonstrated that the effect upon trade of changes in transfer costs cannot be explained in terms of increase or reduction in the total volume: the currents of trade are altogether transformed. Evidently the same may be said of the possible influence of changed costs of transfer upon factor movements. Factors are attracted to

[8] Indirectly, certain investment is required, e.g., housing in the immigration country, which may be more costly than in the emigrants' home country.

regions that now have become suitable for the location of important industries. A study of variations of the price mechanism of several trading regions would naturally explain what happens in each case. The present analysis is an attempt to characterize the relationship in that mechanism as a whole.

§ 5. *Various combinations of commodity and factor movements as alternatives.* It has been demonstrated that under certain circumstances factor and commodity movements are alternatives, and under other conditions new movements of one cause greater movements of the other. Now consider the fact that some factor movements take the place of others just as some commodity movements take the place of others. The latter phenomenon is self-evident: import duties on manufactured goods, for example, often lead to the production of similar goods at home by means of imported raw materials. Thus, raw materials are traded instead of finished goods. In general, transfer costs determine whether under given conditions of production goods at a later or earlier stage of manufacture are traded.

Similarly, one factor may move from A to B, where other factors are relatively abundant. If this movement is made difficult, the result may be that other factors move from B to A. Instead of capital going one way, for instance, labor may move the other as a result of checks on interregional capital movements.

However, capital and labor movements may complement each other. European emigration to South America would have been unthinkable in the last century if European capital had not also moved. Yet even in such cases certain factor movements may be said to replace others. Because natural resources could not go from South America to Europe, other factors had to go in the opposite direction. The outcome has been increased interregional trade, so that it is perhaps more accurate to say that factor movements and trade of one sort have replaced trade of another sort. In general, one combination of factor and commodity movements may take the place of another. Variations in difficulties of transfer may lead to such substitutions, as may all other sorts of economic variation.

Factor and commodity movements are the reactions of the economic mechanism. Both imply a local adaptation of the supply of goods to the conditions of demand. *Factor* movements chiefly reflect adaptation of conditions of production to conditions of transfer and demand[9] and at the same time imply an adaptation of transfer conditions and local distribution of demand. *Commodity* movements, and the interregional distribution of production they express, represent an

---

[9] For the sake of brevity I will not repeat each time that conditions of stability, taxation, and the like play a similar role to that of other conditions of production, demand, etc.

adaptation of local supply to local demand, given certain conditions of production and transfer.

The controlling element in local adaptation is in the long run the fact that natural resources are immobile, whereas labor and capital can be distributed. Most other factors are fairly mobile, and most goods may be transported among many regions. The number of combined movements that are feasible is therefore enormous, which makes tariffs and other hindrances to interregional economic relations in many cases ineffectual.

§ 6. *Some dynamic aspects of factor movements and their relation to trade.* So far this analysis has been concerned with comparisons of the situation before and after a certain change has taken place. Such a comparison is essentially static. Yet factor movements require time. It is not sufficient to inquire into the situation merely when they are completed because new economic variations affecting factor prices may constantly occur, so that factor movements continue indefinitely. Furthermore, certain factor movements have special effects while they are actually in progress, so that the situation must be considered as it develops.

Capital holds a unique position in one respect: it can move from one region to another only in the form of goods or services. Export of capital assumes an excess of commodity exports over imports. By the same token, a region wishing to import capital must either import more goods or export less than before, or do a little of each. It may therefore be said that capital movements are in a sense commodity movements.

The characteristic of capital movements in this respect is that they assume a certain *relation between* commodity movements in the directions of export and import. This relation can only be brought about by a thorough change in the general economic situation of the various regions. The nature of this change (the mechanism of interregional capital movements) will be separately analyzed from the standpoint of domestic and international movement (Part V).

If capital moves while the capitalist does not, the borrowing region must pay interest to the lending one in the form of commodities or services. Such payments affect trade in the same way as do original capital movements, except that they do not give rise to new interest payments. The effects of capital movements and interest payments in opposite directions are obviously neutralized so far as the mechanism of trade is concerned; the net sum alone moves in a given direction in the form of goods or services. An analysis of interregional capital movements must consider the growth of interest payments and the net sums moving at various times, even though the influx of capital proceeds at an even rate. For this and other reasons such an analysis must incorporate time.

Another circumstance is the fact that new changes constantly occur, and that therefore the discrepancy between factor prices in different regions may always be so considerable that factor movements continue. It is true that with some exceptions, and certainly after some time has elapsed, these factor movements tend to reduce the price differences; but other economic changes may increase them as much or more.

Assume that labor moves from *A* to *B*. Wages in the latter tend to fall relative to wages in *A* as well as to other factor prices in *B*. Economic progress and improvements in methods of production may, however, be so much more rapid in *B* that wages there rise in terms of commodities as quickly as in *A;* that is to say, no relative decline occurs. This is self-evident. Greater interest attaches to the fact that the factor movements—and the changes in trade that go hand in hand with them—may be the direct causes of other economic changes, which counterbalance many effects that would otherwise operate.

As has already been pointed out, capital movements imply a transfer of buying power and therefore exercise a far-reaching influence upon interregional pricing as long as the capital movements or interest payments continue. As a result, the relation between factor movements and the basic elements of pricing takes on a dynamic character, which includes elements heretofore ignored. The influence of trade upon factor prices must alter the supply of factors from domestic sources; it may create new savings, increased education, more births, and the like, or vice versa. British export of capital in the nineteenth century not only raised the interest level in Great Britain but also increased the production of food in transatlantic countries, and thus cheapened the food supply of the mother country. This may have had considerable influence upon its economic development, including the volume of savings. Factor movements also affect factor prices and act more or less upon factor supply in the same way. Export of capital tends to raise the rate of interest and thus increase savings; the importation of labor may indirectly reduce the birth rate in the immigrant region. The outcome depends upon the price sensitiveness of such factor supply.

It follows that in a study of economic variations, and particularly of their influence upon interregional trade, attention cannot be confined to the domestic reactions of factor supply to changed factor prices. One must also ask how far interregional factor movements are induced and what is the influence thereby exerted upon factor prices and trade and upon the domestic supply of factors. Some of these reactions come about quickly, others occur after some time;

some last long, others are exhausted within a brief period. An analysis must therefore cover a time-using process consisting of various opposing tendencies.

An investigation into the nature and variations of interregional trade thus becomes a study of variations of the many-market price system in general, including changes in the conditions of production and in the volume and character of output. The part played by interregional factor movements, directly and indirectly, cannot be disregarded. The theories of interregional trade and of interregional factor movements to a great extent overlap; only the special aspects of the latter may be ignored in this treatise.

X

Interior Costs of Transfer and Factor Movements: Some Aspects of a General Location Theory

§ 1. *The Thünen case.* Attention has heretofore been confined to the costs of transfer of commodities and the movements of productive factors *between* regions. The lack of interior mobility of both goods and factors, which has been disregarded, will now be examined.

The basis of study is now a district whose frontiers are not described. How does the lack of mobility of goods and factors affect location of production and trade within this district? For the sake of simplicity it is at first assumed that *labor and capital are completely mobile* in the sense that each quality of them has one price in terms of commodities throughout the district. The subject is the influence exerted by the immobility of nature and of the transfer costs of commodities upon production and trade.

In the first few simple cases the surface of land is assumed to be the same over the whole district so far as suitability for transport of commodities is concerned. This common element is called "uniform transport features." Later the influence both of transport features and of "transport facilities" (transport features as modified by man)—e.g., some parts of the district having railroads, others not—will be analyzed.

The first case is virtually the same as that so admirably studied by von Thünen.[1] In the middle of the district is a center of natural resources such as coal and iron mines, required for key manufacturing industries. It is surrounded by land of uniform quality and suitable for farming. Consequently, a city develops in the center and buys food from the surrounding country, sending manufactured products in exchange.

If only one farm product is produced, the case is simple: its price in each part of the district will be equal to that in the city, corrected for the cost of transport. The rent of land will be lower the farther it is from the city, its intensity of cultivation will be lower, and its

[1] Von Thünen, *Der isolierte Staat* (Jena, 1910).

population will be less. At a certain distance[2] land will be free; still further away no cultivation will take place.

The case is much more complicated if several farm products are produced, but their prices will still be higher in the vicinity of the city because of the costs of transport. The question is, where will each of them be produced? Will heavy products or goods otherwise difficult to transport be produced close to the city, and the others be produced further away? Under the present assumption the answer is in the affirmative. Animal foodstuffs, for example, which are usually more difficult to transport than vegetable foods, will be produced in the neighborhood of the city. If, however, different pieces of land are of varying quality, this statement will not hold. Nor is it certain that each product will be grown on the land best suited for it. If a particular quality of land is best suited for both wine and wheat, for what will it be used? Naturally, for the product that is able to pay the highest rent; the other product will be grown on land that is from its point of view only second-best. The fact that, *ceteris paribus,* heavy goods are produced closer to the city than light ones is only a consequence of the heavy goods' ability to pay a higher rent, owing to the greater saving in transportation costs resulting from nearness to the market.

Determination of which products can pay higher rents is possible only by means of a general price system of mutual interdependence. A simplified picture is obtained when in the ordinary one-market price system various pieces of land of the same quality but different location are dealt with as if their quality were different; in other words, location is regarded so far as land is concerned in much the same way as fertility. The "technical coefficients" indicate how much of other factors each piece of land requires for the production (including transportation to market) of each product. Through such a price system it can be determined how the various productive factors— including land—are to be combined and for what sort of production they should be used.[3]

§ 2. *Relative mobility of raw materials and finished goods in simple cases.* The possibility of dividing production so that the raw material is made in one place and the finished product is made in another should now be considered. The influence of the immobility of nature and the costs of transfer of commodities is dealt with first. Uniform

[2] The question of distance need not be analyzed here.

[3] In most treatises on economic principles the theory of rent is dealt with in this way: it is assumed that consumption takes place only in one place; otherwise the location of consumption—the quantities consumed at various places—has to be considered as it affects the location of production. As shown in the following sections, such a theory at its best is nothing more than a first step toward a real theory of rent.

prices of labor and capital throughout the district are assumed, as well as equal transport features and facilities. First, the location of the industry producing the finished product is dependent upon (*a*) the relative transferability of the raw materials and finished goods and (*b*) the distance from the possible manufacturing centers to the sources of raw materials and to markets. The location both of consumers' markets and of raw material production (including crude food) is assumed to be known.[4] Next, the location of industries[5] producing raw materials and of markets is analyzed, and the conclusions are modified to include differences in transport features and facilities, costs of transfer, and large-scale economies.

In the first case a commodity is made from one raw material only. How is the manufacturing to be located in relation to the source of the raw material and an important market? The answer is simple. There are two different possibilities. If, on the one hand, the finished goods are more difficult to transport than the raw material, as with beer or bread, production tends to be located close to the market. If, on the other hand, the raw material is more difficult to transport than the product made from it, production tends to be placed near the raw material source. In many cases the raw material loses weight during the production process. This is one reason why threshing is usually done on the spot where cereals are harvested. Butter is transported, not milk; and bricks are transported, not clay. Canning industries grow up in districts with a surplus production of vegetables. It follows that improvement in the transportation of finished goods must tend to move industry closer to the raw material sources. Hermetical sealing and artificial refrigeration have moved slaughtering and packing plants from the great consuming centers to the centers of the cattle raising districts.

Next, consider the fact that most commodities are produced from several raw materials found in different places. Materials found everywhere—"ubiquities"—have of course no direct influence because there is no need for transporting them. One must compare the cost of transporting finished goods and that of *localized* raw materials. Note, however, that "ubiquities" in many cases tend to make finished goods relatively heavy compared to localized raw materials. The bread-baking

---

[4] A thorough analysis of this type of case was first made by A. Weber in his well-known work *Ueber den Standort der Industrien* (Tübingen, 1909); it is available in an American edition. This book has profoundly influenced the material presented in the next few pages.

[5] The ideas presented in Chaps. VIII, X, and XI are in some essential ways similar to those presented in Lösch, *The Economics of Location* (New Haven, 1954), and in Isard, *Location and Space Economy* (New York, 1956). For a critical and original development of the Weber type of location theory, see Palander and Hoover.

industry uses several raw materials, but only one is costly to transport. Similarly, paper manufacture uses many raw materials, but pulp predominates. In the eighteenth century the textile industry and some others went where water-power could be found, for wool, cotton, and finished cloth could be more easily transported than power.

In many cases several of the localized raw materials used are costly to transport—more so than the finished product. Both coal and iron ore are weight-losing materials; hence, the iron and coal industry is "raw material located" rather than "market located." But if coal and iron mines are at some distance from one another, where is the best place for the industry?

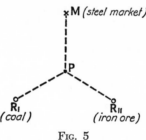

FIG. 5

The answer is that a "point of minimum transportation cost" may be found, as indicated by the adjoining "location figure." The expenses of loading and unloading, however, are often so great that two short journeys cost more than a single long one. For this reason total transportation costs are in many cases lowest if the manufacturing industry is placed in one of the raw material centers, e.g., the iron and steel industry in the coal district (P and R_1 coinciding) because coal is as a rule more costly to transport than iron ore. In this industry the ore usually goes to the coal, whereas in other metal industries—copper, for instance—the coal goes to the ore. Naturally the economies from a reduction of the number of transport journeys may also cause the industry to move from the *neighborhood* of the main market (in cases where its distance from the raw material centers would make such a location advantageous) to the market center itself. If, however, the goods are costly to transport and the lengthening of the journey would be considerable should manufacturing be conducted in one of these centers, it will pay to choose some other place and to carry the expense of a greater number of journeys.[6]

§ 3. *Relative mobility in complicated cases.* A more complicated case is that of several markets and products, with many similar sources of raw materials. I shall call the raw materials *a, b, c,* etc. The sources

[6] An important reason for choosing such intermediate points is that breaks in the journey may be necessary there in any case. See § 7.

of the first are A_I, A_{II}, A_{III}, etc.; the sources of the second are B_I, B_{II}, B_{III}, and so on. The markets are M_I, M_{II}, M_{III}. Is the market M_I to be supplied with goods produced with raw materials from A_I, B_I, and C_I, or some other combination?

Each conceivable combination of raw materials has a minimum cost of transportation to each market. If the raw material prices are equal at all raw material points, the case is simple. The raw materials having the lowest minimum costs of transportation are used for each market, and the industry is located between the raw materials and the market, as above. The same raw material source may of course supply several markets. However, the prices of raw materials may be quite different at the various sources. Furthermore, large-scale economies in production tend to reduce the number of manufacturing points; each of them may supply several markets. Consequently, the points are chosen that ensure a definite scale of output and cause a definite saving in costs of production, with the least possible increase in the costs of transport. The manufacturing units tend to reach a size where further increases would cause greater expenses than economies.

If the markets to be supplied from a given combination of raw material sources lie in different directions from them, the attraction of each market as the manufacturing point is more or less balanced by the attraction of the others, and a location close to the raw materials, particularly if they are weight-losing, is probable. This is another reason why raw material location occurs more frequently than the simple location figure would seem to justify.

Markets are often not concentrated at particular places, and one must speak of "market areas." In each such area a number of consumption points exist or may be conceived to exist, each having the "weight" of the consumption there and in the surrounding district. Each such point may be treated as a concentrated market. Minimum costs of transportation points may be computed and the advantages of large-scale weighted against the increases in transportation costs.

As a matter of fact, production in many cases is divided not into two stages—raw materials and finished goods—but into many. Wood, pulp, and paper furnish an example of three stages. The location of production of the semimanufactured pulp is determined as explained above; the only difference is that the market is not a consumers' market but a producers' buying market. This is the case with all producers' goods; the chief demand for machinery, e.g., comes from the manufacturing industries. Market location means that the semi-manufactured goods and machinery (called "half materials") are produced in the same places as the finished goods. Typical examples are Worcester, Massachusetts, which made textile machinery when the textile industry was located there, and Denver, which still produces heavy mining machinery. An agricultural machinery center is to be found in Chicago. In general, the machine tool industry is located where machines are used and repaired. In this case not only do costs of transport play their part but above all the advantages of easier contact with customers call forth all sorts of so-called subsidiary industries.

The location of producers' buying markets (e.g., the manufacture of paper), however, depends upon the location of "half-material" production (pulp). Thus, the governing elements are (1) the transportability of the various goods and (2) the location of raw material producing industries and consumers' markets, with the modification that production may be divided into several stages, of which each acts as a market for the preceding one. The place where half-materials are manufactured is at the same time a producing point and a "raw material" source. Thus, given a certain local distribution of raw material sources and markets, the location of the later stages of production is governed by the relative transportability of the different sorts of commodities. In other words, it is governed by *the relative transportability of commodities in various stages of production and the distance of different places from raw material supply and markets.*

§ 4. *Location of raw material production.* Even if all raw material sources were of equal quality, demand for some of them would be greater than for others, owing to the difference in distance from important purchasing markets. In some cases only a limited quantity can be supplied; as a rule greater quantities can be extracted, although at higher cost. Consequently the supply prices of a given raw material differ considerably between one source and another.

Iron ore from well-situated mines close to iron and steel centers commands a much higher price at the pit head than ore from out-of-the-way districts without coal mines. Many potential sources of iron ore are so poorly located that they are not used at all. Similarly, most lime and clay deposits are void of economic interest: Portland cement is manufactured almost exclusively in districts that are located close together and not far from a good harbor.

Natural resources differ not only in location but also in quality, yet each may be used for some purpose. An infinite variety of climate and soil is serviceable for agricultural pursuits. Among alternative uses, the producer who offers the highest rent will obtain the site for his own purposes. In this way it is determined where raw materials are produced, in what quantities, and at what costs. The location of raw material industries—given a certain local distribution of markets—is affected by the local distribution of the various natural resources. In other words, it is governed by the distance between markets and different natural resources.[7] The markets for raw materials are the centers of the later stages of production, whose location in turn is determined by the relative transportability of various goods and by the distance between consumers' markets and raw material supply. Evidently the location of the first stage and of the later stages of production affect one another. Elements governing them all are (1) the local distribution of natural resources and consumers' markets and (2) the transportability of goods.

The chief reason for treating separately production of goods of the first order—called "raw materials"—and later stages of production is that natural resources are much more important for the former than for the latter. Coal cannot be produced in places where there are no coal seams, nor can wheat be produced where there is no land suitable for wheat-growing. But iron and wheat flour may be manufactured almost anywhere, and the cooperation of nature is restricted to offering a small area of land for a factory. Many other natural conditions must of course be fulfilled, but they exist equally almost everywhere and hence do not affect the location of production at later stages. The important exceptions concern man's inability or unwillingness to live and work under certain conditions of nature, e.g., in a particular climate.

Apart from this, nature affects the process of manufacturing very little.[8] Cotton-spinning is favorably affected by a moist climate; to provide moisture in a dry climate involves some expense. There are analogous cases, but they need not detain us. On the whole, apart from transportation features, the location of manufacturing industries is affected by nature only through its influence on the local distribution of (1) raw material supply and (2) labor and capital supply.

§ 5. *Location of consumers' markets.* So far the location of production has been investigated on the assumption that the location of consumer's markets is known. As a matter of fact, it is as much a result of the play of economic forces as is the distribution of industry. On the whole, people consume where they live and work and draw incomes; thus, a movement of laborers from one place to another means at the same time a transfer of a consumers' market. In more general terms the local distribution of productive factors governs the location of consumers' markets.

The movements of labor and capital and their influence upon the distribution of productive factors will be analyzed later. If it is as-

---

[7] Raw material production in some cases requires the cooperation of considerable quantities of machinery and other "half-materials." Their places of supply have an influence analogous to that of raw material sources.

[8] It affects transportation a great deal, and transportation and manufacturing go hand in hand. The influence of differences in the transport features of the earth is considered in §§ 6-7.

sumed here that the distribution not only of natural resources but also of labor and capital is known, what is the relation of the location and size of consumers' markets to this distribution of factors? The answer is simple if all incomes are consumed on the spot and nothing is saved, and if the land and capital in a district are owned by the people living there. Incomes are equal to the prices paid during a particular period for the productive factors.[9] Consequently, if the local distribution of these factors and their prices are known, the income or "buying power" in each place may be ascertained. Thus are the character and extent of consumers' markets determined.[10]

However, a part of the incomes generated in any given district is consumed elsewhere, and part of the incomes of other districts is consumed in this district. Some of the natural resources or capital in the district, called A, may be owned by people living and spending outside it, whereas the inhabitants of A may draw incomes from other districts. Such circumstances affect the volume of consumers' goods bought and sold in A and other districts. The size and character of consumers' markets in each place depends not only upon the local distribution of productive factors and upon individual wants and desires[11] but also upon the conditions of ownership of productive factors.

Another complicating fact is that a part of the money earned is not consumed but saved, i.e., used to buy capital goods, not consumers' goods, either inside or outside the place where it is earned. When savings are invested in the same place, the market for consumers' goods is weakened and the market for capital goods is increased. When the money is invested in other places, there is a transfer of buying power—just as when money is consumed "abroad' or incomes are drawn from outside—and the market for capital goods is increased in the places to which the savings move.

To sum up, the local markets for consumers' goods are reduced everywhere by savings, and are increased or reduced by the inflow or outflow of buying power from other markets. The market for capital goods[12] is increased by the amount of new savings invested in each place.

[9] In a more dynamic treatment of this problem the existence of profits must be considered.

[10] The local demand for raw materials, semimanufactured goods, and machinery is governed by the location of production as explained previously.

[11] Traveling and other forms of consumption outside one's "home district" must also be considered in special cases but are as a rule of little importance.

[12] The influence exercised upon the markets for capital goods, by depreciation of old capital goods, etc., should be included, but in this chapter everything not strictly necessary for an understanding of the general trend of the analysis was left out.

§ 6. *Local differences in transportation resources and facilities.* I have shown so far that the location of industry is governed by (1) the local distribution of natural resources and other productive factors, and (2) the transportability of goods, whereas the local distribution of consumers' markets depends chiefly upon the local distribution of natural resources, labor, and capital. I shall return to the distribution of labor and capital in the following chapter.[13]

Some elements that have until now been virtually disregarded should be considered. The surface of the earth does not offer uniform opportunities for transportation, nor are the means of transportation uniformly distributed; on the contrary, important differences in transport features and transport facilities influence location of industry. The costs of transport are not proportional to the distance a commodity is to be moved. The cost per ton-mile, to take the most obvious example, is much higher for traffic on land than on sea. Furthermore, it may be far easier to carry a commodity one way than another. The previous analysis must, therefore, be modified. Instead of transport distance one must think of cost of transport. Von Thünen's "rings" are not circular but extend farther away from the city along good transport lines. Of two points close to each other, one point may have much easier access to resources and markets than the other. Location is affected by the transport facilities between natural resources and markets; these facilities in turn depend upon the local distribution of resources and markets as well as upon the transport features of the earth's surface, other transport resources, and transport facilities.

It has already been mentioned that sea transport is cheaper than land transport, at least when the distance exceeds a certain minimum. For this reason all places close to the sea have relatively favorable transport relations with all other places similarly situated, provided harbor facilities are not lacking. The Atlantic Coast districts of the United States are really nearer in an economic sense to the coastal districts of Europe than to some parts of the Middle West. In general, coastal districts and interior regions of a continent show marked differences in transport facilities. Particularly valuable is a long and irregular coast line offering numerous natural harbors. The economic superiority of Europe in the Middle Ages over Africa was probably due in no small degree to marked differences in this respect.

A similar influence is exercised by the interior waterways, such as lakes, navigable rivers, and canals, especially if they enable ocean-going vessels to reach interior ports. Traffic statistics show the enormous importance of these means of transport. Non-navigable rivers

---

[13] One must keep in mind the assumption in this chapter that labor and capital are completely mobile within the districts under consideration.

also play an important part in transportation, e.g., in the case of timber, as do lakes without communication with the sea. It goes without saying that there are innumerable differences in the quality of such means of water transportation.

The same holds true for land transportation resources, owing to topographical conditions, temperature, and the like. Plains offer less resistance to road or rail transport than mountainous areas. Extremely hot and extremely cold districts offer many obstacles to the construction and operation of transport routes.

The transport resources of a district have to do with more than the surface of the earth. *Power* above all is required for all sorts of transportation, and the cost at which it can be obtained substantially affects costs of transport. The influence of good coal mines or water-power resources is obvious. There is, however, this difference between their influence and that of the earth's surface: power may be procured from other districts. Thus, power holds much the same place in transportation, in a narrow sense, as do raw materials in production. Costs of transport in a district are affected by the availability and the transportability of the various sorts of power. A district that is close to a cheap coal supply and has good communications with it, for example, may have fairly good transport facilities in general, even though the topographical conditions are unfavorable to transportation.

Differences in transport facilities are often not so marked between *districts* as between *places*. Transport facilities do not generally cover whole areas but follow narrow lines, except in the case of seas and lakes. Valleys offer better conditions for railroads than the surrounding regions. A railroad network, like a caravan network, is necessarily a system of lines that incompletely covers an area. Rivers and canals are likewise much more useful to places along the line they follow than to places some distance away.

§ 7. *Local differences in transportation resources and facilities, continued.* Points where transport lines converge have exceptionally intimate transport relations with other places. The most important are the great ports, where seagoing traffic connects with a network of converging railroad lines, and sometimes a navigable river. Such transportation centers offer relatively favorable transport facilities to manufacturing industries for *two* reasons: (1) the existence of a network of transport lines and (2) a reduction in the number of times goods have to be reloaded.

As soon as there is a break[14] in the transportation network, the tendency is to evade the costs of the break by locating production and consumption there. A center of converging transportation routes

[14] For an interesting discussion of these problems see Hawtrey, *The Economic Problem*, x.

of the same sort, e.g., railroad lines, does not constitute such a break: cars may be switched from one line to another. For this reason such centers offer much less attraction to industry than places where different transport systems meet. However, if production on a given scale is much cheaper than in smaller units, and one factory therefore supplies a large district, the transportation center will be the natural location, even if there is no break in the transport route. It is easy to give examples of these influences. Practically all the great cities of the world are also important ports. Manufacturing takes place in them on a large scale, even though in some cases practically all raw materials are transported from far away. The distance to raw materials may be unfavorable, but excellent transport resources and facilities more than make up for this.

Another well-known example of the fact that places where transport lines converge and break may have excellent transport relations with raw material sources, even if the latter are far away, is the iron and steel industry in the Chicago district. It is a center of railroad and interior shipping lines, receiving coal from Kentucky and ore from the Lake Superior district. Other places in the Chicago district have equally good or better access to coal and ore, but Chicago[15] itself profits from a large local market, selling to the agricultural machinery industry, the manufacturers of locomotives, etc. Therefore its transport facilities to markets and raw material resources are on the whole so favorable that the iron and steel industry has rapidly expanded there.[16]

The Scandinavian pulp-exporting industry is chiefly located in the small ports where rivers, on which timber is floated, touch the Baltic Sea—a typical case of "break location." Pulp for paper-manufacturing within Scandinavia is to a large extent produced in other districts, where conditions are good for the location of a paper industry.

The high cost of unloading and reloading, compared with other transportation costs, makes longer journeys relatively much cheaper than short ones. This is particularly true in sea transport, where the length of the journey matters comparatively little. For this reason one long sea transport is much cheaper than two shorter ones of the same combined mileage. It has already been pointed out that whereas the point of minimum transport costs would often lie far away from both raw materials and markets if costs of transport were proportional to distance, it is in fact often advantageous to choose a

[15] "The tendency of the industry to shift to the Lake Shore points is due to the economy that results from having the blast furnace located beside the ore dock where the lake steamer unloads." Russel-Smith, *Industry and Commerce,* p. 179.

[16] "It is one of the surprises of American industry that iron manufacturing on a huge scale should be undertaken at such points, distant alike from ore and from coal." Taussig, *Some Aspects of the Tariff Question,* p. 125.

raw material or market center. The number of journeys is thereby reduced by one, which may more than offset a greater total transport
distance.

The effectiveness of motor transportation for short distances is due
to the fact that goods can be brought directly to the consumer, so
that the unloading and reloading at the railroad station are saved.
Here, too, the initial and final expenses count heavily. For this reason
the superiority as to transport relations of factories in the neighborhood of railroads has largely disappeared: if goods must be transported
from the railroad station by motor trucks in any case, location is of
little importance. But factories with their own side tracks, which bring
the railroad trunks to their doors, can save the costs of reloading.

It is evident, therefore, that the transport facilities of different
districts and places to raw materials and to markets are exceedingly
unequal, even if the districts are not far from each other. This fact
influences location of industry in a decisive way, for it is transport
facilities, not distance itself, that have economic importance. Each
producing unit will be placed where the costs of production are lowest,
i.e., where the total costs of transportation are at a minimum, or
only so little above the minimum that cheaper natural resources
or cheaper raw material supply more than compensate. For each
commodity the total costs of transportation also depend upon the
transportability of the various raw materials and goods of "higher
order." Thus, one may say that *location of industry depends upon
the transport facilities of each place to natural resources and upon
the distribution of productive factors that govern the consumers'
markets.*

§ 8. *Economies of scale in transportation and the pricing of transport
services.* One group of circumstances has as yet only been touched
upon although it exercises a profound influence upon the costs of
transport and the location of industry. So-called large-scale economies
are important in transport industries no less than in production in a
narrow sense. Traffic can be handled much cheaper per unit if there
is a lot of it. This is true, although in a varying and limited degree,
of the loading, etc., done in harbors or railroad stations, and of transport itself, by water or rail. Furthermore, it is important that a large
volume of traffic shall make possible regular and direct lines and
frequent sailings from a given port to other important ports throughout the world. Industries in small harbor cities must either wait for a
suitable shipping opportunity or send goods to a big port and collect
goods there by means of small ships. Similarly, the volume of goods
to be transported by land determines whether a railroad should be
built, how it can be operated, etc.

Other things being equal, places have better transport facilities if the volume of traffic is considerable. Thus, differences in transportation costs depend not only upon differences in distance and transport resources but also upon how far large-scale economies can be utilized in the organization of transport services.

In some desert districts it is impossible even to build roads, and transportation by means of camel caravans is the only possibility. Even so, there is a great difference between places touched by the regular caravan routes and distant points from which camels are occasionally sent down to places along the routes. A fertile agricultural district can as a rule support a scattered railroad network connecting it with a harbor. Only in densely populated manufacturing districts is the amount of traffic so considerable that the most efficient organization and combination of the various means of transport is possible.

In brief, costs of transport, like the prices of other services, are determined by supply and demand. They are affected by distance, by transport resources—the surface of the earth and power sources[17]—and by the character and scale of transport facilities. The character of the commodities is also very important: if, for instance, the goods sent from a district by sea are much heavier and bulkier than goods imported in that way, some ships will return without cargo, and return freights will tend to be low relative to outgoing freights. As a matter of fact, trade is usually fairly reciprocal, both as to value and transport requirements; but where it is not, transportation costs are profoundly "dislocated" and location of industry is consequently affected.

The importance of overhead costs, e.g., in railroads, makes the fixing of rates somewhat indeterminate and leaves room for varied forms of tariff policy—that of "charging what the traffic can bear" and others. Firmly established and prosperous industries in a district may have to pay relatively high railroad charges while less advantageously located and weaker firms in other districts are paying less. In general, the policy of charging higher rates per ton-mile for goods of little bulk and weight in relation to value is disadvantageous to finished goods —as compared with raw materials—and favors market location of industry.

§ 9. *Local distribution of labor and capital.* The movements of labor and capital also have an influence upon transport relations. Just as transport lines adapt themselves to the demand for traffic, so the latter adapts itself to transport conditions. Places with favorable transport facilities, i.e., easy access to raw materials, including food, and markets, attract labor and capital. The conditions for many sorts of activities are better there than elsewhere, and mobile productive factors therefore gather. In this way the volume of traffic is increased, and large-scale economies further reduce the costs of transport. Transport

[17] Local differences in the supply of labor and capital are considered below.

facilities are organized where there is a need for them. They are thus as much the effect as the cause of the local distribution of industry.[18]

Transport facilities are improved by the concentration of labor and capital where they are already advantageous. Such points become important markets and appropriate locations for industries. Furthermore, the nearby supply of semimanufactured goods as well as of tools and machinery is increased. The distance of transportation is thus reduced in many cases. The great ports offer excellent illustrations of the tendency of good transport relations to become still better through the concentration of labor and capital. However, as a manufacturing center grows, raw materials have to be collected from places farther and farther away, and other goods must be sent greater distances to pay for these imported raw materials.

§ 10. *Economies of scale in industry.* The improvement of transport facilities through the concentration of economic activity where they are already good tends to attract population and production still further. There are many other advantages of concentration for the location of industry and the interlocal trade. They are not necessarily related to differences in transport resources and might operate anywhere, but since differences in transport resources tend to draw production to certain places, such economies of concentration augment the effects. They may be considered under three categories: (1) economies of concentration of industry in general, (2) external economies of concentration of a particular industry, and (3) internal large-scale economies of a producing unit.

Economies in the first category almost all depend upon improvement in transport facilities. External economies also fall partly under this heading. Subsidiary industries spring up, which supply the main industry with materials and accessories. A short distance and intimate contact with buyers and sellers are favorable circumstances.[19] External economies consist partly in the existence of a fully developed market of skilled and specialized labor. Internal economies have little to do with transport. Purely technical circumstances, such as the smallest size of a certain machine and other forms of nondivisibility, play a dominating part. All these economies tend to concentrate industry in a small number of places. Other things being equal, the tendency is to place industries where the transport resources are best.

Such agglomerating tendencies are met by opposing deglomerating ones. First, longer transport of raw materials and products means higher costs of transportation. If a factory or a group of factories is to supply a large district, the average distance to the consumer will be much longer than if factories are scattered over the district. Second,

[18] Cf. the conclusions in Chaps. VII and XI concerning the supply of productive factors.
[19] See § 12 concerning *transfer* relations as opposed to transport relations.

agglomeration in a district raises the prices of natural resources, whereby costs of production are increased. This affects chiefly the location of industries requiring considerable land, like agriculture, or specialized natural resources, like the mining industry; the level of land rents in cities influences the location of most manufacturing industries.

A third group of circumstances has to do with some effects of diversification of industry, which have a bearing upon agglomerative and deglomerative tendencies and upon the location of industry in general. I will follow Professor Black in calling the production of a commodity an "enterprise." [20] Clearly, many producing units—a factory or a farm—contain several enterprises which are complementary to one another, in raw materials or in something else. If they use the same raw materials, they are often called joint-product enterprises. A well-known example is the dye industry, which uses tar to manufacture a number of different products. Similarly, cotton and cotton seeds are produced together. Enterprises may also be complementary to one another by making possible a more efficient utilization of labor or tools and implements. One enterprise may use the productive elements in one season more than in another; it is often advantageous to add another enterprise that can use them in the slack season. Since it is not possible to transfer them to another place for a few months, the second enterprise must be located in the same place as the first. Another reason for combining several enterprises in one producing unit (farm or factory) is that important advantages of large-scale production may result. Under certain conditions the production of several commodities may be necessary to keep a minimum-sized plant busy, to use a certain machine, or to utilize marketing organization and management. Important examples of these combinations of complementary enterprises are to be found in agriculture, in the retail trade, and to a surprising degree in manufacturing industries—in fact, in almost every kind of industry and trade.

From the point of view of location it is well to deal with various forms of complementary material in different ways. When by-products are used as raw materials for other processes of production in close connection with the main process, manufacture on the spot is advantageous. The first stage of complementary production, whereby in the *same* process two goods are produced—e.g., coke and gas—may be regarded as a unit; location will be the same as in the case of one product.

To turn to the seasonal variations[21] in labor requirements, which lead to complementary lines of production, the by-product may exist

[20] Black, *Production Economics* (New York, 1926).
[21] Analogous differences in work to be done at different times of the day may be similarly regarded.

within a firm or *between* different firms having their peak requirements for labor at different seasons. In either case production may
be drawn to places where it would not otherwise be located, evidently because the supply of labor in the slack season is cheaper.
This is an instance of insufficient mobility and of local differences in
labor supply.

As to economies of large-scale production which, owing to the limi-
tations of markets, are in some cases available only if several enterprises are combined in one producing unit, their influence on the
location of industry differs little from cases where only one product
is manufactured. Industry is concentrated into a smaller number of
units and places, for the economies more than balance the increase
in costs of transportation. This is a deviating force which somewhat
changes the location that would result from local distribution of
natural resources and transportability of the various goods. It is not
possible to generalize upon such deviation, except to say that it is of
an agglomerating sort.

Disregarding for a moment differences in natural resources and
transport facilities, one may say that the concentration and spread
of industry are so governed that agglomerating and deglomerating
tendencies balance. The greater the costs of transport, the more
evenly each industry is spread over the area and the smaller is the
market area supplied wholly or partly from each productive unit. The
greater is the superiority of large producing units to small, and of
those concentrated in a district to isolated ones, the more is each
industry concentrated in certain places and districts. The greater are
the general economies of concentration, the more are industries located close to one another. The result is that some industries, like
brick manufacturing, are spread over a large area, while others, like
the automobile industry in Detroit, supply practically the whole world.
To sum up, the economies of large-scale production tend to concentrate production of each commodity or group of commodities at
places having the best transfer facilities, both for the natural resources
required for production of raw materials and for the markets that
consume it.

§ 11. *Review of location.* The location elements dealt with here have
been: (1) the distance between natural resources and markets,[22] (2)
the transportability of raw materials and finished goods, and (3) the
local differences in transport resources and facilities. The three together determine the transport facilities of each place and, other
things equal, influence the location of industry thereby. There are,
however, (4) certain agglomerating tendencies whose effects are

[22] The location of markets depends chiefly upon the distribution of the productive factors—natural resources as well as labor and capital.

added to those of the other three elements, and certain deglomerating tendencies that counteract the agglomerative tendencies. Element (4) may cause a deviation of location from what would follow from the first three.

For example, certain districts in California have climatic and other conditions that make them eminently suitable for growing fruit and vegetables (1). Certain of these products are as easily transportable as the goods to be made from them, and are sent for a long distance to various markets, where some of them are prepared for consumption; others, which are relatively difficult to transport, are prepared on the spot and then transported (2). Some parts of the United States and the rest of the world have good transport facilities to these California districts and buy their products, but others buy from competing producers like Florida and Italy (3). Within the fruit- and vegetable-producing parts of California are many small specialized districts that produce citrons, peaches, plums, tomatoes, etc.; this concentration is largely due to external economies (4) and other economies of concentration, including improved transport facilities (3). However, the high rents in some of these districts—and the high costs of transport to many parts of the world—prevent a further concentration of specialized production in them (4).

As for the influence of these four circumstances on the location of industry in general, it has been shown that districts with good transport facilities tend to attract plenty of labor and capital and become important markets; consequently, they tend to specialize in industries that (1) are market-oriented and show important advantages from large-scale production and (2) produce goods difficult to transport. Districts with poor transport facilities are scantily populated and tend to specialize in goods that are easy to transport and can be advantageously produced on a small scale.

This holds true on the assumption that other things are equal, i.e., that the districts have a similar supply and local distribution of natural resources. However, differences in transport facilities are usually to a great extent due to different supply and distribution of natural resources. Consequently, the direct influence of this inequality in factor supply must be considered together with the indirect influence of unequal transport relations.

First of all, it is evident that raw materials and crude food products —goods of the first order—must be produced in districts where nature is favorable. Places that fulfill this condition attract such production if transport facilities are fairly good, which they will be if there is sufficient demand.

"Goods of higher order" are produced close to the raw material sources if these materials are "weight-losing" or if the raw materials are more difficult to transport than the semimanufactured or finished goods. As a rule, several sorts of raw materials are required. Industry tends to be located close to the materials most difficult to transport. However, other goods of a higher order are more conveniently produced close to the main markets. Tailor-made clothes are an example. Of course, the greater are the quantities of labor and capital required to produce a certain concentrated supply of natural resources and the production of the goods of higher order based on them, the more important is the market that is created there from the location standpoint.

Coal is an important raw material in many industries. The mining of coal requires a great quantity of labor and capital in a comparatively narrow district. Being exceedingly weight-losing, it tends to call forth manufacturing industries near the sources of this raw material. Some of these industries are such that large-scale economies play an important part, and concentration of production in large units and manufacturing districts is advantageous. For all these reasons important markets grow up where coal is produced.

The example of wool may be compared to that of coal. It has limited uses, and both wool and its products are easily transported. Sheep-raising and wool-shearing require comparatively little labor and may be conducted on a small scale. This industry is therefore eminently suited for relatively barren agricultural districts with little other natural resources, scanty population, and poor transport facilities. The Falkland Islands, for instance, have 2200 inhabitants and 300 sheep per capita.

If transportation to places where important raw materials can be produced is unfavorable, the attraction of even such goods as coal will naturally be small. Very little coal is produced on Svalbard, for instance, although coal mines there are rich. Yet if other important goods, principally iron ore and food, can be produced in the neighborhood or easily brought there, the coal centers will become centers of population and industry, unless unfavorable climate acts as a deterring element.

To sum up, natural resources influence location of industry, i.e., they have a power of attraction in proportion as (1) the goods produced with their aid are important, difficult to transport, and weight-losing, (2) the use of labor and capital is intensive, and (3) they are situated near other natural resources or have good transport facilities. If the other resources also have a great power of attraction, the combined attraction tends to draw a large part of the world's economic activities to the district. For instance, the combined attracting power of natural resources which fulfill to a high degree the three above-mentioned conditions in Europe has tended to concentrate economic life in this part of the world; and the special attraction of the iron and coal districts has brought to them a colossal concentration of European industry.

§ 12. *Transfer costs other than transportation costs.* Attention has so far been confined to the costs of transport, and other obstacles to commodity movements have been almost completely disregarded. There are many such obstacles, among which are the reduction in quality and value of easily spoiled goods through transportation; the lack of intimate contact with customers consequent upon great distances from the market; and duties on imports and exports. All are included here in the term "costs of transfer."

The costs of transfer are, of course, not proportional to the distance the goods are transferred. For transportation costs this has been abundantly illustrated; in particular, breaks in the journey are expensive since they involve reloading. Similarly, in the case of high import duties, raw materials free of duty or slightly taxed are sent instead of manufactured goods with heavy duty charges. Production is located inside the tariff wall, just as it is at points that can be conveniently reached by trucks inside a district. In both cases location of industry is similarly affected. Duties and breaks are thus important aspects of transfer relations. The earlier analysis of transportation costs thus holds good for other costs of transfer as well. It explains certain aspects of location in districts with scattered transportation routes of different sorts, converging points, breaks, and tariff borders.

It must be borne in mind that transfer costs are of little importance to many leading goods that are easily transportable and not subject to duties. This does not mean, however, that transfer costs in general do not affect them. Transfer costs of other goods affect factor supply and factor prices in various places and hence the location of *all* industries.

XI

Local Differences in Labor and Capital Supply: Location Theory, Continued

§ 1. *Equalizing wages.* The tendency for trade to equalize factor returns means, in the case of labor, that real wages are equalized among regions. This concept poses many difficulties. Real wages refer not to money alone but to the goods and services the wage can buy. Because the retail prices[1] of food, clothing, and housing vary considerably from one place to another, equality of real wages implies lasting and considerable local differences in nominal wages. In Sweden the cost of living was found to be about 50 percent higher in the more expensive places than in the cheaper ones. Nominal wages, of course, tend to be low in the latter places and high in the former.

Assume that nominal wages differ locally in the same way as do the costs of living, with the variations called "equalizing differences in wages." The price of the goods a worker buys is the cost of his labor to the employer. Thus, the wage bill is eliminated from the cost account. This would be a simple way of taking into account the local differences in money wages and their influence on the location of industry. Unfortunately, the meaning of the term equalizing wage differences is vague: the worker's budget is not composed in the same way everywhere even in the same country and is still less so in different countries. Habits of food and clothing naturally adapt themselves to climatic conditions and are strongly influenced by tradition. The standard of living concept is therefore rather loose. Even if this difficulty did not exist, one could not expect freely mobile labor to equalize real wages. Districts with disagreeable climatic conditions, for example, would have to pay an extra high wage to attract people. It would seem natural to take account of this situation by saying that equalizing local wage differences are those that lead to equal attractiveness, but this would be a most unpractical mode of pro-

---

[1] The farming population obtains many food products at wholesale prices, whereby its cost of living is reduced below the level with which other people, even in low-cost towns and villages, have to reckon.

146

cedure. What is agreeable to one is disagreeable to another; taste and habits are different. Two men of different nationality, or coming respectively from an agricultural district and a mountainous district, find it disagreeable to move and settle in each other's habitat. It seems best to treat all such facts as restrictions of mobility, to deal with all inequalities in wages that have to do therewith as real differences, and to regard as equalizing those that correspond to differences in the cost of living. It must, however, be kept in mind that the concept "equalizing difference" is necessarily loose and is most useful for comparisons between places with fairly equal habits of living.

With these reservations real wage differences may be said to exist at any given moment because of lack of mobility, which may cause permanent real differences to a limited extent, and still greater differences temporarily until labor flows have had time to reduce them. Differences of the latter sort may last a long time if new economic changes create them as quickly as the labor flow extinguishes them. This is seen, for example, in a comparison of wages in progressive and declining districts.

§ 2. *Influence of equalizing wages.* It has been indicated that all prices are determined in a mutual-interdependence price system, in which the transfer facilities of each place and commodity to natural resources and markets are included. Now suppose the existence also of local wage differences parallel to the costs of living. From the point of view of locating an industry, districts at a great distance from food resources or having difficulty obtaining it, i.e., an expensive supply of food, are in a position similar to that of districts which pay high prices for coal or other raw materials. They are suitable as places for production only if they have either good natural resources or excellent transfer facilities for raw materials other than food. Of course, if the quantity of labor required in industry is small, food is a relatively unimportant raw material. Places with poor facilities for obtaining food attract such industries rather than industries requiring plenty of labor, i.e., food; the latter are located there only if some special advantages are available with regard to natural resources or raw material supply

Consider a few examples of the influence of equalizing wage differences on location. Densely populated districts generally have poor transfer facilities for food, for they need to draw food from far away. Consequently, nominal wages are high; so are site rents. For these reasons certain industries keep away from densely populated districts, whereas others settle there since they can reap great advantages from (1) good transfer facilities to markets and often also to raw materials, (2) special natural resources, or (3) large-scale economies.[2] The excellence of the district in these three respects is, as a matter of fact, the chief cause of the dense population.

Many scantily populated districts have natural food resources or good facilities for obtaining food but poor ones for other raw materials; consequently, food is cheap and wages are low. The low wages make it possible to manufacture cheaply goods that require plenty of labor. However, scantily populated districts having good natural resources or good transfer facilities for a *small* number of raw materials but poor ones for others, including food, get high wages. They import everything but the goods for which their natural resources are particularly advantageous. In such cases population is scarce because of little employment or poor communications in most respects ("out-of-the-way districts").

Since food is probably the most important raw material (wages are a significant cost item for most productive processes), good natural food resources generally attract a substantial population. Other natural resources have a more specialized use (in the production of special raw materials for special commodities) and hence have less power to attract production and mobile productive factors. Such districts have a relatively monotonous sort of industry and "import" most goods, including food, from other districts; they produce only goods for which their natural resources and transfer facilities give them exceptional advantages.

As an illustration, the following Swedish figures for the price of food entering a worker's budget deserve attention.[3] The first group of districts have good transfer facilities in most respects, a fairly dense population, and diverse industries. The second group are mostly out-of-the-way agricultural districts and are more scantily populated. The third group embraces northern Sweden, where agriculture is handicapped by a severe climate, industry is based on forests and mines, and population is scarce. It will be seen that the differences between the Swedish districts with respect to their retail food price index numbers for 1927 were considerable:

District	Agricultural districts	Manufacturing districts	Towns
I	1462	1526	1593
II	1356	1384	1453
III	1630	1635	1713

Important also are price differences between cities and small towns.

---

[2] Or the existence of a concentrated labor market; see § 3.

[3] The figures are computed from unpublished material collected by the Social Board for 1927.

The following retail price index numbers in Swedish towns in 1927 are illustrative:

Number of inhabitants	Cost of food and fuel	House Rent[4]
<5000	1757	363
5000-20,000	1803	478
>20,000	1840	588

Another difference between various districts that affects price and wage conditions has to do with the transportability of its "export" materials and commodities. If the natural resources and transfer facilities are such that primarily easily transportable goods are "exported," their prices will be only slightly lower at home than in other districts. "Import goods," however, being difficult to transport, cost considerably more than in other districts; the price level and cost of living, and consequently wages, are high, which tends to discourage production. The reverse is the case in a district that exports goods difficult to transport, such as heavy and bulky agricultural products: there they are much cheaper than in the districts that "import" such goods.

§ 3. *Real wage differences.* It is well known not only that local wage differences are "equalizing" but that wages are higher in some districts than in others by much more than what corresponds to higher costs of living. As a matter of fact, the cost of living concept and the real wage concept are both vague. Although differences in nominal wages are easy to establish, a computation of the differences in real wages can never be accurate. For this reason it is best to follow a different course from that used in the last section, to take the existing nominal wage differences as the starting point, and to study differences in the costs of living only as one of several circumstances that explain why labor movements fail to equalize the nominal pay.

Among elements that cause local wage differences are variations in working conditions and climate. The miners in northern Sweden, with its dark, cold, and gloomy winters lasting half the year, receive wages more than twice as high as those of the miners in central Sweden. Professor Russel-Smith mentions an example of the opposite influence, the attraction of the glorious climate in southern California. "The sudden influx of persons attracted by the search for health rather than by resources," he writes, "has caused many occupations to become overcrowded. Salaries, therefore, have become surprisingly low in comparison with the general level in the western country."[5]

[4] The quality of housing is probably higher in the larger towns, which impairs the comparability of the figures.

[5] Russel-Smith, *Industry and Commerce*, p. 170.

He also states, "The farm laborers in the Northern Mississippi Valley near to free land got nearly twice as much wages as those in the valley of the Potomac." [6]

Differences in nominal wages between agriculture and manufacturing are in many countries considerable. It was found that digging and construction of small roads in an agricultural district not far from Stockholm was done by farm laborers as a part of their ordinary job at a rate of pay only about one-third of the wages paid at the same time (1928) for the same work to town laborers belonging to the trade union of building and construction workers.

The average wage in Swedish manufacturing industries is 70 percent higher where costs of living are highest than where they are lowest, whereas the difference in the cost of living is estimated at 50 percent. More complete evidence is found in the tabulation below,[7] in which places in Sweden where manufacturing industries are located are arranged in seven groups, according to the costs of living:

Group	Index of cost of living	Workers' income per hour (in öre, 1st quarter of 1926)
G	>1230	167
F	1171-1230	125
E	1111-1170	115
D	1051-1110	108
C, B, A	<1051	98

The difference is probably due only slightly to the fact that skilled labor forms a larger share of the total in the most expensive places. Denmark—a densely populated country with almost equal costs of living in all manufacturing places—shows much less divergence in nominal wages.

These examples show that nominal wage differences can be important. One must not overlook, however, that in some countries and industries the labor in the cities may be superior in quality to that in small towns and country districts. The employer may be able to pay a higher wage per hour in the former than in the latter and yet get the same labor cost per unit of product. In some countries, at least, there seems to be a tendency for cities to attract the best workers.

It is of course impossible to compare the price of a "unit of productivity" instead of the wage per hour. From the point of view of one industry the higher wages per hour in the cities are more than balanced by greater productivity, but for another industry there is no compensation at all in greater productivity. Moreover, if one worker produces 10 percent more than another, it may pay the employer to

[6] Russel-Smith, *Industry and Commerce*, p. 169.
[7] *Sociala Meddelanden* (Stockholm, 1926).

give him 20-30 percent higher wages because the fixed capital is better utilized. The best way to deal with these qualitative differences is to regard unskilled city labor and country labor, for instance, as different "subfactors." In many cases the differences have little economic importance and may be ignored; when necessary, they are taken into consideration.

In summary, local differences in wages are far from proportional to differences in the prices of food and other commodities and services entering into a worker's budget. Although local differences in the labor supply are largely influenced by the different costs of living, they must be dealt with like local differences in natural resources. Large cities with a concentrated labor market possess qualities of labor entirely absent in the country. The advantage of access to such a labor market, where any quality of worker can be found readily whenever needed, is an important element in the location of many industries. The fact that these advantages are unavailable in small places can be regarded as a lack of mobility of certain labor factors.

Although these differences in labor supply are important and hold a place in the price system analogous to that of differences in natural resources, their ultimate influence on location is somewhat different. They cause certain industries to be located in big cities and others to be located in country districts, but they do not prescribe *where* in the country the cities shall be located. The labor market in a large city in one part of the country may well have the same characteristics as one in another part. The location of cities depends chiefly upon transfer facilities. Apparently labor supply also adapts itself; the agglomerating tendencies that bring together a large number of people in big cities affect also the quality of the labor supply as contrasted with what it is in more scantily populated districts. A similar influence on labor supply is exercised by local specialization of industry in agricultural districts. As has been pointed out, specialization has been carried through to a surprising degree in certain parts of the United States where certain districts concentrate on a single product—no doubt partly because of the special skills that exist in such districts.

This is not the place to inquire more closely into the circumstances that govern local differences in labor supply and wages within a country. It suffices to know that these differences are important and follow no simple rules. The division of labor and trade between two districts is profoundly influenced by the fact that in one of them the transfer facilities lead to the creation of a large city, with a special labor market as the result, whereas in another transfer facilities are such that nothing but small cities develop.

However, in certain industries that use much more labor at some times of the year than at others, labor is cheap in the off seasons, and the conditions of labor supply are favorable for industries that can use labor at that particular time of year. There would be very little agriculture in northern Sweden were it not for the fact that the small farmers work all winter in the forests cutting trees and transporting logs to the rivers. An analogous supplementary relationship is seen in the relatively high wages of female labor and low wages of male labor in some districts that concentrate on the textile industry, with its great demand for female labor. The result is that such districts have attracted mechanical industries that use male workers almost exclusively.

So far this section has dealt exclusively with domestic differences in wages and labor supply. The influence of international differences on the location of industry is of exactly the same character as that of domestic differences in wages and labor supply.

§ 4. *Interest differences.* Local differences in the supply of capital are in most cases of slight importance within a country. Nevertheless, they cannot be altogether disregarded. The interest rates in Danish savings banks in 1927-28 were as follows in some typical districts:[8]

District	*Interest paid on deposits*	*Interest charged on loans, etc.*
Copenhagen	3.83 percent	4.96 percent
North Sjaelland	4.56 percent	5.18 percent
Jutland (except the South)	4.74 percent	5.56 percent
South Jutland	4.69 percent	6.02 percent

The considerable margin between the deposit and the loan rate in South Jutland (the district received from Germany in 1919) was probably due to a greater element of risk, owing to unsettled and less favorable economic conditions there than in the rest of the country. Certainly the interest level in South Jutland would have been higher still if public policy had not directed capital to its credit institutions.

As to conditions in the United States, Professor Black may again be quoted: "Local interest rates are nearly twice as high in Montana as in Massachusetts. They are high in all the Southern States. They are two percent higher in western South Dakota than in eastern South Dakota; and in northern Minnesota than in southern Minnesota. For large enterprises, however, eastern capitalists are willing to invest their capital in the West and South at only slight premiums."[9] Evidently capital is more or less mobile depending on the purpose for which it is to be used.

Another interesting statement is made in the *Bulletin of the Na-*

[8] *Statistiske Meddeleser* (Copenhagen, 1929).
[9] Black, *Production Economics,* p. 199.

tional Conference Board (May 1928): "The lack of industrial employment in the South has been the main cause of lower wages there than in other parts of the country. Wages are uniformly highest where capital is in largest supply, and until comparatively recent years capital was scarce in the South." No doubt there were other reasons than scanty supply of capital and high interest rates that industry did not expand much in the South in the last century, but the character of the capital supply in the South compared to that in the East must have affected the location of industry. Under the influence of a more even supply of capital, certain American industries have over the years shown a tendency to move southward, evidently attracted by the lower wage rates prevailing there. This has been the case particularly with the cotton textile industry.

The considerable international differences in interest rates are too well known to need illustration here. They are, of course, often much larger than the domestic differences, but the latter influence trade and location in the same way.

§ 5. *Influence of local differences in the supply of labor and capital.* Local differences in the supply of labor and capital affect both the rents of natural resources and the prices of commodities in various places. *Ceteris paribus,* rent is lower in a district where the wage or interest level is high than in one where that level is as low as in other districts. A striking proof of the influence of this difference is the fact that rents of agricultural land at a distance from large cities are *lower* than the rents of land further away, in spite of the better position of the former; the reason is that the wage level is higher in the neighborhood of the city.

Land in certain low-wage districts of Sweden would have no value at all if the higher wages elsewhere had to be paid; at present, rents are considerable. In the same way rents are higher south of the Danish-German frontier, and lower north of it, than they would be if the wage level in both districts were more similar.

Obviously, commodity prices also are affected by local differences in labor and capital supply. Wages are an important cost item in the production of most goods. Most personal services, for instance, are very expensive in the cities, except for those services where large scale is a decisive factor. Services are also generally dearer in high-wage countries like the United States than in European countries with their lower income levels.

In brief, the price of any commodity or productive factor in one place depends more or less directly upon the prices of all other commodities and productive factors in that place and upon the prices in all other places. The height of land rents in a district is affected by wages and interest rates and by commodity prices; and all these are the result of the play of all the basic elements in the price system, which governs not only prices but the location of production as well. It is therefore impossible to explain, for example, the influence of the local distribution of natural resources on their value without considering at the same time the local distribution of other productive factors and of markets, as well as local differences in wages, interest rates, and commodity prices. Obviously, *the theory of rent is part of a general location theory* and cannot without extreme simplification be incorporated in a one-market theory of pricing, where the local distribution of natural resources is dealt with in the same way as that of special qualities of the land, and the local distribution of economic life is otherwise disregarded.

How can differences in labor and capital supply be accounted for without the simplifying assumption of parallelism between wage rates and costs of living in different places? Unfortunately, generalization on this basis is difficult; previous results contain an element of truth in spite of such simplification. Industries much hampered by the high wages of cities or other districts avoid them, unless there is some special advantage that more than compensates. This is very often the case: cities have good transfer facilities from the point of view of certain industries, i.e., with regard to raw material sources and markets, or offer a useful labor market. An example of industries that avoid high-wage districts is the hand production of furniture. Only for high quality goods is intimate contact with the customer of paramount importance. In the same way, industries manufacturing ready-made clothes, hats, gloves, or shoes are usually located in cities. Similarly, some industries avoid high-wage countries and dear-capital countries. If transfer facilities are favorable, even commodities requiring relatively great quantities of labor may be produced in high-wage countries. Certain industries, however, may derive such an advantage from low wages that they are to a large extent located in low-wage countries even though transfer facilities are better in other countries. In this way large cities may grow up in countries where only small cities would exist were it not for the international wage differences. This concentration affects the quality of the labor supply and offers increased possibilities of large-scale production, which indirectly affects the international distribution of production.

Location is affected by a number of circumstances: one may draw production to certain places, another may provide low expenses of production elsewhere. It is only natural that the result should be fairly equal costs for the same commodity in many places and countries. It is therefore to be expected that even industries producing easily transferable goods will be found in many places in the world.

§ 6. *Interaction of factor and commodity movements.* The various circumstances affecting the location of industry touched upon here cannot all be regarded as basic elements—known economic data. They are to some extent as much the effect as the cause of location. Local differences in labor and capital supply in particular[10] are due partly to the play of economic forces.

The problem arises as to *why* the supply of labor and capital in various places is what it is. This question was partially answered in Chapter VII through an analysis of the reaction of factor supply within each country, but equally important is the matter of labor and capital movements between districts.

The preceding analysis of the causes of location of industry applies to some extent to the distribution of labor and capital. The same circumstances that make it advantageous to locate industries in given districts tend also to draw labor and capital to them. Assume a certain distribution of productive factors and a certain location of industry at a certain moment; local price differences are considerable but are unable to elicit factor movements, for the mobility of factors is small. Where it is great, factor movements have already reduced price differences to insignificant proportions, assuming that trade is going on. Any change in the price system can, by changing factor prices, bring about factor movements. The consequent new distribution of labor and capital forms the basis for a new location of industry and new trade.

Suppose that costs of transport are reduced for several commodities; interlocal trade is changed and so are factor prices. It may, for example, be advantageous to carry on manufacturing close to the market instead of close to the raw material sources. Demand for labor and capital increases in the former and decreases in the latter; wages and interest rates tend correspondingly to rise and fall; and a movement of capital and labor is induced if the obstacles are not too great. Similarly, a reduction in the obstacles to factor movements may increase this shift.

Such movements affect the distribution of productive factors. Without them the distribution would be equal to factor supply at earlier times as modified by births, deaths, savings, etc. It may therefore be said that the actual distribution at any given moment is a function of (1) location at earlier times, (2) changes in domestic supply through births, savings, etc., and (3) interlocal movements that the local price differences are able to effect. The prices and price differences at any one moment are governed by the mutual interdependence price system, in which all the various elements operate together.

[10] As shown by the previous analysis, local differences in labor and capital supply affect the location of industry in two ways: by changing the conditions both of production and transportation and by the location of consumers' markets.

Evidently no simple explanation or description of the local distribution of mobile factors is possible. The spread of factor supply must be regarded as one of the basic elements of pricing, although partly due to prices of earlier times, and changes in this distribution must be carefully considered in every analysis of economic variations.

Certain general observations should, however, be made. First, as factor movements depend upon the price system, or rather upon all the circumstances affecting it, factor movements imply an adaptation of factor supply to these circumstances which is "advantageous" from the factor's point of view. Districts with excellent transfer facilities or natural resources attract labor and capital. The result is not at all an "equalization of factor supply" everywhere. On the contrary, as districts always differ decisively with regard to transfer and natural resources, so they also differ with regard to labor and capital supply, for the latter adapts itself more or less to the former. Of course, if there are considerable differences in demand conditions, factors adapt to this also.

Second, labor and capital movements are as a rule greater within countries than between them. Thus, the supply of these factors adapts better to domestic differences in natural and transport resources; local conditions of production are more influenced by these differences. Nevertheless, the equipment of productive factors varies greatly between districts in the same country, and these variations exercise the same influence on the location of industry and trade as do international differences on international trade. The problem is the same; only the reactions of factor supply through factor movements are quicker and relatively more effective—although not always much more so—in the case of domestic trade.

Third, labor movements make possible an enormous agglomeration of population in cities, where wages, both nominal and real, are usually higher than in country districts. It is even conceivable under certain circumstances that factor movements lead to increased local differences in factor prices.

How do such factor movements affect trade? In general, factor movements, like commodity movements, tend to equalize factor prices in different districts. These two movements may act as substitutes for each other. If costs of transport of commodities are high, industry—and the necessary labor and capital—may move instead of them.[11] But if factor movements are difficult, industry remains stationary, and trade continues. Such trade is costly, but not costly

---

[11] "The greater the role played by expensive land transport in the economic life of a people, the more numerous and strong the tendencies to industrial wanderings will be." Schumacher, *Die Wanderungen der Grossindustrie in Deutschland und in den Vereinigten Staaten, Schmoller's Jahrbuch* (Leipzig, 1910), p. 2.

enough to permit sufficient factor price differences to make factors move in the place of commodities. Nevertheless, certain factor movements not only enhance the inequality in factor supply between different districts but also increase the local differences in factor prices; insofar as this is the case, trade is increased by factor movements. The advantage of concentration of economic life arising from improved transfer facilities and economies of large-scale production often underlies such a development.

§ 7. *Illustrations.* That changes in the transportability of commodities affect the location of industry and the distribution of labor and capital is seen, for example, in districts with natural facilities for the production of perishable products like vegetables, fruits, meat, and fish. The advent of canning and freezing meant a decisive improvement in transportation, which gave such products and districts access to the world market and meant an enormous stimulus to industrial development.

Better facilities for supplying districts without access to cheap coal with other power sources have contributed much and are likely to contribute more to a changed location of industry. "The utilization of new forms of power such as petroleum or hydroelectric energy, and the new possibilities of electric transmission of power, have made possible the use of machinery in localities not supplied with coal." [12]

Examples of how new railroads have revolutionized economic life in a district are too numerous and well-known to require discussion. In the seventies American industry was concentrated in the Northeast, whereas the Northwest specialized in corn and the South in raw cotton. In the latter districts population was scarce and had small local markets and poor transport facilities. Neither population nor industry could develop much until railroads had been built; the latter were as necessary for migration as for transportation of goods. Thus, the building of railroads, which at first did not pay, was necessary for rapid economic development. When communications had improved and population had increased, conditions were found to be suitable for many manufacturing industries that had formerly been located in the East. Similar shifts of industry may, of course, take place between countries. "The discovery or making practicable of a new trade route may direct trade from one country and give the benefit to others. . . It would be easy to give examples of the decay of towns and cities and of large tracts of country, whilst the rest of a nation flourishes. In precisely the same way, a nation may suffer—though the world may gain—by the transference to another nation of any great staple industry." [13]

The economic history of Germany shows clearly how easier trans-

---

[12] Edie, *Economics, Principles and Problems* (London, 1926), p. 326.
[13] Nicholson, *Principles of Political Economy* (London, 1908), pp. 326, 327.

portation by means of new railroads and improved waterways leads
to a concentration of economic life in certain districts in the west
and the east. Labor and capital were not, as in the United States,
spread more evenly; the reverse took place. This was partly due to
the fact that cheaper transportation increased the size of the most
economical units of production in many industries and therefore tended
to attract industry to the districts where conditions of production
were best, whereas other districts lost their part of these industries.

XII

Interregional Trade Theory as Location Theory

§ 1. *Introduction.* In the preceding pages describing the interrelationship of factor supplies, the location of transportation and production, and the various prices, one fact has been abundantly illustrated—namely, that everything depends upon everything else in economic life. It is important to note that our interregional analysis applies to domestic as well as to international trade. Factors command varying prices in different parts of the same country, and these differences in local factor cost and supply affect the location of production and interregional trade within countries in the same way as international differences affect foreign trade.

Even if there were free mobility for labor and capital between all districts within a country, and no mobility at all between countries, a similar interregional theory would apply to both domestic and international trade. The only difference—although an important one—would be that in the former case greater attention would have to be given to the reactions of factor supply in studies of the effects of economic changes. As a matter of fact, even small and nearby districts show substantial and lasting differences in natural resources, transfer resources and facilities, and labor supply. Such differences are to a large extent causes rather than effects of location of industry.

§ 2. *A bird's-eye view of pricing.* Assume that the world is divided into a great number of districts, so small that the costs of transferring goods within them are conveniently included in the costs of production. Production, of course, always includes much transportation—in a certain sense, it is nothing else—so there is nothing artificial in this assumption. Assume further that the prices of the productive factors are known. The demand from consumers in each place[1] for the various commodities is then also known and can be reckoned as functions of commodity prices. Further, the costs of production and prices of the commodities are known—hence the actual demand—as well as

---

[1] Given certain conditions of ownership and taste. The demand for capital goods from new savings is left out of account for the sake of simplicity in this review.

the costs of transferring[2] them between different places. From this one may infer (1) what commodity each district can supply more cheaply than the others and (2) to which districts it can export it, considering the difference in costs of production and transfer. Since there must be a balance between production and consumption for each commodity, one can also tell how much each district must produce. The productive factors required for this output (at the assumed factor prices) must be equal to the supply of factors in each district.

The foregoing holds true on the assumption that all districts have a common monetary system. If they are in two groups, each with its own currency, there is one more unknown factor: the exchange rate. Another equation, however, also applies: the demand for foreign currency must equal supply, i.e., the balance of payments must be in equilibrium. As to demand for "foreign" goods, the main item in this balance, this derives directly from the character of each individual's demand as a residual after the demand for producers' goods is satisfied. The latter is, of course, directly dependent upon what each district produces and what producers' goods it has to import.

In case many groups of districts exist, each with a separate monetary system, one such equation applies to the relation of each group with the rest. If there are n groups, there are also n equations. However, as the last of them is determined in the $n-1$ first equations, there are just enough to determine the exchange ratios.

§ 3. *Importance of the region concept.* Regions of different types have to be analyzed. Wages and interest rates in some of them differ only slightly, owing either to marked mobility of labor and capital or to original similarity in factor equipment, but they differ sharply in others. Commodities and factors may move easily between some regions and with great difficulty between others. It is convenient, therefore, to think of the world as consisting of a number of large regions, each of which consists of smaller regions (subregions), the latter containing a great number of very small districts. How this regional division can best be effected obviously depends upon the kind of problem under analysis.

Neighboring districts may be regarded as belonging to the same subregion if natural or transfer resources are similar, if labor and capital move easily between them, or if goods move freely between them but with greater difficulty to another group of districts. In each case the grouping is effected in a manner appropriate to the problem

---

[2] When the quantity of the various productive factors in each small district is known, so is the quality of transportation, i.e., what has been called the "transport resources."

in hand. Uniformity with regard to the monetary system, for example, is of little ultimate consequence in a study of location but is very important in a study of the mechanism of trade adjustments.

Special attention should be given to certain large regions (countries), yet the small interior subregions and districts cannot be left out of account. Distribution of productive factors and transfer resources and facilities within the countries affect not only the international location of industry but also the internal distribution of production and trade. Only if the large regions, such as countries, are made up of similar subregions or "cells"[3] can interior location be disregarded in a study of the division of production and trade between large regions. In most cases such similarity does not exist, and an analysis like the classical theory and that given in the first nine chapters of this book, which fails to consider interior location, ignores essential parts of the problem.

§ 4. *Reactions of the so-called basic elements of pricing.* An analysis like the foregoing, where all the so-called "basic elements" are assumed to be known or to vary for noneconomic reasons, tells only part of the story. As already pointed out, such elements react to changes in the price system. In other words, the basic elements react to price variations and are consequently more or less the result of previous location, although they govern the changes in location taking place at present.

To begin with the supply of factors of production, little need be said about the influence of supply of natural resources on the location of industry in by-gone days. It is obvious that mines, for example, may be exhausted or become more difficult to work, forests may be cut down, and agricultural land may be exhausted and made more or less fertile. Such influences play their part in international as well as domestic trade. More important is the fact that the supply of various qualities of labor is affected by the type of industry carried on in each region. The volume of savings also reacts. Further, there is the inflow and outflow of factors. The reactions of such interregional factor movements to changes in the price system have already been analyzed; numerous examples will later be presented to show that such movements are of great consequence as regards international trade. Variations in the price system sometimes affect labor supply within each country considerably, both by causing migrations and by affecting the sources of domestic supply. That labor supply within smaller—or greater—regions than countries reacts to economic variations in similar ways has already been pointed out. These reac-

[3] That is, have similar distribution of productive factors and similar equipment of coast lines, harbors, land surface, and other transfer resources.

tions vary in strength, and few general rules can be given, except that migration seems easier within a country than between nations.[4] The question of how the price system and thus the location are affected must also consider the time element.

So much for factor supply. The transfer facilities, which profoundly affect location and trade, also react to economic variations. Railroads and harbors, for instance, are built where they are needed. This means that transport resources alone do not determine the facilities. The latter are created, for example, by investments of capital. As a matter of fact, many capital investments affect nature permanently or for a long time, from the point of view of transportation and production alike. In other words, no sharp line can be drawn between transport resources and transport facilities, or between natural resources and capital goods. In many discussions it would be best not to attempt to draw any line but to deal with the material means of production under one heading.

The character and distribution of the material means of production and transportation is to a very large extent a result of adaptation to economic conditions of earlier times. Some, such as raw materials, can be moved easily if a new location is found advantageous; others can be transported only with difficulty or not at all. Thus, in a study of economic variations the possibilities of moving material means of production and transportation directly or indirectly from one place to another, and of changing their technical form, must be dealt with in a manner analogous to that of variations in the location and quality of labor.

It follows that an accurate account of the location of industry must describe a historical process, and that the analysis of the price system in more static terms, as in § 2, explains only part of the relationship. That is, however, important, for the direct effects of the various changes in the basic elements on prices and location are indicated by the price system.

It is not necessary to discuss in detail actual cases of present location to demonstrate the influence of earlier location of industry. Inventions may by chance lead to manufacture in one country or place when others would do just as well; yet the industry tends to remain where it was first located, for the quality of the labor factors adapt themselves and so do capital investments in production, transportation, and trade connections. A force of considerable strength

---

[4] Differences in the supply of labor and capital between towns and country districts are the result of factor movements, which are due chiefly to differences in transport resources and economies of concentration. "It has often been observed that in every nation the principal trade is between the towns and the country; it is the exchange of manufactures against food and raw materials." Nicholson, *Principles*, p. 325.

may be required to move production to other places. The ability of a locality to hold an industry greatly exceeds its original ability to attract one. Many industries are still placed in the neighborhood of water power, although a different location would be natural now that electrical energy can be transported cheaply. The household glass industry in many countries has remained in the old forest districts, where it grew up centuries ago because of the supply of cheap fuel; yet coal is nowadays transported to these places from distant mines.

§ 5. *Arbitrary elements in location.* The historical influence can lead to an uneconomical location of industry. Those people who decide, for example, where a factory is to be placed in many cases base their decisions upon deficient knowledge of the actual facts and cannot judge correctly the future changes equally relevant to the location. In a word, mistakes play an important role in location. It is obviously impossible to lay down any principles.[5] Moreover, a mistake in the location of one factory reacts on the location of other lines of production in several ways. The markets for firms that sell raw materials and semimanufactured goods are located where the later stages of production are carried out and move with them. Besides, the demand for productive factors in a district by an industry that would better be located elsewhere may raise the prices of some factors in that district and thus make it unsuitable for industries that would otherwise settle there.

It should be observed in this connection that the location of consumers' markets is to some extent governed by other than economic considerations. The capital and other centers of government, as well as army and navy stations, acquire an extra importance as markets.

The organization of government also affects location profoundly through taxation, particularly in countries where local rates differ considerably between districts without offering corresponding advantages to industry. The post World War I economic development in Great Britain showed many examples of new industries evading the "devastated areas" where the old and unprofitable industries were located, unemployment was excessive, and local rates were burdensome. Such local differences in rates may of course affect local differences in wages and particularly in rents. International inequalities in taxation also affect the prices of productive factors and international trade.

One circumstance which increases the influence of chance on location is that the elements affecting costs of production are so numerous

---

[5] It seems unfruitful to speculate on the difference between the actual location and the optimum location that would give maximum income. Location is governed by what happens in a small number of cases. Hence, chance is likely to exercise a greater influence than it would if the number of elements was great.

and varied that several places may offer nearly equal advantages. One may be more suitable with regard to raw material supply, another with regard to labor. Economies of large-scale production may restrict the number of producing units, in which case it is more or less a question of chance as to which place receives the industry in question.

Firms may produce at very different costs but sell at virtually equal prices.[6] Low-cost firms are generally growing; high-cost firms are as a rule declining. In many cases the latter have a disadvantageous location; as long as they continue to exist, they contribute an element of irregularity to the location map.

A commodity may also be produced by several different processes and the best location for a firm using one of them may be different from that for firms using another. Often, however, the various processes result in goods of differing quality. There is nothing peculiar in the fact that firms producing different grades of goods are differently located; it is, strictly speaking, a matter of different industries. The better grades of men's ready-made clothes are manufactured in Berlin, where there is a specialized market for skilled labor and where it is easy to observe fashion changes. The poorer grades are produced chiefly in villages and small towns in an agricultural district of Germany, where the farmers' families do part of the work. Here, too, certain external economies accrue—for example, the establishment of a labor market—but the preponderant influence is a cheap labor supply.

All these and many other circumstances explain why few manufactured goods or raw materials have well-defined market areas. This analysis applies to international as well as to domestic trade—although in some cases high tariffs make market areas coincide with countries and thus give the former distinct borders. International trade is between firms, not between nations. Some firms export, and others do not; some export only to a few special foreign markets, others to a number of them. Some firms are able to hold a part of the home market against foreign competition; others succumb. One must therefore expect continued importation of goods that the country is well able to produce for itself; and it is only natural that international trade currents should exhibit irregularities that at first sight seem to defy all principles. To what extent this is actually the case only an analysis of concrete examples can demonstrate. Under all circumstances it is clear that the location of industry, whether national or international, cannot be completely explained by an analysis such as the one presented in §§ 1–4.

[6] In the Swedish iron industry the costs of ordinary iron were found to differ in 1927 by almost 50 percent.

§ 6. *Arbitrary local price differences.* Further qualifications help to bridge the gap between abstract theory and reality. For instance, commodity prices for traded goods have here been assumed to differ by the costs of transfer between different places, but as a matter of fact, trade is not enough to guarantee this result. An investigation into local price differences at any time shows irregularities not explained by the costs of transfer.[7] Temporary interlocal price discrepancies are great for commodities affected by seasonal variation, such as agricultural products. These price discrepancies call forth cross transports and other irregular trade currents. Such waves on the price surface are, however, comparatively unimportant. Price averages for long periods—several years—seem to show relations that do not deviate much from what the costs of transfer make natural; and what influences the location of industry is the price situation during a fairly long period, not its daily or irregular variations.[8]

Evidently the time and space elements are interrelated, for surely local forces that may affect prices in an irregular manner for short periods may offset one another during longer periods. Professor Black points out that with regard to daily price averages Chicago and St. Paul are by no means part of the same livestock market, with regard to monthly averages the differences are much less marked, and with regard to yearly averages all significant elements are virtually identical.

[7] See particularly the extensive investigations by the United States Bureau of Railway Economics.

[8] The investigation into the prices of oranges in the United States made by the Bureau of Railway Economics shows very considerable irregularities in prices on any one day but a surprising regularity in price averages for a whole season.

Part Four

*International Trade and Factor
Movements*

XIII

International Trade

§ 1. *Introduction.* The results reached in Part Three will now be utilized in an analysis of international trade problems, particularly those having to do with the obstacles to commodity and factor movements. I do not intend to present a general location theory, even in its outlines, but to deal mainly with international trade, and therefore only so much abstract location theory is included as is needed for the special discussion of international trade problems.

The reason for dealing with such problems to some extent separately from other location and trade problems (e.g., the relation between towns and country districts) is that national borders are different from, and in some respects more important than, borders within countries. They act differently as obstacles to both commodity and factor movements. Furthermore, varying currency systems cause the mechanism of trade between countries to differ from that of other sorts of trade. There is also a community of interest[1] between the members of one nation, which makes such a study interesting in itself and valuable as a guide for national policy. Last, many important economic variations are common to all districts within a country but not to districts in other countries. This makes it natural to treat a country as a unit and to study its relations with other countries. Numerous social institutions concern the inhabitants in a certain country but affect foreigners only indirectly. For instance, collective agreements concerning wages and labor conditions usually affect a whole national industry but do not influence the same industry abroad. Changes in state taxation and state regulations in general also affect economic life within a country more directly than that in other countries.[2]

[1] This community of interest is founded partly on sentiment. However, the factor mobility contributes also; e.g., the great interior mobility of capital creates common interests among all capitalists in a country.

[2] From a certain point of view a "national economy" (*Volkswirtschaft*) is an *organic unity* and must therefore be one of the basic concepts in any location and trade theory. There is a fundamental difference in character between international trade and trade between other regions smaller or larger than individual countries. This viewpoint has not influenced my treatment of international trade. I am convinced that only a purely analytical discussion, which discards the use of such concepts as *organisms* which are different from a sum of the cells that make them,

The object in this part is to explain why trade between nations is what it is and to analyze some problems connected with international economic relations. Some of the explanation was given in Part Two, where a simplified picture of international trade was presented. Now the circumstances disregarded there must be dealt with: mobility of productive factors and transferability of commodities, international transfer facilities, and accumulative and dispersive tendencies related to them. It is well to review the most important conclusions on these questions reached in Part Three and to deal in turn with their international aspects. Import duties play such an important part in determining location and trade that they deserve special treatment. Finally, international movements of the factors of production and their relation to international trade are discussed.

§ 2. *Obstacles to international commodity movements.* Such obstacles as costs of transport reduce trade. The distance commodities go and the ways they pass depend upon the height of these costs and upon the differences in the costs of production in various places. Europe imports enormous quantities of vegetable food from America and Australia but produces a much greater proportion of its animal food within its own borders because the former is relatively much easier to transport.

National frontiers serve as obstacles to international trade. The influence of tariff walls is obvious. Other circumstances are the differences between nations as to language, laws, banking systems, habits, and traditions—in a word, everything that makes it more difficult to trade in foreign countries than in one's own, and more difficult in certain foreign countries than in others. Another class of circumstances is more directly connected with national frontiers: cumbersome customs formalities, government preference for domestic products, movements and preconceptions that induce people to prefer such products to foreign goods, and the like.

These factors all influence more or less the course of international trade. The importance of some, or rather of their absence, is evident from the large extent of trade between different nations within the British Empire, despite the high import duties in some of them. For instance, in 1927 the British Empire outside of Great Britain took 46

can lay a firm basis for international trade theory. An analysis of a nonquantitative, qualitative sort may be added afterwards. There can be no advantage in attacking the problem from two angles and with two different sets of instruments at the same time; confusion is bound to ensue. For a discussion of these questions, see Harms: *Volkswirtschaft und Weltwirtschaft* (Jena, 1915). *Weltwirtschaftslehre* as a new branch of economic science in Harms' opinion has to study international economic relations on the basis of an organic national economy concept. Compare Wieser, *Theorie der gesellschaftlichen Wirtschaft* (Tübingen, 1924).

percent of British exports, and 49 percent of the British exports of fully manufactured goods.

The influence of differences in "economic customs" is difficult to illustrate with figures because statistics for the trade between various parts of one country are almost entirely lacking. It is clear, however, that trade is to a very great extent dependent upon close contact between the producer and his market, and that this contact is difficult to establish in a foreign country. In the 1920's a little country like Denmark with low duties and cheap water transportation from other countries produced about 75 percent of all the manufactured goods it consumed, whereas the export of such commodities was inconsiderable.

For certain goods the impediments are so great that international trade is unprofitable. Differences in the costs of production are insufficient to take goods over tariff walls and other obstacles; each country satisfies its own needs of such goods. These goods, called "home market goods," include everything that is usually produced only for the home market. Commodities that enter into foreign trade are called "international goods." They fall into two categories, import and export goods.

In some cases import goods and home market goods compete for the consumers' demand. A country may produce all the coarse cotton goods it needs but import the finer qualities. For certain uses the question of which quality is to be preferred is governed by the ratio between prices; thus the various qualities are more or less closely competitive. In other cases different goods may easily act as substitutes for each other. Tiles may be a home market commodity, whereas other material for the covering of roofs is imported. They naturally compete for the consumer demand. Evidently prices of such goods tend to move in harmony. When imports are obtained more cheaply, the prices of the corresponding home market goods are also lower. If they were not, demand would turn to the foreign commodities. There are other home market goods that feel no direct competition from foreign commodities, and their prices frequently change quite differently from import prices. They shall be called "noncompeting home market goods" as opposed to the "competing home market goods." This distinction is important in an analysis of relative price variations, for although the latter group feels the influence of variations in import prices and to some extent affects them, the former group has a more independent position. Certain home market goods, of course, compete with goods exported from the country in question. Their prices tend to move like export prices.

In summary, the various classes of goods are as follows: international goods, subject to international trade; competing home market goods, in more or less close competition with international goods; and noncompeting home market goods, a large group with a less direct connection with other goods. International goods may be either import or export goods; consequently, competing home market goods may compete with either imports or exports.

There are no fixed border lines between these groups.[3] Any change in the economic situation may cause international trade in some commodities to cease, or may move others from the home market to the international class. This fact does not impair the usefulness of such distinctions, but it makes discrimination in handling them of paramount importance.

In 1919-1923 exports made up the following percentages of total production: 23 percent in the United Kingdom, 23 percent in Germany. 29 percent in Canada, 20 percent in Japan, and 10 percent in the United States. In German manufacturing industries in 1925, 43 percent of the workers were employed in industries producing export goods, 10 percent produced goods of which small quantities were exported, and the remaining 47 percent were employed in home market industries. In Great Britain 4,300,000 out of 11,600,000 insured persons belonged to the exporting group of industries in 1924, according to estimates by the Balfour Committee.

What kind of commodities belong to the different classes? Are generalizations possible for a number of countries that differ considerably in productive resources? Of course, the import goods of one country are the export goods of another. But what about the line between international and home market goods? Do not certain commodities fall on the same side of it everywhere?

Obviously, commodities that are difficult to move tend to be produced where they are used and thus belong to the home market category. This is true of a large part of the most important goods and services. Cooked food is seldom transported long distances; it is in the literal sense of the word "produced at home." Houses are built where they are to be used. Thus, two very important productive processes are, without significant exceptions, located in the country that uses their results; international division of production is virtually out of the question.

Services are supplied at home. The rendering of a service is almost always effected a short time before its "consumption," which excludes any possibility of importation. Not only cooking but all sorts of house-

---

[3] This classification disregards the fact that owing to the costs of transport a certain commodity may be imported across one frontier and exported across another, as in the case of bricks in Sweden. The classification refers to conditions in the country as a whole and abstracts from minor local circumstances.

work fall within this category. So do retail distribution and practically all of wholesale distribution.

Whether goods belong to one class or the other depends to a great extent upon the tariff system; no generalizations are possible. As a rule, however, import duties on raw materials are fairly low, those on semimanufactured goods are higher, and the highest import duties are levied on finished products. For this reason raw materials in most countries are found among import or export goods, despite the fact that costs of transport weigh more heavily upon them. Finished goods frequently meet such high import duties that domestic production takes the place of importation.

§ 3. *Division of national markets.* It would seem natural to expect impediments to international trade to be either so high that domestic industries get complete control of the home market or so low that foreign producers supply all that is required of a certain commodity. For manufactured products—or rather, goods not at the first stage of production—this is, as a matter of fact, the rule. Although statistics imply that the sort of commodities that are imported are also to a large exent produced at home, the figures are misleading. As Professor Taussig wrote, "A duty on a manufactured product commonly is either so high as to keep out all imports, or so low as to admit all and thus to be in effect merely a revenue duty. True, imports often appear to continue, and a division of the supply between domestic and foreign quotas often appears to be brought about. But the appearance is deceptive; the two sets of goods on examination prove to differ in quality, or to be for other reasons not in reality competitive." [4]

To this statement should be added the fact that foreign and domestic commodities sometimes differ in quality and yet compete so closely that it would be impractical to regard them as different commodities. The difference may even be imaginary, consisting simply in a belief, created through advertising of a certain brand, that the produce of one firm is superior to that of another. Boots and shoes are imported into many countries that produce the larger part of what they need in domestic industries. The home market is divided between foreign and domestic producers. The explanation is to be found, partly at least, in the fact that at existing prices imported grades are preferred for some purposes by some persons and home products are preferred by others. Another example is the fact that the large automobile exporting countries also import foreign motor cars, which differ little in usefulness and price from domestic cars. Thus, certain commodities are at the same time import goods and competing home market goods in the same country.

[4] Taussig, *Some Aspects of the Tariff Question,* p. 10.

The fact that prices of some foreign commodities are neither so low as to make domestic production unprofitable nor so high as to fail to sell in the domestic market is, however, largely to be explained by other circumstances—above all, by the existence of interior costs of transport. The market area over which a certain commodity is distributed from a certain center of production does not stop at the national borders, except insofar as the latter are important obstacles. Often they are not, and goods pass the borders, i.e., enter into international trade. Some of them, like bricks, may not go far into other countries but only to the parts within easy reach. In the case of bricks, producing places are scattered, and the number of more or less communicating markets is great. The market areas for certain producing points in southern Sweden extend into Denmark, and the market areas for some brick factories in Norway and Finland reach into the neighboring parts of Sweden.

No explanation referring to conditions in a country as a whole can explain such trade currents. The analysis must run in terms of conditions in regions or districts, or more exactly, in the places that constitute them. Germany's southwest is part of a district extending through northern France and Belgium which is rich in coal and iron and has excellent transport resources and facilities. It exports goods to surrounding agricultural districts—some within, some outside of Germany. Yet agricultural districts in northern and eastern Germany import similar products from Great Britain and Poland.[5] British coal is sold in northern Germany simply because of lower costs of transport from the British mines than from coal mines in western Germany.

It is evident that division into home market goods and international goods must be handled with caution. Among import goods, some are imported only to certain ports. Even substantial price variations might fail to change very much the proportion of this import to the total domestic consumption. Other import goods easily pervade all parts of the importing country. If they compete closely with goods produced at home, important variations in the volume of imports may follow minor price changes. There are, of course, corresponding differences between the various export goods.

Among other circumstances contributing to the division of national markets for certain goods between domestic and foreign producers is the fact that the domestic industry is unable to satiate the domestic demand for a product. The home-market firms can hold their own against foreign competition and keep part of the home market, but they are unable to drive out foreign goods altogether. The causes of the superiority that these firms have over former or potential competitors among firms of the same nationality include better location, easier access to power and raw materials, and more efficient

[5] Cf. Marshall, *Money, Credit, and Commerce,* pp. 104-105.

management. Some of these circumstances do not permit increased production at equally low cost per unit, so that any attempt to conquer the entire home market is obstructed. In some cases the low costs of production of certain firms may be due to temporary conditions, and as time goes on, these firms may get weaker and disappear, leaving the whole market to the foreign producers. Conversely, a domestic industry may through inventions or other favorable changes win such a superiority over its foreign competitors that the latter are driven out. This process requires time. The best foreign firms, and those having the best hold of the market, fight for some years before they quit the contest. During such periods the home market is supplied partly with domestic and partly with imported goods.

Competition does not depend upon price differences alone, however. The marketing of many products continues successfully, even though competing firms sell similar products at lower prices.[6] This is only partly due to real or imagined differences in quality; it is due also to manifold conditions of modern marketing, which have to do with good will, trademarks, exclusive selling rights given to a limited number of retailers, etc. For example, a firm manufacturing goods like ready-made clothes for women often finds it advantageous to sell its articles through a limited number of retailers in large places and through only one retailer in small places. Since other retailers also carry such articles, one firm cannot capture the whole domestic market; there is room for others, domestic or foreign, selling goods that are of cheaper, or dearer, quality. A Swedish firm that dominates this branch of industry has found it impossible to supply more than 50 percent of the total home demand. The rest is divided between small domestic and large foreign manufacturers.

Last, it should be observed that price discrimination makes it possible for a firm in one country to invade the market in another where costs of production are equally low. Dumping is a means of gaining new markets and is used as a substitute for or supplement to real marketing costs. It may also be a means of disposing more or less regularly of the surplus output that exceeds the requirements in the main market. The Swedish firm mentioned above used to sell its goods 10 percent lower in Denmark, exclusive of import duty, than in Sweden, and it found it profitable to retain the Danish market even during boom periods in Sweden.

These matters are complicated. To give them the cliché "economic friction" explains nothing. The sorts of circumstances that lead to a division of the home market between foreign and domestic producers have only been indicated here.

Manufactured products have been dealt with chiefly so far. The

[6] See Black, *Production Economics*, p. 825, and Schüller, *"Zur Theorie der Handelspolitik,"* p. 51.

case of many primary products from agriculture and mining is in one respect somewhat different. Increasing quantities of such commodities can as a rule be supplied only at increasing prices. Their import price is often one that allows a domestic output short of domestic demand; consumption is therefore partly satisfied with foreign goods. Reduced import prices force a diminution of domestic production but not its cessation. Examples are abundant. Most European countries grow wheat and import it from transatlantic countries, which is due only partly to the fact that mixing imported and European wheat gives a better flour. Access to cheap American wheat in the latter half of the last century did not lead to the disappearance of wheat-growing in Europe. In manufacturing industries, however, cheapened importation often leads to complete cessation of domestic production. The use of machinery for Belgian and American window-glass is at present rapidly driving out hand methods in a number of countries, which must either adopt the new method or give up the industry.

The difference in this respect between agricultural and mining products on the one hand and more highly manufactured products on the other exists only so far as the costs of the former contain large elements of rent of natural resources, which have few competitive uses. Lower wheat prices reduce the price of wheatland, but it may still be profitable to subject certain lands to an extensive cultivation of wheat. The supply of wheatland is low. It is not so with capital and labor, for which there are always many competing uses. Only for a limited period can wages far below the general standard be paid. And the reward to capital can be kept much below the normal rate of interest only if it has been tied up in certain capital goods, which cannot easily be turned to other uses, and only so long as these goods last. Without a sufficient reward, no new capital will be invested in these channels. Reduced prices for a commodity consequently eliminate its production[7] unless rent can be reduced significantly, serving as a buffer for the blows of price reductions. Manufactured goods seldom fulfill this condition, but within limits many agricultural and mining products do. They are often both produced at home and imported at the same time, whereas manufacturing goods, were it not for the circumstances indicated above, would be produced either in sufficient quantities to satisfy the whole home market or not at all.

The elements touched upon here help to explain not only the division of the market in country *A* between producers in *A* and in a foreign country, but also the fact that producers from *several* foreign countries compete in *A*, with or without competition from domestic

---

[7] Cheaper imports, e.g., as a result of a tariff union, may stimulate producers to introduce more efficient methods and to seek further specialization. The developments in Belgium after the creation of Benelux offer several examples.

firms. It is, of course, by no means necessary that costs of production in these several countries be equally high, for the impediments to international trade may put a greater obstacle in the way of export from B to A than from C to A. Ties of common language and habits, tariff preference, etc., may unite the two latter nations. Furthermore, the difference in quality between goods that nevertheless cannot be treated as different commodities tends to create a division of the market so that each competitor can enjoy a share. As regards agricultural and mining products, a division of the market is still more natural. Wheat is exported to many European countries from Argentina and Canada no less than from the United States.

Having dealt chiefly with obstacles to commodity movements across national frontiers, I come to a consideration of lack of mobility in general, first from the point of view of different goods and second from that of different places.

§ 4. *Relative mobility of goods at different stages of their production.* The analysis in Chapter VIII demonstrated that the relative costs of transferring goods at different stages of production deserves special interest from the point of view of the location of production. Other things being equal, certain industries become "market located," i.e., situated close to the market centers, whereas others become "raw material located." If several raw materials are used, industries of the latter type tend to settle near the sources of materials that have the greatest weight.[8] The iron and steel industry is in most cases situated not far from the coal mines; the ore goes to the coal.

It makes no difference whether or not the places are in the same country, except when movements across the national borders meet special difficulties—which they usually do. Such obstacles, e.g., import duties, affect location and trade by changing the relative transferability of raw materials, semimanufactured goods, and finished products. So far as they impede the movements of finished goods more than goods at earlier stages, they make the latter more mobile and thus distribute the various stages of production between countries.

Owing to differences in transferability, some natural resources exercise a much greater influence upon the local distribution of economic activity than others. Resources used to produce raw materials for market-located industries have little power to attract economic activity. However, resources that give rise to raw material-located industries attract not only these industries but also, owing to the implied growth of markets, many market-located industries. Coal mines, for example, have attracted many industries when iron mines are in the neighborhood and transfer facilities are good.

The differences in total costs of transfer when production is located

[8] Not near materials that are most weight-losing, as was pointed out to me by Dr. T. Palander, a specialist in location problems.

in different places are of course only one element in determining location. Differences in productive factor equipment that lead to differences in costs of production contribute their influence as well.

§ 5. *Local differences in transfer facilities.* The transfer facilities of different places also influence international trade. The conclusions regarding interregional trade are now applied to the case of countries, with special emphasis upon the influence of obstacles to international commodity movements. Such obstacles make transfer between countries more difficult, other things being equal, than those within a country. Duties have a similar effect.

First, as to conditions within countries, if the distances to be covered are small (the necessary raw materials are close to one another and to markets) or if transportation between them is easy (owing to navigable rivers, good railroads, etc.), the costs of transportation are low. This is of special advantage in industries using several heavy raw materials. The British iron and steel industry owes much to superiority in this respect. Ore and coal mines, blast furnaces, steel works, and shipping ports are within a ten-mile radius in some areas. In the first half of the century British average haulage distance was under 30 miles, compared with 150 in Germany, 200 in France, and 500 in the United States. "The cost of assembling all the raw materials and then carrying the finished steel to a port of shipment is $14.20 in the United States, and only $5.05 in Great Britain when home ore is used." [9] Even the Belgian steelmakers paid more in transport rates per ton than the British.

In the United States excellent means of transportation in many industries atone to a large extent for the long haulage distances. In Russia, however, the lack of good communication has prevented the utilization of natural resources at some distance from each other. This was one cause of the slow development of manufacturing industries in some parts of that country before the First World War.

Other things being equal, countries with good interior transfer facilities and plenty of natural resources produce relatively great quantities of goods per individual and have a large foreign trade.[10] Both real and nominal wages are high. Countries with poor interior transfer facilities tend to specialize in goods with easily transportable raw materials. The standard of living is, other things being equal, comparatively low.

As to the transfer facilities between countries, countries that consist chiefly of places far from outside raw material sources and markets, or which have poor communications with most of them, primarily

[9] "Trade and Engineering Supplement," *New York Times,* October 1, 1927.
[10] "The expansion of a country's foreign trade depends largely on her facilities for internal transport." Marshall, *Money, Credit, and Commerce,* p. 112.

export easily transportable goods. Sweden specializes in fine cotton and silk fabrics, watches, and machinery of high value. All countries of course produce market-located goods for home consumption. In every country special resources may outweigh advantages or difficulties in transfer facilities. Iron ore of exceptionally high grade is produced in the extreme north of Sweden and the interior of Chile.

The fact that a larger country has a greater number of resources than a smaller one does not of course make it probable that it has better transfer relations, except insofar as tariffs or similar obstacles intervene. A country like Denmark has better transfer relations for most manufacturing industries than certain parts of Great Britain,[11] Germany, and the United States. Coal, iron, steel, and machinery can be obtained relatively cheaply. It is only natural, therefore, that Denmark and Holland should have manufacturing industry although they lack all the important raw materials. They also have a high standard of living.

It is often overlooked that *what is important for goods in higher stages of production is not natural resources but good transfer facilities.* Favorable transportation resources—navigable rivers, etc.—are as important as natural resources. If nature is rich in means of communication, she atones for poverty in raw materials. It is often thought that the so-called law of diminishing returns from land comes into effect when the population of a country increases, and that this explains why the standard of living often falls. Yet the matter is not so simple: it is only for agriculture and mining land that land as such is required in special qualities and in relatively large quantities. Production of goods at later stages is fairly independent of nature and is affected chiefly by transfer facilities and the supply of labor and capital. Thus, what makes for lower economic productivity when population grows is not so much the scarcity of nature as of capital and adequate transfer facilities. Raw materials and food have to be imported from further away, and the manufactured exports have either to be sent in exchange to more distant markets or forced into the usual ones in greater quantity. Since the supply of such a country's export product is increased, its price tends everywhere to fall. Equilibrium is reestablished, but the country has suffered a double loss: from less favorable terms of exchange and from a greater transportation bill for raw materials and finished goods.

To return to comparisons of countries with different transfer facilities, it is obvious that small countries are disadvantageously situated. In large countries there is a greater number of domestic places than in small countries. The use for communication with places abroad is

---

[11] The Portland cement factories in Denmark have a cheaper supply of British coal than do their competitors by the Thames.

therefore smaller, and the obstacles are fewer. This means more to some industries than to others. Of course, commodities that pass the national frontiers with great difficulty and are best produced on a large scale are better situated in large countries than in small ones.

Countries having good international transfer facilities secure a large amount of foreign trade. They have a superiority in industries requiring much transportation for the collection of heavy raw materials from different countries and for the distribution of heavy finished goods. In this respect European countries are better situated than, for example, New Zealand and Australia. In Europe, countries with good harbors have an advantage over countries like Czechoslovakia. If the latter were an island like Great Britain, its industries would certainly be more important and its standard of living distinctly higher than at present.

Changes in transfer facilities, e.g., through new facilities like the Suez or Panama canals or through the growth of important markets in the neighborhood, may affect the economic life of a country profoundly. India and Iran have come economically much closer to Europe through the Suez Canal. The economic growth of the United States has improved the position of Canada much more than that of European countries. However, the Baltic countries suffered decidedly after the First World War from being virtually cut off from the Russian market, which before the war had taken the larger part of their export commodities. They were not, like Finland, able to reorganize their economic life and find new markets in the West.

Any generalizations about transfer relations must of course be made carefully. All countries have transfer relations that are good in some respects and poor in others as regards the supply of raw materials or the marketing of products. Such differences affect profoundly the character of industry and trade.

§ 6. *Transfer facilities, factor supplies, and the character of industry.* The character of industry and trade depend not only upon transfer facilities but also upon factor supplies and other basic elements. The competitive position may be great in spite of unfavorable transfer facilities if the productive factors needed are cheap. Transfer facilities and factor supply also react upon each other. On the one hand, the distribution of labor and capital is governed primarily by economic circumstances, of which transfer facilities are one. Transfer facilities, on the other hand, are affected by factor supply, and costs of transport, like costs of production, are affected by factor prices.

Regions with good transfer facilities attract labor and capital, which move from other districts within the same country and to some extent from other countries. In old times poverty tended to keep back the growth of the population, so that prosperous regions had a more rapid increase than other regions. In general, regions with good transfer facilities become densely populated. They become important markets and profit from large-scale economies in transportation. However, a large part of their raw materials and food supplies must be drawn from far away.

Northwestern Europe has a fully developed transport system: a labyrinth of canals and navigable rivers, excellent harbors, and partly as a result of dense population a network of good railroads and highways. It has a supply of coal and iron deposits, as well as particularly good transport facilities for the iron and steel industry. The latter is important. Obversely, countries with poor transfer facilities and little or no active natural resources tend to be scantily populated and to specialize in goods that can be produced on a small scale and require plenty of the natural resources found there. Goods easily transferred are preferred for export.

To summarize briefly, countries are groups of places. Because of obstacles to commodity movements, inside as well as outside, transfer facilities affect the location of production and international trade. In other words, both the spread of productive factors and markets through the world and the local differences in transfer resources and facilities are important. Thus, not only the supply of productive factors in each country but also its local distribution is a governing element. Similarly, the local distribution of demand and the relative transferability of goods at different stages of their production are also relevant.

In particular cases one or another aspect may dominate. For some location problems the character of nature is decisive, and all other elements may be disregarded. Deserts and arctic zones are "death belts." Among the "life belts," the tropics produce handicraft goods and certain fruits; the cold temperate zones produce wheat, etc. In other cases, one may ignore international differences in transfer facilities and concentrate attention on the supply of productive factors within each country. For many location problems, however, transportation and the transferability of different goods are of decided influence. Furthermore, the location of one sort of economic activity more or less influences the location of the others. Evidently a deeper understanding of the local distribution of industry and international trade is impossible unless transfer facilities are thoroughly analyzed, as well as the forces governing the local distribution of labor and capital.

§ 7. *Location as a product of economic development.* The supply of productive factors is itself the result of economic history. If a country has for one reason or another obtained certain manufacturing industries, technical labor will be educated and trained and other industries will be started because of its supply. Fixed capital takes on a technical form that affects location. In the same way, the local distribution of productive factors and markets, and hence transfer facilities, are results of a historical development. Furthermore, transport facilities such as harbors and railroads grow up where they are needed and tend to remain.

The European economic superiority in the nineteenth century was due much more to the fact that labor had been technically trained and excellent transport facilities had been arranged than to a permanent superiority in natural and transportation resources. Western Europe had almost a monopoly in the manufacturing of many goods from raw materials procured from other parts of the world—raw materials that from the viewpoint of transfer resources alone might have been more advantageously manufactured elsewhere. The rapid economic progress in North America was to be expected when population and capital had grown sufficiently to make possible efficient utilization of its resources.

Evidently some so-called basic elements of location and pricing are more fundamental than others, i.e., adapt themselves less. The character of nature, as "natural resource" or "transportation resource," seems to exercise a lasting influence. Population, taste, capital supply, and transportation facilities are subject to a slow change, which is affected by, at the same time that it influences, economic development, of which the development of international trade is a part.

Look at a few illustrations. Coal and iron mines in districts with good transportation resources have been able to attract other industries to a large extent. This is due not only to the advantages of proximity but also to the fact that the mines originally attracted and held a more educated labor force than that found in agricultural districts. The development of modern manufacturing processes has been to a considerable extent due to the qualities and experience acquired in the iron and steel industry during efforts to utilize its products.[12] These international differences in the quality of labor explain why the machine-producing industries are to be found almost exclusively in the iron and coal districts.

Great Britain got the lead in the eighteenth century, principally because no other country then had excellent transport resources and facilities, interior and exterior, and coal and iron deposits close to one another. Her invention of textile machinery and the locomotive were the result not of inherited technical superiority[13] but of the

[12] To make it possible for this industry to start, a supply of technical labor is of course necessary. This has been lacking in China, where the iron and steel industry has consequently been insignificant until recently.

[13] John Erikson, the Swedish inventor of the propeller, had constructed a locomotive that was in many respects superior to Stephenson's, yet no railroads were built in Sweden. Erikson had to emigrate to the United States to find scope for his genius.

concentration of energies on manufacturing industries in general and the textile industry in particular, which latter had developed in the seventeenth century partly because of the moist air and plentiful supply of water power. When cotton became cheap, England was ready with coal, iron, constantly improving technical labor, and excellent transport resources and facilities. The economic expansion made possible an enormous increase of population—the rise in wages was limited—and the expansion continued. This labor supply can be regarded rather as the response to a stimulus than as an independent cause of the development.

Similar considerations explain why the textile industry has virtually everywhere been the first field for the development of manufacturing industries with modern machinery. This industry profits from contact with the market and uses raw materials that are easy to transport. It tends to be "market located." This, however, is only part of the explanation. A machine-using textile industry, producing standard, low-grade qualities of goods, requires a minimum of technical skill on the part of leaders and workers. This skill has been easy to acquire, partly because the handling of wool and flax was familiar for centuries. As familiarity with the handling of machinery has grown, other industries have been taken up, until a later stage is reached, when the machines are to a large extent manufactured at home instead of imported.

The growth of education and development of skills naturally tend to disseminate industries that have been concentrated in certain localities owing to their superiority therein. The trade resulting from such superiority has been largely in the east-to-west direction. Some authorities believe that in the future trade will be rather in the north-to-south direction, which, owing chiefly to differences in nature, is not likely to be much reduced. "No exchange of culture, no equality in education or skill, no emigration of peoples evening up density of population can change the temperature and make tropic fruit grow in the land of arctic fur, or cotton grow in the land of spring wheat."[14]

Even the east-to-west trade is unlikely to fall off considerably. One reason for its continuance is the lasting difference in transport resources between districts in similar latitudes. It seems probable that these differences will entail others in labor and capital supply, both as to quantity and as to quality. The relative backwardness of certain parts of Asia and Africa, for example, is as great today as fifty years ago, perhaps more so. The trade between highly industrialized countries such as Great Britain and Germany shows no sign of falling

[14] Russel-Smith, *Industry and Commerce*, p. 665. See also Black, *Production Economics*, p. 767.

off,[15] although the trade with other countries is growing more rapidly.

§ 8. *International trade of the United States.* What circumstances govern the exports and imports of the United States and make them different from those of other manufacturing nations? Its exports of finished manufactures in 1928 amounted to $2,260,000,000. Automobiles and machinery were the most important articles. For each, the advantage of a large market and good transfer facilities is great; the automobile industry in particular finds a market in the United States many times greater than that in any other country. Besides, the incentive to invent labor-saving machinery is particularly strong in a high wage country; an unusual supply of highly efficient technical labor has therefore developed. Among the exports of finished manufactures there are also specialties that seem to be produced in the United States simply because by chance some invention originated there and sustained effort maintained technical superiority. All manufacturing nations have such specialties.

The export of crude materials and foodstuffs—such as copper, petroleum, wheat, cotton, and tobacco—is clearly due to the great supply of the corresponding natural resources, just as the importation of such goods—e.g., sugar, raw silk, coffee, rubber, and furs—is due to their absence. Manufactured food stuffs—e.g., meat and wheat flour—are also important export articles. The fact that they are manufactured in the United States and not, like the rest, exported in crude form is chiefly explained by the transfer facilities: easy access to great quantities of the raw materials and to large markets. It is, however, probably also due to some extent to a supply of specialized technical labor,[16] which counts for much, e.g., in the meat-packing industry. The export of semimanufactured goods—iron and steel goods —is also due partly to the transfer facilities, which make manufacturing close to the steel plants advantageous; it is partly due to access to cheap fuel and power and to technical skill.

Next among the imports after crude materials and foodstuffs are finished manufactures, which are imported in considerable quantities across a high tariff wall. Among them are goods that for no obvious reason have become the specialties of one foreign country or another. Chiefly, however, the imports are goods requiring relatively large quantities of labor, such as high-grade textile goods. The high wage

[15] The fear that Europe will be unable to export manufactured goods to pay for its importation of food and raw materials if the economic development and tariff policy in countries exporting the latter continues along present lines is on the whole unfounded. The terms of trade may vary to the disadvantage of European exports, but probably not to any serious extent unless tariff walls are raised many times their present height or population is violently increased.

[16] See the brilliant and instructive analysis by Taussig in *Some Aspects of the Tariff Question.*

level in the United States makes the production of such goods expensive. Because such industries have not, despite high protection, reached full development in the United States, the technique in many cases is not comparable to that in the countries specializing in them.

Some semimanufactured goods, such as pulp, are imported, because they are much more easily transported than the raw materials and the natural resources for production of the latter at home are insufficient.

Many more goods would, of course, be imported were it not for the high tariff. Commodities made from foreign raw materials would in many cases be cheaper produced abroad and transported in finished form. The duties affect the "relative transferability" in such a way that production comes to be located in the United States despite the higher manufacturing costs.

§ 9. *Meaning of the effects of and the gain from international trade.* Various aspects of the location of industry and international trade have been separately discussed. The controlling elements on the demand side were found to be (1) individual tastes and the desire of groups and (2) conditions of ownership of productive factors. On the supply side the controlling factors are (1) the physical properties of nature, i.e., of both productive factors and commodities, (2) the supply of productive factors, (3) the conditions of economic stability, (4) the social conditions of production (taxes on industry, etc.), and (5) the lack of divisibility of the productive factors. In a strict sense, (5) is included in (1). Location is also profoundly affected by (6) transportability of commodities, (7) distance relations, i.e., local distribution of the productive factors, (8) transport resources, and (9) transport facilities and social transfer conditions (e.g., duties). Like (5), element (6) may be included in (1). Element (8) could also be included in (1).

The basic elements governing location may thus be singly described: (*a*) tastes and desires of man, (*b*) physical properties of nature in a wide sense (including the qualities of both goods and factors from the point of view of production and transportation), (*c*) quantity and local distribution of productive factors (including, of course, fixed capital in all forms and transport facilities), and (*d*) the social conditions of ownership, production, stability, and transfer.

These conditions are not independent of price variations. A change in any one of them changes more or less the whole price system—among other things, international trade—and this reacts on the other circumstances. The domestic supply of factors of production, for example, is affected and tastes change. Yet these reactions are on the whole so uncertain in character and extent that it is often best to treat them separately, whereas the reactions of prices and quantities that are not basic to the price system react in a much more direct and predictable way.

In this light the expression "effects of international trade" should be examined. How much would the situation differ in its absence? As the other basic conditions would be very different if there were insurmountable obstacles to international trade, it is not worthwhile to pursue the analysis of the effects of such trade very far on the assumption of fixed basic conditions. Still less is there any reason for discussing the question of the total gain from international trade or its division between the trading nations.[17] An analysis of the effects of international trade as a whole must run largely in terms of the changes in the basic circumstances, e.g., in the amount of population[18] due to such trade.

It is much more worthwhile to speak of the gains and losses of changes in international trade due to reductions and increases in the obstacles to international commodity movements.[19] The effects of such variations can be explained primarily in terms of changes of the price system, on the assumption that other basic circumstances remain unaltered. In other words, it does less violence to reality to abstract from the influence on the number of inhabitants in a country in a study of protective duties, for example, than to assume the disappearance of foreign trade altogether. However, particularly in the long run, all variations in international obstacles cause reactions in the other basic elements. The only satisfactory method for an analysis of the effects of reduced international obstacles is to consider both the changes in the price system that would occur if the other basic elements were unaffected and the changes due to the actual reactions of these elements.

Special interest attaches to the question of how the volume of

[17] Cf. Chapter VII. The usual analysis concerning the total gain from international trade or "the variable distribution of transport costs" evidently offers little of interest. One cannot say how much of the burden of transportation costs each country carries without knowing how much its position would be improved by their disappearance.

[18] The present number of inhabitants in Great Britain for example would be much less if there had been no foreign trade in the last two hundred years.

[19] It is a little artificial to give to these effects of changes in the obstacles to international commodity movements the term "effects of international trade." Variations in demand conditions, factor supply, etc., also cause changes in the price system that involve among other things changes in foreign trade. (Cf. my paper "Protection and Noncompeting Groups," *Weltwirtschaftliches Archiv*, 1931). Yet the changes in the price system caused by a new demand or a new supply are not said to be due to the changes in foreign trade. A treatise on international trade thus differs from a general price and location theory only by giving special attention to changes in the basic conditions insofar as they concern international trade and, *perhaps*, by studying most carefully the effects of variations in that sort of basic element—the obstacles to international transfer—which has most *directly* to do with international trade.

available goods[20] in the various countries is affected. If it increases, one may speak of a "gain," and if it declines, a "loss." Note, however, that these words are not used in any normative sense. It is beyond the scope of this work to inquire how far a gain of this sort means greater "satisfaction" in a case where both the taste of consuming individuals and the distribution of income have changed as a result of the changed transfer conditions.

§ 10. *Effects of and gain from a reduction in transport costs in international trade.* Compare two situations, one with higher and the other with lower costs of transport between countries. According to the previous analysis, the latter situation is characterized by greater international trade and, as a rule, by less international inequality in factor prices. Production can to a greater extent adapt itself locally to the local factor supply and other basic elements. National income in terms of goods and services[21] is increased.

Even if there is no tendency toward equalization of factor prices as a result of increased trade, the tendency to equalize costs of production, actual or potential, in various countries is a sign of a change in the economic situation, which means a greater volume of world output. Consider, for instance, the case where iron and coal mines are more expensive in country A than in country B, and yet the former country is able to produce iron more cheaply because the resources there are much closer to one another, which brings a saving in costs of interior transport. If a reduction in the costs of transport between the countries makes it possible for A to export to B a part of the iron B needs, the prices of resources are raised in the former country still more over their level in the latter. Evidently the saving in cost of transport more than makes up for the more expensive resources in the iron industry in A.

[20] For an individual country this quantity, which is a measure of the national income, is the net volume of production plus imports minus exports and adjusted with regard both to the foreign ownership of certain natural resources and capital and to present international capital movements.

[21] For proof and exceptions see Chapter XV, § 3, where difficulties connected with the different possibilities of weighting, when an index of the volume of goods and services is computed, are also discussed.

XIV

International Price Relations

§ 1. *Commodity prices.* Since this book is an investigation into the character of the price mechanism as it operates in the world, not in the so-called theory of pricing and distribution, special attention has been given to relations between the price systems in different countries. In the light of the previous analysis an attempt will now be made to illuminate a little further the nature and extent of international price differences, beginning with commodity prices.

The following tabulation illustrates the fact that wholesale prices of food are much higher in some countries than in others, even if the comparison is confined to countries with a similar economic life. It shows the wholesale prices of important articles of food in four countries as a percentage of the prices of the same articles in New Zealand.[1]

Country	July 1914	February 1929
United States	129	132
Canada	125	128
Australia	105	115
South Africa	141	110

Before World War I food prices were substantially lower in Australia than in South Africa. By 1929 the situation was rather the reverse.

Retail prices also differ widely. The following figures leave no doubt that even though qualitative differences exist, the price differences are much too large to be due to this factor alone. The figures represent the indices for retail prices of food, fuel, light, and soap in certain towns:[2]

Estonia	78	Portugal	98	Great Britain	100
France	104	Holland	105	Spain	114
Germany	114	Sweden	116	Denmark	118
Canada	120	Australia	123	Italy	125
United States	138				

§ 2. *Wages, interest rates, and rents.* International differences in wages are still more striking. However, since the usefulness, skill, and dependability of workers in various countries differ considerably, the

---

[1] *Statistical Yearbook for New Zealand* (1930), p. 832.
[2] *International Labor Review*, II (1929), 580, 867.

figures are not strictly comparable. An investigation made by the machine industry union in Switzerland[3] into wages in that industry in some manufacturing countries of Europe in 1928 gave the following result. The figures represent earnings per hours in Swedish öre.

Country	Skilled	Semiskilled		Unskilled
Sweden	129	120		107
England	113	—	76[4]	—
Switzerland	109	—	88[4]	—
Holland	102	89		75
Germany	98	89		71
Austria	73	66		58
Italy	71	55		45
France	66	53		44
Belgium	50	47		38

The British Dominions and the United States would, of course, show still higher figures, but comparable statistics are not available. The average weekly income for male workers in manuafcturing industries in 1928 was $13.90 in Sweden,[5] but in the United States it was no less than $31.74 for skilled and semiskilled labor and $25.17 for unskilled labor. In 1926 white laborers in manufacturing industries in South Africa earned more than $32.[6]

For production costs and international competition, the height of *money* wages and the quality of labor are the vital circumstances. The worker, however, is interested in the things his wages can buy, his *real* wages in terms of commodities and services. These differ almost as much as money wages from one country to another. The International Labor Office calculated the following indices of real wages in 1928.[7] It is evident that such figures cannot be regarded as reliable indices for the standard of living of manufacturing workers in different countries because their manner of living differs so radically, but the use of several different sorts of budgets as a basis for real wage computations has demonstrated that the following figures are not markedly altered when the commodities and the weighting are changed to correspond more closely with actual conditions.[8]

Portugal	32	Germany	71	Denmark	104
Estonia	41	Holland	85	Australia	143
Italy	42	Great Britain	100	Canada	171
Spain	45	Sweden	101	United States	191
France	53				

[3] *Verkstäderna* (Stockholm, 1929), 6.

[4] Only figures for unskilled workers, probably including also semiskilled workers, are available.

[5] *Sociala Meddelanden* (Stockholm, 1929), p. 844. The annual income is divided by 52.

[6] *International Labor Review*, II (1929), 113 ff.

[7] *Ibid.*, 580, 867.

[8] Differences in social insurance constitute another complicating factor that must be disregarded.

Real wages were thus in 1930 more than six times as high in the United States as in Portugal, and almost five times as high as in important manufacturing countries like Italy. Money wages were almost nine times as high as in Portugal, and five times as high as in Italy and France.

Statistics of wages in agriculture are still more difficult to obtain in comparable form. It may be worthwhile, however, to quote from Professor Black the following annual wages of farm labor in 1913:[9]

Japan	$ 26 (plus board)	Germany	$200
China	42	England and Wales	222[10]
Italy	100	United States	364
Sweden	180	South Africa	480
Denmark	185		

It is not necessary to add further statistics to show that the short-time and long-time rates of interest—the latter in particular—also differ considerably from one country to another. In northern and western Europe industry was paying about 5 percent for borrowed capital in 1930, whereas not further away than the Baltic nations the level was four or five times as high. Similar differences exist with regard to the rent of land, although figures for comparable grades are difficult to obtain.[11]

§ 3. *Why wages differ in various countries.* How can wages stay at such different levels in countries which compete more or less closely in several lines of industry? The extremely low wages of Asiatic farm labor are, of course, partly to be accounted for by the different kinds of labor there represented. But they are largely due to differences in the equipment of cooperating factors: natural resources, technical labor, and capital. The following table for the 1920's is illuminating:[12]

Country	Agricultural workers per square mile agricultural land	Livestock per 100 agricultural workers
Japan	503	23
China	260	?
Italy	89	117
Germany	80	251
Sweden	50	372
Denmark	44	760
United States	11	878
Australia	1	5360
Argentina	1	8821

Evidently the smaller the area of agricultural land with which each worker cooperates, the smaller the number of livestock per man. We

[9] Black, *Production Economics*, p. 946.
[10] 1910 figures.
[11] Differences in rent play a greater role in determining location within countries —for example, as between cities and villages or within cities.
[12] Black, *Production Economics*, p. 945.

may take this to indicate that the quantity of natural resources and capital per farm worker was lowest in Japan and that it increased as a country was placed lower down on the table. Compare these figures with those of farm wages in the preceding table; it is evident that farm wages rise as the quantity of cooperating factors increases. This must be a causal relationship and not a mere coincidence.[13]

There can be little doubt that the quantity of capital and natural resources per worker in manufacturing industries also differs widely in different countries. Besides, the number of laborers of a technical and organizing sort per hundred manual workers is much higher in certain countries than in others. For these and other reasons the quantity of output per manual worker in certain industries, such as coal, iron, cotton, and window glass,[14] tells very little as to differences in the quality and effectiveness of the manual laborers in various countries. It is certain, however, that such differences exist, although there is no possibility of comparing their direct economic importance.

The best illustration is probably obtained from the cost accounts of firms producing similar articles in many different countries. In most cases the result of cost comparisons is that even substantial wage differences lead to surprisingly small differences in costs per unit produced, in spite of the fact that the technical equipment is almost the same in all the factories. An American firm that puts out a standardized article obtained the following wage and cost figures (in dollars per unit) a few years after World War I.[15]

Costs	United States	England	Germany	Italy	France	Belgium
Wages	$.05½	.02½	.02¼	.00¾	.01	.01
Costs incl. wages	$.20	.20	.18	.14	.12½	.12

As interest and depreciation costs probably differ only slightly, the wage differences in this case lead to substantial differences in wage expenses per unit, although by no means of the same relative magnitude.

Corresponding sets of figures, such as those compiled by the General Motors Company factories, confirm the impression that wage differences are larger than the differences in usefulness of manual labor under equal conditions of production. It would be rash to draw conclusions as to production in general from a small number of rather

[13] One must not expect complete correlation, for the quality of land, transfer conditions, etc., are different. As it is doubtful whether wages were really higher in Germany than in Scandinavia, the only important exception to the expected relation is that wages were higher in the United States than in Australia and Argentina.

[14] Cf. Taussig, *International Trade*, Chap. xv.

[15] These figures were obtained from the firm and have not been formerly printed.

special industries, but such figures give some support to the view that the actual wage differences are to a great extent due to other circumstances than differences in the quality of manual labor, e.g., to the equipment of other productive factors, transfer conditions, etc.

§ 4. *Why the commodity price level is higher in the United States than in Europe.* To return to international differences in commodity price levels, consider the causes of a high price level in a special case: the United States. Why, for example, is this country usually regarded as more "expensive" than Europe?

First of all, international goods are more expensive in the United States than in most European countries. The cause lies not in the greater cost of inward transportation compared with outward transportation, but simply in the high tariff wall. The latter tends to raise not only import prices but also the prices of productive factors, and thus it cannot fail to heighten home market prices. Moreover, a highly protected home market in many cases leads to exportation at dumping prices, which makes prices on some American goods lower in a country such as Great Britain than in the home country.

Protection is, however, only partly responsible for high prices in the United States. Even without protection their general level, measured by ordinary wholesale price indices, would certainly be higher there than in Europe. The supply of factors of production in these two parts of the world is such as to raise relative prices of home market commodities higher in the United States.

The United States is a country having great natural resources and a relatively meager population, measured by European standards. Labor must be regarded as the relatively abundant factor of production in Europe and the relatively scanty one in America. This is true of common labor, both skilled and unskilled. Highly qualified labor with a capacity for organization and technical leadership is less rare in the United States than in Europe, owing to differences in opportunities and training, the customs of society, and the rapid development of economic life. There is at present in the United States a greater wealth of certain types of organizers and technical leaders. In industries where the gifts of nature, such as wheatland and copper mines, together with the type of labor just mentioned are vital factors, American industry has been most successful. Practically all the important export industries belong to this group. In spite of high wages for common labor they have been able to produce as cheaply as or more cheaply than other countries, deriving advantage from the rich supply of nature's gifts and human talent for organization. Dependent to a high degree upon natural resources are such commodities as wheat, cotton, and metals; dependent rather upon administrative talent are machines, automobiles, and possibly films.

Among the home market industries are some that for the same reasons produce rather cheaply, requiring large quantities of the relatively abundant and cheap factors. The cotton-spinning, weaving, and boot and shoe industries are among those dependent upon technical labor; the fruit-growing industry depends chiefly upon a rich supply of natural resources. Yet some goods and services need above all common labor, skilled or unskilled. Most personal services belong to this class, as well as such high quality goods as tailor-made clothing, glass, and furniture. To this group belong most of the products from industries where standardization and mass production play a small part. These commodities are much more expensive in the United States than in Europe.

Retail distribution is another large and expensive group of services that makes little use of automatic machinery. Like restaurant and hotel services, they are on the whole dearer than in Europe.

In Europe, goods requiring large quantities of common labor are relatively cheap, for the simple reason that wages of common labor are so much lower. A great many home market goods and most of the personal services belong to this class. In particular, almost all goods and services bought by the wealthy class cost a great deal less in the Old World. This has much to do with the fact that on the whole the economies of large-scale production, which American manufacturers have been particularly able to make use of, count for less in home market industries than in export industries.

It thus appears that home market prices in the United States are higher than in European countries because of the relatively scanty supply of common labor.[16] A high level for wages usually goes hand in hand with a high commodity price level because wages are by far the most important cost element so far as home market goods and services are concerned.

It would be erroneous, however, to say that because high home market prices always follow high manual wages, the same is true of traded goods. Differences between two countries in the following four respects may well make prices higher in the country with the lower wage level: (1) the grade of labor may be different; (2) the prices and quantities of other productive factors used may differ; (3) interior transfer conditions may cause higher transportation costs; and (4) exterior transfer conditions may raise the price level of international goods. In addition, whether one finds home market prices high or low depends much upon the particular goods desired; and differences in the quality of commodities make clear-cut comparisons

---

[16] Abbreviated statements of this sort must not be taken to mean that one basic element can be considered except in relation to the others. The character of the relationship in the price system should be borne in mind.

impossible. Yet in the case of the United States none of these circumstances tends to depress the level of home market prices below the European level sufficiently to offset the influence of the high wage level[17] and the forbidding tariff wall.

One fact stands out: there is no simple relation between nominal wages and the level of home market prices in different countries. The relation between the prices of labor and other factors and the prices of commodities of all sorts must be described in terms of interrelated price systems.

§ 5. *Note on Ricardo and Senior.* Ricardo and Senior placed more emphasis than did Taussig[18] on costs of transport in explaining international differences in price levels.[19] A country secures a low price level if it obtains its gold dearly in terms of labor, for this means low money wages. High costs of transport for the country's export goods to the gold- or silver-producing countries make the prices of these goods at home lower than they would be if costs of transport were lower. Thus, high transportation costs mean low money wages and a low price level. However, countries close to the gold- or silver-producing countries and having good communication with them attain a high price level.[20]

It is clear that this analysis concerns countries that export the same sorts of goods and sell them to the gold-producing countries. Ricardo made the tacit assumption that the effectiveness of factors in production is the same, but Senior went further and examined the influence of differences in this respect,[21] leaving it to Taussig to discuss the different relative effectiveness in export and home market industries.

Other things being equal, high costs of transport for export goods certainly do make for low prices compared with other countries that can carry the same export goods more cheaply to the market. But the costs of transport to the gold-producing countries are irrelevant. Any country may obtain the gold it wants through indirect exchange, selling goods to other countries who in their turn sell to the gold-producing ones, obtain gold in payment, and send it to the first. From the point of view of international trade, gold is a commodity like all the others. Ricardo was right in stressing the influence of

---

[17] See the end § 5 below.

[18] Taussig, *International Trade* (1928).

[19] Ricardo, *Principles of Political Economy and Taxation,* ed. Gonner (London, 1925); Senior, *Lectures on the High Cost of Obtaining Money* (London, 1830).

[20] "In a country not possessing mines the value in gold and silver of all those commodities which are not subject of a monopoly [depends] on the gold and silver which can be obtained by exporting the result of a given quantity of labor at the current rate of profit." Senior, *Lectures,* p. 13.

[21] *Ibid.,* p. 11.

transfer conditions on relative price levels but gives an all too simple analysis of them.

§ 6. *Domestic price differences.* The relation between price conditions in various countries cannot be adequately described in terms of price levels or individual prices that refer to each country as a whole; prices in different districts within the same country differ considerably. In many cases such domestic differences are greater than the price differences between different countries, in spite of the fact that labor and capital are usually more mobile within countries than between them. Out-of-the-way districts tend to have low prices if the goods they send to other districts are difficult to transport. Regions with a very one-sided productive factor endowment tend to be expensive. The agglomeration of population has much to do with regional price conditions. All these and other factors have been analyzed in Part Three; it suffices to emphasize that it is an exaggerated simplification to assume in international price comparisons that price conditions are uniform throughout each country.

There is as little tendency for domestic as for international price differences to disappear. They are founded upon differences in the basic status quo and change only with these circumstances; and there is certainly no tendency for factor equipment and transfer facilities, or other basic elements, to become equal everywhere.

XV

Some Effects of Import Duties

§ 1. *On tariffs and the location of industry.* Like all other impediments to international trade, tariffs exercise a restricting influence.[1] The international division of production goes less far than it would under free trade. In each country industry becomes less specialized and more diversified. The price equalizing tendency of trade is thereby weakened. This is true both of commodity and factor prices. Greater international differences in commodity prices exist behind the shelter of tariff walls. In each country demand for the relatively scarce factors is increased and demand for the relatively abundant factors is reduced. The character and location of industry is adapted to the conditions of productive equipment, transfer, and other basic elements in a different way.

Import duties, like other duties, affect transferability of commodities. The tariff problem is one aspect of the problem of changed transfer conditions, which affect the location of industry, nationally and internationally, and perhaps the distribution of labor and capital.

In some important respects this influence is different from that of other impediments to international trade. The costs of transport, for instance, are as a rule greater for raw materials than for the goods made from them, which obviously tends to restrict trade in raw materials. Import duties, however, are often relatively heavier on goods in later stages of manufacture and therefore tend to make raw materials move, so that their manufacture into finished goods takes place in the countries where they are consumed. Internationally, market location is favored over raw material location.

All countries seem to think it an advantage to produce a multiplicity of finished goods for themselves, even if suitable conditions are lacking, but are much less eager to produce a variety of raw materials. Even though the location of raw material industries is very little affected by protective duties on such materials, the indirect

[1] The analysis in this chapter is expressed chiefly in static terms, i.e., compares a given duty with conditions if it were increased, decreased, or eliminated. A more dynamic viewpoint is taken in Chap. XXI.

196

effects of other duties are considerable. Free trade countries are made to produce more of them because manufacturing is encouraged in countries with high protection.

Evidently countries with special facilities for the later stages of manufacture and countries specializing in food, also heavily taxed, are particularly sensitive to protection in foreign countries, which tends to reduce the demand from abroad for the very services that they are best qualified to render. For instance, protection affects the location of the mechanical industries much more than that of coal and copper mining. Although countries with plenty of natural resources clearly feel the effects of a protectionist policy of this sort abroad less than others, it is also clear that the attracting power of such resources for industries at later stages of production is considerably reduced.

Because international trade is largely handled by sea transport, countries with great shipping industries are also affected by protection. However, it is uncertain whether protection causes an increase or reduction in demand for shipping services.

§ 2. *On imports and exports.* In a protectionist country the ability of certain industries to charge much higher prices more than compensates for the increased expenses of production through higher prices of raw materials, higher nominal wages,[2] etc. Such industries profit from protection and expand accordingly. Others, however, are incompletely compensated for increased costs, and the export industries are generally not compensated at all.

Different firms have quite different costs of production. Low cost firms, which would be able to supply a part of the home market needs without protection, expand somewhat behind the tariff walls, but for reasons mentioned in Chapter XII there are limits to this expansion. Firms with somewhat higher costs are able to compete, but there may still be room for importation from other countries. In the export industries the low cost firms continue to export in spite of the handicap of increased costs, but certain firms with higher costs drop out of the market. For goods difficult to transport the exporting industries may continue to hold that part of the foreign markets most easily accessible but relinquish the markets that can only be supplied at the price of heavy transportation charges.[3]

Evidently both imports and exports are reduced. How much they decline depends on the slope of the domestic supply curves[4] in pro-

[2] The influence of protection on the prices of the factors of production is discussed later.
[3] It is not necessary to repeat here why differences in the quality of the articles and other circumstances also lead to lasting divisions of national markets.
[4] Their character is governed not only by the factor equipment but also by the whole price system.

tected industries, the reaction of demand toward price increases, and the corresponding supply and demand reactions abroad.

From a short-term point of view, the object of the duty is only to make possible a full utilization of capacity and a consequent reduction in costs per unit. The possibility of increasing exports in this way cannot be denied. Duties may enable growing firms quickly to reach the size where full economies of large-scale production are enjoyed and exportation is rendered feasible. In both cases, however, the same result can be reached in other ways. The increase in exports is almost certain to be slight and temporary compared to what it would be under free trade; the percentage of capacity used will fall after the next period of good general business conditions and expansion; the foreign firms driven out of the protected market will turn with greater energy to other markets to which the protected industry used to export. Therefore, this intensified competition can in many cases result in reduced instead of increased exportation.

In the long run—barring the case of "educating duties" that increase the national income—exports from protected industries are reduced. That *total* exportation is reduced when imports are restricted through tariffs is obvious for the simple reason that in the long run imports pay for exports.[5]

§ 3. *On national income.* It follows from the analysis in Chapter XIII of the effect of trade obstacles on the national income that duties, like other obstacles to international trade, reduce the national income and thus in a certain sense cause a loss. It may be useful to demonstrate this more clearly. The ordinary argument that a greater quantity of labor or "productive power" is used to produce protected goods than would be necessary to produce export goods to pay for their import is not conclusive, since the proportions in which the productive factors are used in the different industries are different. Furthermore, relative factor prices, thus the combination of the factors, are changed by protection. The case should be put another way. If a free trade country applies a new duty to encourage domestic production of a certain commodity *a* at a cost 50 percent higher than the import price, then the loss is approximately 50 percent of what the import value would have been. If a number of other duties have already been introduced, the level of factor prices will have increased, and the commodity *a* will cost not 50 but, say, 90 percent more to produce than to import.[6] Thus, reasoning at the "margin of protec-

---

[5] Except in the rare cases where other items in the balance of payments are considerably affected for a long period. See Chaps. XVI and XXI.

[6] If *e* is increased factor prices as a percentage of costs of production, the actual cost when only one duty is introduced will be $(50 + e)$ percent after the duty has been in force a certain period of time.

tion" gives a higher figure for the loss from each individual duty. Yet if the "free trade margin losses" are added up, a figure for the quantity of productive factors "lost" through protection is obtained, which is not increased by the rise in the general level of factor prices through the tariff wall. This figure is a minimum expression for the total loss, which corresponds approximately to the figure for the total loss obtained by a calculation of the index of available goods, using free trade commodity prices as weights. If prices in the state of protection are used as weights, the figure for the loss becomes greater. Which system of weighting should be used depends upon the special aspect of the question one has in mind. It may be quite as natural to use the situation in a state of protection for a basis as to use the free trade position. The latter is in most countries much affected by state interference of different sorts, e.g., taxation, and by trade unions, monopolies, etc.[7]

This analysis has not accounted for the fact that in certain cases the terms of trade are changed by the duties, usually to the advantage of the protectionist country, and that this gain may more than offset the above-mentioned tendency toward a loss. However, as later analysis will demonstrate, it is not probable that any country can gain much in this way. The slight changes in terms of trade are likely to mean no more than a reduction of the loss that would otherwise fall on the protectionist countries, and an increase of the loss accruing to outside countries.[8] In any case, the duties reduce the combined incomes of the countries concerned.

Although the "division of the total gain" from international trade has little real meaning, there is evidently some justification for asking how the loss from trade restrictions is divided between trading nations. It seems artificial, however, to portray first a certain loss to the world, and then its division. In reality there is no such division. There is a reduction of the index of available goods in each country,

---

[7] The existence of labor groups, between which the flow is restricted through monopolistic measures, may be an argument not only for temporary protection (see Manoilesco, *The Theory of Protection and International Trade* [London, 1930], and Ohlin, "Protection and Noncompeting Groups," *Weltw. Archiv*, 1930), but also for long-lasting protection, if the monopolistic measures are long-lasting, on condition that the duties make the distribution of labor and production change in the direction it would have in the absence of the monopolistic policy. This fact has been ignored in the orthodox theory.

[8] Barone-Staehle (*Grundzüge der Theoretischen Nationalökonomie* [Bonn, 1927], §§ 93-97) expresses the opinion that a country may gain from protection if considerable and frequent fluctuations in world market prices would lead to corresponding shifts in demand during free trade and thus to losses on fixed capital, which one cannot transfer from one industry to another. Closer analysis of the problem, however, shows that this can be so only if and when the firms refuse to produce and sell at prices that cover the variable expenses. For certain aspects of this question see Chap. XXI, § 6.

caused by the shift of production as well as by changes in trade terms.[9] These changes will be analyzed in Chapter XXI. At present it is assumed that no considerable variations in these terms take place.

The loss of national income as a result of protection is relatively much greater for some countries than for others. Tariffs split markets into smaller ones; industry must therefore be carried on in smaller productive units. This is true of all countries. Industries produce exclusively for the home market when under free trade they would also manufacture for export; and goods which would otherwise be imported are produced at home on a small scale. In a word, tariffs discourage large-scale production,[10] most of all in small countries. Large nations can produce most goods in big units in any case. Corroborative statistics are abundant; in the United States (in 1923) 40 percent of the workers were employed in factories with a staff of 500 or more, whereas the corresponding figure in Switzerland, a small manufacturing country, was 20 percent.

Small countries consequently lose relatively more because protection causes an inefficient organization of industry. If an industry cannot achieve sufficient scale by exporting at once, all attempts to start it will fail. This is not so in countries where the home market is large enough to support one or more firms of adequate size; in that case it is relatively easy to build up firms with sufficient strength to take care of the export trade. In other words, freer trade would be of particular benefit to small countries.

§ 4. *On distribution of income.* The question how protection affects the real income of various classes in society is important from the point of view of economic policy. Unfortunately, it can only be analyzed in general terms. The money prices of productive factors tend to rise (although some may fall slightly), but commodity prices also rise. The real income of an individual is moved upward if his income rises more than the prices of the commodities he buys.

Consider first the manufacturing laborer. His real wage is most likely to increase if protection is given to industries that use excep-

[9] It is incorrect to say that there is a loss from less efficient production in each country, which is increased or reduced by changes in the terms of trade. It is not at all certain that protection reduces the volume of *production* if the volume index uses as weights the commodity prices in the state of protection. This was pointed out to me by Professor Myrdal. As a matter of fact, it is the volume of available goods (including imports) and not the volume of production in an individual country that is of interest.

[10] It is conceivable in special cases that an import duty might increase the size of a certain industry, which would exist anyhow, and thus give it some advantages of large-scale production. It is improbable, however, that these external advantages would be so large as to make the extra production a cheaper way of procuring the commodity than by importation. In my opinion Graham makes far too much of the theoretical possibility. See his article "Some Aspects of Protection Further Considered," *Quarterly Journal of Economics,* Feb. 1923.

tionally large quantities of labor and produce goods of little importance in a worker's budget. Freer trade in such a case would reduce the standard of living of the manufacturing laboring class. If manufacturing and agricultural laborers form two noncompeting groups, protection of manufacturing industries may raise the real wages of its workers at the expense of agricultural laborers. It is wrong, however, to assert that the country as a whole may get a lower income if protection is given up; this is possible only under special conditions (see § 3 above).[11]

Questions of this sort have been curiously neglected in economic literature.[12] One of the few economists to touch upon them—and along lines similar to mine—is Professor Cassel, who discusses the following case.[13] A scantily populated country in which gold production is the important industry decides upon protection of its agricultural products. Factors of production tend in general to get higher prices, especially those that are in relatively greater demand than before, namely, labor and agricultural land. However, the value of factors used principally in the gold industry, which are in a relatively less advantageous position, may drop substantially. Such is the case with capital and the gold mines. In agriculture, labor is offered higher wages than before. Wages rise then in the gold industry, a part of it becomes unprofitable, and the working of certain mines is terminated. Concomitant with this reduction of gold production is a drop in the value of the mines. As demand for capital is reduced, the rate of interest also tends to fall.

Commodity prices naturally rise, except the price of gold and perhaps of some goods requiring exceptionally great proportions of capital. Professor Cassel nevertheless thinks that real wages may now be higher than before the introduction of protection. This would be the case, so far as I can see, only under very special conditions. As workers buy much of the agricultural products and little gold, the higher prices of the former work to their disadvantage. Even though other goods the workers buy may not rise much in price, an increase of real wages assumes that nominal wages rise at least as much as agricultural prices.

It seems beyond doubt that the tariff policy pursued in the early

---

[11] See Nicholson, *Principles of Political Economy,* II, pp. 315 ff.

[12] International trade theory has in my opinion given far too much attention to the effects of certain variations, such as those of duties, on national incomes and too little attention to their effects on individual incomes. National incomes, however, are not units to be divided but sums of individual incomes. In many cases changes in the sums count for very little, but changes in the individual incomes are distinctly relevant. For a similar opinion, see Cannan, "Was der allgemeinen Wirtschaftstheorie gegenwärtig Not tut," *Die Wirtschaftstheorie der Gegenwart* (Vienna, 1928), Vol. IV.

[13] Cassel, *Theoretische sozialökonomie* (Leipzig, 1927), § 87.

1900's did not raise the standard of living of the laboring classes. It is doubtful if agricultural duties increased the relative scarcity of manual labor compared with other factors, and they certainly raised the cost of living for the working classes. In Switzerland import duties were calculated to have raised the cost of food by 12 percent.[14]

It is true, however, that manufacturing duties tend to depress the rent of farm land. Some sources of raw materials for manufacturing industries probably increase in value, whereas others decrease. It is likely that the sum total of rent is reduced in countries with high manufacturing duties. In free trade countries, of course, the foreign manufacturing duties affect rents in the opposite way. But in most countries the sum of rents is small compared with the sum of wages to manual workers. Even a substantial reduction of rents brings only a slight increase in wages.

The effect of manufacturing duties upon the relative scarcity of labor and capital is rather to the advantage of the latter, although lack of statistical material prevents reliable conclusions. It seems probable, however, that manufacturing industries in Europe require a greater amount of capital per laborer than does agriculture. Therefore, a shift in production from agriculture to manufacturing in Europe would mean a relative increase in the demand for capital and a rise in the rate of interest.

One must conclude that the share of the laboring class in the national income was not increased by the tariff policy around 1900 sufficiently to offset the depressing effect of that policy on the national income. On the contrary, free trade seems to be in the interest of the working classes. Certainly the poorest classes benefited when Great Britain turned to free trade in the middle of the last century. They obtained a double advantage from (1) the tendency toward increased scarcity of manual labor at the expense of land and (2) the marked cheapening of imported goods, of which they were large consumers.

The chances of an improved standard of living for certain small protected groups are much greater than for the laboring class as a whole. Protection may favor them at the expense of other labor groups, and perhaps of capital and natural resources. Skilled workers in the United States, for instance, may profit from protection. The gap between skilled and unskilled wages in this country is unusually large, which is no doubt partly due to the inflow of unskilled immigrant labor, which tends to depress the remuneration of this factor. The relatively high expenses incurred as soon as skilled labor is employed would tend to limit industries that use much of this factor if protection did not prevent competition from foreign industries

[14] Reichlin, "Die Zollbelastung der schweizerischen Lebenshaltungskosten," *Zeitschrift für schweizerische Statistik und Volkwirtschaft* (1925).

with lower costs of production. As a matter of fact, among American manufacturing industries more or less dependent upon tariff protection, a large place is taken by those producing high quality goods (textiles, shoes) and using much skilled labor. The tariff, therefore, increases the demand for this factor and tends to keep its remuneration on a higher level than under free trade.

> It is among the characteristics of our general industrial conditions that the gap between the wages of skilled and unskilled is greater than in other countries. The mechanic, the craftsman, the man of quick eye and deft hand, gets an unusually high rate of pay . . . Any industry which calls for such men must pay wages at the current rates; and if it cannot secure from them results commensurable to the pay, and if its products are subject to foreign competition, it "needs" protection and clamors for it. Precisely this seems to be the case in the woolen manufacture.[15]

If the skilled workers are favored by the American tariff, the owners of natural resources are almost certainly put in a less favorable position. The rise in nominal wages that is the inevitable outcome of such extensive protection lowers the prices of other factors used in export industries. Agricultural land and mineral resources, such as copper, belong to this category.

The chances of favoring manufacturing laborers at the expense of farmers and landowners are particularly good in countries that export agricultural products. High duties on finished manufactures in a country like Denmark, for instance, would probably raise nominal wages in manufacturing industries but would not greatly increase the costs of living of the working population. They might raise real wages of manufacturing laborers while seriously depressing the standard of living of the farming population.[16]

§ 5. *On the supply of productive factors.* Protection tends to change the relative scarcity of factors to a considerable degree, at least if the duties are high. The effect of protection, therefore, consists to a large extent in the changes brought about in the supply of productive factors.[17]

When new duties are imposed or old ones increased, certain industries expand and increase their demand for labor. The situation becomes favorable for a trade union policy tending to raise wages. Although at the same time labor flows from other occupations and

---

[15] Taussig, *Some Aspects of the Tariff Question,* p. 359.

[16] Comments on the effects of the Swedish tariff—based on figures computed by the Swedish Tariff Commission—may be found in the original edition of this book.

[17] This question has been analyzed along similar lines in Professor Heckscher's "The Effect of Foreign Trade on the Distribution of Income" and in my own *Theory of Trade,* as well as in Cassel's *Theoretische sozialökonomie.* Building chiefly on Cassel, Dr. Mackenroth, then a student in Stockholm, presented a similar analysis in "Zollpolitik und Produktionsmittelversogung," *Weltw. Archiv* (1929).

young people turn to the expanding trades, the unions may succeed in maintaining a somewhat higher wage level than formerly, relative to wages elsewhere. In other words, the supply of labor of the quality needed may fail to adapt itself completely to the new conditions.

In many European countries industries insensitive to foreign competition pay higher wages than industries which feel that competition more directly. If the tariff is increased, some industries move to the former group, and the chances of raising wages in them are considerable. The experience of Australia after World War I offers numerous examples of this. In most countries, however, protection is not so high that the protected industries fail to feel foreign competition. On the contrary, duties are often raised because and when these industries have difficulties,[18] so as to offset the advantages of foreign competitors while leaving a certain amount of competition between them and domestic firms.

In the case of noncompeting groups of a more permanent kind—such as skilled and unskilled manufacturing labor—the reaction of labor supply if protection raises the reward to one group is necessarily slow. Yet in the long run it may be considerable. Take, for instance, the case of skilled labor in the United States. Protection not only increases the demand for it and its market price but also the opportunities for acquiring training and experience. A much greater number of people get a chance to join its ranks. Probably the number gifted by nature with the necessary qualities for such work is great. It is not certain, therefore, that the relation between wages of skilled and unskilled labor is in the long run changed by protection much to the advantage of the former. It is even possible that the flexibility of supply is so great as to make only temporary changes in the scale of remuneration necessary to induce people to undergo the required training, in which case the old wage ratio returns. As a matter of fact, supply reactions, once started, may go even further and cause a relative decline in skilled wages.

Since World War I manufacturing and agricultural laborers in many countries have formed two fairly noncompeting groups because excessive unemployment in the factories has discouraged farm laborers, in spite of the much higher wages. The high tariff in countries like Canada and Australia seems to have been effective in raising the demand for manufacturing workers and their corresponding reward, while exercising a depressing influence on real wages in agriculture by raising the costs of manufactured products and of transportation. Unemployment, trade union policy, and immigration of farm labor

[18] The effects of duties of course differ to some extent according to the business situation existing when they are imposed. A special analysis of the tariff problem would have to give much attention to such dynamic circumstances.

have so far prevented an adjustment of labor supply that would restore the old scale of wages.

The most direct influence of protection is exercised on the supply of so-called technical or organizing labor. The quality of such labor needed in one industry differs from that required in others. By stimulating the growth of certain industries, the tariff encourages education and training for the technical labor required. In many cases, however, the technical labor is more specialized in certain directions, but its total supply is not increased. The so-called "infant industry argument" is based largely on the fact that the necessary qualities of technical and skilled labor are created. Note that successful experiments of this sort do not with any certainty imply a gain. The "educated" industry should be able not only to stand on its own legs but also to repay the indirect support it has received through protection in its youth. Even then it is doubtful whether the effect is more than to turn a certain amount of technical labor—inventive and organizing ability—into other channels than would have been the case under free trade. If it had not gone to the protected industries, it would in industrialized countries have been used in other industries— and probably to as good effect. Insofar as concentration means increased efficiency, the effect would have been still more marked.

For the education of technical skill to represent a gain from protection, it must be such that the total quantity of skilled and technical labor is increased and the quality of labor is improved. This may occur when a "new" country introduces protection for manufacturing industries. It attracts the labor force in a technical direction rather than toward agriculture. At the same time the opportunities for acquiring the qualities called for are much increased. It is therefore uncertain whether after a period of transition the reward to technical labor is relatively higher than before the imposition of the duties. But the quantity of such labor may be much increased, which may conceivably mean a greater national income if its wages are higher than those of agricultural labor.

It is even possible that the sum of the various national incomes— world income—may rise. Education that improves the quality of labor can, of course, increase incomes. Since protection is one way of educating labor under given circumstances, it may, although involving some misapplication of productive energy, be worth what it costs and more.

The situation differs considerably between old and new manufacturing countries. The effect of protection on the quality of labor is probably greater, the more primitive is the stage of industrial development, after a definite level has been reached. The "infant industry argument" should be called instead the "infant country argu-

ment." This influence on the quality of labor may in the long run
be far and away the most important aspect of protection. Friedrich
List had in mind something of this sort when he said that the wealth-
creating forces are more important than wealth itself. Future incomes
may be greatly increased if present incomes are somewhat reduced
and wealth-creating forces are thereby developed.

In countries that have reached a certain standard of industrial
development, having passed the "infant" state, there seems to be
little chance of improving the quality of labor, in particular of increasing the supply of technical labor. On the contrary, the custom
in some protectionist countries of meeting all industrial difficulties
with tariff increases—making the tariff a "sleeping cushion"—cannot but
prevent the invigorating influence of serious competition from exercising its favorable influence upon quality.

It is evidently impossible to prophesy how labor will react toward
changes in the scale of reward and other circumstances brought
about by protection. And the influence of tariff policy upon the
growth of population is absolutely unpredictable, for which reason
it has heretofore been assumed to be nonexistent. The difficulties
are not much less in analyzing the reaction of capital supply to changes
in the rate of interest brought about by protection. These reactions
are probably similar to those that occur when the interest rate
changes for other reasons, so that the reader may refer to the analysis
given in Chapter VII. However, if a change in the distribution of
income, to the advantage of the capitalist and at the cost of relatively
lower wages, leads to increased savings (which seems rather likely
to happen), labor will in the long run benefit more or less from a
tendency to increased scarcity. Changes in the total supply of labor
and capital due to international movements of these factors because
of tariff policy have been omitted from the analysis so far and will
be dealt with in the next chapter.

Finally, it should be observed that the reaction of factor supply to
protection takes time. The effects of protection in this respect differ
at different periods. The first three or four years will certainly see
changes in the relative incomes of different factors of production,
with no change in relative supply. After a decade or two supply
reactions will probably be so important that their character will dominate the situation and determine whether or not one factor maintains an improved position relative to the other. As supply reactions
grow even more uncertain with the passage of time, it is impossible
to forecast the effects of protection on the distribution of income
and the supply of industrial agents a half-century later.

§ 6. *On interior location.* So far the effects of tariff policy on the
location of industry *within* countries have not been considered. Interior local differences in price conditions as affected by protection

have also been disregarded and will be discussed in Chapter XXI. As to the former phenomenon, it is obvious that if a country chooses to impose a tariff of some significance, the location of industry will be affected: some industries are stimulated, others are retarded. There is no reason to assume that those stimulated will be located in the same way as the others. Export industries tend to locate near good transfer facilities to other countries, e.g., close to good ports. Market-located home market industries, however, which may well expand owing to protection at the expense of export industries, locate to a large extent in the interior of the country. Protection may thus move industry away from the coastal districts to those in the interior.

Even among home market industries or industries producing goods that are also imported, the effects of protection are distinct and various. The Swedish Tariff Commission in its final report of 1924 furnished evidence indicating that the Swedish tariff favored agriculture in the South and checked it in the North. Grain was cultivated almost exclusively in the southern district because farmers in the North, who worked in the forests during the winter, were unable to produce enough even for their own consumption. They did not, therefore, derive any advantage from the duties on grain. The duties on animal food, however, were low and largely ineffective. It seems probable that in most countries the tariff wall leads to a redistribution of national wealth among geographical districts. Space does not allow further analysis of this problem, which is analogous to that of tariff unions and preferential duties.[19]

Protection abroad must also influence location within the country. Foreign tariff walls change the transfer relations with foreign markets, acting very much as expensive breaks in the journey. Given certain raw material supply sources, such changes cannot but affect the location of manufacturing industries. The location of raw material production may be influenced as well. Foreign tariffs also cause home market industries to expand at the expense of export industries. The raising of many tariff walls since World War I has tended to retard the British export industries located principally in the North, and to stimulate home market industries, which tend to settle in the South.[20]

Such variations cause an adaptation of interior transport facilities, which in turn paves the way for a changed location. A closer analysis of such problems falls outside the scope of this book. The above suffices to indicate that in specific cases an important part of the effect of protection may be a change in the interior location of industry.

[19] See H. G. Brown, *International Trade and Exchange* (New York, 1914), V, § 6.
[20] During 1924-26 the number of persons insured under the Unemployment Insurance Acts increased by 11.6 percent in southern England, as compared with 5.2 percent in the Midlands, 2.6 percent in the northeastern district, and 3.4 percent in the northwestern district.

XVI

International Capital and Labor Movements

§ 1. *Incentives and obstacles.* The circumstances that encourage or obstruct international labor and capital movements should be dealt with first. To begin with labor, its international mobility is reduced by all the ties that unite a citizen with his native land and its culture. The inevitable uncertainty as to his fortunes in a new country also tends to keep him from emigrating, especially if he is temperamentally disinclined to undertake risks. As Adam Smith wrote, "Man is of all sorts of luggage the most difficult to be transported."

The obstacles to emigration thus differ greatly among countries, as does the ease with which immigration may be accomplished. Racial kinship exercises a great influence. There are, for instance, few Italians and Greeks in the British Empire and few British in South America. Similarity of political and cultural institutions tends to affect the streams of migration in an analogous manner. Discriminatory immigration legislation also retards the influx of people of different races and with very different institutions. Since World War I almost all countries have been regulating immigration in some way, generally exercising a restrictive influence.

Nevertheless, the lust for adventure may lead enterprising youths to make their way in countries where conditions are less settled than in their own. A failure of some sort may lead them to try a new country rather than to continue at home under the handicap that failure often imposes. Inferior or restrictive political or religious institutions have in some cases made people move to countries where greater liberty obtains.

Migration movements vary from one time to another as well. Waves of migration rise and fall for a variety of reasons. When emigration has once started, its organization improves. Knowledge of conditions in the receiving country is increased through such avenues as letters to relatives in the old country. The stimulus to migration may thus grow stronger, while deterrent psychological factors may diminish in importance. After some years, the receiving regions may begin to fill up, so that no free land is available, for instance. Migration then becomes less alluring, and the wave recedes.

Cyclical variations in business conditions also cause variations in international labor movements. Excessive unemployment in the receiving countries is a powerful deterrent. An analysis of the variations in immigration into the United States brings out clearly the fact that good business conditions lead to high immigration figures. The experience of Argentina is also pertinent. During the nineties the policy of monetary deflation brought poor business conditions. At the same time the net immigration fell from 885,000 in the preceding decade to 397,000, only to rise again to 1,177,000 in the first decade of this century, when good business conditions prevailed. In Brazil the inflation and good business conditions of 1887-98 brought immigration to an annual figure of 83,000, as against 24,000 in the six preceding years. During the following period of deflation, 1899-1905, it fell again to 55,000.

Seasonal economic variations also lead to seasonal migrations back and forth. Each year Belgians and Spaniards work for a few months in French vineyards. Before World War I, Germany used to receive almost a million farm laborers each summer, chiefly from Poland.

Economic conditions in the emigrant countries seem to exercise much less influence on migration. Only in times of exceptional economic crisis is any increase of emigration noticeable. The "pull" is stronger than the "push." [1] The fact that labor movements react so readily to changing conditions is of importance in a study of variations in international trade.[2]

On the whole, people migrate because they expect an improvement in their economic position. Emigration goes from low-wage countries to high-wage countries. This does not mean, however, that the poorest countries have supplied the greatest number of emigrants. Great poverty is often an obstacle to migration because it prevents the accumulation of funds to defray the necessary expenses.

One important qualification must be made. Laborers are interested in real wages or real incomes rather than nominal wages or incomes. The standard of living, not the sum of money obtained, is of consequence. As costs of living differ considerably from one country to another, money incomes may well be higher in one of them than in others without the standard of living being higher. It is even conceivable that this standard could be higher in a country where money wages are lower. Consequently, labor would migrate from the latter country to the former. Nevertheless, the standard of living concept is open to serious criticism owing to its elasticity, particularly in international comparisons. Simple statements concerning real incomes do

---

[1] See Jerome, *Migration and Business Cycles* (New York, 1926).
[2] On the whole, the aspects of international trade concerned with the business cycle are left out of account in this book.

not give a much more adequate explanation of migrations than do statements in terms of money incomes.

Fortunately such difficulties are negligible in this investigation. As a matter of fact, the important labor movements have always been from countries with low money incomes to countries with higher ones. It thus appears that where nominal wages and incomes are high, real wages and incomes are also as a rule higher than they are in countries with lower nominal figures. Since I do not here attempt a general treatment of international labor and capital movements, I shall ignore the difficulties involved in a precise terminology and reason from the fact that labor moves from countries where its monetary reward is low to places where it is higher.

To turn now to the circumstances that govern international capital movements, the most important stimulus to export and import of capital is certainly differences in the rate of interest. Countries where the rate of interest is low find it profitable to export capital to countries where the rate is high. Often, however, capital movements may not be explained wholly in this way: other elements enter in. The chief explanation of the ease with which before World War I Russian state bonds could be sold abroad, mainly in France, lay in the higher rates of interest in Russia. But if it had not been for the political harmony between France and Russia, it is doubtful whether these capital movements would have been so extensive. Certainly the propaganda conducted by French banks in favor of Russian bonds, with the consent and approval of the French government, in addition to the higher Russian rate of interest helped to sell these bonds. The importance of such political considerations should not be ignored: by prejudicing the market in favor of the borrowers, state institutions may decisively influence the flow of capital. The result is that important movements may take place between two countries although the difference in the rate of interest is not greater than that between the lending country and a third to which there is no such movement. Great Britain, for instance, favors investments in other parts of the British Empire. The Colonial Stock Acts make the national debts of the Dominions trustee investments in the United Kingdom on certain conditions.[3]

Among circumstances other than political regulations that affect international capital transactions is the natural preference of capitalists for a diversity of investments. This may lead to important capital movements, even between countries that have the same interest level. Investment trusts in particular attempt to spread their capital over securities in such a way as to reduce the risks, and partly

[3] Hawtrey, *The Economic Problem*, p. 281. See also Viner, "Political Aspects of International Finance," *The Journal of Business Economics* (Chicago, 1928).

for this reason they buy foreign securities as well as domestic. Such trusts have been important instruments for the exportation of British capital.

Another important element is the policy of establishing branch offices and factories abroad, which is resorted to increasingly by manufacturing firms. Capital comes in most cases from the home country of the firm concerned. Tariff policies that place obstacles in the way of international trade have in many cases induced firms to establish production in the protected country. The superiority of American industry in the production of cheap automobiles and the high import duties on cars in most countries led the Ford Motor Company and other automobile firms to establish branch factories in Europe. Therefore, instead of trading goods, a country may both import and export capital.

As with the establishment of branch factories, a desire to guarantee the supply of foreign raw materials through a controlling interest in the industries producing them has led to considerable foreign investment, e.g., in the production of iron ore, copper ore, and oil. The manufacturers of electrical machinery have similarly found it profitable to secure control of electrical power companies all over the world in order to ensure the obtaining of orders.

The establishment of great international enterprises does not, however, invariably cause capital to leave the firm's home country. Firms such as the Dutch Shell Company and the Swedish Match Company, with branches in a dozen countries, find it easy to borrow capital in different countries, wherever the rate of interest is low. This means simply that capital is exported from countries with a low rate of interest—a circumstance that has already been considered.

During some periods the opportunity to make substantial profits by placing capital in new countries has served as an even more powerful inducement to foreign investments than have interest differences; many foreign shares are bought and new companies are created for this reason. The investment of capital in Russian industries by a great number of European countries during the 1920's and 1930's is not to be explained solely by the higher rate of interest in Russia; the important factor was the possibility of a rapid economic development in that country, with consequent high profits. The same was true of a considerable part of English and American investment in railroads and new industries in South America during the early 1900's. Such export of capital is usually irregular, assuming enormous proportions during boom periods and then ceasing abruptly.

A good illustration of the difference between export of capital for extraordinary profits and that caused by interest differences is the flow of capital from Great Britain to the United States while the latter country was exporting hundreds of millions of dollars to Canada. The flow of capital between Great Britain and the United States in the decades before World War I was almost wholly caused by the difference in the rate of interest. Investments in American railroad bonds were more remunerative than corresponding investments in Great Britain. At the same time the interest rate in Canada was not much higher than that in the United States, but Canada offered distinct possibilities for American enterprise and technique. Large profits were to be reaped by placing capital in Canadian industries and giving them the advantage of experienced American leadership.

A special sort of profit is obtained by investing in foreign countries to evade high domestic taxation. After World War I, in particular, much capital was exported for this reason from Germany and probably also from France and Great Britain. Switzerland and Holland received large portions of it.

There are also circumstances that retard international capital movements; otherwise considerable international interest differences could not exist. For instance, many states put special obstacles in the way of an export of capital. Heavy stamp duties on foreign issues in France after World War I checked the French export of capital. The temporary British embargo on foreign loans reduced foreign investments from £153,000,000 in 1923 to £63,000,000 in 1924, and to £28,000,000 in 1925. Other states, such as Italy, restricted the import of capital by political means.

The ordinary investor also prefers to put his money in things he knows something about, such as bonds or shares of companies, whose development he is, or thinks he is, able to follow. As he knows much more about his own country than about others, he is inclined to export his capital only if stimulated by a higher yield. To him foreign investments seem more risky than domestic ones. His valuation of this extra risk governs his investment policy in the face of existing interest differences. It is possible that under certain conditions the risk may be estimated lower for foreign than for domestic investments. Such was the case in France during the years before the monetary stabilization, when the "flight from the franc" meant an important export of capital. As a rule, however, the risk is estimated to be greater when capital is invested abroad.[4] Such considerations tend to restrict the export of capital. They are similar to those that retard emigration.

Special types of capital movement are those due to absentee ownership. These include remittances from Great Britain to British people living in southern France and remittances by immigrants to their old countries.

---

[4] Note that many "international" securities are bought by capitalists in countries with widely different interest levels; this fact is partly owing to differences in the estimates of the risks involved.

Turn now from what may be called "long-term capital movements" to "short-term capital transactions." On the border line between the two are commercial credits given by exporting firms to their customers, chiefly in manufacturing industries. Goods are often sold against six months' credit. All countries that export manufactured goods have large amounts of such credit outstanding. They are only slightly affected by changes in interest levels.

Short-term transactions are usually speculative. Their object is to profit from expected variations in foreign exchange or from arbitrage in international securities between the leading stock exchanges. Capital also moves back and forth between different money markets in accordance with strictly temporary differences in short-term money rates. Such short-term capital movements play a decisive part in the maintenance of equilibrium in the balance of payments and are therefore discussed later. The discussion here concerns not the mechanism of trade variations but the mutual relationships of such movements and of international trade from a long-term point of view.

Finally, capital movements, like migrations, vary decidedly from one phase of the business cycle to another. They are affected by the state of trade in general. The largest capital movements occur during boom periods.

§ 2. *Economic causes.* Before passing to a more detailed analysis, I shall explain the necessity for international labor and capital movements. In so doing, I shall concentrate upon movements due chiefly to international wage and interest differences. These are sufficiently different to cause productive factors to move from one country to another because the basic elements of the price system—factor equipment and other conditions of production, demand conditions, and transfer facilities—differ internationally.

Labor and capital movements adapt the supply of these factors among countries to the differences in the supply of other factors, and to differences in demand and transfer conditions. Above all, they adapt to international differences in natural resources. Regions where nature is benevolent as a means of production or transport become thickly populated. In arid districts, for instance, population is much lower than in more humid regions. Railroad maps show a surprising degree of correlation with rainfall. Similarly, districts with irregular coastlines and navigable rivers and lakes are the homes of a much larger number of people than districts with inferior transport resources. The discovery of new natural resources and of new methods to utilize old ones will cause factors to move. New oil wells in Venezuela, for example, attracted American capital and technical labor during the first half of the century.

The supply of capital and labor also adjusts to tariffs and other obstacles to international trade, as well as to differences in the social conditions of production, the supply of technical labor, and the like. Were it not for the obstacles to international labor and capital movements, the distribution of productive factors would be even more rational from an economic viewpoint. No doubt, parts of the world now populated would be deserted, while others would lose and still others would gain inhabitants and capital.

The rest of this chapter deals with the influence of international labor and capital movements on their prices and on the volume and character of trade.[5] We shall also analyze the reactions to such movements when any of the basic elements change, particularly those that lead directly to variations in international trade.

§ 3. *Relation between international factor movements and international trade.* Any change in the economic system that affects the prices of the mobile productive factors may lead to international factor movements, provided the international difference in the factor prices is made great enough. In addition, a change in the mobility of the factors may also change their international movement, other things being equal.

Since factors move from countries where their prices are low to those where they are dear, their scarcity and reward in the former are increased, while their prices in the latter fall, unless there is some counteracting tendency.[6] International factor mobility tends to make prices more uniform between the countries concerned, just as do international movements of commodities. Since the exchange of goods is unable to bring about a complete equalization of factor prices, international differences remain and, if they are sufficiently large, call forth factor movements. International price equalization thus appears to be furthered either by both goods and factor movements or by the one that meets with the least resistance.

If the mobility of factors increases, a new transfer takes place, and the consequent increased harmony between their prices in different countries renders needless part of the former exchange of commodi-

---

[5] One aspect of international capital movements is left entirely out of account. When capital moves in the form of goods and services, such movements affect the mechanism of international trade. A study of this phenomenon is postponed until Part Five. The present discussion involves only the fact that a transfer of capital, like migration, changes the supply of the productive factors and thus the international distribution of production and trade. An increase in the quantity of capital in a country, whether brought about through borrowings abroad or domestic savings, tends to raise the prices of the other factors. Thus, the increase in the quantity of capital goods is relatively much less than the increase in the money value of these goods because part of the new capital "evaporates" into increased wages and rents. See Wicksell, *Vorlesungen über Nationalökonomie* (Jena, 1914), Vol. I.

[6] Export of capital tends to raise the rate of interest and thus to depress wages. If the wage level is temporarily fixed through wage agreements between employers and trade unions, unemployment is increased. This fact, which was important for a discussion of post-World War I economic problems, cannot be further analyzed here.

ties. However, a reduction in the costs of transport for commodities through improvements in the technique of transportation increases trade, and thus diminishes the need for international factor movements. Everything depends both upon the intensity of the reaction of factor prices and thereby factor movements when trade varies, and upon the intensity of the reaction of commodity prices and thereby trade when factor movements vary.

This preliminary analysis rests on the assumption that the national income in each country is about the same as it was before the factor movements. In progressive countries increases in the domestic supply of labor and capital lead to an expansion of output and incomes, which tends to increase international trade.

A more important qualification is that factor movements in only one direction increase the quantity of productive factors and the national income in the importer relative to the exporter. In such cases the influence of factor movements on the *character* of international trade conforms to the previous analysis, but its influence on the *volume* of such trade is uncertain. The tendency toward a reduction of trade may be counteracted by a tendency to increased trade if the national income is increased in a small country.[7] Trade between Great Britain and Australia would grow if a few million British people and much capital moved to the latter. But trade would be reduced if the national income were lowered in a small country. Emigration and export of capital from Scandinavia to the United States would probably diminish trade between them. Whether national income in the two countries is changed or not, factor movements tend to reduce the percentage of the national income used in each country to buy goods from the other. In that sense the need for international trade is reduced by international factor movements.

In a third type of case these conclusions do not hold true. The quantity of certain productive factors in a country may be so small that an increased supply does not reduce but increases their prices. For instance, wages may rise owing to external economies as labor flows into a scantily populated country. In such cases relative scarcity, e.g., of labor and land, need not be affected by the *factor movement* in the opposite direction between the emigrant and immigrant countries; wages may rise relative to rent in both. The character of trade is not affected in the same way as it is by a tendency toward international equalization of factor prices; nor is the volume of trade reduced. The new country may continue to send out agricultural products in growing quantities in exchange for manufactured goods.

Any change in the relation between the quantities of productive

---

[7] The fact that economies of large-scale production become available in this country may reduce the growth of trade but not prevent it altogether.

factors in the two countries will affect the volume of trade as indicated above. Thus, an influx of labor and capital into new countries may increase international trade for two reasons. Even after a point has been reached at which the percentage of the income used to buy foreign goods falls off, the total volume of trade may continue to rise owing to the growth of economic life due to the influx of labor and capital. As a matter of fact, this is what has happened between Europe and the United States since 1800.

In summary, it is evidently necessary to distinguish between cases where increased mobility of labor and capital reduce the differences in their prices internationally and cases where in the beginning no such equalization takes place. In all cases, however, factor movements mean an economic adaptation such that the world income is increased.[8]

§ 4. *Effect of capital movements on trade and income.* A few representative cases may now be described at greater length. The first is international capital movements caused by a sudden increase in the mobility of capital unaccompanied by labor migration. In such cases the borrowing nation (*B*) has a relatively abundant and cheap supply of labor compared to the lending country (*A*). The increase of capital in *B* and the reduction of it in *A* tend, respectively, to reduce and to raise the rate of interest.[9] Industry in both countries is affected. *B* acquires greater competitive power in the production of capital goods, while the costs of production of the same goods in *A* tend to rise. At the same time, the increased prices of other productive factors in *B* and their reduction in *A* raise the costs of the corresponding goods in *B* and reduce them in *A*. For this reason part of the trade between *A* and *B* tends to disappear. It is impossible to say generally whether the terms of trade move to the advantage of either.

Will the transfer of capital from *A* to *B* increase or decrease world trade? Is it likely that the borrowed capital in *B* will lead to increased output of the same sort of goods that *A* is used to exporting? Are the expanding industries in *B* from this point of view *competing* or *cooperative* with *A*? If the two countries are on the same level of industrial development, the first alternative seems probable, although important capital movements have never taken place between

---

[8] For qualifications of this observation, see Chapter XIV. So far as the number of people in the world or their taste is concerned, an opinion concerning world income has little relevance. This is one reason why it serves no useful purpose to speak of the "advantages" or "disadvantages" of international factor movements in the long run. Think of the effects if Japanese and Chinese had emigrated to North America and Australia in great numbers a hundred years ago. The analysis here should be compared with the corresponding one about commodity movements in Chapter IV and should be qualified similarly.

[9] Countries that export capital and not labor can be assumed to have passed the point of diminishing return for capital.

similarly endowed countries except during wars and postwar rehabilitation. However, if A and B are at a quite different stage of industrial development—if B, for example, is an agricultural country—the chances are that B will increase its output of goods *other* than those that A is exporting. In the case of capital lending from developed to developing countries, the question is: will the stimulus afforded by foreign capital in the latter countries lead to an expansion of industries competing with or complementing export industries in the creditor states?

If the natural resources, transfer facilities, and actual or potential quality of technical labor are similar in these states, the chances are that the new industries will compete. There can be little doubt that foreign capital in Italy around 1920 stimulated the expansion of manufacturing industries in general. The penetration of the Italian textile industry into many foreign markets formerly held by the British industry was thus accelerated by British loans to Italy. Such developments tended to make the terms of trade less favorable to Great Britain and to reduce Britain's volume of trade.

Investments in countries with different natural resources and transfer facilities from those of the capital-exporting country are likely to lead to an expansion of industries producing goods that the latter is wont to import. French and British lending to Sweden, Norway, and Finland made possible the building of numerous important railroads in the last third of the nineteenth century, which was a condition of the rapid economic growth in these countries, including the increased export of wood, pulp, and paper. These goods were thus cheapened for Western Europe. The foreign borrowing of Denmark was also used to some extent to reorganize agriculture and transform it to a butter-and-bacon industry, which must have reduced the supply prices of these goods in Great Britain and thus increased trade.

If terms of trade are ignored, it is obvious that the transfer of capital means an increase in the combined national incomes of the borrower and lender countries. Capital is moved from places where its marginal productivity is low to places where it is high. This conclusion must of course be qualified insofar as the terms of trade vary to the advantage of one country when the capital is transferred.

To judge the influence of factor movements on the national income in each country, one must consider another element. All countries profit from economic growth anywhere in the world. In the long run prosperous neighbors are likely to be the best customers. The capital-exporting countries, which in most cases have intimate trade relations with borrowing nations, profit in many indirect ways from the prosperity caused or stimulated in the borrowers by their capital. The manufacturing industries of Great Britain owe their development to some extent to trade with countries where economic expansion has been furthered by the influx of British capital. Countries other than those immediately concerned with the borrowing are also affected. Countries with the same export industries as the borrowing nations stand to lose, but those that import such goods are likely to gain substantially. Apart from the above effects, capital movements affect trade directly in other ways, which will be described later.

§ 5. *International migrations.* With regard to the effects of migration between two countries, it is natural to assume that the receiving country has a relatively abundant supply of many natural resources, as well as of capital and technical labor, since this creates high wages for ordinary labor, skilled or unskilled. Whereas capital by itself moves from countries with fully developed manufacturing industries to those with industries in the early stages of growth, labor moves in the opposite direction. The general effect on factor prices is analogous to that on interest rates: a tendency to lower wages in the receiving country and higher wages in the emigrant country. Similarly, the combined income of the two countries is increased. It is improbable, however, that the emigrant country, like the lending one, will see its national income grow, for the earnings of expatriated labor do not accrue to the mother country. If they did, the case would be entirely parallel to that of capital. The simplest possible observation seems to be that the decline in total income of the emigrant country is less than the immigrants earn in the new country, but the increase in the total income of the new country is greater.

As to the possible effects on international trade and the terms of trade, they are analogous to those regarding capital movements. There is this difference: immigrants' wages are spent where they live, but interest on borrowed capital is usually spent in the lending country. This tends to increase the prices of productive factors in the borrowing country, i.e., to affect the terms of trade in a direction favorable to the lender, although the opposite tendency due to the transfer of capital may be stronger.[10]

The analysis so far has not considered that the immigrants are in some respects different from the native citizens of the immigrant country, which affects trade directly in several ways. Immigrants often maintain for long periods a preference for their former habits and for some of the goods of their mother country. The demand for the latter is thus greater than if the population in the new country had grown in another way. Immigrants also affect the tastes and habits of their new country and thereby turn its demand in a channel favorable to the old country. Immigrant engineers and tradesmen in

[10] Cf. the analysis of the mechanism of international capital movements in Part Five.

particular often create a demand for goods from firms in their mother country. Dutch merchants were already scattered widely in foreign countries in the seventeenth century, and this circumstance is thought to have deeply influenced the foreign trade of Holland. Without being formal representatives of exporting industries in their mother country, British all over the world have greatly contributed to the growth of British exports.[11] The growing German population before World War I in both German and British colonies seems to have had some influence upon German trade.

When technical and highly skilled workers immigrate, the economic life in the new country may be revolutionized. The classic example is the emigration of the French Huguenots in the seventeenth century to Germany and Holland, with its resultant stimulus to the textile and other industries in those countries. It is obvious that in such cases the emigrant country may lose heavily from increased competition in its export trades. In modern times technical labor rarely moves because of religious or political discontent. An outstanding exception is Russia. The growth of the rubber shoe industry in Germany was helped by expatriated Russian technicians, whereas the Russian export industry, which formerly dominated the export market, declined. The migrations of engineers between nations in response to higher wage offerings are no doubt less in volume and in effect than might be expected. Many efforts to create competing industries by moving a few technical leaders from old industries have unaccountably failed.

Even when such attempts are successful, it is by no means certain that international trade is thereby ultimately reduced. All countries profit from economic progress elsewhere, and the spread of technical knowledge is a powerful stimulus in that direction. The best clients of leading manufacturing countries are the other manufacturing countries. As technique is improved and the standard of living is raised in a country, its need of specialized goods of high quality—in both technical appliances and consumers' goods—tends to increase, and the scope of domestic and international trade is accordingly enlarged.

The majority of immigrants have been unskilled[12] and less well educated and nourished than the home-born unskilled laborers in the immigration countries. This makes them undertake much of the disagreeable and lowest paid work. Such has been the case with

[11] "I say that for provisions, clothes, and household goods, seamen and all others employed about materials for building, fitting and victualling of ships, every Englishman in Barbados or Jamaica creates employment for four men at home." Sir Josiah Child, 1962.

[12] Before World War I, 10 percent of the immigrants to the United States belonged to the professional and skilled artisan class. Among the emigrants from Western and Northern Europe skilled labor was no less than 40 percent.

Southern Europeans in the United States. They thus compete much less with native labor than one would suppose; the influence on the wages of the latter is comparatively slight. Foreign and native-born labor are to a large extent and for a considerable time not competitive but cooperative factors. This was certainly true of Chinese immigration into Australia and the western part of the United States, where their work was in practice confined to a small number of trades like laundering. It is also probable that the immigration of Italian farm workers into Australia, for instance, where they were admitted only if they went to work on the farms, tended for many years to raise rather than depress real wages for factory labor. Trade union policy also makes the manufacturing jobs very difficult to secure, even when the immigrants have become naturalized citizens. In the long run, however, a number of immigrants, and certainly their children, acquire qualities that enable them to compete effectively for the better paid jobs of the native born.

Countries that receive an incessant flow of immigrants obtain a supply of low priced labor that they would not otherwise have. Industries requiring such labor in large quantities are enabled to continue producing goods that would otherwise be imported. A good example is the American beet-growing industry.

§ 6. *Movements of capital and labor.* The cases where labor or capital alone move to a country have been much less important than those where the transfer of capital is accompanied by a flow of some sort of labor. In the case of a joint movement of capital and technical labor, what classes of country are likely to export and import these productive factors? Capital can be exported only from countries with large savings, resulting in most cases from the use of modern production methods. Great Britain, for example, owed its position as the capitalist of the world in the middle of the last century to its early adoption of machine technology. It is therefore only natural that the leading manufacturing nations, which are for the most part the leading exporters of capital as well, should send out some of their technical labor with investments. Investments in which new firms are created call particularly for emigration of experienced organizers and technicians. These labor movements evidently are due less to higher pay abroad than to the fact that foreign investments make them necessary.

Concerning the effects of capital movements accompanied by a transfer of technical labor, Professor Edie has made the following significant statement: "What the export of capital has fundamentally meant has been the export of the industrial revolution from the industrialized countries to the 'undeveloped countries' . . . The automatic machines dispensed in large part with the necessity for skilled labor, and thus made possible the operation of machinery by the untrained labor masses of such countries as India, China, and Japan." [13] The effects on export industries in the lending country are uncertain. Much depends upon whether capital is invested in industries competing directly with export industries in the lending country. In the case where technical labor moves also the great probability is that industries will compete, for the technical labor in many cases comes from industries in which the prosperous country excels, and these industries are often the basis of production for export. Yet it is by no means certain that such will be the case.

If it is assumed that the borrowing country has relatively low wages for ordinary labor and low rents for certain natural resources, capital and technical labor from the lender will be used to establish industries requiring such resources. Examples are numerous. American technicians, for instance, have used American capital to develop the oil industry in Mexico and South America. If the resources do not exist in the lender country, the new industries will not compete but will rather supply the lender with raw materials or food for workers at relatively low prices. Most tropical products are grown on plantations under European leadership with the aid of European capital. Cotton-growing in Egypt on land of special quality has been stimulated both directly and still more indirectly by European technique and capital. The influence of the Aswan Dam, for instance, has been great. The cases of tea, rice, and cotton-growing in India are similar. Improvements in communications due to imported technique and capital have often greatly increased the output of goods that the lending countries could only with great difficulty produce for themselves. Iron mines in the interior of Chile and in North Africa, for instance, have come within reach, and the supply of high grade ores has thereby been increased. It is not necessary to dwell further upon the obvious fact that a growth of industries that are cooperative rather than competitive with industries in the capital-exporting country tends to turn the terms of trade of the lender in a favorable direction.

If capital and labor emigrate to join industries in the later stages of production, competition generally ensues between borrower and lender and the terms of trade move in a direction disadvantageous to the lender. The growth of cotton-spinning and weaving in India narrowed the market there for British goods of the coarser grades. If a country's transfer relations are good, this fact, together with the cheap supply of labor, can attract large amounts of capital and technical labor. Will the industries be chiefly cooperative or chiefly competitive? If the movement was due solely to advantages in transfer relations—often import duties—with wages and interest rates similar in both the borrowing and lending countries, the establishment of

[13] Edie, *Economics: Principles and Problems* (London, 1926), p. 660.

competing firms is almost certain to follow. It is conceivable, however, that when very strong firms establish branch factories abroad, the influence of such firms on the leading markets is so much increased that exports from the parent factory are not reduced but increased. This was the experience of the Swedish Ball Bearing Company and many others.

In the nineteenth century European capital and labor emigrated to the United States to exploit the natural resources that were scarce in Europe. Later on, the United States, aided by excellent natural resources and transfer relations, developed industries that competed with the European ones in most of the export markets of the world. In many cases this development was possible only because technical methods as well as ordinary labor and capital came from Europe. The dried fruit industry, for example, grew up in southern California after a number of Southern Europeans had settled there.

In general, when the supply of labor and capital in new countries has reached a definite level and the relative scarcity of land has begun to rise, manufacturing industries expand. An excellent illustration is the case of Canada, where the quantity of labor and still more of capital was greatly increased in the first decade of this century. Statistics show that certain products requiring much land were at the beginning of the period of borrowing exported to a considerable extent, but importation was slight. Toward the end of the period, imports and exports of these products almost balanced. The following Canadian figures are in millions of dollars:

Period	Imports	Exports
1900-1903	2.6	35.0
1911-1913	9.8	12.3

There was a general shift in imports from fully manufactured products to machinery, raw materials, and partly manufactured goods. In other words, importation was concentrated upon products requiring highly technical labor and upon certain natural resources, as contrasted with products requiring capital and labor of ordinary grades. No doubt the increased supply of capital and labor was the fundamental cause, although tariff policy worked in the same direction.

It was pointed out that immigration countries are often good markets for exports from emigration countries. Trade between capital-importing and capital-exporting countries is affected in a similar way, particularly when technical labor moves as well as capital. This is perhaps most obvious when capital and labor are used to build up a sales organization for large exporting firms and when orders from abroad are received chiefly because long credit is given.

Another consideration is the fact that trade follows the investment.

This is true not only when it is expressly stipulated that a majority of loans, e.g., for railroad building, shall be used to buy goods in the lending country, but also in other cases. The American Federal Trade Commission, after prolonged and detailed studies, expressed its opinion in the following words: "In general, the demand for foreign goods follows the nationality of the investment. It is the almost invariable rule that where such public utilities as railroads, light and power plants, street railways and the like, are financed by foreign capital, the equipment and supplies must come from the country financing the investment. And in industries not of the public utility type, this rule largely holds true." [14]

The combined effects of British emigration to the dominions and of investments there are seen in the extent of dominion trade with the mother country. In 1927 New Zealand purchased British goods up to £ 14 per head .

§ 7. *Effects on "outside" countries.* From a world point of view, it is fairly obvious that the redistribution of productive factors throughout the world, whereby a different utilization of various natural resources is made possible, means an increase in the volume of production.[15] The spread of machine technique, which goes hand in hand with the movements of capital and labor, is a dynamic force contributing markedly to the hastening of economic progress, from which all countries stand to gain. As to the share in this benefit that accrues to capital-exporting countries, which often supply technical labor also, the character of the competition from new industries is important. Exporting industries in other manufacturing countries also feel this competition, just as they receive the benefit of widening markets for manufactured products. For instance, old food-exporting countries such as Rumania, Hungary, and Russia see the prices of their exports reduced, owing to the increased supply of transoceanic food.

To get a bird's-eye-view of these and similar effects, one should ask: How is the world scarcity of productive factors affected? If European manufacturing workers become farmers in Australia and Argentina, the scarcity of manufacturing labor relative to that of agricultural labor will be intensified there, in Europe, and on other continents. The world will not consume relatively less manufactures and more food. A shift in relative prices will retard food production in Europe and encourage that of manufactured goods, partly for export to the transoceanic countries. The total production of both sorts of commodities will rise.

If the farming population in Australia is drawn to factories erected

---

[14] Federal Trade Commission, *Cooperation in our Export Trade*, I, 173.
[15] For the arbitrary element in such calculations, see the discussion of national income in Chapter XV.

by European capital and technical labor, the tendency is for factory wages, outside of Australia at least, to fall. In spite of the fact that world production will grow, the standard of living of the factory workers in the world at large will fall; food will be made more expensive. In the long run, farming and manufacturing labor cannot be regarded as noncompeting groups whose incomes may vary in opposite directions. Changes in the position of industrial workers in Europe tend to cause corresponding changes in the standard of European farmers. This result may come about quite slowly, as experience during this century has shown.

The British export of capital and labor has been of a sort to raise the standard of living both in Great Britain and in other manufacturing countries. It has gone to regions with abundant natural resources, which have been converted into raw materials and food transported by means of railroads: 60 percent of British foreign investments before World War I were used in this way. Rents in Europe were reduced, and the goods the workers bought were cheapened. Great Britain of course profited more than other countries from this development; it was more dependent than they upon export of manufactures and import of food and raw materials. Furthermore, it had especially intimate trade connections with countries that received its capital and emigrants.

§ 8. *Connection between different types of international factor movements.* It is now obvious that capital and labor movements are intimately related. If one factor moves, the economic situation, particularly with regard to factor prices, may be so affected that another factor moves also. Migration to new countries has increased the demand for capital there, whereas capital investments—e.g., in the form of railroads opening up vast new districts—have stimulated immigration. Immigration into Canada before World War I would have been unthinkable without enormous borrowings abroad. In other words, British investments in Canada led to a greater emigration to that country. An increased supply of either capital or labor must enhance the relative scarcity of the other and encourage its influx. If the relative supply of nature, on the one hand, and capital and labor, on the other, are very different in the countries involved, capital and labor movements go hand in hand.

It is often impossible to say that capital movement is the cause of labor movement more than the reverse. In Canada capital investments in the railroads may be regarded as a cause rather than an effect; but in South America the inflow of labor from Southern Europe has led to increased investments of British and American capital.

In all such cases of interrelated factor movements a check on one tends to check the others. If immigration into Australia is restricted, the inflow of capital will be reduced. A falling off in European investments in South America would retard economic progress and diminish immigration. Similarly, restrictions on the English export of capital to its former colonies would narrow the field for English emigrants in these countries. Obstacles to capital or labor movement need not of course prevent them but may only divert them in other directions. Immigration restrictions in the United States have increased the flow of European labor to South America, which has probably stimulated investments there both of European and American capital.

That capital flows out when labor is not allowed to flow in is particularly interesting. This phenomenon occurs when capital and labor move in opposite directions[16] and when such movements to a large extent complement each other. Consider two countries, of which A has a rich supply of capital and B of labor. Either A may lend to B, or B may send labor to A, or each may send a little to the other. The situation will of course be very different if many of the mobile factors are gathered in A than if they move to B. In any case, wages and interest rates may be so nearly equalized that no further movements occur.

The supply of natural resources and technical labor and the social conditions of production affect the outcome, as do the transfer relations, such as tariffs. If these circumstances alter, the margin between interest rates may rise and the margin between wage rates may fall so much that capital flows to B instead of labor to A, or the margin may vary in the opposite way and more labor and capital be concentrated in A. Furthermore, if the international mobility of any factor changes, the movements may also vary. Greater willingness of A's capitalists to invest in B may lead to considerable investments there and to a reduction in emigration from B to A. Restrictions on the export of capital from A may cause an immigration of labor.

In Australia the inflow of manufacturing labor is in many ways kept back, but the immigration of people willing to do farm work is encouraged, so that the market for protected Australian manufactured goods is extended. The scope for a high-wage trade union policy for factory labor is widened, while the standard of living among farm laborers tends to fall. The high price of factory labor keeps back the expansion of manufacturing industries and probably reduces the inflow of foreign capital.

Changes in factor supply following from variations in the obstacles to international factor movements affect international trade. The character of this influence upon trade varies from case to case, and to

[16] In these cases the relative supply of capital and labor is very different in the countries concerned, and this difference is more important than the differences in natural resources.

discover it, one must use the theory concerning the relation between "basic" elements and international trade.

§ 9. *Reactions of international factor movements and trade to changed mobility of commodities.* In many cases an increase in the obstacles to international trade reduces trade and therefore raises the international differences in factor prices, which tends to stimulate factor movements. Commodity and factor movements in such cases are alternative possibilities. In other cases increased obstacles, by making trade with certain countries more difficult, render those countries less suitable for economic life. The inflow of labor and capital is reduced.

Most important of the obstacles to trade are restrictions on imports. Import duties in country A raise the relative prices of the productive factors used in great quantities for protected goods. These factors are likely to be the ones relatively expensive in A. Most of the cheap factors are employed in industries that do not need protection (unless their transfer relations are very unfavorable). Since, after an increase in protection, exports will diminish, the cheap factors' price will fall. Factor prices abroad tend to move in the opposite direction. Unless A forms a large part of the world or of the countries particularly affected, this influence is likely to be small.

How does this affect factor movements? One would expect the factors whose scarcity is enhanced in A to flow in. If labor is favored by protection in A, its relative scarcity, and therefore its wage, is enhanced. But labor is interested in real wages, and in a higher standard of living, not in nominal wages. Since production in A is made less effective as a result of the protection, it is unlikely that labor's income in terms of commodities will rise. Abroad, the relative scarcity of labor will fall and production will become less effective. For both reasons real wages tend to fall. In most cases this decline is slight, but real wages are not considerably raised in A relative to their level in other countries. If in exceptional cases real wages in A do rise, and if the change is decided, an inflow of labor to A will be stimulated. If capital is favored by protection, the rate of interest may rise in A while declining abroad. Capital may flow in, or in capital-exporting countries the outflow may be reduced or stopped.

But what of the factors whose relative scarcity is reduced? When labor is favored, capital and various sorts of land are affected. Real interest and rent incomes fall in A for a double reason: lower relative scarcity and reduced general levels of incomes. Abroad, the tendency to increased scarcity is met by a tendency to lower total income. If the percentage reduction of total incomes is greater in A than abroad, the interest level there may be considerably reduced compared with the level elsewhere and capital may flow out of A. Evidently, whether labor moves in or capital moves out of A—or whether existing movements are affected in a corresponding way—depends upon the special circumstances in each case.

When capital is favored, the result is the reverse. There is a tendency for labor to leave A and perhaps for capital to enter A. In general the former tendency is stronger, but it is quite possible that the mobility conditions and factor prices will be such that a slight stimulus makes capital flow in, whereas a stronger stimulus will have no influence upon labor. Evidently, if the supply of productive factors in a country is to be increased by means of a tariff, the latter should be so constructed as to raise the relative scarcity of the mobile factors and place the burden of reduced scarcity upon the immobile factors, e.g., natural resources.

Now turn to some cases in which reduced obstacles and increased trade might increase factor price differences. Lower obstacles to trade (improved communications in certain countries) may improve a country's industry and increase the inflow of labor and capital.

It is only the *relative* factor prices that are made more nearly equal through increased trade when obstacles are reduced. For some factors the differences in their price in different countries may be increased. Higher productivity may tend to raise all incomes in terms of goods much more in one country than in another country. Assume labor in A to be relatively scarce and wages to be higher than in B. A reduction in the scarcity of labor in A does not prevent wages from rising in terms of goods *more* in A than in B. The increased relative scarcity of labor and the tendency to higher income levels in B may not suffice to raise wages there in absolute terms as much as does the strong tendency to higher income levels in A, in spite of the counteracting tendency of reduced relative scarcity of labor. The wage difference may thus be increased, and a labor flow may be called forth.

Cases in which a decrease in the relative scarcity of a factor increases its reward are exceptional, albeit of decided importance. They can come about only when economic life as a whole is decisively affected in some countries, but not in others, by reduction in the obstacles to international trade. New countries, for instance, sometimes possess improved communications, and extended trade would make them suitable for many new industries, which would tend to create an influx of mobile factors. Tariffs and other obstacles to trade work in the opposite direction.

It may be objected that import duties check only the *inward* movement of goods and therefore do not make the protected countries less suitable for production. As a matter of fact, such duties indirectly serve also as obstacles to export trade. If so, the differences in the prices of the mobile factors (labor and capital) are reduced by the duties. This may be the case in spite of the fact that import duties on manufactured goods in new countries raise the scarcity of labor and capital relative to the scarcity of land, while affecting the relative scarcity in old countries in the opposite direction. However, the obstacles to trade may substantially reduce the advantages of locating industries in the new countries. In other words, the potential income level may be considerably reduced. Consequently, wages need not rise and may well fall in the new countries, much more so than in the old ones. The tendency toward immigration is weakened, and a tendency in the opposite direction may be evoked.

These ideas may be expressed in a slightly different way. Factories intended to supply a great number of countries naturally tend to be placed where costs are low. Protection tends to raise nominal factor prices and to repel such factories. The demand for the factors in protected countries is reduced, and their prices in terms of goods are lowered. This is the same as a reduction in the attracting power of such countries or of their natural resources.

The general indication of this analysis is that except in special cases protection in a country does not increase its productive factors. But a tariff policy that consistently aims at increasing the income of the most mobile factor might succeed to some extent. If the price of an easily mobile factor is already relatively high, a slight tendency to raise its scarcity may suffice to cause an inflow. An import duty on goods that use much of this factor may bring about such a result. Other mobile factors will be cheapened, but their prices may have such a relation to prices abroad that an outflow is improbable.

A country with a fairly high rate of interest may raise it further by stimulating the expansion of industries using much capital. Real wages and rents would fall for a double reason—lower relative scarcity and decreased effectiveness of production—but this need not lead to emigration. In addition, new or higher duties in country A threaten foreign manufacturers with a loss of their former markets. Rather than lose that market and the resultant profit, those producers in many cases establish branch factories in A, bringing capital and technical labor of their own for building and operation.

Twentieth-century economic history abounds in examples. In 1922 Canada had more than 700 American companies, of which, no doubt, a large part owed their existence to the Canadian tariff. The British preferential tariff policy and the wage level in Canada, lower than that in the United States, also stimulated this development. Swedish ball-bearing factories are found in many countries that have high tariffs on their products. Swiss and British textile plants have been erected in Australia for similar reasons. Obstacles to international trade other than duties, such as the "buy-British-goods" movement, may bring about the same result in important free-trade markets like Great Britain's; but there can be no doubt that import duties strengthen the tendency.

Export duties and other export restrictions may serve a purpose similar to that of import duties. As a matter of fact, they have been imposed much more than import duties to achieve this aim. Legislation in some Canadian provinces in the last years of the nineteenth century prohibited the export of pulpwood from Crown lands. Some people think that this had an influence in bringing pulp and paper mills to Canada. Export duties on hydroelectric power were imposed to make the location of factories on the Canadian side of the border more favorable than on the American side.

Another case of export restrictions is offered by the Brazilian state of Minas Geraes, which prohibited the export of high-grade iron ore. In spite of the fact that there is no coal and that the mines are situated two hundred miles from the shore, by the early thirties Americans invested some $200,000,000 in the iron industry in this state, using technique and coal from the United States and producing annually 150,000 tons of rolled iron. Part of this iron was exported to pay for the import of 600,000 tons of American coal. Freight rates were fairly cheap, as carriers sail southward with coal and northward with ore. It seems probable that this development was decisively influenced by the export prohibition.

In the previous analysis the "educating" effect of protection was not mentioned. Successful education of certain grades of labor in protected industries may raise the general level of incomes and the incomes of certain factors in the protected country relative to their rewards in other countries. This may lead to an inflow of capital or labor or both.

The effects of import duties in one country on conditions and prices abroad has so far been assumed to be slight. In exceptional cases the effects may be considerable in countries having intimate trade relations with the one imposing the tariff. After 1876 sugar was admitted free of duty into the United States from the Hawaiian Islands. Production expanded from 11,000 tons to about 800,000 tons in 1925. Immigration of both unskilled labor and white skilled labor increased rapidly. Much capital was imported and invested in irrigation arrangements. The development was similar in Cuba, which exported chiefly sugar to the United States. This export increased greatly after the creation of the partly reciprocal tariff with the United States, which permitted the import of Cuban sugar at a much lower duty than that on sugar from other countries. There can be little doubt that the expansion in the Cuban sugar industry was partly due to this preferential position: it had become possible through a considerable inflow of American capital and technical labor, which was partly the result of the lower tariff. Immigration of ordinary labor also seems to have been stimulated. The number of immigrants was 38,000 in the years 1909-1913, and 84,000 in the years 1920-1924. A substantial increase in the American duty on Cuban sugar[17] would have given economic life in Cuba a setback and reduced the immigration of capital and labor. This is a case in which reduced mobility of commodities tends to reduce the movements of capital and labor.

A similar case is to be found in the position of Ireland in the middle of the last century. The reciprocal tariff with Great Britain, with its high protection of food, stimulated the expansion of agriculture in Ireland and led to an enormous increase of population in the first half of the century. When the Corn Law was repealed in 1846, food prices fell, and the scarcity of land and agricultural labor was reduced. For Ireland this was disastrous. The reduction in incomes fell chiefly upon the small tenant farmers, who had to pay their rents to the landlords according to old contracts. The inevitable result was poverty and misery, further increased when the potato crop failed. Thus, the sudden surge of emigration, which in six years reduced the Irish population by 20 percent, was partly the result of the British free-trade policy.

§ 10. *Effect of labor movements on quality of labor.*[18] A not unimportant aspect of the effects of international labor movements is the fact that the status of the immigrant often turns out after a time to be different from that of the emigrant, even though the same individual is concerned. The immigrant's efforts to adapt himself to new conditions exercise an educating influence. An energetic spirit and dash, which is such a characteristic of the United States, seize him. For these and other reasons the immigrant after a year or two often proves to be a more efficient worker than he was at home. This is one reason why international labor movements increase the volume of world production and why they fail to bring wage levels in immigrant and emigrant countries closer together. They also tend to keep international trade at a higher volume than it would be if the character of labor did not change after migration.

From a long-term point of view it is still more evident that international migrations in many cases lead to changes in the quality of

[17] Such an increase was decided upon by the House of Representatives in 1929 but was not accepted by the Senate.

[18] The remainder of this chapter deals with some aspects of the effects of international factor movements on factor supply and prices without pursuing the analysis to the reactions of trade. The effects of such movements on economic conditions in general deserve attention for their own sake.

labor. Man is affected by his environment, particularly by climate, which to some extent makes him what he is. Comparing the north and south of Europe, it is hard to believe that the climate in Greece and Spain does not contribute to the pleasure in doing nothing, which a man in the cold north would not share in the slightest. Such things may have much to do with the Nordic peoples' greater willingness to face hard work. In short, climatic conditions may affect the efficiency of labor considerably.

Another fact that makes labor change its quality when it moves is the influence of the higher standard of living in the immigrant countries. A high standard reacts favorably upon the intensity with which a man is able to work. In some nations the people are still so poor that a rise in their standard of living would mean an important increase in their productive capacity. Modern research indicates that the influence of food and housing accommodations on health and strength is great. A characteristic and conclusive example is the substantial decrease in efficiency of manual laborers in Germany in 1923, when inflation and the consequently low wages forced them to subsist on the minimum necessary to exist. There followed a significant improvement when a rise in real wages took place.

§ 11. *Reactions of domestic factor supply.* Not only the quality but also the quantity of domestic factors are affected by international movements of capital and labor. With regard to labor, in the emigrant countries the death rate may fall if the standard of living is raised. A higher standard of living may either reduce or raise the birth rate. The fact that emigrants are as a rule of reproductive ages tends to reduce it. Such effects were apparent in Ireland in the last half of the nineteenth century, when the earlier excess of births over deaths disappeared for a long period. In many cases emigration of technical labor leads to the education and training of a greater number of them, and reduction of the supply is thus avoided.

In immigrant countries the inflow of technical labor—as a rule accompanied by capital—hastens industrial development and is therefore likely to increase rather than to decrease the domestic education and training of such labor. How far the domestic increase in population through an excess of births over deaths is affected by immigration is impossible to say. The facts support the impression that the population in the United States would now be much smaller but for the inflow from other countries. It is not improbable, however, that if immigration had been stopped, say at the middle of the last century, the increase of births over deaths would have been greater than it has proved to be.

Similar considerations apply to the influence of international capital movements upon savings. The British export of capital has tended to keep up the rate of interest. In view of the fact that a large part of the savings comes from interest incomes, it seems almost certain that savings have been increased by the export of capital. In addition, the exported capital earned a higher profit abroad, and this too added to domestic savings. All in all, the supply of capital must have been increased. In borrowing countries the rate of interest moves downward, which probably tends to reduce savings. However, the economic development may be so much stimulated that the ability to save is increased.

§ 12. *Special aspects.* In examining the effects of international factor movements, e.g., on factor prices, I have been careful to describe them as *tendencies* to price changes in one direction or another. Other tendencies may of course operate, and the development may be correspondingly different. International migration, for instance, from A to B may fail to reduce the wage difference if the tendency of wages to rise for domestic reasons is stronger in B than in A. Although comparisons of standards of living are unsatisfactory, there is some truth in the observation that the difference between the American and British level of real wages is greater now than fifty years ago. Yet there can be no doubt that emigration from Great Britain has tended to reduce American wages.[19]

To a large extent the foregoing analysis has a static character: various situations are compared at different dates after a change has occurred. A static investigation can serve only as an introduction to a more dynamic study of the process of change, the order of events, and the speed of the different reactions. But a dynamic study would require consideration of the factual circumstances in concrete cases and is, therefore, monographic rather than general.[20]

[19] In the first half of the last century external economies of all sorts may have counted for so much that immigration raised the wage level, but it does not seem likely that this has continued.

[20] I am now, in 1964, more optimistic about the usefulness of dynamic theoretical models. Parts of this chapter and of Chap. IX appeared in "Das Verhältnis zwischen dem internationalen Handel und den internationalen Bewegungen von Kapital und Arbeit," *Zeitschrift für Nationalökonomie* (1930).

Part Five

*Mechanism of International Trade
Variations and Capital Movements*

XVII

Equilibrium in International Trade

§ 1. *Governing elements.* In the price system depicted in Appendix I and discussed above the foreign exchange rates are determined in relation to one another. For all other price ratios there corresponds —in a state of equilibrium—a definite set of foreign exchange rates i.e., of prices for each currency in terms of other currencies.

There seems no need of a special foreign exchange theory to explain how these rates are governed in the long run. The foreign exchange rates, just like other prices, are determined by the conditions of demand, supply, and transfer relations of goods and places (it is convenient to group together the basic elements under these three headings). The foreign exchange theory is as much a part of the general price theory as, for example, the theory of wages, and an investigation into the changes of the price system when the basic circumstances vary will throw light upon it as upon other price reactions. The only difference is that attention is concentrated on demand and supply in the foreign exchange market.

For the sake of clarity in the discussion that follows certain terms should be defined. The meaning of "aggregate money incomes" [1] in a country has already been partly explained: it is the sum total paid to the owners of the productive factors during a given period, to which is added the sum of profits. Patent rights, monopoly rights, etc., are for the purpose of this analysis, wherein they play no special part, dealt with as ownership of physical factors. The expression "buying power" and the synonym "purchasing power," when used with reference to a country, mean the aggregate of money incomes and the flow of liquid capital during a certain period of time,[2] increased by (1) the income drawn from the ownership of productive

---

[1] Cf. Bastable, "Some Applications of the Theory of International Trade," *The Quarterly Journal of Economics* (1889). It is a pity that Bastable did not pursue this line of analysis further. I am convinced—and hope that this volume demonstrates— that the concept "aggregate of money incomes" is more useful than others, such as "the height of money wages" (Taussig), or "the rate of efficiency earnings" (Keynes). The basic concepts and approach used here are well suited for a study of the influence of employment variations.

[2] The portion of the flow of incomes that is saved and thus becomes liquid capital must not, of course, be counted twice.

factors abroad, (2) new borrowings abroad, and (3) credit inflation; and reduced by (1) the incomes that people living abroad draw from productive factors in this country, (2) new lendings to other countries, and (3) credit deflation. Changes in international capital transactions and credit policy affect the aggregate of money incomes at some later date and affect one another mutually, but this does not impair the distinction made.

Buying power is partly that of consumers, partly that of traders—both merchants and producers. Traders' buying power is used for investment, not consumption, and corresponds to savings plus the other "free" capital if new borrowings abroad (2) and credit inflation (3) don't exist and if consumers who buy durable capital goods, such as new houses, are regarded as traders.

"Volume of industrial transactions" is the sum of all dealings in commodities and services during a stated period. A reduction of the aggregate of money incomes leads directly to an equivalent reduction of the total of industrial transactions, but indirectly to a much greater reduction of this total, for the people who sell less are able in their turn to buy a smaller amount. Changes in buying power and industrial transactions in the case of changes in international capital movements are discussed in the following chapters. Changes in the "volume of credit" are connected with changes in buying power and industrial transactions, and with variations in the aggregate of money incomes. The volume of credit multiplied by its velocity during a definite period is equal to "total circulation." Each individual has *command* over a certain sum of money and uses it to buy commodities, services, real estate, bonds and stocks, etc. The total circulation thus embraces all transactions in commodities, titles of wealth, and productive factors in any country.[3]

One of the principles underlying this price system is that at any time, in the absence of lending or borrowing by any region or country, imports of goods and services should exactly balance exports.[4] Buying power in terms of money may be acquired in two other ways than by earning or by borrowing. In the process of production a part of the capital that has been invested is made "free," i.e., liquid. This is a normal and important source of buying power. (The term "invested" is here used in a wide sense; every sale of a commodity means that

----

[3] Keynes distinguishes between "industrial" and "financial" circulation (*A Treatise on Money* [London, 1930], XV). My expressions "buying power" and "industrial transactions" refer to the same field of economic activity as his "industrial circulation." The uncertainty, under given circumstances, as to how much the effects of changes in the volume and use of credit concern this activity and how much they concern the financial transactions is a source of many theoretical difficulties.

[4] Gold exports and imports for monetary purposes can be dealt with later as a modification of this reasoning.

the monetary capital invested in that commodity is made liquid.) Second, banks may create or destroy buying power. If the former happens, prices tend to rise, but in the latter case they tend to fall—unless other individuals or institutions increase their credit arrangements accordingly or the volume of trade increases.

In the absence of any assumption about monetary conditions, the price system as outlined above evidently determines only relative prices of commodities, services, and productive factors. Assume that the sum total of all incomes—the amounts paid for all the factors of production, including profits, during a period of time—is kept constant because no new buying power is created by the banks, nor is existing buying power extinguished. If prices vary under these conditions, that can be ascribed to changes in the basic elements—technique, demand, etc.—not to monetary policy.[5] If, however, the quantity of labor and capital changes, a corresponding change in the volume of income is called for if the prices are to be unaffected. If the quantity of factors has increased, the aggregate of money incomes should be increased by as much as the income of the new factors, and vice versa if the factor supply has been reduced.[6] So long as such a policy is pursued, all price variations are due to changes in the basic elements. Further price changes may be regarded as due to deviations of the monetary policy from this principle.

Now consider the fact that individuals may acquire buying power by borrowing and may reduce it by lending. A borrowing individual or group of individuals may buy for more than their incomes and the flow of liquid capital, while lending ones buy for less. Hence, in the case of a country, international capital transactions disturb the balance between imports and exports,[7] and the difference is equal to the amount of capital transferred during the period.

The transfer of credit and buying power from one individual to another and from one place to another cannot but affect the price system. Other goods are demanded, and at different places. The relative scarcity of productive factors and goods is changed, both because of the new character or direction of demand and because of its location.

[5] There is not space to expound the monetary theory underlying such statements. In brief, it is a neo-*Wicksell* theory influenced by Lindahl, *Penningpolitikens medel* (Stockholm, 1930), and Keynes, *A Treatise on Money*. The concept of "buying power" is not found in their writings.

[6] Another way to express this is that the general price level of productive factors should be kept constant. The commodity price level, however, may well vary. Technical progress, for instance, will reduce it. The policy assumed here is conventional; it has been chosen because it provides a natural starting point for the following analysis.

[7] The so-called "invisible" exports are included. Interest is paid for the service of "waiting" and is classed with commissions for sundry services, freight charges for transportation services, etc.

Hence, each condition of capital transactions between individuals and places corresponds to a unique price system.

To sum up, the price system is changed when any of the basic elements vary, as well as when monetary policy or the transfer of capital is changed.[8] The problem of pricing from the long-term point of view is to discover how the new equilibrium of the price system differs from the previous one when one or several of such changes have occurred.

§ 2. *The foreign exchange problem.* The price system does not vary with friction. The equilibrium position toward which it tends is never completely realized, and new changes in demand, supply, transfer conditions, monetary policy, and transfer of buying power require time before the full effects are worked out. Changes in basic circumstances, monetary policy, and transfer of capital give rise to a number of counteracting tendencies. To disentangle the net result at various stages is an impossible process.

Some of these tendencies directly affect the foreign exchange rates. This is true above all of international transfers of buying power that directly involve changes in supply and demand in the foreign exchange market. Such international transfers of capital, which are more or less temporary in nature, generally occur—thanks to the slowness of other reactions—as a result of substantial variations in the basic circumstances. For this reason a study of the dynamic process by which the price system varies must give special attention to the foreign exchange market. It is all the more necessary to do so when changes in the price system involve substantial alterations in international trade and therefore directly affect the demand for and supply of foreign exchange.

The outcome of variations in basic circumstances and in capital transfers is necessarily dependent upon the reactions of monetary policy. If such variations are associated with a policy of inflation, not only the ultimate result but also the process of development will be quite different from what they prove to be when the same variations are accompanied by neutral or deflationary monetary measures. The organization of monetary systems and the traditional rules of policy are therefore fundamental in variations of the price system.

Most foreign exchange is at present based upon a gold standard or gold exchange standard. One result is that foreign exchange rates

---

[8] Keynes (*A Treatise on Money*, xx) seems to think that there are only two reasons for changes in the system, namely, changes in capital movements and in the relation between the price levels of various countries. The latter, otherwise known as inflation or deflation, which is not parallel in all countries, can also be included in monetary policy. Why should one ignore the fact that such changes may affect the quantities of imported or exported goods as quickly as or quicker than their prices, and not these quantities only via the prices? And why leave out of account changes in the basic elements or study their effects in terms of price level variations?

vary only slightly. The long-term problem thus becomes: How does the price system change under varying conditions when the foreign exchange rate is kept almost fixed? The following chapters are chiefly concerned with this problem. From a short-term point of view the problem becomes: How is the equilibrium on the foreign exchange market maintained when there are almost constant foreign exchange rates in a world full of variations?

§ 3. *Interrelations of various elements in the balance of payments.* The balance of payments embraces all the international transactions that must be settled during a definite period, usually one year.[9] The various entries may be grouped as follows:

A. Balance of trade and services
  1. Visible items (commodity trade)
  2. Invisible items (services, speculative gains and losses, interest payments)
B. Balance of capital transactions
  1. Long-term loans, regular business credits, immigrants' remittances, etc.
  2. Short-term transactions (mostly by professional dealers)
C. Gold movements

For reasons analyzed below, it is best to separate gold movements from other commodity transactions. Short-term transactions, *B2,* and gold movements, *C,* are chiefly balancing elements, which change in response to changes in the other items. Considerable variations in commodity, service, and long-term capital transactions,[10] however, ultimately call for more permanent balancing adustments than those under *B2* and *C.* Floating balances and gold reserves can be used only temporarily to equalize transactions.

As for the more permanent readjustments, with few exceptions they involve a balancing change in the commodity and service transactions *A1* and *A2,* principally in the former.[11] In other words, commodity

[9] It must be sharply distinguished from the balance of international indebtedness *at a certain date.*

[10] Short-term capital movements and gold movements may also provide the original disturbance instead of exercising a stabilizing effect and call for readjustments in the other items. The history after World War I offers interesting examples, like the "flight from the franc," which meant the piling up of enormous floating balances chiefly in London and New York. The gold imports by the Banque de France in 1928 and 1929 are another example. Short-term lending by London and the removal of French balances brought the sterling exchange below par in the first eight months of 1929, when all other items were better than in 1928, at which time sterling was high. It was cheaper to borrow in London than in other financial centers but was more remunerative to invest elsewhere.

[11] In this respect *A2* holds a position similar to that of *B1.* Of course, certain elements in the balance of trade *(A1)* are more elastic than others. Not only is the elasticity of consumers' demand relevant, but also the size of stocks and other factors.

trade adjusts itself to variations in the long-term capital movements, but the capital movements do not as a rule adjust themselves to trade variations. International capital movements of this sort are due to differences in long-term interest rates and and other comparatively permanent circumstances, which are not often affected by changes in the volume of imports and exports of goods and services. It is interesting to note that in general long-term capital movements are considerable in both directions, which proves that circumstances other than interest differences exercise a considerable influence. While in 1928 the United States made new investments abroad on a large scale—$2,070,000,000—other countries invested $1,704,000,000 in the United States.

In the relation between capital movements and trade, it is well to bear in mind that changes in the basic elements of pricing may at the same time affect both trade and capital movements. This may happen, for instance, on the discovery of new natural resources, which give rise to new industries and enhance the scarcity of capital in the country concerned. In other cases the capital movements are entirely unaffected by the basic alterations that create tendencies to changed trade. The point is that basic changes which primarily affect imports and exports seldom call forth secondary readjustments with regard to long-term lending, whereas the reverse always happens.[12]

Basic changes that tend to increase imports into a country relative to exports from it are as likely in the long run to reduce as to increase the long-term lending from this country. The change in this sort of capital movement is not in the nature of a readjustment restoring the equilibrium temporarily disturbed but may, on the contrary, make still greater readjustments in the field of trade necessary. In brief, primary changes in trade or long-term capital movements, or in both, cause secondary readjustments, chiefly in trade and in the short-term capital transactions. The part played by gold movements will be touched upon below.

§ 4. *Short-term international capital movements.* The object of dealings in the foreign exchange market is obviously to exchange buying power in terms of one currency for buying power in terms of another. In other words, one sum of money is exchanged for a sum of a different sort of money. If one buys 1,000 pounds sterling, it is usually either a cable transfer, a check, or a 60- to 90-day draft or remittance. In the first case the buying power is available at once; in the second,

[12] In a few cases long-term borrowings have had the express object of repaying short-term indebtedness incurred because of trade variations, but this is certainly an exception to the rule. I fundamentally disagree with the statement by Mr. Keynes: "Historically, the volume of foreign investment has tended, I think, to adjust itself—at least to a certain extent—to the balance of trade, rather than the other way round." This is true only of temporary, i.e., short-term capital transactions, unless "a certain extent" means "a very small extent." *The Economic Journal* (1929), p. 6.

after as many days as it takes a letter to reach London; in the last, after 60 or 90 days. Naturally the rates quoted in each case differ. The dealers in exchange, in order to cover their expenses, have separate buyer's and seller's quotations which include their fee for transforming buying power in one currency into buying power in another. Such a fee used to be charged by the banks when buying power in one place was exchanged for credit in another within the same country.[13] Nowadays banks in most countries render this service to their customers gratuitously. Nevertheless, this service is essentially the same as that rendered by the dealers in foreign exchange.

Assume some sort of disturbance to occur by which the demand for foreign exchange tends to exceed the supply. In which way is the equilibrium between demand and supply maintained? What kind of reactions are called forth to guarantee it? First, a tendency of the demand for foreign exchange to exceed the supply will raise the rates. They cannot rise much, for the countries concerned have either a gold or a gold exchange standard. I shall deal only with the former, although with slight alterations this analysis holds true for a gold exchange standard also. The gold standard fixes the amount of gold that a unit of currency can buy, and the "gold points" set the limits for possible deviations from this ratio. The upper gold point is the quotation at which it becomes arbitrary if one buys exchange or exports gold, and the lower point expresses the rate that makes gold import just as advantageous as selling foreign exchange.

With this monetary system people as a rule do not expect the foreign exchange rate to deviate much from par or from some slightly different position that experience shows to be a typical average. There are, however, profits to be gained by anticipating such changes and by buying or selling foreign exchange or credit accordingly. Those who undertake such deals are almost exclusively the banks and bankers, i.e., the professional dealers in exchange.

The most important of these transactions are as follows. Foreign central and private banks hold demand deposits in financial centers, chiefly London and New York. They draw on these accounts and thus increase the supply of foreign exchange when the rates are high and a drop is expected, and vice versa. The practice of having such floating balances extended widely after World War I, particularly among central banks which found that it enabled them to reduce that part of their gold reserves in excess of legal requirements. In 1930 the floating international balances in New York were estimated at $3,000,000,000, and the American balances of the same type in London and elsewhere were estimated at half this figure. Another important form of short-

[13] See Arnauné, *La Monnaie, le Credit et le Change* (Paris, 1922), p. 117, and Marshall, *Money, Credit and Commerce*, p. 142.

term international capital movements is the variations in the holdings of foreign bills. The banks also resort to borrowing and lending abroad to profit from fluctuations in the exchange rates.

The greater the certainty with which future fluctuations can be foreseen, the smaller are the variations necessary to call forth such speculative adaptations in supply, and the more stable are the rates. For this reason seasonal changes in international trade cause extremely slight exchange fluctuations. "Industrial countries tend to owe money to agricultural countries in the second half of the year, and to repay it in the first half . . . The seasonal transference of short-term credits from one center to another was carried out for a moderate commission." [14]

In the case of less regular variations in trade an extra stimulus to short-term credit movements usually arises from changes in the relation between the interest rates quoted in the money markets at home and abroad. Tendencies toward a negative balance of payments almost always go hand in hand with stringent conditions on the money market. This is partly due to the fact that the selling of foreign exchange extinguishes part of the existing credit, and the banks are unwilling to grant it again under these conditions. While supply of credit is in this way reduced, demand is often increased. Inevitably the interest rates on the money market rise, and foreign liquid balances flow into the country, whereby demand and supply on the exchange market are equalized.

A rise in interest rates leads to capital transfers in yet another way. International securities, particularly those quoted on the leading stock exchanges, tend to become cheaper at home. The higher money rates exercise a direct influence, and it becomes more difficult and expensive to hold securities by means of borrowed money. Consequently, professional dealers send such securities abroad, where their quotations have not suffered a corresponding depreciation. These security movements are sensitive even to extremely small differences in prices. One may well speak of a regular arbitrage, at least in the most fungible of them.

It is primarily the willingness of professional dealers to respond to the stimulus of small variations in exchange and interest rates that governs the extent of the exchange variations. However, merchants also react in a way that exercises a stabilizing influence on the foreign exchange market. Bills on 90 days are a common way of financing international trade. When the foreign exchange rates rise and monetary conditions in a certain country are tight, exporters tend to have these bills discounted at once in the country on which they are drawn.

---

[14] Keynes, *A Tract on Monetary Reform* (London, 1923), p. 108. This book contains a clarifying analysis of the forward market in foreign exchange.

Importers, however, try to arrange for prolonged credit abroad because it is difficult to find money at home.

Such are the principal reactions in short-term international capital movements, which are, as it were, "automatically" elicited.[15] When the original disturbance is considerable and lasts more than a very brief period, these reactions may prove insufficient to maintain the foreign exchange rates within the gold points; or rather, they threaten to become insufficient. In such cases the central banking authorities find it necessary to resort to special measures, principally to an increase in the official discount rate.[16] The unfavorable movement of the exchanges, the reduction in liquid foreign assets held by the banks, and most of all the tightening of the money market, make the need for such a measure self-evident, if there are no signs that the situation will normalize itself.

The raising of the discount rate tends to tighten the money market still further. If necessary to guarantee correspondence between market rates and the discount rate, the central bank may sell part of its securities—for example, national state bonds—and thereby withdraw funds from the money market. In many cases, however, the selling of foreign securities and foreign exchange from the reserves of the central bank and the private banks is sufficient to tighten the money market.

The higher discount rate and the generally more restrictive policy of the central bank toward the private banks make the latter also pursue a more cautious credit policy. Besides, the higher rate is felt as a warning by the business world, and a certain reticence colors its activities for the time being, so that the demand for credit is kept back. Thus, in general credit is restricted and its volume and velocity declines.[17] The demand for foreign exchange is reduced while supply increases in response to the higher interest rates. The tendency to a rise in the foreign exchange rate is counteracted.

§ 5. *International gold movements.* The development of foreign exchanges depends, on the one hand, upon the strength of the disturbances and, on the other, upon the extent of the short-term capital movements, the change in credit policy, and the reactions of trade. It

[15] The difference between "barter" and "trade under a money régime," which has been so much discussed, seems to be the difference between trade with and without credit. I fail to see the use of analyzing this difference and demonstrating that it is on the whole insignificant. It would be an example of unfruitful "Fragestellung."

[16] Some central banks make frequent changes in their discount rates. Others, like the Banque de France, do it more or less reluctantly and only after strong indications. In the same way reactions toward an inflow of gold differ. The monetary system of the United States has been relatively insensitive to gold flows since World War I.

[17] The effect of this change in the credit situation upon the general economic situation cannot be described here, as it must rest on a theory of money and discount policy, which would carry us too far even to indicate briefly.

depends, in other words, upon the elasticity of supply and demand. In general, the more easily floating capital moves to and from a financial center, the less need there is for changes in the discount rate, and the smaller the variations in the exchange rates caused by a disturbance of a given intensity. However, this does not mean that the quotations of, for example, the pound sterling or the dollar (the currencies in the leading financial centers) vary less than the quotations of other currencies. The disturbances in these centers are often more severe than elsewhere, partly because they serve as bankers and reserves for other countries.

When the balancing reactions are weak relative to the original disturbance the foreign exchange rates rise to the upper gold point and gold begins to flow out.[18] This is an added reason for the central bank to restrict its credit policy, for other banks to follow suit, and for the business community to take a cautious attitude. The efflux of gold leads to a restriction of credit and a rise in the interest rates, which in turn stimulate short-term capital inflows.

Evidently a reduction of the gold reserves affects the situation very much in the same way as a decline in the liquid foreign assets of the central bank. These assets can at any time be transformed into gold and really serve the same purpose as gold reserves, i.e., the maintenance of the currency in a certain vague relation with other currencies.

The similarity between gold reserves and demand deposits in foreign financial centers under the gold standard becomes evident after a consideration of the so-called "earmarked" gold reserves. They consist of gold that a central bank keeps on deposit in a financial center, usually in the Bank of England or the Federal Reserve Bank of New York. The monetary laws in many countries now permit this earmarked gold to be included in the gold reserves legally required as note cover. Thus, for all practical purposes this gold is the same as gold kept in the cellars of the central banks themselves. Yet there is little real difference between such gold deposits and ordinary demand deposits in London or New York which can be exchanged for gold without delay.

In brief, international gold movements are part of the mechanism for equilibrating the foreign exchange market. They play a role similar to that of floating balances but usually come into play at a later stage.

§ 6. *Reactions of credit volume and buying power.* Indirectly all foreign exchange transactions, and the changes in credit policy that go with them, affect other items in the balance of payments through their influence on the volume and velocity of credit and on buying power. When the banks sell part of the foreign assets that they have in re-

---

[18] The development depends much upon the willingness of bankers and others to speculate through short-term capital transfers. In this way "psychological" reactions affect the course of events.

serve and are paid either in cash or by domestic credit, the volume of cash and credit tends of course to decline. For the sake of simplicity I shall speak of credit only, since there has been practically no gold coin in circulation since World War I, and the distinction here between notes and demand deposits is not important. The volume of credit also declines as a result of a more restrictive credit policy, which is often pursued when the foreign exchange rates rise. Finally, the credit restriction and decline in the demand for credit that result from an efflux of gold further reduce the volume of credit and buying power.

The inevitable outcome is a fall in demand for goods and services in general. Imports are reduced, and exporting industries try to force their sales abroad at the expense of slightly lower prices or increased selling costs.

Credit reductions also come into play. Traders find their credit supply reduced and are forced to cut down their purchases accordingly. They may even voluntarily reduce purchases more, and the "velocity" of the bank deposits may decline, which reduces the buying power of other traders. This happens if they find it wise to reduce stocks because of difficulty in selling and thus fail to use their money and credit as quickly as usual. On the whole, traders' purchases are very sensitive to changes in the credit situation. Since practically all dealings in international trade are carried on by traders, the volume of imports may be speedily reduced much more than the decline in consumers' purchases warrant per se. Traders' purchases may be simply postponed for a few months, until the business situation has again become normal and stocks must be replenished. In the case of a more prolonged disturbance, the restrictions in traders' purchases will lower consumers' incomes and thus make the purchases of the latter fall off in a double way, which again reacts on traders' dealings.

All these shifts in demand cannot but tend to bring about changes in production and prices, which differ in accordance with the character of the original disturbance. They will be described, as well as their reaction on the balance of trade, in the following chapters. Only the most immediate reactions, whereby the equilibrium on the foreign exchange market is maintained during a fairly brief period, say half a year or so, are so similar in almost all cases that they can be described appropriately here. If the disturbance is only temporary, no other and more profound readjustments may be required. But if it is a severe and prolonged disturbance—for example, a substantial increase in long-term lending during several years—there will be a need for thorough readjustments in production and trade.

To sum up, the rise in foreign exchange tends to retard imports and stimulate exports, although probably with little effect. Much more important—at least in the first stage—are the international short-term capital transactions of various sorts that are stimulated by differences in international interest rates and by speculative profits. When these transactions prove insufficient, the upper gold point is reached, and gold movements create greater interest differences. At the same time the risk in exchange speculation is reduced, since the rates cannot rise further, and capital movements therefore tend to increase. All these reactions involve changes in the volume of credit and of buying power, whereby imports are restricted and exports are to some extent increased. Part of such variations in trade result quickly, others slowly.

§ 7. *Criticism of the orthodox view of the role of gold movements.* The mechanism outlined above differs in certain respects from what has been considered the orthodox view. Above all, the international gold movements hold a less central position. Nowadays debts and credits are settled by changes in the volume of liquid balances in financial centers, and in many cases there is no need of foreign exchange variations so pronounced that gold movements are necessary. It is usually only in the case of marked disturbances, when the volume of credit has to be reduced for a long period of time, that gold exports occur as a result of the disturbance.

The chief differences between the theory above and the orthodox view may be summarized thus:

(1) In most cases international gold movements are not part of the mechanism of equilibrium.

(2) The change in the volume of credit and buying power, which in the orthodox view is due to gold movements, is brought about, at least to a certain extent, much more quickly in other ways—through changes in floating balances and foreign exchange reserves, etc. There is always a tendency toward an original change in buying power prior to any gold movement.

(3) It is uncertain whether and how much gold movements affect the credit policy of central banks and are thus responsible for secondary changes in buying power. The outstanding example of a case where extensive gold movements have not led to a proportionate increase in the credit structure, and on certain occasions have not led to any increase in industrial transactions at all, is the policy of the Federal Reserve System.

(4) Finally, when gold moves, it is often less as a *causa efficiens* with regard to the credit policy of central banks than as a restorer of gold reserves to a percentage that is considered desirable or normal. Variations in the total of liquid debts and credits govern credit policy, and it is of little consequence whether a part of the other assets—say, demand deposits in New York—are exchanged for gold, or vice versa.[19]

A study of the gold movements between the Continental central

[19] Cf. Viner, *Canada's Balance of International Indebtedness, 1900–13* (Cambridge, Mass., 1924).

banks before World War I suggests that they had little influence on credit. After the war it became still more apparent that they were primarily for special purposes, for example, to distribute the new gold from the gold-producing countries, which proceeds in rather irregular currents. In brief, there is relatively little difference between the gold standard and the gold exchange standard, so far as the mechanism of equilibrium is concerned.

The truth of the foregoing description[20] of the role of gold movements does not rest on any form of the quantity theory of money. To avoid misunderstanding, it may also be added that when several disturbances occur at the same time and affect the balance of payments primarily in opposite ways, the mechanism of equilibrium is colored thereby. For instance, the commencement of extensive lendings to foreign countries does not cause the above-mentioned reactions if credit has already been severely contracted; the sequence of events is affected. To modify the description of the mechanism accordingly, however, presents little difficulty.

[20] Similar descriptions have been published by Angell, Feis, Graham, Hawtrey, Keynes, Viner, and others.

XVIII

The Mechanism of Domestic Capital Movements

§ 1. *A simple case.*[1] Assume that English capitalists lend money to Scottish industrial enterprises to build new factories. The capitalists' balances in English banks are immediately reduced, whereas the balances of the Scottish concerns in Scottish banks increase. Apart from what happens later, the buying power has obviously diminished in England and increased in Scotland. This may seem self-evident, but it is often overlooked.[2]

The demand for goods thus rises in the latter country and falls off in the former. In a measure the new Scottish demand is for English import commodities and Scottish export commodities; imports increase and exports decline. The Scottish trade balance becomes in a corresponding degree negative, if it had previously been in equilibrium. The money borrowed from England is partly used to pay for this import surplus.

Some of the borrowed money is, however, used for the purchase of home market goods, i.e., goods in which there is no trade between England and Scotland, such as bricks, or for the payment of wages to workmen employed in building the factories. Thus, part of the loan creates a demand for Scottish "home market goods," whereas the money would otherwise have been employed in purchasing English home market goods. The demand for the Scottish goods rises, while that for the English declines; there is a tendency for prices to rise in the one case and fall in the other.

The result is twofold. Productive factor prices as well as profits rise in Scotland, i.e., incomes and buying power grow and the trade balance moves further in a negative direction. Second, labor, capital, and natural resources are to some extent withdrawn from other operations and applied to production of noncompeting home market goods in Scotland; the volume of manufactured export goods and articles that compete with English import goods thus becomes smaller than it would

[1] Full employment is assumed.
[2] Keynes explicitly refuses to admit it. See *The Economic Journal* (June, 1929).

otherwise have been. The contrary process takes place in England. In this way exports fall off and imports rise in Scotland, whose trade balance becomes still more negative. As before, the import surplus is paid for with the borrowed money.

The increased deposits in Scotland and reduced deposits in England naturally tend to affect the volume of credit granted by the banks. The Scottish banks find that they have plenty of money and are more ready than before to grant credit, whereas the English banks restrict their credit accommodation. This process causes a secondary inflation[3] of credit and buying power in Scotland and a deflation of credit in England. Such a shift of buying power naturally tends to influence demand, production, and trade in the same way as does the primary and direct shift. There gradually arises a situation in which Scotland's import surplus is about as large as the sums borrowed from England, and the position of the banks in the two countries again becomes normal. When this occurs, the transfer of capital can proceed at an even rate without any further adjustment of production. The adjustment that has taken place merely implies that, when all the commodities and services the Scots desire to purchase with the borrowed funds cannot conveniently be imported from England, the production of home market goods is increased in Scotland, whereas to counterbalance this, the Scots produce less goods for export to England and less articles that compete with English import goods.

§ 2. *Relative price variations.* This adjustment in Scotland means that the price of home market goods will probably rise somewhat as compared with the prices of the others, which for the sake of simplicity may be called interregional goods. It is probable that the former goods in England will fall somewhat in price as compared with the latter. But it does not follow that English export goods will fall in price in comparison with Scottish ones.[4]

It is conceivable that the increase in buying power in Scotland will also raise the prices of export goods produced there, while the reduced buying power in England will to some extent force the latter's export prices down. In proportion as this takes place, the tendencies making for an English export surplus naturally become stronger. But if it is assumed that the transfer of capital is on a reasonable scale and that the adjustment may take place gradually, such an alteration—to England's disadvantage—in her terms of trade with Scotland is by no means certain and may in some cases be negligible.

---

[3] The primary inflation of credit accompanied the sale of English bills to Scottish banks and the increase in prices of certain commodities and productive factors.

[4] Pigou, Keynes, and others reached the opposite conclusion because they failed to consider the changes in buying power and paid little or no attention to the difference between home market and export prices.

The changes in buying power involve in many cases not only increased demand for home market goods in Scotland and reduced demand for the same goods in England but also a shift of demand in favor of the export goods of one of these regions. There is no more reason for assuming that Scotland's export goods will be favored than England's. Consequently, so far as this shift in demand is concerned, the terms of trade may move to the advantage of England just as well as to the advantage of Scotland. However, the readjustments in the use of the productive factors tend to reduce the supply of Scotland's export goods and to increase the supply of England's, which tends to move the terms of trade in favor of Scotland. Naturally the elasticity of demand determines to what extent tendencies of a certain strength are able to change relative prices.

§ 3. *Mobility of labor and capital instruments.* There are two ways in which the real transfer of capital to Scotland comes about. England may (1) export its own goods and services, or refrain from importing so many of Scotland's goods and services, which the Scots now want in greater quantities than before, thereby setting free productive factors in Scotland to produce the goods and services it wants in greater quantities than before; or (2) send productive factors or capital instruments or both for a certain period of time to produce these goods and services in Scotland. In many cases migration of labor is a concomitant to capital movements and a part of the process of adjustment. It is rare, however, that capital instruments wander about; there is only one important case where this happens. Ships from England may help to transport—i.e., to produce—what is wanted in Scotland. When capital instruments are in this way temporarily "lent" to the borrowing region, its productive activity is made easier in the same way as when labor is sent. In such cases the movements of commodities—capital instruments are commodities—evidently works in two different ways to make the real transfer of capital possible.

§ 4. *Illustrations.* When a Welsh baron decides to live in London the year round and not, as before, to live eight months in his home castle, a stream of money begins to flow from his tenants to London; this means a decline in Welsh buying power. He no longer uses this money in Wales to buy both "imported" and local goods and services. Consequently, the level of incomes on his estate drops, buying power is further reduced, and the demand for all sorts of home market goods and services in the district falls. Since the supply of houses, for instance, is not easily reduced, rents drop considerably as a result of the general impoverishment of the villages on his estate.

The creation of a new industry in an out-of-the-way agricultural region has an opposite effect. An export surplus of milk, for instance, may be turned into an import surplus, and the price of this product may thus be much increased. Land rents rise, as do the costs of living and nominal wages. If the mobility of labor to this region is not complete, there is also an increase in real wages, and the price level of the whole region moves further upwards.

The buying power is transferred across the country, as it were, by a net of invisible wires. Goods and services have to follow either directly or indirectly through changes in production, which are sometimes made easier through movements of labor and capital goods.

XIX

The Mechanism of International Capital Movements

§ 1. *Transfer of buying power.* In principle the chief difference between domestic and international capital movements is in the monetary mechanism. Buying power and credit cannot be transferred without being, so to speak, transformed from one monetary system to another, which gives rise to certain complications. Capital, whether or not it passes across a national frontier, moves only in the form of goods or services, neither of which is freely mobile geographically; hence, a cumbersome readjustment of production becomes necessary. The difficulties in the way of such a readjustment depend upon special circumstances in each case—for instance, the character of trade relations between the regions, the sort of goods that are wanted in the borrowing region, the elasticity of demand, and the size of the capital transaction compared with other sides of economic life.

I shall first consider two countries only and, disregarding the difficulties of transition, concentrate on the situation *after* the process of adaptation to a continued movement of capital has been carried out in some way or other. The buying power in A has been increased, while that in B has been reduced.[1] For simplicity's sake I shall disre-

[1] Buying power may exceed the flow of liquid capital plus the aggregate of money incomes without tending to raise this aggregate if foreign money, borrowings or gifts, is used to buy foreign goods or home-produced export goods for which the foreign demand has declined. Such buying power does not create an increased demand for productive factors in the borrowing country and therefore fails to raise the sum total of their prices, i.e., the sum of incomes. It is much the same thing if money that has been held in foreign countries—for instance, as deposits in some financial center—is used to buy foreign goods. In that case also the total buying power is greater than the country's income plus its liquid capital. Moreover, new buying power can be created by inflating credit, whether on the basis of an increased supply of foreign exchange or not; this buying power can purchase commodities and services *before* it has had any effect on the aggregate of money incomes. The increased demand for home market goods and services necessarily causes increased money incomes, but certainly this comes later and is a secondary circumstance, leading to a further increase in the demand for various sorts of goods. Primarily buying power has sprung not only from ownership of productive factors but also from the note printing press and from the creation of new bank credits. The increased incomes are the consequence of the increased buying power and of the

gard other countries and reason as though these two countries alone existed. *There is thus a market in A for more of B's goods than formerly,* while the market in *B* for *A*'s goods is not as big as it was before. The local distribution of the total demand has changed. *A* has become a better market and *B* a worse one for goods of all kinds.

This is perhaps most clearly seen if one imagines what the situation would be if there were no transport charges or other obstacles in the way of the exchange of goods. All kinds of goods would then be exchanged between *A* and *B*, each country specializing in the goods that could be produced at least cost. But after the capital movement starts, *A* buys more and *B* buys less of their combined production than before. The monetary transfer of purchasing power from *B*'s to *A*'s currency cannot entail any difficulty because *A* automatically acquires an import surplus corresponding to the size of the loans.

To the extent that the borrowers in *A* buy goods from *B*, they pay for them in *B*'s currency. Similarly, to the extent that they buy goods produced in *A*, the export of these goods falls off, the exporters have correspondingly less *B* currency to offer and the importers have to obtain *B* currency from the borrowers, paying them in *A* currency, which is just what the borrowers need in order to buy *A* goods.

If the borrowing individuals in *A* demand goods other than those demanded by the lenders in *B*, the *direction* of the total demand has obviously undergone a change. This results in a change also in the relative scarcity of the factors of production and in the relative prices of goods. The goods for which there is a greater demand than before become somewhat dearer, and the others become somewhat cheaper. It may just as well be *A*'s as *B*'s goods that have become cheaper, and if the direction of the demand does not materially change, the relative prices of goods also remains the same as before. It is therefore not at all necessary under the assumptions made that the capital exporting country *B* should offer its goods at lower prices than before in order to find a market for a greater quantity and obtain an export surplus corresponding to the sum of money lent abroad.

§ 2. *Nature of international capital movements.* In reality the transfer of buying power is more complicated, mainly on account of the costs of transport, customs, and other obstacles in the way of free com-

---

greater demand for goods and services. Whether the aggregate of incomes rises or not, buying power during the period of borrowing is increased. It would be doubly misleading in a description of *the sequence of events* to say that the higher incomes are the cause of the increased demand. This note should clear up certain fundamental and common misunderstandings from which observers such as Keynes seem to suffer. See Keynes, *The Economic Journal* (1929), and *A Treatise on Money,* xxi. In the late 1930's Mrs. Joan Robinson suggested that the influence of *changes in national incomes* was an essential part of the international mechanism, which had heretofore been neglected.

modity movements. Owing, in fact, to these obstacles, the transfer of buying power cannot produce the automatic redistribution of the goods between A and B that characterizes the simplified case. The necessity arises for a more complicated adaptation in both countries to enable A to acquire a greater share of the total production of the two countries. The character of this adaptation has already been briefly described in the domestic case. As another illustration, consider a numerical example.

Assume that A has borrowed $100,000,000 in B and uses $30,000,000 to make further purchases of cotton and wheat from B and a like amount to purchase more of A's own export goods, machinery and textiles. Its trade balance thus contains a $60,000,000 deficit, and the borrowed capital goes to make up the deficit, i.e., to pay for the import surplus. The borrowers in A then use the remaining $40,000,000 to purchase noncompeting home market bricks, whose output must be increased, and to which productive factors must be directed from other spheres of activity. In a progressive country this means that industrial agents that would otherwise have passed to the export industries (the machinery and textile industry) and to the production of home market goods that compete with imports (wheat of the lower quality) now go to the noncompeting home market industry (the brick industry). The production of export goods and competing home market goods (textiles, machinery, and low-grade wheat) in A will thus expand less than it otherwise would. Exports will decrease and imports increase, and the trade balance will become an additional $40,000,000 or so more passive.[2] Practically all the borrowed money consequently pays for a temporary import surplus. When this process of adaptation has once been carried out, the monetary transformation of the loans clearly proceeds automatically, just as in the simple case where transport costs were disregarded.

A corresponding adjustment takes place in B. Demand is reduced by $100,000,000. This loss devolves on some of B's home market goods (bricks). Industries that produce these goods expand less than they otherwise would, and the factors of production are instead directed toward a further expansion of the export industries (cotton and wheat growing) and the production of competing home market goods (textiles). This reacts favorably on exports, which rise, and unfavorably on imports, which fall off—just the reverse of the process of development in A.

The reorganization of production here described—an increase in the manufacture of noncompeting home market goods (bricks) in A and of international goods (wheat and cotton) and competing

---

[2] A may more or less permanently increase the foreign exchange reserves that it keeps in financial centers abroad.

home market goods[3] (other textiles) in *B*—is quite natural, since the movement of capital involves *B*'s ceding a certain amount of goods to *A*. As the home market and competing home market goods cannot economically be transferred to *A*, the entire transference of goods must be effected through the international goods (cotton, wheat, textiles, and machinery), with *B* exporting more and importing less of them. *A* imports more and exports less, which enables it to expand its production of home market goods (bricks) and in that way to obtain an increased supply of all goods, or of substitutes for them (foreign wheat instead of home grown of a different quality). *B* reduces its output of home market goods and gets a diminished supply of all the goods, for which its demand has declined.

§ 3. *Monetary mechanism.* After this general account of the nature of international capital movements, a more detailed analysis is appropriate, especially of the process of adaptation that they necessitate.[4] The monetary mechanism varies with the organization of the monetary system and the habits and traditions of the central banks with regard to credit policy. For instance, the size of the gold and the foreign exchange reserves above legal minimum or normal figures and the traditions of discount policy (compare the different practices of the French and English central banks) cannot fail to affect the monetary mechanism. A surface analysis of this mechanism in various cases of a disturbed balance of payments was presented in Chapter XVII, where special attention was given to the short-term capital movements as balancing elements. The changes in credit volume and buying power, which are an important part of the mechanism in all cases, were scarcely touched upon there. They will be more closely analyzed here with reference to a special kind of disturbance. The matter to be examined is the effect of an original disturbance in the form of a changed or new capital movement, which exercises pressure during at least a few years in a certain direction and consequently has time to exercise profound effects on the price system.

First, it should be observed that there is a change in buying power,

[3] Competing home market goods are rather sensitive to changes in international trade though they are not subject to it themselves to any considerable extent. Noncompeting home market goods are here called only home market goods.

[4] The following analysis is similar in several ways to the theory of international capital movements that was worked out at the Harvard School of Economics—on the basis of the Thornton-Mill theory—under the leadership of Professor Taussig. My theory is best regarded as a modification of the Harvard theory. In certain important respects it differs from Taussig's theory, e.g., in stressing the changes in demand through buying power variations. I am not certain whether there is any important difference in principle between my analysis and that presented by Professor Viner, to whom I am much indebted for an interesting discussion of the problem in private correspondence. Taussig's and Viner's theories are different, which I hope to demonstrate elsewhere.

a monetary transfer, *before* the real transfer of goods and services, just as in the domestic case. This *monetary* transfer is the direct and indirect cause of the readjustments involved in the *real* transfer.

Consider the actual monetary mechanism in the borrowing country.[5] Through a loan A obtains $100,000,000 in B currency, of which in the first place $60,000,000 is used for the purchase of B's goods. The remaining $40,000,000 in B exchange is sold by the borrowers to A's central bank, which pays the same amount in A's own currency. The central bank increases its foreign exchange reserves and in payment releases more notes or increases the deposits placed at the disposal of its customers. There is no reason to expect it to restrict the credit to other customers, which would offset the effect of the purchasers of foreign exchange. It is as a rule in this simple way that the borrowers obtain buying power in their own country's currency.[6]

Such an increase in credit and buying power tends to affect the prices of various sorts of commodities and industrial agents. Directly and indirectly it also tends to increase imports, while curtailing exports. It is sometimes objected that the effects of this increased purchasing power on the balance of trade are necessarily insignificant. This opinion overlooks a very important aspect. Buying power is increased not only by the amount of the borrowings but later by an increase in the flow of liquid capital and of money incomes. The new means of payment pass from one individual to another. If $40,000,000 of foreign bills is sold to the banks in A, the volume of credit is immediately increased by $40,000,000. The effect of this greater volume of credit is to raise buying power by a much larger amount as soon as the secondary effects have begun to appear.

The $40,000,000 is used to purchase home market goods. Either greater quantities of them are produced by means of formerly unemployed workers and unused capacity in machinery, or their prices must rise. In both cases the manufacturers of such goods have their incomes increased. This income is used to buy international or home market goods. To the extent that the former is bought, a deficit in the balance of trade and a demand for foreign exchange is created; the rest of the money goes to buy home market goods. Hence, the producers of these goods see their incomes rise still further, part of which they use to buy international goods, whereby the deficit in the trade balance is increased. The total increase in the buying power during a year, for instance, far exceeds the expansion of credit. If the borrowed amount is called a "primary" increase in buying power,

---

[5] This expression is used in the same sense as "capital importing" country, in spite of the fact that capital may serve as reparations, gifts, etc.

[6] Whether or not this transaction takes place through the intermediary of a private bank is immaterial.

the further increase in buying power may be called "secondary," as it is due to the effects of this credit expansion.

There is a further increase in buying power as a result of a "third" increase in credit of a slightly different sort. The increase in the foreign currency reserves in *A* is likely to lead to a change in credit policy[7] and thus to bring about an auxiliary change in purchasing power. *A*'s central bank begins to find its currency reserves unnecessarily large and is unwilling to make further purchases of *B* currency, the exchange rate of which consequently tends to fall. At the same time, a more liberal credit policy is adopted in *A*. *B*'s central bank, however, views with anxiety the growing short-term indebtedness and the tendency of the *B* currency to fall below par; and it tightens its credit accommodations.

The slower the adjustment of the balance of trade proceeds, and the more the foreign exchange reserves continue to grow, the greater is the probability that a secondary increase in *A*'s buying power will be brought about. In other words, the incomes of home market producers rise more quickly if the deficit in the balance of trade is minimized. Rising prices make home market industries pay exceedingly well, and a strong tendency to an expansion of productive activity is inevitable.

Production cannot be expanded without larger credit. Evidently, even if the credit policy of the central and private banks were not changed, the increased demand from home market producers would probably lead to an extension of credit. As a matter of fact, credit policy is made more liberal, and the volume of credit grows for that reason also. If the gold reserves are not sufficient to allow such an extension of credit, the foreign exchanges will be allowed to drop below the gold point, a portion of the foreign bills will be exchanged for gold, and the necessary cover will thereby be provided. Both theoretical reasoning and the evidence of experience[8] indicate that this influx of gold is due to the increase in credit rather than the contrary.

The mechanism of changes in buying power described above is likely to be more influential in one country than in another. In general, if the loan is contracted in the currency of *A*, the money market will be more directly and more effectively tightened in *B* than it will be stimulated in *A*.[9] However, it is quite possible that this influence will be stronger in *B*, since it depends upon a number of circumstances

[7] The expansion of credit dealt with here will occur even if the discount and the willingness to give credit are unchanged.

[8] See, e.g., Canada's experience as described by Viner.

[9] Angell, in "Reparations and the Cash Transfer Problem," *Political Science Quarterly* (1926), pp. 349-351, in my opinion attaches far too much weight to the currency in which the loans are contracted.

touching upon such elements as credit policy, connection between various financial centers, and ability and willingness to part with gold.[10]

The readjustment is easier and the sequence of events is somewhat different if credit is inflated beforehand in the borrowing country in anticipation of the loans. In that case there need be no growth whatever in the foreign exchange reserves. Such growth comes about because of the slowness with which credit and buying power increase in A and decline in B, and it becomes superfluous if the readjustment of buying power occurs earlier than it would in the usual course of events.

§ 4. *Preliminary analysis of terms of trade.* The increased demand for home market goods in A and the reduced demand for such goods in B implies a shift in demand from B factors to A factors. These variations in relative factor prices are accompanied by corresponding changes in commodity prices. Assume that all goods produced in a country require for their manufacture identical "units of productive power" consisting of a fixed combination of productive factors. The shift in demand raises the scarcity of the A unit, which means that every commodity produced in A becomes dearer than before compared with every commodity produced in B. The terms of trade between A's export goods and B's change in favor of A. Income levels rise in the latter country and fall in B.

Consider first the conditions of supply and then the conditions of demand for international goods. When certain industrial agents are drawn to home market industries in A, the output in export industries declines in relation to what it would otherwise have been. In B, the supply of export articles tends to grow when productive factors flow over from home market industries. These changes in supply cannot fail to move prices in the direction indicated above, on the assumption that the combined demand of A and B for the export goods from either is in the first place unchanged by the borrowings.

How much a certain shift of the supply curve will change prices depends upon the elasticity of demand in both countries. As to the elasticity of demand, there is no reason for assuming that it is either great or small. In one case it is greater than unity, in another less. But the competition from other sources of supply makes it probable that demand is in most cases highly elastic. It is only in the short run that demand is likely to be inelastic under certain conditions. If prices fall and further price reductions are anticipated, buyers may hold back and the volume of sales be reduced. When this happens in the case of a commodity very important to a country's trade, such as coffee in Brazil, the effects on the balance of payments are considerable. The drop in export prices, instead of raising the total value of exports,

[10] See Keynes, *A Treatise on Money*, p. 341.

reduces it. There can be no doubt, however, that after some time a reduction in the costs and price levels in a certain country in almost all cases enables it to export considerably increased volumes of its usual export goods and some quantities of goods that have not been exported at all. Usually this increase in volume more than balances the effects of lower prices and thereby increases the value of exports.

It must be stressed that a relative change in costs—B's falling in comparison with A's—enables B to export certain goods that before belonged to the home market or competing home market group, whereas some of A's goods disappear from its export trade. If the whole of a country's export goods is considered, it is safe to say that the foreign demand is highly elastic, and therefore the tendency to changed terms of international trade is strong only in exceptional cases. For this reason detailed studies of the influence of different degrees of elasticity of demand upon the terms of trade in international trade appear to be of little practical importance. Such studies served as a diversion for some of the acutest intellects among nineteenth-century economists but, in my opinion, have added little to our real knowledge of international trade.[11]

The fact that the level of factor prices and incomes and the flow of liquid capital in terms of money is as a rule increased in A and reduced in B means that demand conditions have changed for all sorts of commodities, international and others. This makes it all the more certain that in most cases only a slight change in the terms of trade will occur, even if a large shift in the trade balance is created. But it cannot prevent the terms of trade from moving a little in favor of A, to the extent that the relative prices of A factors and B factors have changed. The problem becomes somewhat different and more complicated when the variations of *relative* factor prices and of sectional commodity price levels in A and B are taken into account.

§ 5. *Relative prices of factors of production.* The increased demand for home market goods in A tends to draw industrial agents from export industries to home market industries. Competing home market industries keep an intermediate position and may expand or decline a little, but they certainly expand less than the demand for their goods, since more import goods are used than before. In a progressive country, where most industries expand more or less each year, industrial agents need not be actually drawn from the declining industries. The readjustment simply means that *new* capital, labor, and natural resources, which would normally have gone to them, are directed instead to home market industries. Thereby the output of the home market industries is increased. Production at full capacity is often extremely

---

[11] See Edgeworth's admirable paper "The Pure Theory of International Trade" in *Papers Relating to Political Economy* (London, 1925), II.

profitable, even though prices have not been raised substantially above the average level.

Such a readjustment naturally involves a change in the prices of the factors of production. Thus, some factors of production are less in demand than before, others more. The result of the change in the direction of production is a changed relative scarcity of the corresponding factors. It seems safe to state that factors used in comparatively great quantities in the production of export and competing home market goods will be less in demand and will fall in price in relation to factors used in home market industries. This movement corresponds to a similar movement of commodity prices; home market goods' prices will rise compared to those of export and competing home market goods.

In such a situation the prices of some factors of production in the developing industries may rise and stay for a considerable time above the prices of the same kind of factors in declining industries. Wages of unskilled labor, for example, may in domestic industries stay for a long while on a higher level than wages of unskilled labor in declining industries. Thus, not only is there a tendency for the kinds of factors used in great quantities in home market industries to rise in price in relation to other factors, but there is also a tendency for the reward given to the units of any factor employed in home market industries to rise in relation to the reward given to the units of the same factor employed in other industries.

These two tendencies arise, or at least they are made possible, because of a lack of factor mobility between industries and trades. It is obvious that if labor of a certain quality could flow without friction from one industry to another and from one place to another, there could at any given time be only one price for that grade of labor in the country. The absence of such mobility makes it possible for wages to be higher in some industries than in others.

Similarly, the lack of mobility of land and capital influences the reward given to these factors in different industries. Capital goods such as buildings and machinery can only with great difficulty and slowly, if at all, be made free and available for use in another industry than the one in which they were first invested. For some time they may be kept unprofitably in the latter industry. Land, too, may for some time be used in one line of production even though another use would be more profitable, although it is in many cases much more easily shifted from one use to another than is fixed capital.

As time goes on, the relative prices of the factors of production, and hence relative commodity prices also, tend to recede toward their position before the borrowings started. The flow of new labor is into occupations that have become relatively well paid. If some capital goods get a higher reward than others, more of the former will be produced and an equalization of the reward effected. If the rent of a certain quality of land rises, it will be profitable to apply capital on other qualities of land in order to give it the qualities of the first, i.e., such land will be "produced" and its rent will fall.

§ 6. *Commodity price levels and terms of trade.* Commodity prices and factor prices move to a great extent hand in hand. However, commodity prices do not bear the same relation to costs of production in all industries, and costs of production as commonly calculated depend not only upon factor prices but also upon the extent to which the productive capacity of a plant is utilized.

The expansion of home market industries, and possibly of competing home market industries as well, may take place to a certain extent without any restriction of output in export industries if unemployed workers and surplus plant capacity are available. One cannot say with certainty which factors will eventually become scarce relative to others. However, the expanding home market industries generally use factors in different proportions than do the declining export industries. Therefore the shift of demand will favor certain types of home market factors over others. Furthermore, expanding industries generally have to pay higher prices for all their factors. For these two reasons costs of production in home market industries rise compared with those in export industries.[12] It is entirely conceivable that there will be no rise in average prices of export products during the period of borrowing. In other words, A may not raise the supply curve of export goods at all.[13] Home market prices and, to a lesser extent, competing home market prices rise, however, in comparison with export prices not only for the above two reasons but also because prices in expanding in-

[12] Costs of transfer are disregarded here.

[13] Thus, the conclusion that terms of trades move in favor of the borrowing country is substantially modified. The orthodox methods of expressing costs in terms of "units of productive power" and similar concepts are responsible for the fact that men like Bastable, Keynes, Pigou, and Taussig found a variation in the terms of trade certain in all cases, at least where the direction of demand is not of a very special sort. The fact that they ignored more or less completely the changes in buying power is another reason why they seem to me to *exaggerate* the changes in trade terms. It is surprising that Keynes should ignore these changes in relative costs and prices because he stressed their importance in the case of an inflationary credit policy of "domestic" origin. Why should the case differ when the expansion of credit and buying power is connected with an import of capital? A typical illustration of how the artificial assumption of units of productive power can make an otherwise acute analysis inconclusive appears in Pigou, "Disturbances of Equilibrium in International Trade." *The Economic Journal* (September, 1929); see e.g., p. 355. Another example of the same mistake appears in a paper by Losch, "Eine Auseinandersetzung über das Transferproblem," *Schmollers Jahrbuch,* 6 (1930). Views similar to mine on the changes in commodity price levels are presented in Wilson, *Capital Imports and the Terms of Trade* (Melbourne, Australia, 1931), e.g., p. 81.

dustries have a tendency to run ahead of costs, with consequent rising profits.

Evidently the buying power in *A* may rise considerably in connection with a change in commodity price levels without any tendency, or only a weak one, for its export prices to rise. And buying power may decline in *B* without its export prices tending to fall. It is not impossible for *A*'s export prices to fall relative to *B*'s. It all depends upon the direction of the new demand in *A* compared with the disappearing demand in *B*. There is at any rate no justification for assuming that a noticeable change in the terms of trade in favor of *A* is the normal or probable outcome, either in the beginning of the borrowing period or later.[14]

In brief, the shift in demand from *B* factors, regarded as a whole, to *A* factors, which the borrowing implies, need not enhance the scarcity of the various productive factors used in *A*'s export industries compared with those used in *B*'s. *How much* the terms of trade vary, when they do vary under the influence of a movement of capital, evidently depends upon circumstances such as the mobility of labor between different trades and places, other reactions of factor supply, or the elasticity of demand.

The price situation does not remain unchanged all through the period of borrowing, assuming that it continues at an even rate. The supply reactions require time. To the extent that they are carried out, prices tend toward the old relationship. It is to be expected, therefore, that considerable price changes will come about a year or two after the borrowing starts, but that as time goes on prices will return more or less to their old position.

Finally, the size of the capital movements in comparison with other aspects of economic life in the countries concerned has an important bearing on the dimensions of the changes in the price system. Other things being equal, the larger the transfer of capital and the greater the readjustment of industry required, the more considerable are the price dislocations. It is much easier to bring about a relative increase of imports and reduction of exports by 5 percent than by 50 percent. The general indication of the analysis above is that changes of the lesser dimension will in most cases not require any noticeable change in the terms of trade in international trade.

§7. *Situation in the capital exporting country.* As for the capital exporting country, *B*, assume that it hands over the borrowed amount to *A* in the form of checks or bills on a third country. Its reserves of foreign exchange decline, the outstanding volume of credit is directly reduced, and the secondary reaction of buying power is brought

---

[14] Individual prices in the international as well as the home market group of commodities may vary considerably.

about in a way analogous to that in which the buying power is increased in *A*. This reduction in buying power must affect commodity and factor prices. Production expands in export industries, whereas it is reduced in home market industries. Competing home market goods hold an intermediate position. The output of such goods is increased in comparison with their consumption, a part replacing imports from *A*.

All in all, the process of readjustment is almost exactly the opposite of that in *A*. However, the difficulties in the way of the necessary readjustment are usually much greater in the lending than in the borrowing country. In many cases a tendency to wage reductions arises, at least temporarily, in certain industries in the former country, while wages in the borrowing country tend rather to increase. If, however, trade unions are strong in *B*, workers belonging to home market industries, where employment is falling off, may prefer a period of unemployment to working in export industries or competing home market industries at lower wages. The readjustment of production may thus cause a certain economic disorganization, and some of the reactions of the balance of payments described may fail for a time to come about. Instead, the reduced production will tend to reduce commodity exports. It is uncertain, however, whether this tendency is nearly as strong as the otherwise existing tendencies to a shift in the balance of trade. If not, the reduction of the foreign exchange reserves continues, and restriction of credit and buying power reaches greater proportions.[15] In that way the trade balance is ultimately adjusted in spite of friction. The adjustments entail losses for *B* not only because of relatively fixed wage rates but also because capital goods cannot easily be transferred from use in one industry to another.

Through friction of this sort, readjustment of the balance of trade is impeded. In some cases this is only partly compensated by the reduction of imports that follows the decrease in buying power. Insofar as this reaction is insufficient, the tendency toward an unfavorable balance of payments persists; interest rates rise, and foreign short term capital flows in. The situation may continue while adjustment proceeds in *A* and in other countries. In this way the burden of readjustment may to some extent be transferred to *A*. It is also conceivable that a financial crisis in *B* might break down either the gold standard or the resistance of the trade unions to wage reductions. In any case—and this is important—*B* may well lose much more from unemployment and other disturbances than from less favorable terms of trade in international trade.

[15] The owners of fixed capital get lower quasi-rents, while unemployment makes the working class decline. The former circumstance is as important as the latter one and should not, as often happens, be ignored. To describe the changes in the aggregate of money incomes solely in terms of wage levels is inaccurate.

The readjustment is naturally much easier in a progressive country where population expands every year than in one where it is stationary or decreasing. In the former there is no need of an absolute reduction of the number of workers in home market industries. The difficulties are also lessened if prices in the world at large are rising during the years when the reorganization of economic life in the capital-exporting country takes place.

In general, secondary effects of different kinds are certain to arise, and their nature depends upon the special characteristics of economic life in the borrowing and lending countries. For instance, if the economies of large scale production are not already entirely available, the expansion of output in certain industries as a result of the borrowings may tend to depress costs. Finally, it cannot be too often emphasized that a description of the mechanism is an account of a *process* and that the situation changes all the time, even if the borrowings continue at an even rate. The difficulty is that goods have to be moved and production adjusted. Like all other adjustments, this requires time, and as time passes, it is more completely effected.

§ 8. *A controversial point.* There is nothing mystical about the creation of sufficient markets for B goods in A, as has sometimes been suggested. Many writers express the opinion that the readjustment has come about surprisingly quickly in some well-known cases of international capital movements. Such surprise is justified in the light of the classical description of the mechanism, where everything centers around the assertion that the lending country must offer its goods on cheaper terms in order to induce the borrowing country to buy a greater quantity of them and thus create an export surplus corresponding to the capital exports.[16] The mechanism outlined above makes much more understandable how the adjustment is brought about so smoothly.

In Sweden an import of capital that had been going on for about a decade at a rate of about 10 percent of the annual commodity imports was changed a few years before World War I into an export surplus of capital of about 5 percent of commodity exports. The necessary readjustment of economic life, which implied among other things an increase of exports by about 30 percent in the course of three years while imports remained almost constant, attracted prac-

[16] Cf. Taussig, *International Trade* (New York, 1927), pp. 239, 261; and Keynes, Rueff, and Ohlin in the *Economic Journal* (September 1929). In *A Treatise on Money* Keynes makes a reference to this discussion but states that credit changes may take place chiefly in A or chiefly in B. He does not seem to have grasped the idea that, independent of the changes in the volume of credit, there is a transfer of buying power to the extent that the borrowers use their money for purchases abroad. He states, "the foreign balance depends on relative price levels at home and abroad," which not even Taussig, the principal defender of the classical doctrine, would be willing to uphold.

tically no attention at the time, and there is no evidence that it met with friction or caused noticeable changes in relative price and income levels. Similar cases have been observed in other countries. Although this proves nothing—foreign demand for Swedish goods may have risen for reasons that have nothing to do with the change in capital movements—it increases the probability that a theory of smooth-working mechanism fits reality.[17]

To understand the true character of international capital movements, it is important to keep in mind that in most cases the monetary transfer precedes both the real transfer and the price changes. The term "monetary transfer" covers those changes in buying power that are the direct outcome of borrowing operations; it includes the "primary" change in the credit volume. These changes in buying power are the ever-present *causa efficiens*, while the character of the price variations varies from case to case. Changes in buying power affect the balance of payments directly in several ways, even in the quite conceivable case where, owing to great mobility and fluidity, there are no relative price changes at all. It is true that in most cases price changes occur, although they need not be considerable and need not involve changed terms of trade. Such changes exercise a further stimulating influence toward adjustment of production and demand—partly by calling forth further changes in buying power—but they hold a secondary position relative to the primary changes in buying power.

[17] Professor Viner has pointed out to me that borrowings may even increase A's demand for import goods more than by the whole borrowed amount. Argentina may borrow $50,000,000 and build a railroad for $100,000,000, of which $80,000,000 may go to pay for foreign goods, whereas in the case of no borrowings the domestic capital would have bought chiefly Argentine goods.

XX

The Mechanism of International Capital Movements, Continued

§ 1. *Size of buying power variations.* I have stressed that changes in the supply price of commodities and in buying power are different aspects of the process of adjustment. Changes in buying power are due in part directly to borrowings and in part to changes in the prices of productive factors, i.e., in the aggregate of money incomes and the flow of liquid capital.[1] One may well inquire which circumstances govern the relative proportions of these two reactions: changes in buying power and in supply prices.

If commodity prices are at all times governed by costs of production, and if every productive factor always commands the same price in all industries in the same country, the relation between the prices of export goods and of home market and competing home market goods will vary only with changes in the relative prices of the various productive factors. If the productive factors used in export industries in the borrowing country are to a large extent different from those used in other industries, export prices will rise only slightly, if at all, whereas the prices of many other goods will rise considerably.

Because certain productive factors may temporarily receive a much higher reward in home market industries than in export industries, and because prices may differ from costs of production, the chance of important increases in the relative prices of home market goods in the borrowing countries is increased. In general, one may say that when the prices of other goods rise much compared to export prices in the borrowing country, while falling much compared with export prices in the lending country, the changes in buying power are correspondingly great. In this case the trade balance is sensitive even to slight changes in the terms of trade, or rather to the variations in buying power that accompany them.

The development of commodity prices and the total volume of buy-

---

[1] In the following I sometimes refer only to the "aggregate of money incomes" when the words "and the flow of liquid capital" should be added to make the statement complete.

ing power depend a great deal upon the credit policy pursued. Whatever policy A adopts in the beginning, it is certain that they will be forced to liberalize unless they can force other outside countries to carry out a definite deflation. If this is done, the lending country has to restrict credit and deflate still further. If, however, there is no reason for outside countries to deflate, increasing reserves of foreign exchange and gold cause a credit expansion in A, in the manner indicated in previous chapters. In the case of German reparations after World War I it was evidently a matter of great importance that the transactions of the international banks should be handled in such a way as to give the countries that were ultimately to receive the reparation payments—namely, France and the United States—a feeling of easy monetary conditions and to cause them to follow a liberal credit policy during the years when the principal readjustment was to take place and a surplus of German commodity exports were to be provided.

§ 2. *Terms of trade.* In many different ways the transfer of buying power tends to turn the trade balances in A and B in such a direction that a real transfer of capital is possible. Alteration in the relation between import and export prices offers special interest from a national point of view. When variations in the price system favor the borrowing country, the lending one dispenses with a greater volume of goods than the transferred sum of money would have bought before the capital transaction began, whereas the borrowing country and outside countries receive more. This outcome is, however, by no means certain. Demand conditions may be so affected that the terms of trade move in favor of B, not A. Even if they change to the disadvantage of B, the corresponding gain may fall to other countries (C), not A.

Considerable capital movements,[2] which primarily reduce demand for goods and productive factors from the lending country, do not cause substantial changes in the export prices of the countries concerned if they have a many-sided production and trade with a large part of the world. Such was certainly the position of Germany after World War II, so there was every reason for assuming that reparation payments would not change the terms of trade greatly to its disadvantage. The situation is different with regard to countries which, like Brazil, export chiefly goods with a comparatively inelastic foreign demand, such as coffee, and which, being industrially one-sided, possess few potential export goods and experience great difficulty in substituting domestic semi-international goods for import goods. An export of capital from Brazil—or the sudden disappearance of its borrowings abroad while the payments of interest and dividends continued

[2] I have in mind borrowings and reparation payments of 10 to 15 percent of the export trade of the countries concerned.

—might cause a substantial drop in the Brazilian export price index.

§ 3. *Influence of tariffs.* Like other obstacles to commodity movements, tariffs impede the international transfer of capital. Trade in international goods is restricted and hence also the means by which capital is transferred. The direct effect of variations in the total buying power upon the trade balance is reduced. It takes a stronger stimulus to make goods move over a tariff wall than under freer trade conditions; a more pronounced shift in prices is essential. In other words, there is opportunity for greater changes in the relation between home market, competing home market, and export prices, with slighter effects upon trade balances. In brief, the connection between national price systems is weakened by tariffs, and the transfer of buying power and goods between them is rendered more difficult. There can be no doubt that the post-World War I protectionist policy throughout the world, as well as the "buy-British-goods" and similar movements, made the payment of the German reparations a much more difficult affair than it would otherwise have been.

If a country that for noneconomic reasons has a large net inflow of capital (reparation payments, for instance) places exceedingly high duties upon all imports, the volume of imports declines. The surplus of foreign exchange causes a credit expansion in one way or another, and the prices of the productive factors and thence the costs of production in all industries rise. There is nothing to prevent them from rising to a level many times as high as formerly. An equilibrium is reached only when the rising price level has so increased imports in spite of duties that these goods discharge the reparation payments.[3]

There was a widespread opinion, expressed in many financial papers and periodicals, that high American import duties were the cause of the American export of capital in the 1920's. The United States, it is said, refused to receive goods as interest and amortization payments and hence had no choice but to invest the money abroad. Behind this view lurks the quasi-mercantilist idea that if a country has a surplus in its balance of trade and at the same time lends abroad, the surplus is due to other circumstances than the loans and that the latter are necessary in order to equalize the balance of payments. An increase of commodity imports will, it is thought, make part of the loans superfluous in a creditor state. As indicated in Chapter XVII, this may be true of temporary variations, but from a long-term point of view capital movement is the cause, and the position of the trade balances the effect.

To prove that the American tariff wall increases American lending abroad it is necessary to demonstrate that the interest level in the

[3] If this country is an important part of the world, other countries may be forced to reduce their price levels.

United States is lower than interest rates abroad, or that the willingness of American capitalists to invest abroad is for other reasons increased, or that of other capitalists to invest in the United States is reduced. There seems no reason for assuming that any of these conditions is fulfilled. It is hence impossible to say whether the United States would export more or less capital if its tariff walls were lower.

§ 4. *Transport costs.* Because capital movements affect the demand for transportation services and thence the costs of transportation, it is conceivable that in certain cases outward freight rates will be substantially increased for *B* compared with inward freight rates. The price level for commodities and factors of production tend downward, but this increases the demand for *B* factors, which more or less offsets the former tendency.

Obstacles to international capital movement consist largely in the difficulties of moving commodities. Import duties and costs of transport between countries are only part of such difficulties; the cost of transport *within* countries plays its part as well. In my location theory I showed that a transfer of buying power and demand from one place to another brings changes in local supply. Goods are moved locally, and the productive factors in each place are put to different uses in producing commodities and services. Both capital and labor are able to move, so that conditions of production are changed. The difficulties of moving goods from the interior to the frontiers exercise the same sort of influence as do the costs of moving them across frontiers and from one frontier to another.

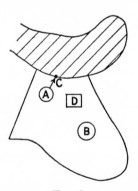

FIG. 6

Fig. 6 may serve as an illustration. Assume that potatoes are exported from region *A* via the harbor *C*, whereas region *B* produces potatoes for the southern part of the country. Their price is *higher* than the price in *C*, reduced by the costs of transport from *B* to *C*. A transfer of buying power from region *B* to other countries, which increases the demand for potatoes in *C*, will depress the price in *B* until it reaches that in *C*, reduced by the costs of transport. Price levels for commodities and productive factors consequently tend more or less downward in regions situated like *B*. Similarly, the regions in capital-importing countries that must have recourse to goods from more distant places of production experience increased price levels.

There is a tendency to avoid sending goods with the highest transportation charges, as well as goods that can be sold abroad in greater quantities only if prices are heavily reduced. Production shifts, and other goods are sent. Region *B* may also send goods to a region better situated for export production (*D*), and the latter may send other goods to the export harbors. This is likely to happen if *B* concentrates on home market goods. In this way the readjustment of commodity movements takes place gradually.[4] In general, the location of industry is changed, as well as prices, within the country. Other things being equal, the industries that produce export goods tend to concentrate in regions favorable for export, because a smaller part of their output is now sold at home. Labor and capital and general economic activity tend to move to such regions. Such factor movements counteract the tendency of prices of mobile productive factors in unfavorably situated regions to fall, but they further reduce the value of natural resources and other immobile factors. It is uncertain, therefore, whether they counteract the tendency of commodity prices to fall in such regions compared with others. At any rate, a tendency toward lower prices in the lending country and higher prices in the borrowing country is inevitable. This is true not only of market prices but of export prices as well.

The preceding analysis, wherein interior costs of transport are disregarded, holds good for regions that from an economic point of view are close to the frontiers. When price conditions in all regions are measured by general price indices, the drop in the lending and the rise in the borrowing country is greater than the analysis indicates. But the terms of trade—the relation between f.o.b. prices of export goods from various countries—are not affected thereby.[5] Evidently export of capital from districts situated like *B* to other countries tends to depress the price level in the lending country more than if the capital were lent by a region like *A*.

§ 5. *Changes in volume of capital movements.* In Great Britain there is a tendency for lending to other countries to incease at the same time that an intensified foreign demand for British goods raises ex-

---

[4] Export of capital from a certain country, i.e., from various parts of it, means a domestic transfer of buying power from one part to another and from the latter to foreign countries.

[5] Nevertheless, the lending country suffers an extra "loss" from the greater transportation costs it has to carry. Variations in the terms of trade are unsatisfactory indices of changes in the national income in each country.

ports relative to imports. Good business conditions increase British savings as well as foreign demand for loans, while British export goods are in greater demand during times of large capital investments abroad. During times of poor business, savings decline, as well as the demand for British goods. Only partly is the change in demand for commodities a direct result of the change in lending. There is a tendency toward a covariation, which to a certain extent keeps a balance between commodity and capital movements.

The close parallelism between capital movements and changes in trade balances cannot, however, be due to this fact alone. Some smoothly operating mechanism working through changes in buying power rather than changes in terms of trade is a contributory factor. The fact that this cannot be easily explained by means of the classical change in relative price levels and trade terms is stressed even by Taussig, the chief protagonist of the classical theory in a revised form.

One thing stands out in the British phenomena. This is the unmistakably close connection between international payments and the movements of commodity imports and exports. This close connection, striking in the case of Great Britain, is found again and again in other countries. International payments, though they involve nothing more between the individuals directly concerned than remittances in terms of money, lead almost at once to transfers of goods. The movement of exports and imports—the substantive course of international trade—responds with surprising promptness to the balance of international payments as a whole. The recorded transactions between countries show surprisingly little transfer of the only "money" that moves from one to the other—gold. It is the goods that move, and they seem to move at once, almost as if there was an automatic connection between these financial operations and the commodity exports or imports.

The fact that changes in international capital movements often appear at the same time as other changes in the economic situation influences the effects of the former. A full analysis, which would require a special volume, would have to consider a great number of different cases. It is particularly worthwhile to examine the cases where changes in capital movements and in other phases of economic life are elicited by a common cause. If the rate of savings increases in country B and the interest level consequently falls, although the fall is reduced through lending abroad, the development is rather different from what it is if the export of capital starts simply because capitalists in B become more willing to invest abroad and the interest level in B consequently rises.

Turn now to another aspect of changes in the volume of international capital movements. During times when the chief lending nations restrict their exports of capital, the world's demand declines for goods like rails, which are needed much more in new countries than in old ones. A serious drop in the export prices of the lending countries may ensue. This is an instance of the case where A buys more of B's export goods than B itself would, and where consequently reduced lending diminishes the demand for B's export goods.

It is probable that British export industries suffered a great deal after World War I from the fact that the French and German export of capital disappeared and that of Great Britain declined; American lending was not able to make up for this. The world demand for British rails, machinery, ships, etc., was kept down. The consequent unemployment and loss in British exporting firms still further reduced savings and thus indirectly the British export of capital.

The restriction of British and American lending in 1929 compared with preceding years may also partly explain how countries that export primary products, such as wheat and coffee, were unable to continue the policy of regulating supply through storing. Sudden increases in the quantity for sale led to a violent drop in the prices of such goods. Such things disturbed economic life in the countries concerned, and the effects spread throughout the world. It is self-evident that a sudden and far-reaching change in the economic system can create various sorts of disturbances.

XXI

Import Duties and Price Adjustments

§ 1. *Effect of duties on relative prices.* An analysis of the mechanism of variations in international trade other than those of capital movements should begin with changes in import duties. I shall disregard their possible influence on the quantity or quality of productive factors or other elements and confine myself to the question of how prices and quantities are affected and how the balance of payments is kept in equilibrium.

Assume that in country A a duty is imposed on a commodity not produced in that country—for example, coffee. The demand for coffee falls off, while demand for other goods, both domestic and foreign, increases.[1] Demand tends to enhance the scarcity of A's goods and productive factors in comparison with all foreign goods and factors, taken as a whole.[2] The aggregate of money incomes in A consequently rises in comparison with that in B. If the combined national income of both countries in terms of money is kept constant by a monetary policy, the imposition of the duty leads to an absolute increase of A's income and buying power and a reduction of B's. This may mean that A buys a larger share of the output of the two countries than before, but this is not necessarily true. The prices of home market goods in A rise relative to prices of similar goods in B. The increase of monetary income in A is partly, in some cases wholly, offset by this fact and thus may not signify an increase in the volume of goods at its disposal.

The change in favor of the productive factors in A at the expense of those in B means also that as coffee-growing becomes unremunerative in B, productive factors flow to other occupations, where costs of production and prices fall also. The average level of commodity prices in B thus declines, while it rises in A.

It is often practical to study changes in commodity prices under

[1] In this analysis coffee stands for a group of commodities that are of considerable importance in A. Otherwise the effects of the duty would be rather small. The amount collected as duty reduces other taxes and increases the net buying power of the tax payers.

[2] In § 1, the rest of the world is referred to as if it were one country, B. Later B means the countries that export goods on which A imposes duties.

three headings. First, how much would demand for various commodities be changed, when their prices vary, if the buying power of the consumers were unchanged? This is sometimes spoken of as "elasticity of demand." Second, how is the buying power of various individuals— and *thereby* their demand for various commodities—affected? Third, how do the schedules of supply prices for commodities change? An analysis of these three reactions may throw light upon the nature and extent of price variations caused by an import duty, notably the variation in the "terms of trade," i.e., the relation between import and export prices.

As to the elasticity of demand, one must ask how much demand in A will react toward (1) the higher price the consumers have to pay for coffee as a result of the duty, and (2) the lower prices of B's other export goods. Importation of coffee falls off, while the purchases of other goods increase; the question is by *how much*, assuming a certain change in prices to have taken place. Furthermore, one must inquire how B's demand for A's export goods reacts when they become more expensive.

The more A's demand for coffee is reduced and the less its demand for other goods is increased, the greater must be the fall in all B prices to equalize the balance between imports and exports, which has been disturbed by the duty. Similarly, the less B's own demand for A's export goods falls off when their prices rise, the greater is the change in prices required to bring about equilibrium—in brief, the more do the terms of trade in international trade move in favor of A. However, the less A reduces its coffee consumption, the slighter is the price variation required to establish equilibrium. The more urgent is the foreign demand for the products from a country at a certain time ("urgent" in the sense that purchases are much increased when prices fall and are slightly reduced when prices rise), and the less urgent is its own demand for foreign products, the less chance there is that the terms of trade will turn to the country's disadvantage, and the greater chance there is that they will change to its advantage.

To turn to the second reaction, changes in buying power in the two countries, they tend to affect imports and exports in the same way as do changes in commodity prices. Reduction of the prices of B's goods increases A's demand for them, and the increased buying power in A augments this. Similarly, the higher prices of A's goods tend to diminish B's purchases, and this tendency is strengthened by the reduction of buying power in B.

Clearly, changes in commodity prices, on the one hand, and variations in buying power, on the other, are two aspects of the same process. The price variation necessary to equilibrate the balance of payments when the import from A to B has been diminished by a duty works by affecting buying power no less than elasticity of demand. The elasticity of international demand is a combination of these two tendencies.[3]

The outcome depends also upon the third reaction, supply. The schedules of supply prices are moved upward in B and downward in A. The extent of their variations for different commodities is the result of several tendencies, of which the change in factor prices is one. The more factor prices fall in B and rise in A, the more supply prices are changed in a corresponding manner and the more the *quantity* of imports to A tends to be increased and the quantity of imports to B tends to fall.[4] Not only are greater quantities of the old import goods sent from B to A and smaller ones in the opposite direction, but new goods pass from B to A, while some of A's old export goods can no longer be marketed in B with a profit, so that trade in them ceases.

In general, when changes in demand caused by the duty have brought about a new economic situation, forces on the supply side exert resistance and tend more or less slowly to return prices to their earlier status. The greater is the adaptability of productive resources, the less effect on prices the new impediment can have. In the long run the forces at work behind the supply of various factors may exercise the deciding influence. Equilibrium between imports and exports in spite of the new duty is maintained by a price variation that evokes reactions of demand and supply just sufficient to offset the reduction of A's coffee imports. How far these price variations need go in each particular case evidently depends upon the conditions of demand and supply. The more sensitive are the latter, the less the prices vary.

Such adaptations of production tend to equalize the price changes of various goods in the same country and minimize the change in the relative price levels of A and B that is necessary to establish equilibrium in the case of a certain import duty. These adaptations of supply also influence the different factor prices and hence the changes in buying power and demand in each country.[5]

§ 2. *Protective duties.* If duties are levied on goods that are or can be produced at home in such a way that their output increases, the

---

[3] When the effects of taxes on imports are studied on the supposition of "barter" by means of the well-known Marshallian curves, both these reactions are handled under one head. Discussions in monetary terms have in almost all cases neglected the changes in buying power.

[4] As to the total *value* of imports, see below.

[5] "The demand of each (country) is made effective by its own supply . . . All trade, either between nations or individuals, is an interchange of things: those which either side is prepared to part with constitute its means of purchase." Marshall, *Money, Credit and Commerce*, p. 160.

effects are not confined to those outlined above in the case of a duty on coffee. Protective duties may naturally cause a shift in production in A directly and thus bring about somewhat different results.

Assume that substantial import duties are imposed on textile goods in country A. As a result, textile industries expand in this country. Demand for *foreign* textiles is thus reduced in two ways: through smaller total demand under the influence of higher prices upon textiles in A, and through a relative cheapening of the home supply. Demand is shifted somewhat from foreign to domestic factors of production; consequently, prices of A factors tend to rise compared with factors in countries producing the taxed commodities. If textile workers successfully pursue a closed-shop policy, their wages may remain on a much higher level than formerly. Home market prices are raised and the corresponding factor prices follow them, as shown in the case of revenue duties. Thus, factors used particularly in home market industries, like those in the protected industries, may have their relative scarcity and their reward increased compared with those of other factors in A. In B a development in the opposite direction takes place. The outcome depends upon the reactions of factor supply, both the mobility of labor from one group to another, and of land and capital from one use to another, and the creation of a new supply of factors by means of savings, education, and the like.

Despite the tendency toward a relative increase in the price level in protectionist countries, prices of some factors and goods produced in these countries may fall. This might happen, for instance, to some of the factors used little or not at all in the protected industries and extensively in the production of export commodities. Since export industries use some of the factors that have become more expensive than before, inability to raise prices on the foreign markets appreciably may well signify that factors used largely in the relatively declining export industries command lower prices than formerly. The price of forest land in countries such as Finland and Sweden is a possible example.

It is also conceivable that certain home market commodities may use relatively as much of these cheapened factors as do export goods, or even more. The prices of such commodities may consequently not only fail to rise but even decline. Suppose, for example, that wheat is an export article, while rye is produced only for the home market. A reduction in wheat-growing lowers the rent of agricultural land; hence, costs of producing rye may not rise at all, in spite of the fact that other factors of production have become more expensive.

It is evident that such reductions of commodity prices in the protectionist country can only be exceptions and that, insofar as they occur, prices of other goods rise all the more. There can be no doubt that the changed direction of demand, the most direct effect of the duties, raises the money prices of productive factors in general and thus the average price level for all commodities produced by these factors. Because import goods are not likely to be much cheapened, both commodity and factor price levels are raised.[6]

England, a free trade country, saw its price level fall almost continuously in the three decades before World War I compared with that of two protectionist countries, Germany and Sweden. The margin was widened especially in the 'eighties and the beginning of the 'nineties. It seems probable that this was due principally to the Swedish and German corn duties. The index numbers include too few manufactured products to tell much concerning the duties upon them.

§ 3. *Terms of trade.* Although it seems certain that home market prices and, inclusive of duties, import prices in a protectionist country can be considerably raised in comparison with export prices, it is much less sure that export prices can be appreciably raised relative to import prices, exclusive of duty, which would improve the terms of trade. It is often asserted that import duties restrict imports and tend to depress import prices, exclusive of duty, so that a rise in export prices is necessary to affect a corresponding reduction of the volume of exports. It is implied that this shift in the terms of trade may substantially affect the size of the national incomes of various states.[7] As a matter of fact, there are several reasons for assuming that in most cases only a slight change in the terms is caused even by a fairly high general tariff wall.

Some import duties tend to reduce exports from A, even if export prices fail to rise. Productive factors are shifted to the protected industries. For export industries fewer factors are available, some of them only at increased prices. Some raw material or semifinished goods are also rendered more expensive. Hence, such industries do not pay well, and less effort and capital is spent to expand sales of their products abroad. Commodities do not sell themselves; foreign demand is not a question solely of prices but depends also upon the effectiveness of marketing. In a word, less energy is devoted to the export trade and more to domestic trade.

The inevitable outcome is a *falling off in A's volume of exports, even if both foreign demand and export prices are unchanged.* In dis-

[6] Changes in the relation between transports to and from a country may alter this conclusion. If the importation of bulky goods is restricted, inward freights may fall and outward freights may rise, which would depress prices in that country. Economies of large-scale production, however, do not seem to necessitate any substantial modifications.

[7] Cf. Taussig, *International Trade*, pp. 142-144. Curiously, most writers in this question make no attempt at estimating the relative importance of changes in the terms of trade.

cussions of the opposite case (the effects upon exports of a return to free trade or low duties), it is sometimes asserted that a small reduction of costs and export prices would have no appreciable influence upon the quantity of exports. Such an assertion neglects that productive factors would be turned from home market to world market production and that much energy and enterprise now used in domestic trade would be devoted to foreign trade. Given a period of transition, the volume of exports might increase substantially, yet their prices would not necessarily be lowered.[8]

Whereas exports decline, imports tend to grow.[9] The increased cost levels in A retard the development of industries manufacturing goods that compete with imports but which do not have supporting duties. In B, however, the corresponding industries profit from reduced cost levels, and there is less need for imports. Second, the home market prices and buying power, higher in A and lower in B, incline demand toward international goods in the former country and away from such goods in the latter country, regardless of any reduction of B's export prices compared with A's.

How much the terms of trade vary depends upon the conditions of supply and demand. It may be well to stress once more that foreign demand is in most cases elastic in the long run. A small rise in A's export prices will be sufficient to turn demand abroad decidedly away from them to similar products from other countries, C,[10] particularly when supply in the other countries reacts easily. A's competitors increase their exports at A's expense. Besides, both B and other countries, called D,[11] will increase their own output of such goods and reduce the sum total of imports. Yet a slight reduction of the prices at which B exports nonprotected goods will increase its exports at the expense of the producers of these goods or competing goods in D. The closer the competition between A and other countries (C), the less probable is it that an import duty is able to affect the terms of trade noticeably in favor of A. The consumers in A will have to pay practically the whole duty, and B will suffer little or not at all from less favorable terms of trade.

Some of A's export goods may drop out of international trade alto-

---

[8] Since markets for most good are not perfect, the share of foreign demand that is satisfied through supply from a certain country depends on sales organization. Unless such selling expenditure is offset through savings from economies of large-scale production when output is increased, the terms of trade, calculated in terms of productive factors, move in an unfavorable direction.

[9] If many goods are protected, imports of those having relatively low duties will grow.

[10] If the prices at which other countries export such goods rise also, the total consumption of them will decline.

[11] These countries do not export protected goods to A, as B does, and do not compete with A, as C does.

gether as a result of slight price increases, which means pronounced elasticity in the foreign demand, but *B* will be able to export goods that before were produced only for the home market. A reduction of the costs of production by, for example, 10 percent would permit many new goods, so far marketed abroad little or not at all, to sell in large quantities; and thus existing export industries would be able to expand at the expense of foreign competitors. For this reason, and because of the other reactions, such a country would be able to increase its volume of exports by much more than 10 percent, even if the sort of goods exported were only *consumed* in 5 percent greater quantities as a result of such a price reduction.

A is able to achieve a considerably better ratio between export and import prices only when the following conditions obtain: (1) foreign countries have an insistent demand for the sort of goods *A* exports and thus restrict their consumption very slightly when *A*'s export prices are raised and buying power is reduced in *B*;[12] (2) the supply of such goods from other countries is small, or cannot be easily increased without markedly raising costs; (3) foreign countries reduce their export prices for the goods upon which *A* has imposed a duty, because *A* is an important market with elastic demand and the productive factors in these industries cannot readily be shifted to other industries;[13] and (4) *A*'s demand for nonprotected foreign goods is not much increased when they can be obtained more cheaply and *A*'s buying power has grown.[14]

It is conceivable that *some* of *A*'s goods might fulfill the first two conditions, but it is practically impossible that the majority of a country's exports would do so. And only when this happens, and the third and fourth conditions are also fulfilled, could the terms of trade be much improved from *A*'s point of view. This can only happen in quite unusual cases.

One must, however, except the situation soon after the imposition of the duty. Industries producing for certain markets do not easily

[12] The influence of reduced buying power in the countries exporting the goods on which *A* levies import duties must be stressed. The chances of turning the trade terms in favor of *A* are greater when countries selling the protected goods purchase very little from *A* than when they are important customers of *A*. The British Labor party's preference for duties or import prohibitions against countries with low wages would probably fall off if it were remembered that these countries happen to be good customers in Great Britain.

[13] The productive factors may have few competitive uses, like certain natural resources, and the reduction of *A*'s demand may therefore reduce the supply price of certain foreign goods considerably. This circumstance is ignored by Pigou, *A Study in Public Finance* (London, 1928), xix-xx.

[14] Marshall's statement in *Money, Credit and Commerce* (p. 198) is incomplete because he omits this fourth element. He apparently has in mind a case where *all* imports have been subject to considerable duties in *A*.

swing to others, even though prices are unremunerative because of import duties. Foreign countries may continue to supply A with taxed goods at considerably lower prices than before. A may continue for some time to export its goods to their former markets, even though their prices are higher than those of competitors. But this situation will not last: A will gradually be driven from some of its markets or be forced to sell at competitive prices; and foreign producers will turn away from the unprofitable sales in A unless the latter is willing to pay a price approximately as high as that paid by other customers. Except for such temporary quasi-monopolistic phenomena it is safe to say that no country has much chance of turning the terms of trade greatly in its favor by means of import duties. Marshall supports this view as follows:

> There has indeed never been a country, the whole of whose exports were in such urgent demand abroad, that she could compel foreigners to pay any large part of any taxes which she imposes on her imports. But England's exports approached to it twice. Once they consisted chiefly of wool, which was indispensable to Flemish weavers. And, again, in the first half of the nineteenth century, they consisted chiefly of manufactures made by steam machinery, which was not in general use anywhere else; together with tropical products, which she had special facilities for obtaining. It is possible that the rest of the world would have given twice as much of their own goods as it did give for many of them, rather than go wholly without them.[15]

So far I have dealt only with the case where *one* country uses a high tariff. Will the conclusion that no country has much chance to move the terms of trade in its favor by means of a protective tariff hold also when *many* countries pursue a similar policy? Will free trade countries under the cumulative influence of many hostile tariff barriers see their terms of trade substantially affected?

As a matter of fact, there are many countries with tariff walls not only against free trade nations but also against each other. Does this improve the position of the free trade countries? The answer is in the affirmative. If there were one large group of protectionist countries only, surrounded by a common tariff, demand would be shifted from the productive factors in outside countries toward interior productive factors. The countries behind the tariff wall would have a favorable position when exporting to one another, compared to the countries outside, which would have to send their goods across the barrier. The fact that there is no such tariff union but a number of independent tariff districts deprives the protectionist countries of this favorable position in their competition with free trade countries. In the export trade they are obliged to compete on an equal footing.

When exporting to the European continent British industry is much

---

[15] Marshall, *Money, Credit, and Commerce*, p. 192.

hampered by the high tariffs prevalent almost everywhere. Its difficulties are increased by the Continental tariff union giving a preferential
position to the Continental competitors of British firms. In a word, if
the protectionist countries direct their weapons exclusively against a
small number of free trade or low tariff countries, they have some
chance of success in the form of favorably altered terms of trade.
But fighting as they are against one another as well, the effects are
likely to be slight.[16]

So far only the elasticity in the demand for and supply of commodities has been dealt with. However, the elasticity of the demand
for services that appear in the balance of payments but not in the
trade balance is also relevant. A creditor nation with large interest
incomes from abroad, for example, may assume that the foreign demand for its currency is relatively inelastic, for foreign nations have
to supply a fixed sum of the creditor country's currency as a supplement to the variable sum they need to pay for their commodity imports. Thus, the interest payments increase the creditor nation's chances
of altering the terms of trade in its favor through import duties.[17]

§ 4. *The monetary mechanism.* Turn now to the way in which the
balance of payments is kept in equilibrium when new or increased
import duties are imposed. As in the case of other disturbances, short-
term capital movements are called into play until the trade balance
has been adjusted.

Immediately after the change in tariff policy the situation is uncertain. If the tariff variation has come unexpectedly, A will have an
excess of exports in the beginning and a temporary increase in the
reserves of foreign exchange. This leads directly and indirectly to an
increase in buying power. If, however, imports increase materially in
anticipation of the imposition of duties, an excess of imports may arise
and a temporary reduction in the exchange reserves may follow. In
that case the increase in buying power comes about in a different
manner from that described in the discussion of capital imports. A

---

[16] These conclusions suggest one thing concerning the methods to be pursued in
attempts to bring about conditions of freer trade in the world. If a number of nations, which are much interested in the success of such an attempt, formed a
large tariff union, the other countries, whatever tariff policy they pursued, would
find themselves unfavorably situated when competing in this important market. They
would have every inducement to join the tariff union, which would have a chance
of growing to embrace the majority of nations. Those who obstinately remained outside would be in a more and more difficult position. Would not the chances of
some sort of universal free trade agreement under such conditions be as great as
they can ever be as long as the inherent mercantilist tendencies of man, exploited
by powerful vested interests, remain one of the principal governing factors in the
tariff policy of all nations?

[17] Cf. my conclusions in Chap. XX that tariff walls strengthen the tendencies to
changes in trade terms in the case of international capital movements. See Pigou,
A Study in Public Finance, xx.

description of the various possibilities would be too lengthy but the fact to be stressed here is that, unless the volume of credit is increased in the protecting country, the trade balance is not sufficiently altered in a negative direction to offset the restricting influence on imports which protection is bound in the long run to have. Thus, foreign exchange reserves grow, and a credit expansion ultimately develops.

§ 5. *Duties as means of better utilizing productive capacity.* The effects of a higher tariff in a period of depression differ much from their effects in a period of intense business activity. A distinct practical interest attaches to duties imposed during periods of depression. As an example, assume that the boot and shoe industry in a country is using only 60 percent of its capacity, while 90 percent is the ordinary rate. A corresponding part of the workers are unemployed. Imports of foreign shoes in greater quantities than formerly have been going on for some time. In this situation most domestic firms find it difficult to meet their expenses and earn no interest on the share capital. Through pressure upon politicians an increased or revised import duty is secured.

To simplify the analysis, assume that the estimated price difference between domestic and foreign shoes of equal quality is 25 percent. The former cost 15s. wholesale, whereas the latter sell for only 12s.[18] After the duty is imposed, imports decline, and the domestic industry, while maintaining its price at 15s., succeeds in increasing its sales by one-half, which brings the utilization of its productive capacity up to the normal 90 percent.

What extra expenses are involved in this increase of output from, say, two to three million pairs? No new buildings or machines are needed, no new directors or officers, and very little addition to the office staff. However, the number of workers must be increased and the purchases of leather and other raw materials must grow in proportion with the increase in output.

Assume that the variable expenses amount to 8s. per pair. The producers consequently earn no less than 7s. on each pair of shoes by which their sales are increased. Yet the consumers pay 3s. more than before. From the point of view of the whole nation there is a gain of 4s. per pair, or 4,000,000s. in all.[19] But this is not all. A con-

---

[18] The fact that domestic shoes nevertheless sell may be explained by old trade connections with retail stores and the preference for homemade goods.

[19] Of course, nothing prevents the domestic industry from reducing its price to twelve shillings and thereby increasing its sales without the aid of an import duty. This would lead to the same immediate gain as the one resulting from the duty. However, shoe manufacturers may prefer not to do so because they would receive only four shillings instead of seven above their variable expenses. An increase in sales by 50 percent would not compensate for this reduction in the amount per pair which goes to cover overhead costs.

siderable part of the so-called variable expenses are so only from the point of view of the individual firm, not from that of society as a whole; this is the case with wages, at least in part. The workers have to live whether they are employed or not. Assume that they received a dole of about 1,000,000s. per year before the duty was imposed. This sum is no longer paid—a clear gain to the taxpayers. Furthermore, the workers earn twice as much when working as they received when unemployed. They too have their economic position improved by a similar amount. The total gain to society is 6,000,000s. Look at it another way. Instead of being imported at a price of 12s., shoes are being produced at home at an extra cost to the nation of only 6s. The difference is net gain.[20]

What would have happened if no duties had been imposed? If it is assumed that several other industries are in a position similar to that of the boot and shoe industry, it is natural to suppose that the balance of payments has a tendency to become negative. Consider first some cases of this type. The usual mechanism comes into play, short-term capital moves out, credit policy is restricted, and wages and prices fall.[21] In this way competitive power is increased all round, with some industries expanding and either enlarging their exports or reducing competitive imports. Equilibrium in the balance of payments is obtained without further loan transactions, and the conditions of employment and utilization of productive capacity are much the same as before the crisis began. Some industries of the least effective class—e.g., the boot and shoe industry—are probably much reduced, their laborers having found employment in other more productive fields. The process of readjustment completed, the volume of available goods will be greater than under a system of permanent duties.

Some readjustments, however, are slow and troublesome. Trade unions, for instance, may prevent the wage reductions that are an essential part. In the retail trade, prices fall slowly. In the meantime, losses from unemployment and a general lack of balance in economic life are likely to be great. During this period of transition import duties of a temporary character may bring advantages of the sort indicated in the example from the boot and shoe industry. Theoretically they may be so constructed (e.g., if they are gradually falling) as not seriously to obstruct or retard the natural redistribution of economic forces among various lines of production. They would keep employed part of the otherwise idle machines and laborers without reducing the stimulus for the rest to shift to more effective industries.

In cases where the balance of payments does not tend in a negative

---

[20] The possible effects on the terms of trade in international trade are left out of account in this section.

[21] In other words, there is need of a certain deflation.

direction before the duties are imposed, and in cases where the tendency of the duties to turn the balance in the other direction is stronger, the reduction in imports must in some way be balanced wholly or partly either by a corresponding reduction in exports or by an export of capital. All such cases differ from that of a protectionist duty under normal conditions in at least one important respect. The factors of production used to increase output in the protected industries come from the ranks of the unemployed. There is, therefore, no diminution of production in other industries, no unoccupied commodity space to be filled through greater imports or smaller exports. This element in the mechanism of readjustment of the balance of payments is absent.

However, the better utilization of productive factors tends to increase the aggregate of money incomes and hence also the demand for foreign goods. The prices of productive factors are maintained on a higher level than would in the long run have been possible without the duties. This implies two things: the buying power is kept so high that an import surplus would be created were it not for the duties; and the schedules of supply prices of export commodities and goods competing with import goods are higher than they would be later if there had been no duties. The exports fail to grow, and demand is turned from competing home market goods to import goods, so that imports are increased.

In brief, so long as protection is maintained, the otherwise inevitable deflation may be unnecessary or may be effected more slowly. If the duties are only temporary, deflation must, it is true, come, but the temporary stimulus afforded by them may be directed toward the industries that respond by increasing their productive activity, and the readjustment may be accomplished with less disturbance to economic activity.

This analysis applies above all to cases where the unemployment or incomplete utilization of productive capacity is due chiefly to monetary causes, e.g., deflation in other gold standard countries not balanced by a corresponding general deflation of prices and wages at home. The conclusions may hold true also when there is no need for or tendency toward deflation, but simply severe unemployment owing to the occurrence of frequent and profound disturbances such as dumping, new tariff walls, and technical progress. The increased aggregate of money incomes will raise the demand for foreign goods and increase exports, whereas the foreign countries will have less buying power and will for other reasons as well buy less from the protecting nation. In this way the trade balance will be restored. It is extremely probable that the trade balance will thereafter maintain a positive tendency. The ordinary mechanism of credit expansion will come into play, prices and cost levels will rise, and exports will decline, so that unemployment and surplus capacity will be created in export industries, perhaps as much as had disappeared in the protected industries.

If savings and capital exports increase, there is no need of a decline in exports. Assume, for example, that the output of protected goods is increased by $100,000,000, that they take the place of imports, and that the rise of incomes increases imports of other goods by $40,000,000. If so much capital is lent to other countries that the balance of payments is moved $60,000,000 in a negative direction, the two tendencies offset one another and the balance of payments is not disturbed.

Some such thing may happen. If the foreign exchange reserves grow, the money market in the protecting country will be easy, interest rates may fall, and floating balances will tend to move to other financial centers.[22] It is nevertheless difficult to see how this can be more than a passing episode. Probably, after a year or two, the ordinary mechanism that contributes to a reduction of exports, at least relatively, will begin to function. Even then unemployment may be less than it would otherwise have been, if export industries expand only a little less than they would have done. When that is so, no unemployment is created to offset its reduction in the protected industries.

In the long run unemployment is probably not helped by the duties. Without duties a readjustment would take place, laborers would be transferred, etc., in such a way as to reduce unemployment—perhaps as much as do the duties, or more so. However, the chances of avoiding an increase of unemployment in export industries for some time after new duties have been imposed are considerable if a short-term movement of floating balances is elicited.

To sum up, in a situation characterized by a lack of balance in economic life, the introduction of a new element may perhaps bring about a better balance, even though this element by itself would cause an unfavorable change. If one disturbance has occurred, it may be better to introduce another in a different direction than to leave the first one to work out its effects. An obvious example is the prevention of sudden and short-lived foreign dumping.

One consequence of this analysis is that in a disturbed economic state trade with other countries may continue undiminished, even though part of it is in reality not advantageous. The cause of this

[22] A very similar, perhaps identical, opinion was advocated in the *Nation* (London) during 1928-29 in a discussion of Great Britain's economic position. "We suggest that, for moderate changes in the import volume, the classical reactions . . . are intercepted by the cushions of international indebtedness and do not actually work through to exports. . . That certainly is the moral suggested by our post-war experience, with its undiminished imports and its largely diminished exports." *The Nation and the Atheneum* (September 1, 1928), p. 700.

peculiar trade phenomenon is the existence of fixed costs and the occurrence of unpredictable disturbances. These circumstances frequently prevent the full utilization of productive capacity. In themselves they have nothing special to do with international trade; nevertheless, a small part of the loss from such incomplete utilization may under certain circumstances be transferred to foreign countries.

In the example above, the duty has been imposed on consumers' goods. If producers' goods are protected, the development is somewhat different. The foregoing has dealt only with the effects of import duties, the object being to demonstrate how the price mechanism works when such duties are introduced under ordinary conditions or in times of unemployment.

XXII

International Price Variations

§ 1. *Monetary variations.* It remains to consider briefly the price variations due wholly or partly to changes in the monetary system.[1] As
before, the discussion is confined to the development in countries
with a gold or a gold exchange standard. In this case, as opposed to
those already touched upon, it is perhaps less the differences than
the similarity of price variations in various countries which has to be
explained.

Why do wholesale commodity price levels go up and down in very
much the same way and at the same time in the European and American countries during different phases of the business cycle? What are
the causes of this surprising parallelism in the price movements, which
was clearly demonstrated in the years 1928-30, for example, for countries with settled monetary conditions? The explanation is often given
roughly as follows: if prices rise in certain countries and not in others,
the trade balance in the latter will move in a positive direction, the
foreign exchanges will drop, and gold will flow into the central banks,
which will reduce their discount rates and expand credit, whereby
prices will be raised in these countries as well. This explanation is
to a certain extent correct, for if nothing else happens *before* all
these reactions, they will come into play.[2] As a matter of fact, however, there are other reactions which in most cases tend to equalize
prices in a quicker and smoother way.

When credit expands and prices rise in A, home market prices in B
tend to rise to the extent that they use raw or semifinished materials
which are, or could be, imported from A, or are potentially competitive with similar goods produced by A. In addition, A will demand
more of B's export goods, and the increase in foreign orders exercises
a stimulating influence on economic life in B in general. The credit

[1] Such changes in buying power, and hence in demand, may be regarded as a
special sort of variation. They are similar to those described above for the cases
of capital movements and import duties. The mechanism of changes in international
demand, in technique and the discovery of new natural resources, trade union
policy, etc., are not dealt with in this book.
[2] Cf. Keynes, *A Treatise on Money*, pp. 336 ff.; and Ohlin, "The Future of the
World Price Level," *Index* (Stockholm, 1927).

volume expands automatically in response to the increased need, unless some restrictive action is taken to keep it at its former level. But this happens only in rare cases. If the central bank in A has reduced its discount rate and has in that way made the price level tend upward, the central bank in B is inclined to follow suit and in the absence of special circumstances will certainly not pursue the opposite credit policy. Should it for some time attempt to do so, short-term capital transactions will lead to a surplus of foreign exchange in B and will soon make the central bank reverse its policy.

Thus, the parallelism of price movements depends upon the connection between certain commodity prices in different countries (above all, the prices of international goods), upon the influence of changes in the volume of foreign orders, and upon the connection between discount rates, which is partly due to the international mobility of capital. This does not exclude the possibility that forces of a non-monetary character lying behind the business cycle also have something to do with the parallel price movement. The mere belief that a business boom abroad will spread to one's own country leads to optimism in buying and thus hastens the development.

Since central banks, when an improvement in business begins, usually have greater gold reserves than legally called for, they are able to expand credit without any increase in gold stocks. Thus, no gold flow need be caused. A business depression and drop in the wholesale price level may also spread without any gold flow, through the direct connection between certain prices, the influence of a changed volume of orders, etc.

An international inflation due to an increased supply of gold develops in essentially the same way. The rise in the price level during times of good business is simply a little stronger than it would otherwise have been. The only difference in the mechanism is that the new gold has to be distributed among the various countries. Assume that it goes in the first place to the United States and Great Britain, and leads to credit expansion there. Central banks in other countries will not be able to increase their credit volumes to the same extent until they have somewhat increased their gold reserves. For some time, therefore, their credit policy may remain relatively restrictive; their balance of payments becomes positive (through capital transactions and, if the situation lasts long enough, through an adjustment of trade), the foreign exchanges fall, and gold flows in, which leads to the delayed expansion of credit (cf. Chapter XVII). But it is by no means certain that such will be the case. If credit expansion has started under the influence of rising prices and order reserves, the central bank may be reluctant to retard it because of insufficient gold reserves. It may proceed to increase gold reserves in a more deliberate, some would say a more artificial, way than the one just indicated. By reducing its foreign exchange reserves, it may temporarily depress the foreign exchange rates and make gold flow in. Or it may dispense with pressure on rates and simply use a part of its foreign exchange reserves to buy gold, incurring in that way a small loss, but saving the business world from a short-lived exchange rate fluctuation. Such an exchange of foreign bills for gold is a transaction of no great interest in itself, and apart from it, the mechanism that brings about the spread of inflation is identical with the one described above.

In summary, whether the gold reserves are adjusted in one way or the other is relatively unimportant. The international character of the price movement is due to the direct connection between the various national commodity price systems and volumes of orders and to the forces affecting discount and interest rates. The gold flow mechanism is of great potential but usually little actual influence,[3] to be used only in the last resort to prevent considerable international price discrepancies under the conditions here discussed.[4]

§ 2. *Determination of foreign exchange rates.* The conditions governing foreign exchange rates have often been discussed in connection with international price relations. I have stressed that anything which affects the supply of or demand for foreign exchange can influence

---

[3] Great Britain is a notable exception to this rule. The gold movements between that country and the United States and France after 1926 influenced British credit policy in every phase of the business cycle.

[4] This analysis differs in several respects from the one presented by Angell, *The Theory of International Prices,* xvi, especially pp. 416-418. The correlation between the short-term fluctuations of prices in different countries seems to me sufficiently explained by my analysis and need not, as Angell suggests, be "due either to some peculiarity in the case selected, or to the interdependence of the price indices used." Neither can I agree that the explanation of the correlation in long-term price tendencies should run exclusively "in terms of the effects of differences in price movements upon the balance of payments." It seems unfortunate to speak, on the one hand, of "disturbances that originate in the balance of payments itself" and, on the other, of disturbances originating in "discrepancies between the movements of general prices in different countries." Changes in credit policy may well affect the balance of payments much earlier than they affect the wholesale price level and do not, therefore, lead to the second type of disturbance. (Keynes, perhaps also Cassel, take an attitude similar to Angell's. The former speaks of changes that "originate in discrepancies of price levels.") But credit changes may affect prices first, and the balance of trade and balance of payments only indirectly. Thus, the distinction between the two types of cases seems unprofitable. It is more natural to classify according to the changes in basic circumstances, capital movements and monetary policy. In other respects my views here are in close accord with Angell's, which have so far been expressed only sketchily. He writes (p. 418): "The ultimate key to the maintenance of equilibrium in the balance of payments in the face of enduring disturbances, and the key to the problem of international equilibrium at large . . . lies in the effect that a persisting change in the relation between the demand and supply of bills of foreign exchange produces upon the volume of purchasing power in circulation, and through it upon the general level of prices." I should like only to add: "and upon imports and exports."

the price paid for it, and that consequently *all* elements in the price system directly or indirectly affect the foreign exchange rates. There is a fixed relation between foreign exchange rates and other prices. If the basic circumstances vary, however, that relation varies also. For instance, under periods of practically constant foreign exchange rates, the relation between commodity and productive factor prices in different countries has been subject to considerable variations, in a way that cannot possibly be due to capital movements or to monetary disturbances.

In principle, foreign exchange rates have nothing to do with the wholesale commodity price *level* as such but only with individual prices. Changes in individual prices may be relevant even though the level of commodity prices happens to remain constant. Only for the sake of simplicity do variations in price *levels* have their place in a discussion of foreign exchange problems, for the main subject of interest is the individual prices, i.e., more or less the whole price mechanism. Of course, the fact that international trade is a wholesale trade puts the foreign exchange rates in a specially intimate relation to the wholesale prices of certain commodities. But the prices of certain services that citizens of one country render to citizens of other countries—shipping, insurance—and the height of short-term and long-term interest rates are equally influential, as they also directly affect supply and demand on the foreign exchange market. The wholesale prices of other goods, as well as the retail prices and the prices of productive factors in general, exercise an indirect influence, so that it is impossible to regard their variations as of no consequence for prices in the exchange market. As soon as one sees the foreign exchange rates as prices in the system of mutual interdependence, the idea of a fixed relation between these rates and some sort of average for a certain group of commodity prices becomes evident.

It follows that the so-called "purchasing power parity" doctrine, at least in certain formulations, is untenable. After years of intensive discussion Cassel gave a condensation of his reconsidered opinion as follows:[5]

> The main reason why we pay anything for a foreign currency is of course that this currency represents in the foreign country a purchasing power which can be used for acquiring the goods or for paying for the services of that country. Thus it is clear that the amount we can pay for the unit of the foreign currency must, broadly speaking, be in direct proportion to the internal purchasing power of that currency, i.e., in the inverse proportion to the country's general level of prices. On the other hand, it is clear that we can afford to pay more in our own currency the more abundant this currency is, i.e., the lower

---

[5] Cassel, "Foreign Exchanges," *Encyclopaedia Britannica*, 13th ed. (1926), first supplementary volume, p. 1086. Cf. his *Theoretische Sozialökonomie*, § 60, where the same opinion is expressed.

its internal purchasing power, and the higher the general level of home prices. This is easily seen if we reflect on the fact that the price paid for a foreign currency is ultimately a price for foreign commodities, a price which must stand in a certain relation to the prices of commodities on the home market. Thus, we arrive at the conclusion that the rate of exchange between two currencies must depend essentially on the quotient of the internal purchasing powers of these currencies.

The idea that people demand foreign currency because it has a certain purchasing power for commodities *in general* on the wholesale market is not in accordance with facts. The importer wants foreign bills to buy and pay for certain foreign goods and is not interested in the prices of other goods. The man who is to transport commodities is interested in the height of shipping rates charged by different shipping companies and not in commodity prices. It is not true that a rise in certain commodity prices in a country—i.e., a reduction in the purchasing power of that country's currency—in all cases reduces the foreign demand for bills on that country. If the price of coal is raised and the foreign demand has a low elasticity—as it proved to be when Great Britain maintained high prices immediately after World War I—a greater sum of money will be needed for the same amount of coal. The pound sterling quotation tends to rise, not fall.

The weakness of the idea that foreign exchanges are an expression for the relation between commodity price levels is perhaps most clearly seen if one considers two countries, each of which produces only goods not manufactured at all in the other. There are no common market goods, and no possibility of comparing the height of the general price levels at a certain time in the two countries. Nevertheless, all prices in both countries form part of a system of mutual interdependence, so that there is a certain relation between the foreign exchange rate and the prices in each country. But this relation cannot be expressed in terms of price levels, e.g., by saying that they are of the same height (cf. Appendix I, § 4).

So much for the simple form of the purchasing power parity doctrine. There is another and more qualified form, which is limited to the assertion that the foreign exchange rates reflect the price level *changes*. Thus, the question whether or not prices before World War I were higher in the United States than in England is irrelevant. A rise in the English price index to 400 and in the American one to 200 goes hand in hand with a drop in the sterling exchange in New York to half its previous rate. The real parity changes with the relation between the price index numbers. It follows that if the foreign exchange rates are kept constant, the relation between the price indices is fixed also.

Clearly this assumes that all basic circumstances, including capital movements, are unchanged. When this is so, all relative prices in each country are unchanged if sufficient time has passed for a read-justment after the monetary changes. If Great Britain chooses to use a fourth of a pound as unit of reckoning, and the United States one-half a dollar, the New York quotation of the new British currency in terms of the new American currency will of course be half the previous sterling rate. In other words, if nothing has changed but the absolute height of the price levels, it is a truism that the exchange rates vary as indicated. However, other things never are quite equal at different times, so that relative commodity and factor prices, and hence the relation between the price indices, change, even if the foreign exchange rates are kept stable through a gold standard. In brief, changes in the basic circumstances of the price system alter the relation between the foreign exchange rates and other prices in the various countries. Even when these rates are kept constant, the relation between the prices in different countries may vary.

To an analysis of this sort it is sometimes objected that as a matter of fact changes in basic circumstances are not able to cause considerable variations in relative price levels in countries with a many-sided and well-developed international trade. Experience shows that this assertion is justified for short periods and "normal" times in countries such as the United States, Great Britain, Sweden, and Holland, but it is not true for long periods nor for periods of "abnormal" transfer conditions, such as the years 1914-21.[6] Neither is it true for countries with a one-sided economic life, such as Egypt, Chile, and Brazil. The deviations of relative price levels in cases of the latter type—e.g., owing to demand changes—are not abnormal deviations from a true equilibrium (the purchasing power parity) but rather changes in the equilibrium itself.

In some cases of foreign exchange and price variation during and after World War I it proved fruitful to disregard at first the variations in basic circumstances and to concentrate upon the relative degrees of inflation. But in other cases changes in demand, transfer, and international credit conditions were as potent elements as even the violent inflation in neutral countries during that period.[7] In any case, the most fruitful and most correct way of explaining foreign exchanges is to show their place in the general price system and the influence of variations in basic circumstances, including capital movements, and

[6] Changes in the monetary systems are another "abnormal" element that influences relative price levels in terms of gold.

[7] See Heckscher, *Sweden's Monetary History, 1914-25, in its Relations to Foreign Trade and Shipping*, in the Scandinavian volume of the *Economic and Social History of the World War* (New Haven, 1930). Heckscher shows that the sterling quotation in Stockholm at one date was exactly half the purchasing power parity. Nobody interested in problems of international trade during a paper standard regime can afford to overlook his study.

in monetary conditions. In specific cases, sometimes one, sometimes another, element may be for all practical purposes disregarded. But to do so in the presentation of fundamental principles, or to present their influence as abnormal deviations from a normal position, is misleading.[8]

Another observation on the post-World War I discussion of the foreign exchanges may be made. Since anything that affects the balance of payments *ipso facto* influences the foreign exchange rates, and since all changes in basic circumstances, in capital movements, and in monetary policy may exercise such an influence, there is no contradiction between the theories of foreign exchanges that seek the causes of their variations in the balance of payments—i.e., in demand, supply, and transfer conditions—and those that stress the influence of monetary policy and price level variations.[9] There is only a difference in emphasis, which has been largely justified by the differences in concrete circumstances at various times. The former theories have been prevalent during periods of settled monetary conditions; the latter, during times of inflation and deflation.

Changes in monetary policy, like other variations, alter the supply and demand schedules in the foreign exchange market and thereby the exchange rates. Commodity prices are of course altered also, but it is uncertain whether the trade balance, the international movement of capital, or the price level is affected first. Changes in the volume of credit often affect the volume of imports or the size of capital transfers much more quickly than they affect the height of home market prices.[10] Experience does not justify making changes in the price level the first step or changes in the balance of payments the consequence of price variations.

[8] In *Theoretische Sozialökonomie*, Part V, § 88, which was added in the 1926 edition, Cassel discusses international trade on the basis of a mutual interdependence price system in a way with which I am in substantial agreement. There seems to be no harmony between this analysis and his old treatment of the foreign exchanges in Part III, § 60. Taken in a broad sense, the theory of foreign exchanges is the same as the theory of international trade. In a narrow sense it explains the details of the pricing on the foreign exchange market, in particular the short-term capital and gold movements, credit policy, etc. But this explanation must rest on the basis of a theory of international trade and capital movements; i.e., it requires as a background the whole price mechanism in trading countries.

[9] The unfortunate terminology of both kinds of theories is partly responsible for the misunderstandings.

[10] Cf. Ohlin, "Stabilizeringsproblemet i Mellaneuropa," *Valutakommissionens Betankning* (Copenhagen, 1925), where numerous examples are given.

Appendices

Index

Appendix I

Simple Mathematical Illustration of Pricing in Trading Regions

§ 1. *An isolated region.* There is much disagreement among economists concerning the value of mathematical formulae in expositions of the complicated relationships of pricing. I believe that they, better than words, can serve a useful purpose in giving a bird's-eye view of the mutual relationship of prices under somewhat simplified conditions. However, attempts to make the formulae more and more complicated in order to bring them into closer accord with actual life and thus make them usable for the solution of economic problems have so far rarely been fruitful—which does not, of course, preclude the possibility of a better result in the future. I shall try to illustrate the nature of pricing in trading regions under simplified conditions by means of some simple equations, without going further and introducing all complicating circumstances. Such circumstances would make no fundamental change in the nature of the relationship to be illuminated and would render the mathematical exposition difficult for most readers to understand.

The system of equations given below resembles closely the one first presented by Cassel in *Theoretische Sozialökonomie.* It is simpler than those of the Walràs-Pareto school and can therefore serve better for the present purpose.[1]

The following analysis is built on the assumption of full mobility and divisibility. Thus, among other things, the economies of large-scale production are ignored. Furthermore, the supply of various factors of productions is assumed to be constant and known. With a preliminary illustration of the nature of pricing in trading regions in view, it is unnecessary to add that this supply is really a function of (1) the prices of the factors and (2) the psychology of effort and sacrifice of the various individuals, however important this fact may be from other points of view (cf. Chapter VII).

First, look at the price system in an isolated region, which produces *n* commodities and has *r* factors of production and *s* inhabitants. The production of each of these commodities requires certain quantities of some or all productive

---

[1] Unlike Cassel I have introduced the individual incomes, the variability of the technical coefficients, and the value of money into the system. Like Cassel I do not consider the difficulties due to the fact that capital as a factor of production cannot be treated in the same way as can other factors. Cf. Lindahl, "Prisbildningsproblements unppläggning från kapitalteoretisk synpunkt" (The problem of pricing from the point of view of the theory of capital), *Ekonomisk Tidskrift* (1929).

factors. The quantities $a_{11}\ a_{12}\ \cdots\ a_{1r}$ of the different factors of production are needed for the production of one unit of the first commodity, the quantities $a_{21}\ a_{22}\ \cdots\ a_{2r}$ are needed for the production of one unit of the second commodity and the quantities $a_{n1}\ a_{n2}\ \cdots\ a_{nr}$ for the production of one unit of the nth commodity. These terms, of which some are equal to 0, are called "technical coefficients." They express the quantities of any factor that are needed for the production of any commodity. They are obviously dependent on the relative prices of the factors, for these prices determine the proportions in which the different factors are combined in a certain production. If the prices of the factors are given, one commodity needs for its production certain proportions of certain factors, and another commodity needs other proportions. The "physical conditions of production" refer to the purely physical properties of nature (both commodities and factors of production), which are to be regarded as known in this economic examination.

Thus, the *technical coefficients* are functions of the prices of the factors of production $q_1\ q_2\ \cdots\ q_r$; and the forms of the function are known, because they are determined by the physical conditions:

$$(1)\qquad a_{11} = f_{11}\,(q_1\ q_2 \cdots q_r)$$
$$\cdot\quad\cdot\quad\cdot\quad\cdot\quad\cdot\quad\cdot$$
$$\cdot\quad\cdot\quad\cdot\quad\cdot\quad\cdot\quad\cdot$$
$$a_{nr} = f_{nr}\,(q_1\ q_2 \cdots q_r)$$

With this the cost of production of the commodities $p_1\ p_2\ \cdots\ p_n$ may easily be obtained.

$$(2)\qquad a_{11}q_1 + a_{12}q_2 + \cdots + a_{1r}q_r = p_1$$
$$a_{21}q_1 + a_{22}q_2 + \cdots + a_{2r}q_r = p_2$$
$$\cdot\quad\cdot\quad\cdot\quad\cdot\quad\cdot\quad\cdot$$
$$a_{n1}q_1 + a_{n2}q_2 + \cdots + a_{nr}q_r = p_n$$

As in any state of equilibrium and perfect mobility prices equal costs of production, $p_1\ \cdots\ p_n$.

The demand for the different commodities is determined by these prices, $p_1\ \cdots\ p_n$, by the income of each consumer, and by his "scale of requirements" or "scale of wants" (the psychic side of demand). If the prices of the commodities and his income were given, his "scale of wants" would determine how much he would buy of each commodity. Each individual's demand for a certain commodity may thus be expressed as a function of the prices of all commodities and services and of his income. The form of the function is determined by his "scale of wants."

Now add together the demands of all individuals, and express the total demand for each commodity, $D_1\ D_2\ \cdots\ D_n$, as a function of commodity prices and the various individual incomes, $I_1\ I_2\ \cdots\ I_s$.[2]

$$(3)\qquad D_1 = F_1\,(p_1 \cdots p_{n1}, I_1 \cdots I_s)$$
$$D_2 = F_2\,(p_1 \cdots p_{n1}, I_1 \cdots I_s)$$
$$\cdot\quad\cdot\quad\cdot\quad\cdot\quad\cdot\quad\cdot$$
$$D_n = F_n\,(p_1 \cdots p_{n1}, I_1 \cdots I_s)$$

[2] All incomes are assumed to be "used." ($\Sigma I = \Sigma D$. This equation is implied in equations (2), (4), and (5).

The individual incomes are determined by the rewards to factors of production. It is as a seller of a certain quantity of such factors—e.g., the use of labor or land, or goods or services produced with them—that an individual acquires his purchasing power. In this examination the conditions of ownership of the different factors are supposed to be known. The individual, m, owns t_{m1} units of the first factor, t_{m2} of the second factor, etc. The incomes of the various individuals, $I_1 \, I_2 \cdots I_s$, may be written:

$$(4) \quad I_1 = t_{11}\, q_1 + t_{12}\, q_2 + \cdots + t_{1r}\, q_r$$
$$I_2 = t_{21}\, q_1 + t_{22}\, q_2 + \cdots + t_{2r}\, q_r$$
$$\cdots$$
$$I_s = t_{s1}\, q_1 + t_{s2}\, q_2 + \cdots + t_{sr}\, q_r$$

If the price-mechanism is in equilibrium, the production of commodities is just sufficient to satisfy the demand. It is now easy to go on to express the demand for the different factors of production as an equation. The quantity a_{11} of the first factor is needed for the production of one unit of the first commodity; for the production of D_1 units $a_{11} D_1$ units are therefore required. The production of D_2 units of the second commodity requires $a_{21} D_2$ units of the same factor, etc., and the production of D_n units of the nth commodity requires $a_{n1} D_n$ of this factor. By summing up these quantities, the total demand for this factor of production may be computed as: $a_{11} D_1 + a_{21} D_2 + \cdots + a_{n1} D_n$. The amount of the first factor of production that is wanted for the production of all commodities must be the whole available quantity of this factor—that is, R_1, which is equal to $t_{11} + t_{21} + \cdots + t_{s1}$. Since the demand for the other factors of production may be computed in the same way, we obtain:

$$(5) \quad a_{11} D_1 + a_{21} D_2 + \cdots + a_{n1} D_n = R_1$$
$$a_{12} D_1 + a_{22} D_2 + \cdots + a_{n2} D_n = R_2$$
$$\cdots$$
$$a_{1r} D_1 + a_{2r} D_2 + \cdots + a_{nr} D_n = R_r;$$

Now the demand for each commodity is, according to equations (3), a function of its price and individuals' incomes. By means of the systems of equations (2) and (4) this demand can be expressed in terms of factor quantities and prices. Further, by aid of the system of equations (1) the different quantities of each factor may be expressed in terms of their prices. The number of "independent variables" is thus reduced to r, namely the number of factor prices, $q_1 \, q_2 \cdots q_r$, and the series of equations (5), which contains r equations, is sufficient for the solution of the problem. The price system under the assumed conditions thus seems to be determinate. The basic data governing it are the supply of productive factors owned by each individual[3] and the two sets of circumstances that determine the forms of the functions, i.e., the physical conditions of production and the wants and desires of the consumers.

As a matter of fact, however, one of the equations is not independent of the

[3] In Part One this is called (1) the supply of productive factors and (2) the conditions of ownership.

others[4]; hence, any multiple of the correct prices will satisfy it. All prices may be twice as high in one situation as in another, and yet all basic circumstances and the equations may be unchanged. To determine the prices, one must introduce an assumption about the monetary system, e.g., that a certain quantity of a certain commodity (gold) is used as unit of reckoning. If the price of this commodity is called p_g, one obtains the equation $p_g = 1$. Thus, the number of equations is equal to the number of independent variables and the system is determinate.

§ 2. *Trading regions.* A similar survey of the price formation under simplified conditions may now be given for two exchanging regions, which are called regions A and B. The symbols employed are as follows:

	A	B
Technical coefficients	$a = f(\quad)$	$a = f(\quad)$
Prices of factors of production	q	g
Prices of commodities	p	v
Incomes of the various individuals	$I = \sum_{1}^{r} t_h q_h$	$J = \sum_{1}^{r} d_h g_h$
Demand for commodities	$D = F(\quad)$	$\delta = \psi(\quad)$
Supply of factors of production	R	S

The only things that are common in the two regions before the commencement of trade are "the physical conditions of production," that is, the forms of the functions. These conditions are determined solely by the physical properties of nature (commodities and factors of production), which are wholly independent of the locality of these factors and commodities.

The price-mechanism in the isolated region A is just the same as that presented in § 1 above. The mechanism of the region B is obtained merely by changing all symbols according to the chart above. Now the problem is, what change takes place when the exchange of commodities between the two regions is opened?

The "foreign exchange," that is, the relation between the money units of the two regions, is represented by x. One unit of A's money now corresponds to x units of B's money, and the prices of commodities in the region B, $v_1 \, v_2 \cdots v_n$, become $\dfrac{v_1}{x} \, \dfrac{v_2}{x} \cdots \dfrac{v_n}{x}$ in A's money. The inhabitants in A compare these prices with $p_1 \, p_2 \cdots p_n$, which are the costs in home-production, and import the commodities they can buy cheaper in B and export the commodities they can produce cheaper than B. If x is given a certain arbitrary value, a certain number of commodity prices will be lower in A and the rest will be lower in B. Take another value of x. Then *another* set of commodities will be cheaper in A and the rest will be cheaper in B. Every possible value of x corresponds to a certain definite number of commodities that are cheaper in A and thus produced there, while the rest is produced in B.

If one knew the equilibrium foreign exchange x, one would also know which goods can be obtained at lowest cost in A and which in B. Give the former

[4]Cf. Walràs, *Éléments d'Économie politique pure* (4th ed., 1900), pp. 122ff.

goods the numbers $1, 2 \cdots m$, and the latter $m + 1, m + 2, \cdots n$. The equations showing that the costs of production are equal to the prices thus become: [5]

(II)
$$a_{11} q_1 + \cdots + a_{1r} q_r = p_1$$
$$\cdot \quad \cdot \quad \cdot$$
$$a_{m1} q_1 + \cdots + a_m q_r = p_m$$
$$a_{m+1,1} g_1 + \cdots + a_{m+1,r} g_r = v_{m+1}$$
$$\cdot \quad \cdot \quad \cdot$$
$$a_{n1} g_1 + \cdots + a_{nr} g_r = v_n$$

This series is almost the same as (2), the only difference being that $a_{11} \cdots a_{n1}$ are changed to $a_{11} \cdots a_{m1}, a_{m+1,1} \cdots a_{n1}$, and the corresponding $q_1 \cdots q_r$ into $q_1 \cdots q_r, g_1 \cdots g_r$, and $p_1 \cdots p_n$ into $p_1 \cdots p_m, v_{m+1} \cdots v_n$.

The equations for the demand for commodities are also a little changed. Since the demand for any commodity is a function of the prices of *all* commodities, and these prices are now $p_1 \cdots p_m, \dfrac{v_{m+1}}{x} \cdots \dfrac{v_n}{x}$ in A and $p_1 x \cdots p_m x, v_{m+1} \cdots v_n$ in B, the demand for the different commodities may be expressed thus:

(III)
$$D_1 = F_1 (I_1 \cdots I_s; p_1 \cdots p_m; v_{m+1} \cdots v_n; x)$$
$$\delta_1 = \psi_1 (J_1 \cdots J_s; p_1 \cdots p_m; v_{m+1} \cdots v_n; x)$$
$$D_n = F_n (I_1 \cdots I_s; p_1 \cdots p_m; v_{m+1} \cdots v_n; x)$$
$$\delta_n = \psi_n (J_1 \cdots J_s; p_1 \cdots p_m; v_{m+1} \cdots v_n; x)$$

The equations expressing the various individual incomes as functions of factor prices are the same as in the isolated state. It is therefore superfluous to write down system (IV). For each of the two countries one equation in IV is dependent on the others. In their place are the equations for the price of gold: $p_g = 1$ and $v_g = x$. The price in B of the quantity of gold, which costs 1 in A, is of course equal to the foreign exchange rate.

With regard to the demand for the factors of production, it must be remembered that region A now has to produce a quantity of the commodities 1, $2 \cdots m$ sufficient not only for its own consumption but also for the *total* consumption of these commodities in A and B, while B has to satisfy the total wants in both regions for the commodities $(m + 1) \cdots n$. The quantities of the factors of production being in A: $R_1 \cdots R_r$ and in B: $S_1 \cdots S_r$, one gets:

(V)
$$a_{11} (D_1 + \delta_1) + \cdots + a_{m1} (D_m + \delta_m) = R_1$$
$$\cdot$$
$$a_{1r} (D_1 + \delta_1) + \cdots + a_{mr} (D_m + \delta_m) = R_r$$
$$a_{m+1,1} (D_{m+1} + \delta_{m+1}) + \cdots + a_{n1} (D_n + \delta_n) = S_1$$
$$\cdot$$
$$a_{m+1,r} (D_{m+1} + \delta_{m+1}) + \cdots + a_{nr} (D_n + \delta_n) = S_r$$

Finally, the equations expressing the technical coefficients as a function of the prices of the factors of production are of the same nature as in the series of equations (1) above.

[5] Each commodity is supposed to be produced only in one region.

(I)
$$a_{11} = f_{11}\,(q_1 \cdots q_r)$$

$$\begin{aligned}&\quad\cdot\qquad\qquad\cdot\\&\quad\cdot\qquad\qquad\cdot\\&\quad\cdot\qquad\qquad\cdot\end{aligned}$$

$$a_{mr} = f_{mr}\,(q_1 \cdots q_r)$$
$$a_{m+1,1} = f_{m+1,\,1}\,(g_1 \cdots g_r)$$

$$\begin{aligned}&\quad\cdot\qquad\qquad\cdot\\&\quad\cdot\qquad\qquad\cdot\\&\quad\cdot\qquad\qquad\cdot\end{aligned}$$

$$a_{nr} = f_{nr}\,(g_1 \cdots g_r)$$

With the aid of equations (II) and (IV) it is possible to express the different commodity prices and individual incomes in terms of factor prices. If in the system III these factor prices are substituted, the different demand equations will be expressed in factor prices and the exchange rate. By putting these expressions in the series of equations V, where the supply of factors are constants, the independent variables are reduced again to the factor prices in A and B and the exchange rate. For the computation of these variables there is the series of equations in the system V. But as the number of unknowns is $2r + 1$, there must still be one equation in order to complete the circle.

The required equation is supplied by the fact that the imports and the exports in the region must balance, for as no credit transactions, etc., are taken into consideration, exports are the only means of paying for the imports:

(VI) $$\delta_1 p_1\, x + \delta_2\, p_2\, x + \cdots + \delta_m\, p_m\, x = D_{m+1}\, v_{m+1} + \cdots + D_n\, v_n$$

This equation, which may be called "the equation of interregional exchange," signifies, in terms of B's money, that the imports balance the exports. Of the first commodity B imports the quantity δ_1, and since the price is p_1 in A, B has to pay $\delta_1\, p_1\, x_1$ reckoned in B's money. Of the nth commodity B exports, and consequently A imports, the quantity D_n at the price v_n, etc.

By these six sets of equations the price system in two exchanging regions under simplified conditions is illustrated; that is to say, a general idea of the nature of the interdependence of the different elements is provided. Evidently any change in any part of the system may cause a change in any other part.

§ 3. *Certain conditions of trade.* This system of equations can also be used to throw light on the question under what conditions two regions do *not* trade with each other. If relative commodity prices coincide in the isolated state, no trade can occur. Under what conditions do they coincide?

Start from the equations expressing the costs and prices of the various commodities.

A	B

(1) $a_{11}q_1 + a_{12}q_2 + \cdots + a_{1r}q_r = p_1;$ $\quad a_{11}g_1 + a_{12}g_2 + \cdots + a_{12}g_r = v_1$
$a_{21}q_1 + a_{22}q_2 + \cdots + a_{2r}q_r = p_2;$ $\quad a_{21}g_1 + a_{22}g_2 + \cdots + a_{2r}g_r = v_2$
$a_{n1}q_1 + a_{n2}q_2 + \cdots + a_{nr}q_r = p_n;$ $\quad a_{n1}g_1 + a_{n2}g_2 + \cdots + a_{nr}g_r = v_n$

As soon as the two regions come into communication, exchange arises if the relative commodity prices are different, that is, if the following condition is *not* fulfilled:

(2) $$p_1 : p_2 : \cdots : p_n = v_1 : v_2 : \cdots : v_n$$

This condition is satisfied and hence trade is impossible in two cases, which will now be analyzed.

Assume that the relative prices of *the factors of production* are the same in both regions. This can be expressed:

(3) $q_1 = l_{g1};\ q_2 = l_{g2};\ \cdots;\ q_r = l_{gr}$ (where l is an arbitrary positive quantity

When this is the case, the factors[6] will be used in the same proportions in the production of any commodity in both regions. The "technical coefficients" coincide:

$$(4) \quad a_{ij} = a_{ij}; \quad (i = 1, 2 \cdots n; \; j = 1, 2 \cdots r)$$

By the aid of the equations (3) and (4) the expression (1) is converted into:

$$(5) \qquad p_1 = l_{v_1}; \; p_2 = l v_2; \cdots; \; p_n = l v_n$$

which is exactly the same as (2). Consequently, the condition (2) holds good; relative commodity prices coincide, and no trade arises if the condition (3) is fulfilled. It may therefore be stated that *no trade arises if the relative prices of the factors of production coincide in the two regions.*

The condition (2) can, however, be fulfilled in another way, namely:

$$(6) \qquad \begin{aligned} a_{11} : a_{12} : \cdots : a_{1r} &= \\ = \quad \cdots \quad &= \\ = a_{n1} : a_{n2} : \cdots : a_{nr} &= \\ = a_{11} : a_{12} : \cdots : a_{1r} &= \\ = \quad \cdots \quad &= \\ = a_{n1} : a_{n2} : \cdots : a_{nr} \end{aligned}$$

In other words, it is fulfilled if the factors of production are combined in exactly the same proportions in *all* commodities in *both* regions. However, this is unthinkable if the relative prices of the factors of production do not coincide. Condition (6) is therefore in fact the same as condition (3).

These conditions, (3) and (6), which are of course never satisfied in the real world, resemble somewhat two assumptions of which considerable use is made in the classical theory of international trade. When dealing with non-competing groups, Taussig bases his final conclusions concerning their small importance for international trade on the presumed fact that "in the occidental countries . . . as a rule the stratification of industrial groups proceeds on the same lines," i.e., relative wages are fairly equal in different countries.[7] It is fortunate that he does not make this assumption for *all* the productive factors, in which case international trade would be impossible, except insofar as it would be called into existence by economies of large-scale production.

In other cases Taussig and others assume that the various labor qualities and capital, but not land, enter in the same proportions in all commodities, and that therefore relative costs are known when the relative quantities of un-skilled labor used for their production are known. Bastable expressed the same thing, when he assumed that a "unit of productive power" can be used as a basis in cost calculations. It is fortunate that this assumption does not include land and that equal proportions in *both* countries are not assumed, for otherwise trade would be impossible except when due to economies of large-scale production.

§ 4. *A generalization.* Assume that the productive factors existing in A and B as well as the sort of commodities produced in these countries in the isolated state are entirely different. It is not difficult to change the system of

---

[6] Only factors of identical quality in the two regions are treated as being the same factor. The economies of large-scale production are disregarded.

[7] Taussig, *International Trade*, p. 56.

equations so as to correspond to these circumstances. The forms of the technical coefficients will be different in the two countries; the supply in B of all
the factors that exist in A will be zero, and vice versa. Nevertheless, a system
of equations is obtained which describes the equilibrium of international trade
under these simple assumptions.[8]

The conditions that have to be fulfilled if trade is to arise are obviously not
different relative commodity and factor prices. Nor can one speak of a tendency toward an equalization of factor prices when trade has started. Nevertheless, the reactions of the supply prices of commodities to an increase in foreign
demand will be essentially as described in the text. They depend upon the
change in relative factor prices under the influence of the new demand conditions and the reactions of factor supply, as well as upon the economies of
large-scale production. For a treatment of practical problems it is, in my
opinion, beyond doubt most practical to use the assumptions underlying
Part I of the text and §§1-3 of this appendix as a first approximation, and to
deal with the differences in the quantity of commodities and factors as explained in Chapter V.

[8] Neither the comparative cost reasoning nor the "factor proportion model" is
applicable in this case.

Appendix II

Reflections on Contemporary International Trade Theories

§ 1. Anyone who has tried to follow and evaluate the development of the theory of international economic relations in the last three decades cannot fail to be impressed. Much progress has been made. Excellent surveys of recent developments have been published, above all Caves' very careful and skillful summary and analysis.[1]

For this new, abbreviated edition of my own *Interregional and International Trade*, first published in 1933, I should therefore like to characterize the theory of international trade as I now see it. Only a few observations on certain aspects of recent developments will be made, and these will be related to my own attempts to change and modify older theory. I shall then be in a position to indicate some essential modifications of my position, particularly concerning the general approach to international trade theory.

It still seems very obvious to me that the most natural and advantageous approach to international trade theory is to start from the mutual interdependence price theory that was developed in the last decades of the nineteenth century. The simplest form is probably the Walràs system as modified by Cassel. It can survey prices in several trading countries, inside which the factors of production are fully mobile. The problem is to analyze and describe the circumstances that lie behind the differences in relative money costs and prices among countries.

Within the framework of a static theory these are the "basic circumstances" in the mutual interdependence system in each country—the data that are regarded as fixed from the outside: (1) the supply of productive factors; (2) the technical knowledge which, with the relative factor prices, governs the combination of factors; (3) the character and structure of tastes, or demand; and (4) the conditions of ownership with regard to the factors. This last, with the factor prices, determines the distribution of income and thus the buying power of each individual.[2]

[1] Caves, *Trade and Economic Structure: Models and Methods* (Cambridge, Mass., 1960). See also an important and penetrating survey by Bhagwati, "The Pure Theory of International Trade," *The Economic Journal* (1964). As an introduction to existing doctrine Haberler's booklet, *A Survey of International Trade Theory* (2nd ed., Princeton, 1961), still remains the most useful, although his modesty forbids enough stress on his own contributions.

[2] Later, taxation and the aims and goals of the public bodies that direct their purchases must of course be considered.

A mutual interdependence theory of some sort is the only system that explains the connection between factor supply, price conditions, and trade. But, for a more concrete picture it is necessary to construct simplified models. Such simplified models also lend themselves better to an analysis of important aspects of development in international economic relations.

One such model is the classical comparative cost model. It has contributed greatly to our knowledge of international relations. For certain types of problems it is probably the most useful one because a relatively simple application is possible.

Another important model is the "factor proportion theorem," which is expounded in the first part of this book.[3] It can convey a more concrete impression of the influence on trade of certain aspects of the conditions of production, to wit, the supply of productive factors. In 1933 I thought that this theorem would be such an essential part of the mutual interdependence theory that it might become as much the foundation of the theory of international trade as the classical comparative cost theory had been. My present views are indicated below.

§ 2. In the 1930's a large number of theoretical models were constructed, each adapted to the solution of one or several problems but none claiming to be *the* basic theory. The incomplete nature of these models became most evident in the theory of business cycles. Nobody asks any more if the overproduction *or* the underconsumption theory is the correct one. It soon became apparent that attempts to make the theory more dynamic necessitated so many simplifications that the outcome would be useful only for a study of certain problems. Other simplifications and other models would be more useful for the analysis of other problems. The same holds good for all parts of price theory. It seems to me unquestionable that the theory of international trade and factor movements must consist of a number of different theoretical models, but none claiming to be the most essential part of the theory.

It is, however, not unreasonable to regard certain models as more useful for the understanding of the general nature of international trade than others. The former are in this limited sense "basic." As I have tried to explain in this book, such a limited basic model seems to me to be the mutual interdependence price theory, extended to cover several trading countries and supplemented by the factor proportion model and some others mentioned below. Each supplementary model is less generally applicable than the mutual interdependence system. The factor proportion theorem has the advantage over the comparative cost theory in that it can be modified in the direction of realism by the introduction of other cost items, such as taxes and various social overheads. One could express the same idea by stating that other models, constructed to illuminate other essential problems like the influence of taxa-

---

[3] I took over several fundamental ideas from Eli F. Heckscher's 1919 paper "The Effect of Foreign Trade on the Distribution of Income" and built them after some modification into a mutual interdependence theory of international trade, on which I had earlier started working. I found that they went well together. Heckscher was rather averse to coordinating the factor proportion analysis with the Walràs-Cassel theory.

tion, cooperate better with the factor proportion model and the interdependence price theory than with the classical comparative cost theory.

In 1933 I still regarded the mutual interdependence model and the factor proportion model as the foundation of a huge building. All the upper floors in the building had to rest on this base. I now realize that one cannot construct such a building containing all the essential parts of the theory. This becomes most evident when development aspects are the subject of analysis. Yet it would be a mistake to assume that a number of different theoretical models *without any natural contact or harmonious relation between them* can be accepted as a satisfactory theoretical structure. It is a great merit if the strategic simplifications in each model can be made in such a way that a natural coherence between them becomes evident. In this respect I still maintain that a consistent price theory is superior to a conglomerate of price and real cost analyses of the neoclassical type.

Even Jacob Viner, that unbelievably skillful advocate of the classical and neoclassical theory, seems to have failed singularly in his attempts to demonstrate the opposite. He tried to defend the classical approach against criticism by pointing out: "The classical theory of international trade was formulated primarily with a view to its providing guidance on questions of national policy." Referring to my criticism of the classical doctrine as an explanation of international trade, he added that I had "given no sign of recognition that this was not the sole or even the main purpose of the doctrine." [4] Caves adds, "Viner is no doubt correct in saying that Ohlin failed to realize that classical comparative cost doctrine was a system of welfare and not a positive theory designed to explain national specialization." [5] Let me answer by saying that, strangely enough, Viner—a prominent pupil of Taussig's—has given no sign of recognition that the doctrine of comparative real costs and Mill's reciprocal demand theory were used by Taussig and practically all other textbook writers before World War II as *an explanation of the character of specialization and international trade.* For any misunderstanding on this point I have, of course, to accept the blame for not expressing myself clearly.

§ 3. As indicated above, the theory of international trade is a "multi-market theory." Other kinds of multi-market theory are found in the theory of *price differentiation* and in the theory of *rent.* Above all, however, international trade theory verges on *location theory.* Instead of asking why certain countries exchange certain goods with one another, one can ask why production is divided between these countries in a certain way. On the whole, the exchange of goods is determined once the location of production has been fixed. Differing degrees of utilization of the productive equipment, and changes in weather conditions from one year to the next, can naturally affect output and international trade, but its general character is established by the location of production.

[4] Viner, *Studies in the Theory of International Trade* (New York, 1937), pp. 437, 501 ff.
[5] Caves, *Trade and Economic Structure,* p. 23.

Location theory is more extensive than international trade theory. A large part of trade theory can be regarded as a small part of location theory wherein certain aspects are emphasized more than others. Special attention is given, for instance, to the influence of political borders on trade. Furthermore, only *certain* location conditions are considered and rather limited attention is devoted to the siting of production in a particular location *within* a certain country, whereas international movements of the factors of production are emphasized. With regard to economic policy, the problems are different since "national interest" plays a great role.

A survey of the mutual equilibrium system of pricing, where there are not *one* but *many* markets, can be given with the aid of equation systems of the Walràs-Cassel type. Here I would refer the reader to Yntema[6] and other mathematically-inclined authors. In addition to my own account, which was published in English at about the same time as Yntema's, I would mention Haberler's theory,[7] which admittedly does not delve more deeply into this line of thought but which clearly assumes mutual interdependence. It was inevitable that the price theory for many markets would be seen in the light of, and based on, the mutual interdependence system of pricing for one market developed by Walràs, Jevons, Menger, and Marshall. However, the equation systems relating to the general price system are a clumsy instrument. They must be supplemented by simpler models that can be more easily used for concrete cases and development problems.

To those who are skeptical regarding the usefulness of the mutual interdependence theory as a basis for a study of international trade, I would point out that this general model elucidates very clearly something that is of great importance and is often ignored. International trade can take place and have roughly the same form as it does today even if there are no factors common to or goods produced in more than one of the various trading countries.[8] What is necessary is that, when trade is opened, a demand arises in each country for the goods of the other country because there are buyers who want the goods and because the goods can be produced more cheaply in the other country than in the home country. This is obviously possible even if there are no common types of factors or products prior to the opening of trade. In this case it is not the difference in relative costs that gives rise to international trade, for when there are no common products, it is not possible to compare relative costs. The construction of this model—a mutual interdependence price system—shows with great clarity that one has to focus on cost calculations in the same way as in the rest of the price theory. The obstinate conservatism with which the classical comparative cost thinking has been retained in theory as something more than a pedagogical introduction—or a model for the treatment of a few special problems—is evidence that, even to-

[6] Yntema, *A Mathematical Reformulation of the Theory of International Trade* (New York, 1932). My work, *Handelns teori*, was published in 1924 but can hardly have influenced non-Scandinavian economists, with the exception of G. Mackenroth, who studied in Sweden.

[7] Haberler, *The Theory of International Trade* (London, 1936; German ed. 1933).

[8] See the end of Appendix I.

day, there is in many quarters an insufficient understanding of this fundamental fact.

It follows that not only the comparative cost model but also the factor proportions model can only be applied in special cases and used as a general introduction to illuminate the character of trade in some essential respects. One is forced to ignore significant quality differences between countries as regards both factors of production and products. Furthermore, particular consideration must be paid to those cases where certain factors of production—especially natural resources—do not exist at all in certain countries. Evidently both these theoretical models presuppose so many simplifying assumptions that they make up only a minor part of the fundamental theory of international trade. However, I maintain that the factor proportion model, built into the mutual interdependence system, is a better introduction than the comparative cost model.

§ 4. It is characteristic of *the developing countries* that a good many factors do not exist at all and that the quality of others differs from factors in the industrialized countries. This means that a simple method of analysis—such as the factor proportions model—which does not take this into account is to some extent unrealistic.

In favor of this simplified theoretical model is the fact that it explains a large number of the conditions underlying the differences in prices and costs —actual or potential—between various countries. But there are many other conditions to take into account if the differences in prices and costs are to be properly explained. Besides the costs for the use of certain quantities of the factors of production—quantities needed for production and transportation— the costs of production also include *taxes and social welfare fees,* many of which bear an important relation to international trade and yet are not included in general systems.[9] It has long been a mystery to me why existing accounts of international trade pay so little attention to these problems. So many books and articles discuss the impact of a certain type of taxation, viz., tariffs levied at the border when goods are imported, yet they devote no space to the question of how *other kinds of taxation* can affect trade. This is of course an extremely difficult problem, but as the world markets increase in size, it is probable that differences in the construction of tax systems and in the level of taxes will attract more and more attention. This question can also be of importance in constructing an appropriate tax system in the developing countries. Certainly much remains to be done.

§ 5. As far as I know, no one has overlooked the fact that there are many other conditions of fundamental importance—in particular, the *advantages of specialization and large-scale operations.* Even in a case where the endowment of factors is the same in various countries, trade is possible between them—as well as between different regions within each country—because specialization and large-scale operations entail advantages. These conditions have been regarded in this book as independent causes, along with the relative scarcity of

---

[9] See Chapter VI, § 10. A more detailed account appears in my appendix "Taxation and International Trade" in *Social Aspects of European Economic Cooperation: A Report by a Committee of Experts* (International Labor Office, Geneva, 1956).

factors of production. This viewpoint is considered in practically all earlier, more well-known accounts of international trade.[10]

Since international trade would arise even if factor endowments and demand conditions were the same in the various countries, it causes differences in the prices of factors of production. Such differences can also result if the *direction of demand* in the one country deviates from that in the other country. This relationship is made evident by the simple Walràs-Cassel model applied to international trade. Differences in factor prices caused in this way give rise in turn to more international trade. There is an element of chance in the line of specialization chosen in a small country. But the character of domestic demand and, therefore, domestic markets often gives an impetus to growth and to exports. This has been rightly emphasized by S. Burensham Linder in *An Essay on Trade and Transformation.*

§ 6. The situation is less clear with respect to another simplifying assumption of the factor proportions model—that of *identical production functions* in the various countries. The combination in which the factors are used is then entirely dependent on their relative prices. An assumption of differing production functions is superfluous because the complete absence of certain kinds of labor or natural resources has the same effect as if their prices were so high that demand was zero. All observed differences in the technique used can then be explained by reference to different relative prices for the factors of production, including differences in the prices of managerial labor of certain qualities. The differing quality of the managerial labor between countries is a kind of *deus ex machina,* which takes care of most of the difficulties that do not properly fit into the simple framework.

Such a procedure involves a risk that a more accurate explanation may be overlooked. There are many reasons for using instead a model that permits different production functions in different countries. But such a model would fail to give the precise conclusions regarding, on the one hand, the relationship between the supply of factors of production and the direction of demand and, on the other hand, the nature and effects of international trade. An understanding of this should constitute some protection against exaggerating the importance of the model in question.[11] It is reasonable, however, to believe

[10] Quite another matter is the fact that a number of authors of older books on international trade—e.g., Taussig—confuse the advantages of large-scale operations with "increasing returns." This was a step backward since the principles for an economic combination of the factors of production were mostly laid down as early as the 1890's. At the beginning of the century surveys of this theory were published by J. B. Clark, Landru, and many others.

[11] It is because of these conditions and the importance of taxes, social costs, transport costs, etc., that I have found the intensive preoccupation with the factor proportions model after World War II—which started with Paul Samuelson's penetrating article, "International Trade and the Equalization of Factor Prices" (*Economic Journal,* 1948)—to have a gradually declining "marginal utility" compared to the results that could be obtained with the same acumen, intelligence, and work if it were directed, e.g., toward a study of transportation costs and taxation in their relation to international trade. An attitude similar to my own appears in Viner, "Relative Abundance of the Factors and International Trade," *Ekonomi Politik* (Samhalle, Stockholm, 1959). See also J. L. Ford, "The Ohlin-Heckscher Theory of the Basis of Commodity Trade," *The Economic Journal* (1963), p. 460.

that some tendencies of the sort described by means of the model will appear in "the real world." [12]

An interesting difference between a series of models, on the one hand, and a more descriptive analytical exposition, on the other, is sometimes that he who produces the latter is conscious of the inexactitude of his analysis, whereas constructors of models—or of *a* model—sometimes seem to believe that their theory has superior precision. A number of mistakes made in theory during the past decade originate in this fallacy. Simple models covering changes in the terms of trade—e.g., resulting from international movements of capital—have been built up on the assumption of two goods and two factors of production and have nonetheless formed the basis for conclusions regarding the effect of capital movements on the terms of trade in concrete cases. Such models are sometimes incautiously based, for instance, on the unrealistic assumption of a relatively low foreign demand elasticity. Hence, one might conclude that the payment of considerable war indemnities is in practice impossible. In reality, it is of course a fact that in the long run foreign demand for the products of one country can be sold on the world market in competition with goods from other countries. It is therefore not at all the demand elasticity of the consumers that is of prime importance, but the elasticity of the demand for products from just this country. By means of a permanent cost reduction—leading to, say, a lowering of prices so that they are 10 percent below the prices commanded by similar products from other countries—it is perhaps possible to multiply exports many times over. A reduction of the cost level may also make it possible to introduce completely new export commodities.

§ 7. I have so far discussed the factor proportions model and shown the need for its extension to include the advantages of large-scale operations and different production functions. There is a need for other models too, e.g., in attempts to explain variations in the terms of trade. But there is one problem that deserves more attention than has so far been given to it in international theory: the *effect of transport conditions* on trade between regions or countries. Here probably more than one model is needed. Very briefly I would like to mention two. Regions with good conditions for transport offer favorable opportunities for many kinds of business activity. I refer here to *nonspecific* transport conditions, such as a relatively even surface area or a net of navigable rivers and natural harbors.

There are also more *specific* transport conditions, which are associated with the location of raw materials and which are therefore of importance for the industries using these raw materials. The distances from the sites of manufacturing to the coal and iron deposits are an example. This location theory has been developed by Weber, Palander, Lösch, Hoover, and Isard. What is primarily analyzed by them is the *possibility of siting different parts of the production process in different localities and the influence of transport costs.* In ordinary international trade theory it is far too frequently assumed that the

[12] It should be kept in mind that in Leontief's well-known and important attempt at statistical testing of the factor proportion model he considers only two factors of production. Each of the simplifications made in the model constitutes a more or less important deviation from reality, and therefore no "close fit" can be expected.

whole of the production process is located in one and the same country or in
one and the same place. When more realistic assumptions are made, transport
costs enter the picture in a more complicated way. In this book I attempted
to clarify some important aspects of this problem with application to international trade. A good many post-World War II textbooks in international trade
now deal with this question.

When the influence of various transport conditions is combined with the
advantages of large-scale production, conclusions are reached regarding the
location of production and the character and effects of international trade
that deviate considerably from those that would have been arrived at if only
the scarcity of the factors of production had been taken into account.

§ 8. It is impossible to formulate a satisfactory theory of international trade
without dealing with the *interregional and international mobility and movements of the factors of production.* This has probably been quite generally
recognized in the last decades, but much remains to be done. For instance,
labor and capital flow to regions where there are favorable transport conditions—general or specific according to the above definition. The mobile factors
are particularly attracted to regions where there is a supply of raw materials
that are relatively difficult to transport, i.e., in instances when the finished
products or semi-manufactures are easier to transport than the necessary raw
materials. Such movements of mobile factors of production can accentuate
the differences in factor endowments between various regions and countries.
This is particularly true if the advantages of large-scale operations are substantial. The explanation of these phenomena requires a theory of trade and
a theory of factor movements. There is also a relationship between the movements of the different factors of production, i.e., as regards transfers of capital
and technical know-how.

When the theory of international trade is combined with the theory of
international factor movements, and when the agglomerative tendencies are
taken into account, one comes to interesting conclusions as to the effects of
international trade on the supply of the factors of production in the various
nations and thus on the structure of international trade in the future. Improved conditions for trade between Europe and Australia in the nineteenth
century led to an influx of labor and capital into Australia, an increased national income, and *thereby* an increased foreign trade.[13] This is one of the
many instances in which current theory is sufficient, although the event occurred over a period of time.

The French economist Byé has criticized current international trade theory
on the grounds that it is based on the assumption that the factors of production are immobile between countries.[14] However, to the extent that, say, labor
is available from other countries—Belgian workers travel every morning to
factories in northern France and back again in the evening—French industrial
activity is not determined by the supply of factors in France. One can agree

[13] I have discussed this type of problem in *Utrikeshandel och Handelspolitik,*
6th ed., pp. 46–47.

[14] A summary of Byé's arguments can be found in an appendix to *Social Aspects
of European Economic Cooperation.* The main report also contains some elements
of a dynamic analysis.

with Byé that very little explicit and formalized analysis is available regarding the effect on international trade of various degrees of international mobility of the factors of production, but such an analysis would hardly overthrow the main body of existing doctrine. In the short run, labor supply is almost fixed. In the long run it varies under the influence of changes in the demand for labor in each country, and it is not difficult to pay due attention to the possibility of migration.

§ 9. The fact that international trade affects not only the use of the factors of production but also their *supply*—both total quantities and qualities—has been recognized by many writers. For a long time, however, this recognition occurred only in the form of scattered observations and primarily in discussing the effects of tariff policy. Protectionist writers emphasized the effect that tariff protection can have in transforming the quality of the labor force in a direction favorable for, *inter alia*, the protected industry. Such effects may be more probable in "underdeveloped" countries than in industrialized countries. This can be explained without any "new theory," simply by applying the old one. But formalized and simple models are certainly useful, as demonstrated already by several very competent economists.

The theory of international trade naturally cannot neglect the effect of changes in prices of factors of production on the supply of factors. A positive supply reaction can often be expected, but basically very little is known about this relationship. It is, for instance, quite possible that in many countries a wage increase leads to demands for shorter working hours.

Since international trade generally has the effect of *raising the national income* and thus the level of factor prices, a certain impact on the supply of factors can be expected. The higher income usually leads to increased capital formation. In this book, however, less attention has been devoted to the effect of the increased national income on the supply of the factors of production than to the impact of the changed relative factor prices.

§ 10. As is the case with price theory and the theory of income distribution, the theory of international trade belongs in large measure to the realm of "comparative statics." In the first theoretical stages, at least, the supply of factors of production is generally considered as given—this is true of the classical English literature (with certain simple assumptions added regarding the supply of labor). Older writers were not blind to the fact that changes in the supply of factors and their quality were associated with the general economic development in the countries concerned, and that this was closely tied up with the conditions for and growth of international trade. It is simply not possible to imagine what sort of economic development would have taken place over the last hundred years without international trade. The classical economists were aware that the expansion of international trade starting in the middle of the nineteenth century greatly stimulated capital formation and led to international movements of capital—e.g., to the investment of English capital in primary producing nations.

§ 11. In order to explain the location of production and the character and extent of international trade, it is often necessary to study a time-using process and to combine the effects of factor movements, transport conditions and the slow change in the qualities of the factors of production under the pressure of specialized employment. For instance, labor and capital flow to regions where the transport conditions for industrial production are favorable. There the labor force acquires qualities that are valuable for this kind of production, and capital is invested in a suitable technical form and in such a way that the transport conditions are further improved.

In other words, if one wants to examine how an increase in international trade—brought about through a radical reduction of the trade obstacles, for instance—affects the national income and factor prices, use of the proportions model and the "terms of trade model" is not very fruitful. This is a *development through time*. It is obvious that no simple and general conclusions can be drawn—whether or not explicit models for the analyses are built.[15] It is not difficult to construct cases where an increase in international trade leads to an increase in international differences in the prices of certain factors of production.

Many development problems can be fruitfully analyzed with the aid of a theory of interregional and international trade such as the one in this book. The creation of a more effective national commodity market and capital market can have the effect, e.g., of increasing real wages in one part of a country and reducing real wages in other parts. One case of this sort that has attracted special attention is Italy: the emergence of an Italian market after the unification of the country is considered to have stimulated the industrialization of northern Italy, while the economic development of the southern parts of the country was affected adversely. There seems to be no real gap between the theories of economic development that have played so great a role in the scientific discussions since World War II and the theoretical approach and methods of this book. But formalized models can, of course, be used with great advantage. The attempts at dynamic model-building that have been made since World War II are still more promising for the future. Primarily they represent an attempt to develop further and analyze more precisely the ideas that earlier economists did not think could be profitably analyzed with theoretical, greatly simplified models. It seems that a great deal can be gained through such models, as indicated by the rapidly growing literature on international trade and growth problems.

§ 12. By affecting the size of the national income, the amount of individual incomes, and the distribution of incomes, international trade must also influence the *direction of demand*. Demand is changed through the general economic development of a nonspecified kind, of which the growth in international trade is a part.

There is a specific effect on demand when the increase in national income leads to increased savings; it thus indirectly causes demand to be devoted to capital goods to a greater extent. That international movements of capital

[15] Some people have exaggerated the importance of the factor proportions model in my account of international trade and referred to it as an equilibrium analysis of international trade after the neoclassical pattern. See, e.g., Myrdal, *Economic Theory and Underdeveloped Regions* (London, 1957), p. 146 *et seq.* A more dynamic type of thinking than in the neoclassical theory was presented by J. H. Williams in his justly celebrated article, "The Theory of International Trade Reconsidered," *Economic Journal* (1929). I was influenced by this article and similar ideas presented by Williams in his lectures.

change the direction of demand is well known and has been thoroughly analyzed by a number of writers. Special attention should be paid to the impact on the pattern of demand made by a general rise in living standards. This is perhaps of particular importance for the developing countries. It should not be difficult to cover such questions within the framework of existing international trade theory.

§ 13. It is well known that the theory of international trade emerged principally to explain trade between industrialized countries and between these countries and primary producers like Australia and New Zealand. Very little attention was focused before World War II on problems that are met chiefly in the foreign trade of countries like many present African states—although certain aspects of the trade of the Latin American countries were analyzed.

Can a theory such as mine be used for a more thorough analysis of the trade of underdeveloped countries? It is evident that when it comes to studying the division of labor and trade between countries at very different stages of cultural, political, and economic development, the considerable international quality differences with regard to labor have to be considered. Therefore, account has to be taken of a substantial number of factors of production. The classical model, with only one kind of labor, and some modern models, with two goods and two factors of production, do not seem to be well suited for such problems, except perhaps for a very general indication of the character of the foreign trade. A theory that includes a considerable number of factors can probably be more easily adapted. Such a theory is also more suitable for studying a time-consuming process that causes changes in the supply and quality of factors.

A theory should not be criticized on the grounds that it must be significantly varied and extended in order to be applied to radically different conditions than those for which it was constructed. If the analysis concerns the division of labor between the developing countries and the industrialized nations, it is natural that *at the very outset* greater attention should be paid to the effect on the supply of factors, partly through their international movements and partly through the change in quality and quantity of factors that can result from an incipient industrialization process. Unfortunately, it is very difficult in concrete cases to state anything definite about quantitative effects of this kind. Precise assumptions in dynamic models are attractive but may sometimes lead to excessive optimism.

In developing countries there are probably instances where completely different kinds of factors—working with different techniques—produce similar and competing products. The effect of international trade is different in such cases from the effect according to the ordinary factor proportions model. Particular attention should be paid to the economic consequences of risks and risk-bearing, because the political risks will probably be greater there than in industrialized countries.[16]

Perhaps the most important difference between cases of this type and those envisaged by current international trade theory is that in the developing

[16] A short discussion of both these problems appears in Chap. VI, §§ 6 and 7. See also Chap. V, § 5.

countries the mobility of factors between various occupations can be extremely restricted. Reallocation possibilities are in the short and medium run very limited. This can mean that the effect of increased international trade is such that a certain productive activity in a developing country has to be discontinued, and the factors find themselves to a large extent unemployed since they cannot be transferred to some other activity. As far as I know, theory prior to the Second World War generally neglected problems of this kind. The fact that they have now been taken up represents an important step forward.[17]

Other kinds of imperfect reallocation were analyzed in detail in pre-World War II theory. I am referring here to the so-called "noncompeting groups," who move from one occupation to another with great difficulty on account of trade union regulations or social barriers. This phenomenon can lead to income differences for certain kinds of labor as a result of the variations in trade. I would here refer the reader to Manoilesco's well-known work.[18]

On the whole, I think that a study of the international trade of the developing countries under present and future conditions must be dominated by an investigation of their *general* production possibilities—their administration, political stability, legal security—and of the possibilities for education and inflow of qualified labor. The supply of domestic capital and of capital from abroad is important, but an analysis of its influence is easier. The main investigation should be a "production analysis" more than a "trade theory." For this reason I am inclined to believe that dynamic trade models can reveal little about the possibilities of increasing the international trade of such countries.

Some economists who in the last fifteen years have dealt extensively with the foreign trade problems of "new" countries by means of a number of simple theoretical models have contrasted these models with one or two of the models used in the neoclassical theory of international trade—such as the comparative cost model or the factor proportion model. They have often implied that these static models constitute the essential part of the neoclassical theory and have then criticized the theory for ignoring a great many other aspects. It is, I hope, now clear that existing theory consists of many different parts—whether it has been given the form of specific models or not—and that *all these parts* have to be considered with regard to their applicability to old problems and new. In itself, it is not surprising that new problems to some extent require new tools of analysis.

§ 14. The world economic depression in the 1930's directed attention to the great importance of economic policies to combat unemployment. The use of import duties and restrictions for this purpose became widespread. Before that time the theoretical analysis had been concerned chiefly with the short-run effects of such a policy on temporary unemployment and unused capacity —e.g., in connection with the theory of dumping. Medium- and long-run

[17] See, e.g., articles by J. N. Bhagwati in the *Review of Economic Studies* (1958) and the *American Economic Review* (1958). Haberler studied some aspects of this problem as early as 1950 in "Some Problems in the Pure Theory of International Trade," *The Economic Journal*. Recent literature about this and similar problems is abundant.

[18] Manoilesco, *The Theory of Protection and International Trade* (London, 1931). This subject was also discussed by Taussig in *International Trade*, and in reviews of Manoilesco's book by Viner, Haberler, and me.

effects had been touched upon in the writing of protectionist economists who were interested in and optimistic about the possibility of increasing employment thereby.

It is not difficult to construct cases in which the obstacles to imports in one country, which are unaccompanied by retaliatory measures from other countries, lead to a reduction of unemployment in that country through the increase in domestic investment that may be called forth in an otherwise depressed state of affairs.[19] The long-run effects on employment and income are more difficult to ascertain. An analysis of such cases represents an addition to and a modification of earlier theory, but the problems in question do not call for radically different theoretical constructions.

§ 15. In addition to these problems, which mainly concern the long-run effects, economists have to study questions regarding the influence of changes in international trade on the *payments mechanism*. The usual analyses, quite correctly, study how the various items in the balance of payments vary under the influence of different kinds of changes in supply and demand. A good many penetrating analyses have been produced in recent decades.[20] In this work I have stressed that variations in the buying power of various nations are of central importance with respect not only to international capital movements but also to variations in supply and demand. By "buying power" I have meant not only variations in the national income of the different countries but also variations in the ability to make purchases that are directly associated with international capital transfers and with an inflationary or deflationary credit policy.

The end of the 1930's witnessed the emergence of a theory dealing with the international payments mechanism, in which changes in the size of the national income were assigned decisive importance. Some people considered this to be a new and important application of Keynes' general theory, but this view is hardly tenable. A study of these problems leads to the problem of business cycle fluctuations as they affect international trading relations—an area to which not nearly enough attention has been paid.[21] I deliberately left it out altogether in this book, which is already rather voluminous.

§ 16. International trade theory has hitherto paid relatively little attention to *imperfect competition* and the effects of price and sales policies, with the exception of the thoroughly discussed dumping case. If one takes into account the fact that there are also transport costs *within* countries influencing the size of the markets, a good many other cases spring up. These have to some extent been discussed within the framework of location theory, e.g., in the works of Lösch and Isard. But a lot remains to be done. The literature is more

[19] This possibility was emphasized, e.g., by Keynes in 1931 in numerous articles in the *Nation*, the London *Times*, and elsewhere advocating the transition of Great Britain to a generally protectionist policy. A relatively extensive but not formalized analysis is in my Swedish report, *Monetary Policy, Public Works, Subsidies and Tariffs as Remedies for Unemployment* (Stockholm, 1934).

[20] See, e.g., Meade, *The Balance of Payments* (New York, 1951).

[21] A clear account of the importance to the payments mechanism of variations in the national income is in Kindleberger, *International Economics* (1958), x. For variations in business cycles, see Neisser, *Some International Aspects of the Business Cycle* (1936), and Polak, *An International Economic System* (1954).

complete on the subject of international cartels. A closely related problem concerns the effect on competitive ability of the size of the national market. Businessmen seem to agree that conditions in this regard are of very great importance for the division of labor between countries. The theoretical analysis has so far hardly given us any explanation of this complex problem, although the analysis of customs unions has begun to make valuable contributions. A theoretical model dealing with economies of scale can hardly ignore the question of market size. It is certainly of the greatest importance for the small, unindustrialized countries.

§ 17. What does one really expect of international trade theory? Presumably, more or less the same things that are expected from the rest of price theory. In the first place, it should contribute to a general understanding of existing economic conditions and the process of economic development. It should provide the same kind of insights as economic history.

Second, these insights should make it easier to pursue an economic policy that attains the desired ends. Thus, a theory of trade should indicate the effects of a tariff or other trade policy, including customs unions. Since many kinds of *internal* economic policy also influence the extent and nature of trade, the theory should be able to indicate their effects also. Otherwise, knowledge of the various effects of a policy will be imperfect, and serious mistakes will be made. This is particularly true when a time-consuming process is analyzed.[22] The post-World War II theoretical discussion is in some respects rather conservative since it has given only scant attention to such problems as transportation, taxation, and social legislation in their relation to international trade.[23]

Third, the theory of international trade should naturally include theories relating to the adjustment of the domestic supply of the factors of production and international factor movements, since these are of great interest for the formulation of economic policy. Theories that analyze factor supplies touch upon the impact of trade on the size of the population and on human qualities. It is obvious that value criteria are necessary when people change their valuation and number under the influence of trade.

With respect to conditions in the developing countries in particular, an analysis of the direct and indirect effects of international trade on production conditions and demand is not enough. If it is not known how political conditions will be affected, our account will be very imperfect. Sociologists and

---

[22] In this book I have discussed some more dynamic aspects in Ch. VII, §§ 4-6; Ch. VIII, §§ 4, 7, 9; Ch. IX, § 6; Ch. X, §§ 9-11; Ch. XI, §§ 6-7; Ch. XII, §§ 4-5; Ch. XIII, § 7; Ch. XV, §§ 1, 5, 6; and Ch. XVI, §§ 8-12. Myrdal's assertion in *Economic Theory and Under-developed Regions* (London, 1957) that such problems have been overlooked by current international trade theory is therefore not justified. A theory that is not intended to solve the problems of the developing countries must be modified, extended, and revised in order to be suitable for such a task. Great use can be made of the knowledge of transport conditions, factor movements, noncompeting groups, other supply reactions of the factors of production, the risk factor, and many other things that have hitherto been treated with a varying degree of dynamics. Yet I have never been able to see that the attempts to discuss in *quantitative terms* the *total* gain from international trade are of any interest.

[23] See Caves and Bhagwati.

political scientists of various kinds will have to step in and try to analyze poorly defined problems of a completely different nature from those that international trade theory tackles. Yet one can hardly criticize writers who devote their attention to economic theory because they cannot achieve things that only sociologists could achieve—in decades. A division of work followed by cooperation between economists and sociologists seems to be required.[24]

§ 18. New types of theoretical models may of course give a more explicit account of the economic aspects of *development*. The theory of international capital movements has long taken dynamic aspects into consideration. The discussion of the effects of tariffs has also done so to quite a considerable extent. It is nevertheless evident that a multi-market theory—like a single-market theory—should be built in a much more dynamic direction than has hitherto been the case.[25] The emphasis in international trade analysis should be placed on problems relating to specialization, the supply of the factors of production and their changing quality, transport conditions, international factor movements, etc. It should also attempt to use formalized models. However, it would hardly be scientific practice to fail to make use of, and further develop, the insights that existing theory has provided; it will be primarily a question of following up lines of thought that have been not neglected but insufficiently studied, or analyzed far too vaguely, in the past. There will definitely not be any question of throwing overboard everything that is old and starting from scratch.[26]

One must avoid the error, which in the natural sciences would be considered unforgivable but which in economics has not been so uncommon, of overemphasizing the differences between the treatment of new problems and of earlier, more or less closely related problems. Nor should one believe that only results presented in the form of explicit theoretical models of an extremely simplified nature are of scientific value. To the extent that one is tempted to exaggerate the precision and utility of conclusions from such models, one runs the risk of being less scientific than if a less formalized analysis were presented, in which the uncertainty about the strength and direction of various tendencies was clearly pointed out. Economic theory models are a good thing—indeed, quite necessary—but a "model mania" that rejects other methods of analysis must be shunned.

[24] Concerning the importance of administrative and legal institutions as preconditions for industrialization, see my *"Taxation and International Trade."*

[25] As far as I know, nobody has come up with the idea of declaring the ordinary single-market theory useless because it is not dynamic. Looking far into the future, I predict that the dynamic theories of price formation within a country—on which a number of writers are presently engaged under the leadership of economists such as Tinbergen and Frisch—can be developed so as to embrace many markets and have such a high degree of thoroughness that they are of some practical use.

[26] For excellent samples of the value of a scientific continuity utilizing earlier theoretical advances, see Nurkse, *Patterns of Trade and Development* (Stockholm, 1959), and Haberler, *International Trade and Economic Development* (Cairo, 1959).

Index